There weren't quite enough pages available in the
magazine release to end the Universe Survival arc
the way I wanted to, so I've added a little bit here. It's
great that I have the opportunity to do that when the
chapters are compiled for the graphic novel release.

—Toyotarou, 2018

Toyotarou

Toyotarou created the manga adaptation for the *Dragon Ball Z*
anime's 2015 film, *Dragon Ball Z: Resurrection F*. He is also the
author of the spin-off series *Dragon Ball Heroes: Victory Mission*,
which debuted in *V-Jump* in Japan in November 2012.

Akira Toriyama

Renowned worldwide for his playful, innovative storytelling and
humorous, distinctive art style, Akira Toriyama burst onto the manga
scene in 1980 with the wildly popular *Dr. Slump*. His hit series *Dragon Ball*
(published in the U.S. as *Dragon Ball* and *Dragon Ball Z*) ran from 1984
to 1995 in Shueisha's *Weekly Shonen Jump* magazine. He is also known
for his design work on video games such as *Dragon Quest*, *Chrono Trigger*,
Tobal No. 1 and *Blue Dragon*. His recent manga works include *COWA!*, *Kajika*,
Sand Land, *Neko Majin*, *Jaco the Galactic Patrolman* and a children's book,
Toccio the Angel. He lives with his family in Japan.

FOR Max
welcome.

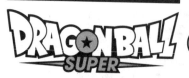

DRAGON BALL SUPER 9

SHONEN JUMP Manga Edition

STORY BY **Akira Toriyama**
ART BY **Toyotarou**

TRANSLATION **Caleb Cook**
LETTERING **James Gaubatz**
TOUCH-UP & ADDITIONAL LETTERING **Brandon Bovia**
DESIGN **Shawn Carrico**
EDITOR **Rae First**

Printed in the U.S.A.

Published by VIZ Media, LLC
P.O. Box 77010
San Francisco, CA 94107

10 9 8 7 6 5
First printing, June 2020
Fifth printing, June 2023

VIZ MEDIA
viz.com

SHONEN JUMP

ratings.viz.com RATED T TEEN

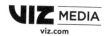

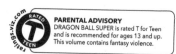

PARENTAL ADVISORY
DRAGON BALL SUPER is rated T for Teen and is recommended for ages 13 and up. This volume contains fantasy violence.

DRAGON BALL SUPER

BATTLE'S END AND AFTERMATH 9

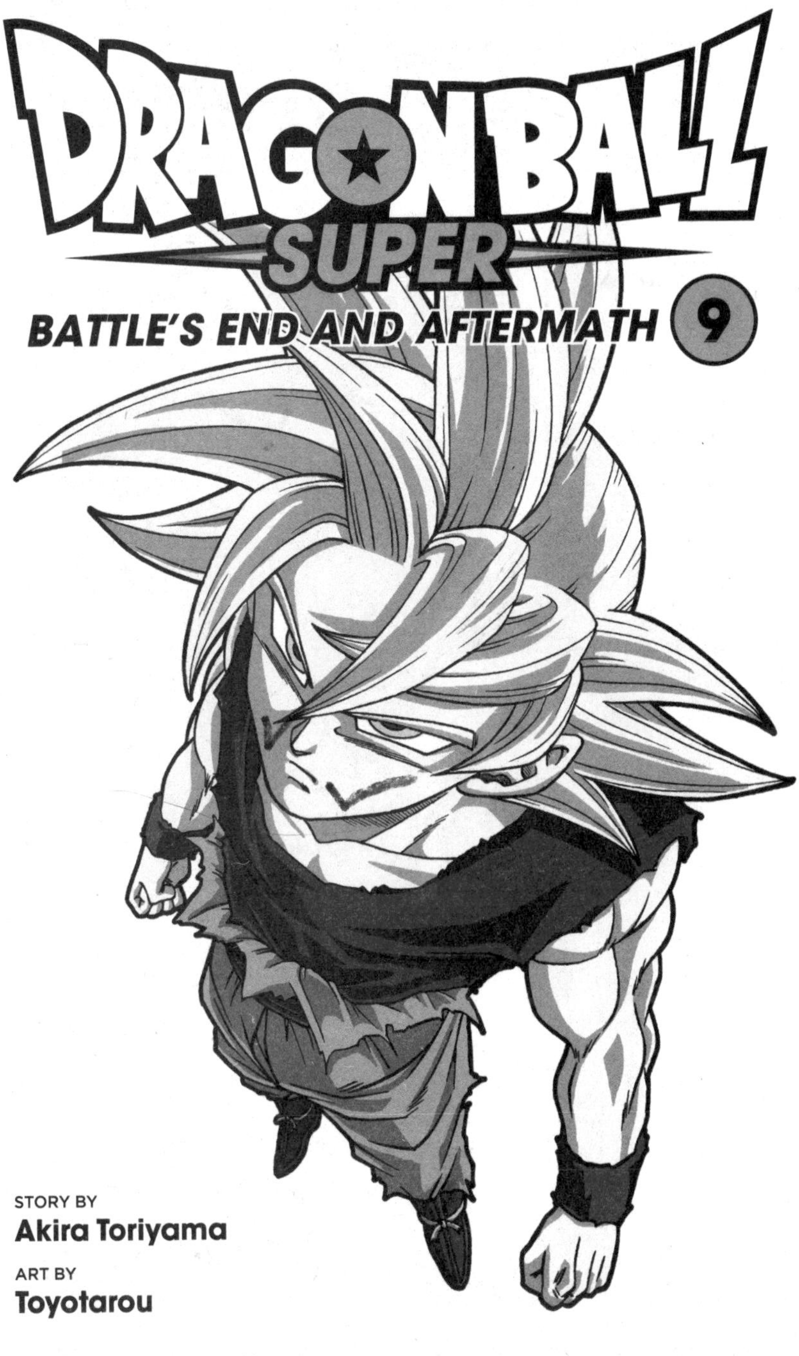

STORY BY
Akira Toriyama
ART BY
Toyotarou

CAST OF CHARACTERS

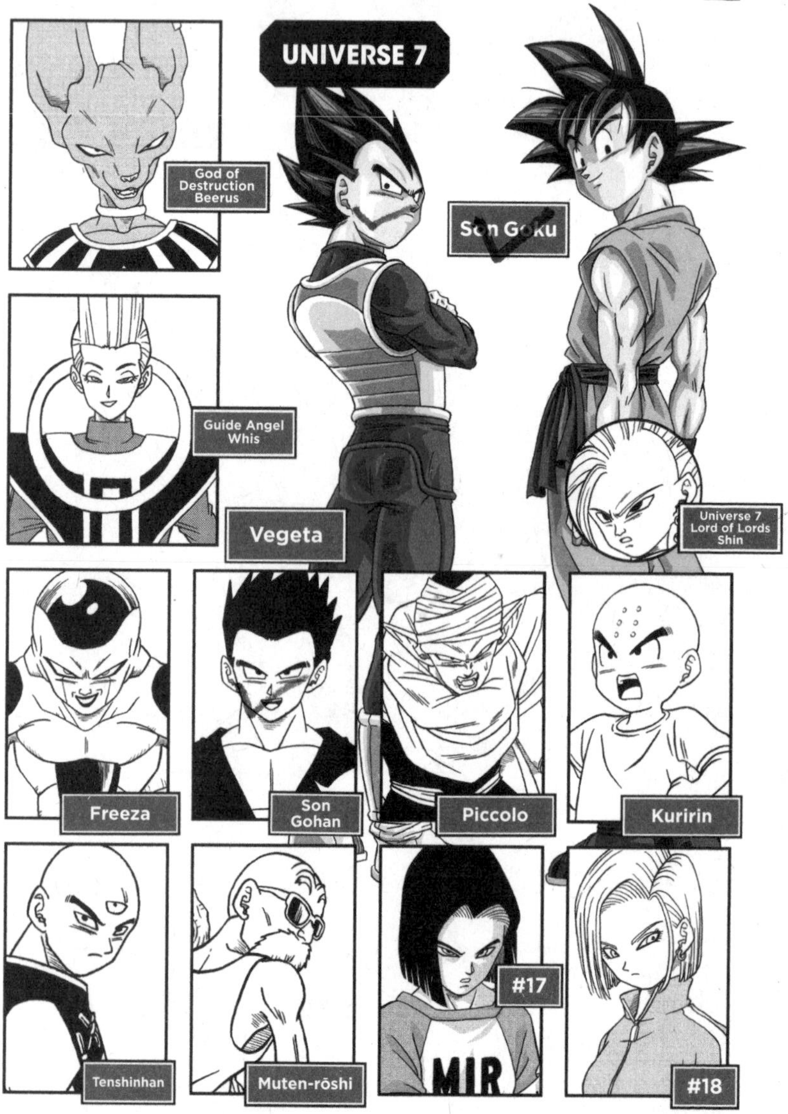
UNIVERSE 7
Son Goku
God of Destruction Beerus
Universe 7 Lord of Lords Shin
Vegeta
Guide Angel Whis
Kuririn
Piccolo
Son Gohan
Freeza
#18
#17
MIR
Muten-rōshi
Tenshinhan

messi

From Other Universes

Jiren (Universe 11)

Toppo (Universe 11)

Grand Priest

Jaco

Belmod
(Universe 11
God of Dusctruction)

Lords of Everything

STORY THUS FAR

A long, long time ago, Son Goku left on a journey in search of the legendary Dragon Balls—a set of seven balls that, when gathered, would summon the dragon Shenlong to grant any wish. After a great adventure, he collects them all. Later, he becomes the apprentice of Kame-Sen'nin, fights a number of vicious enemies, defeats the great Majin Boo and restores peace on Earth. Some time passes, and then Lord Beerus, the God of Destruction, suddenly awakens and sets out in search of the Super Saiyan God. Goku, by becoming the Super Saiyan God, manages to stop Beerus from destroying the Earth and starts training under him with Vegeta. One day, Trunks appears hoping to save the future. Goku and Vegeta travel to his future, but they soon find themselves struggling against Goku Black and Zamas from the parallel world. Things get even worse when Goku Black and Zamas perform Potara fusion to become the immortal God Zamas. With little hope remaining, Goku ends up asking for help from the Lord of Everything, who erases the entire future world, along with Zamas. After some time, the Lord of Everything decides to host a Tournament of Power, where all losing universes are to be obliterated. Now, only a handful of our heroes from Universe 7 and Universe 11's Jiren remain. Who will prevail?!

9

DRAGON BALL SUPER

TABLE OF CON-TENTS

CHAPTER 41 **Ultra Instinct**..................................07

CHAPTER 42 **Battle's End and Aftermath**..........53

CHAPTER 43 **Joining the Galactic Patrol!**.......101

CHAPTER 44 **Escaped Prisoner Moro**...............147

DRAGON BALL SUPER

CHAPTER 41: ULTRA INSTINCT

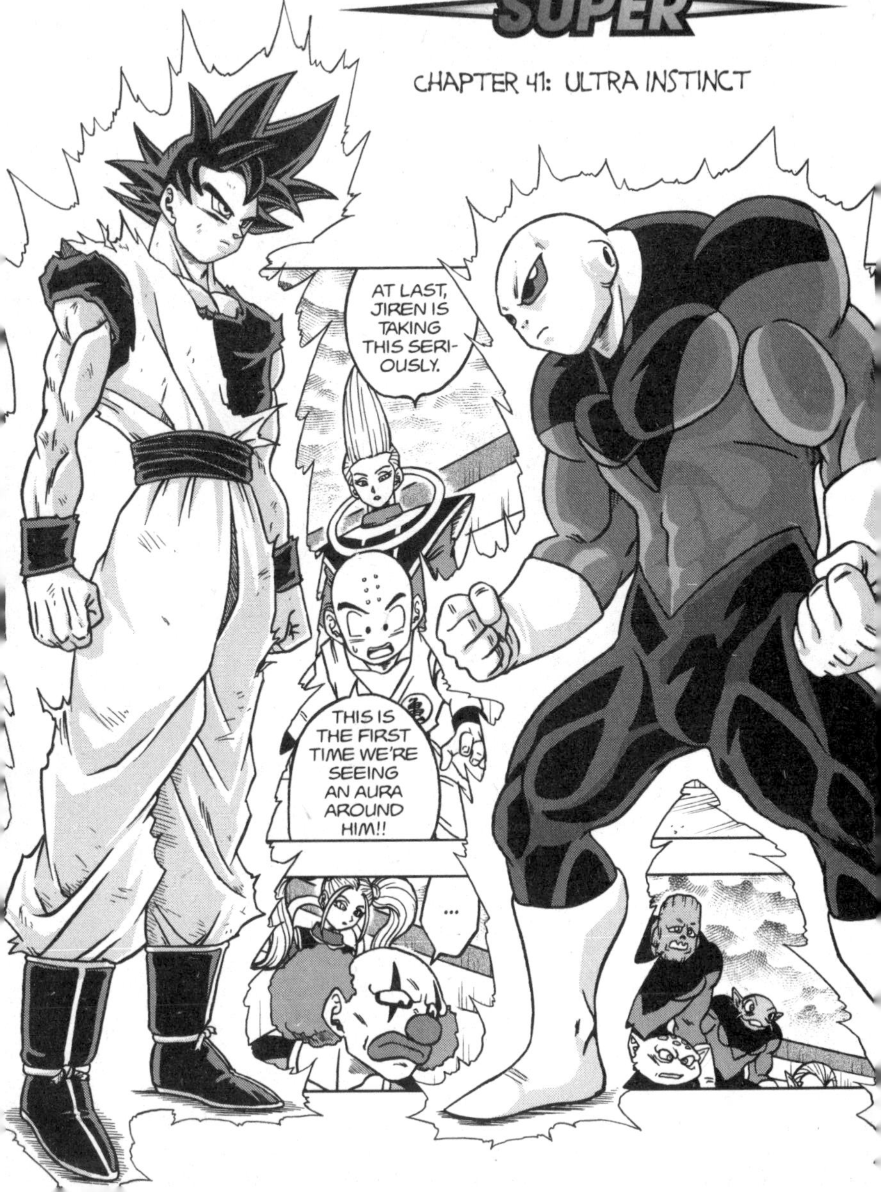
AT LAST, JIREN IS TAKING THIS SERIOUSLY.
THIS IS THE FIRST TIME WE'RE SEEING AN AURA AROUND HIM!!
...

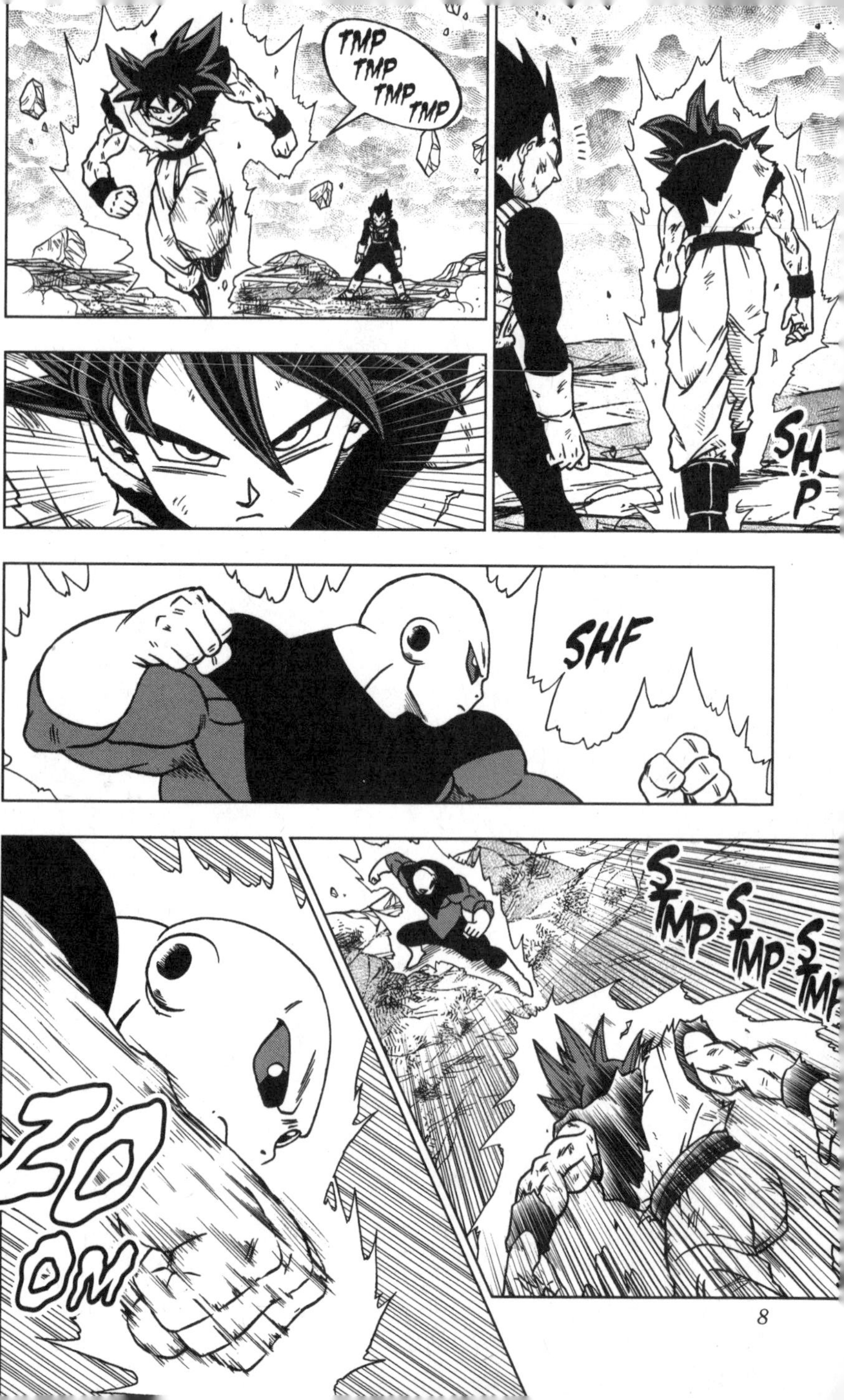

SHP
TMP TMP TMP TMP
SHF
STMP STMP STMP
ZOOM

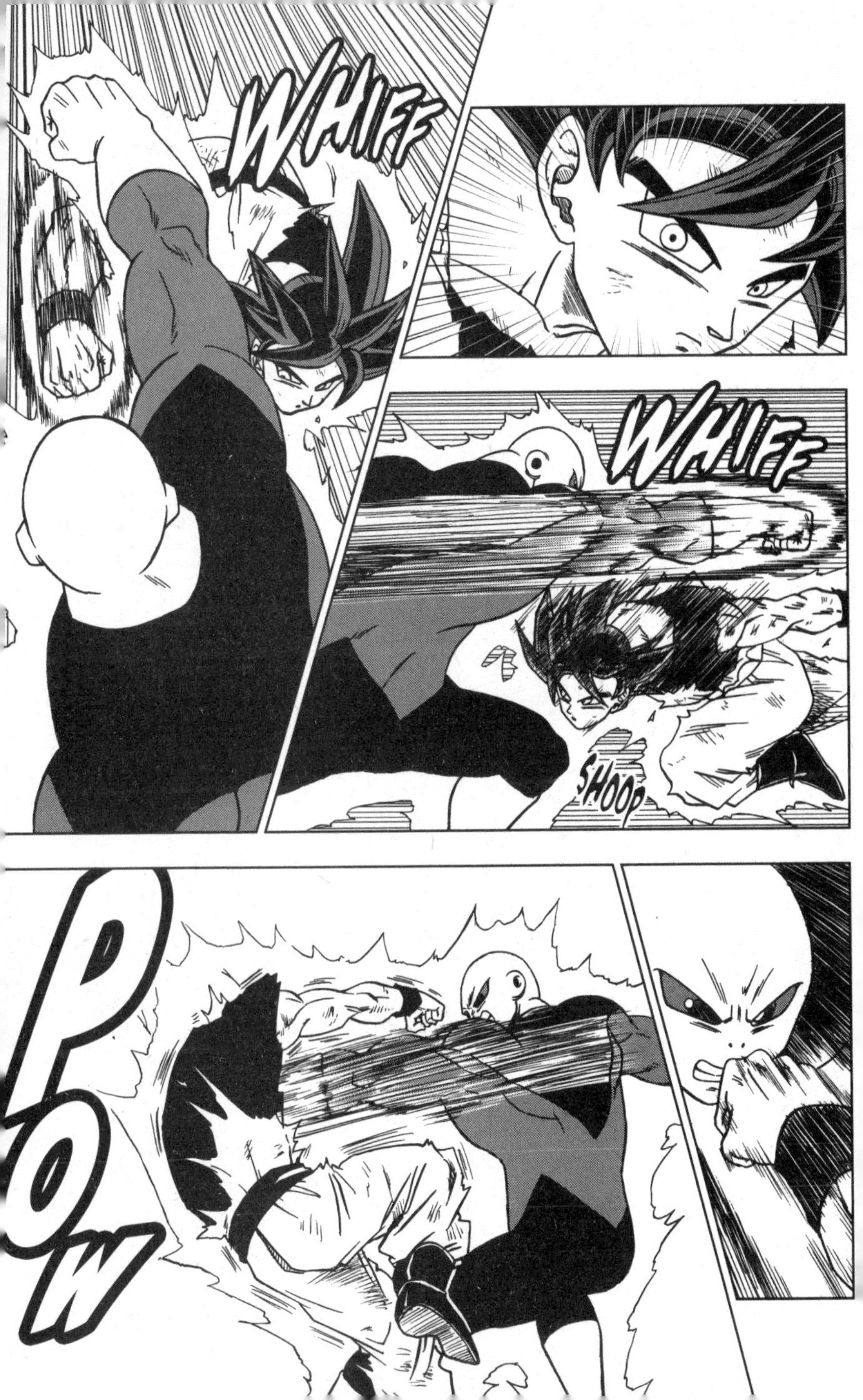
WHIFF
SHOOP
WHIFF
POW

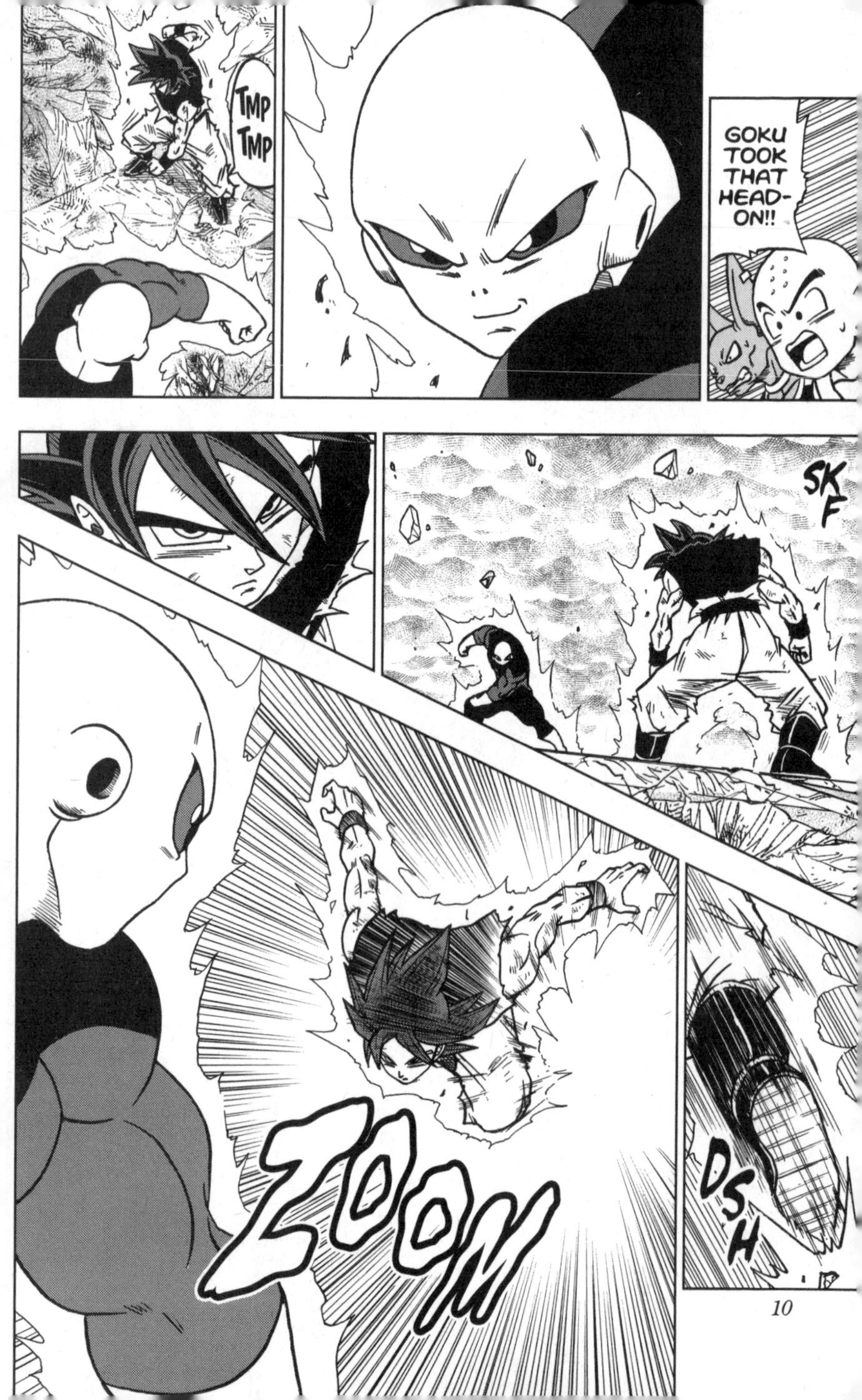

GOKU TOOK THAT HEAD-ON!!
TMP TMP
SKF
DSH
ZOOM

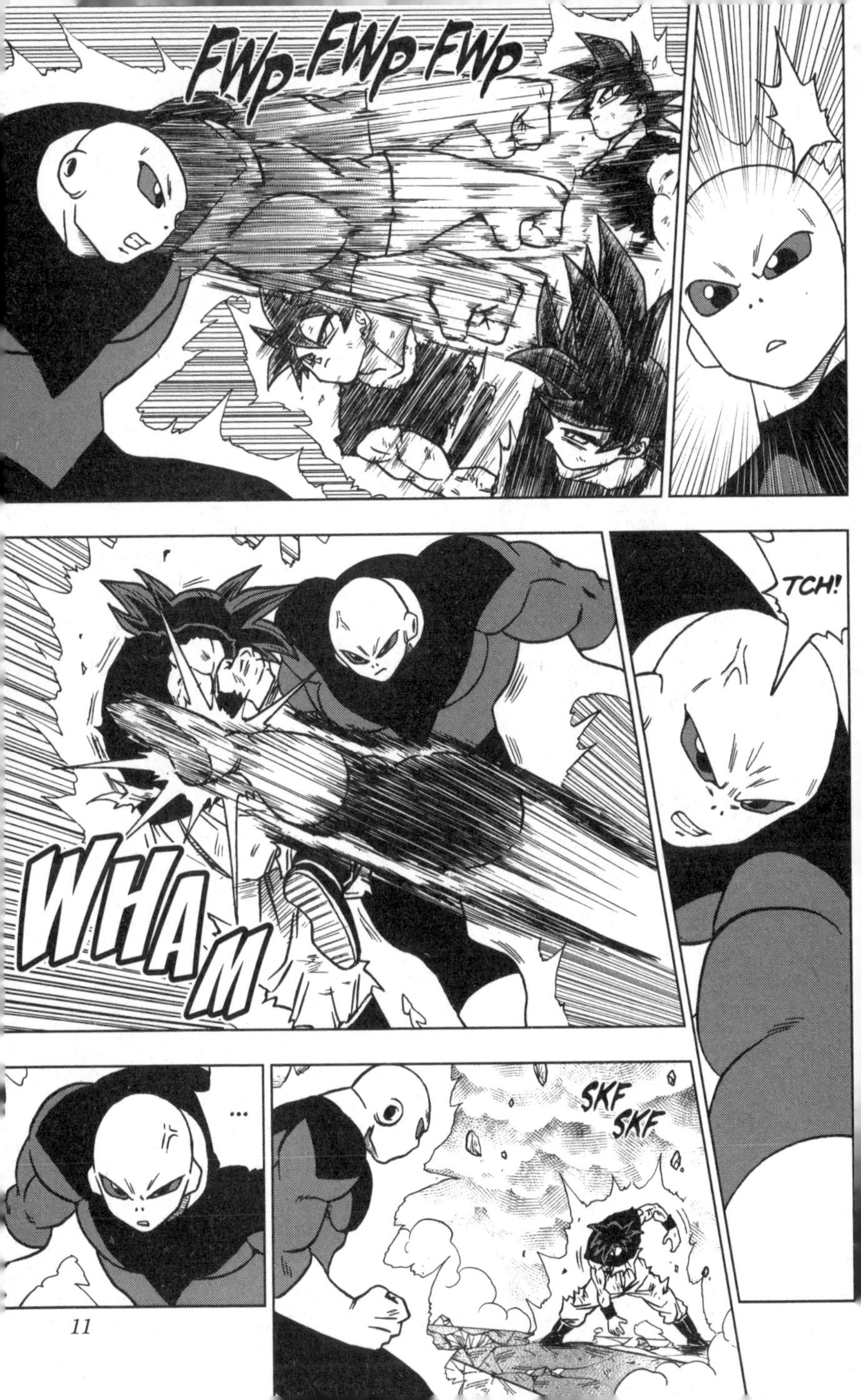
FWP FWP FWP
TCH!
WHAM
SKF
SKF
...

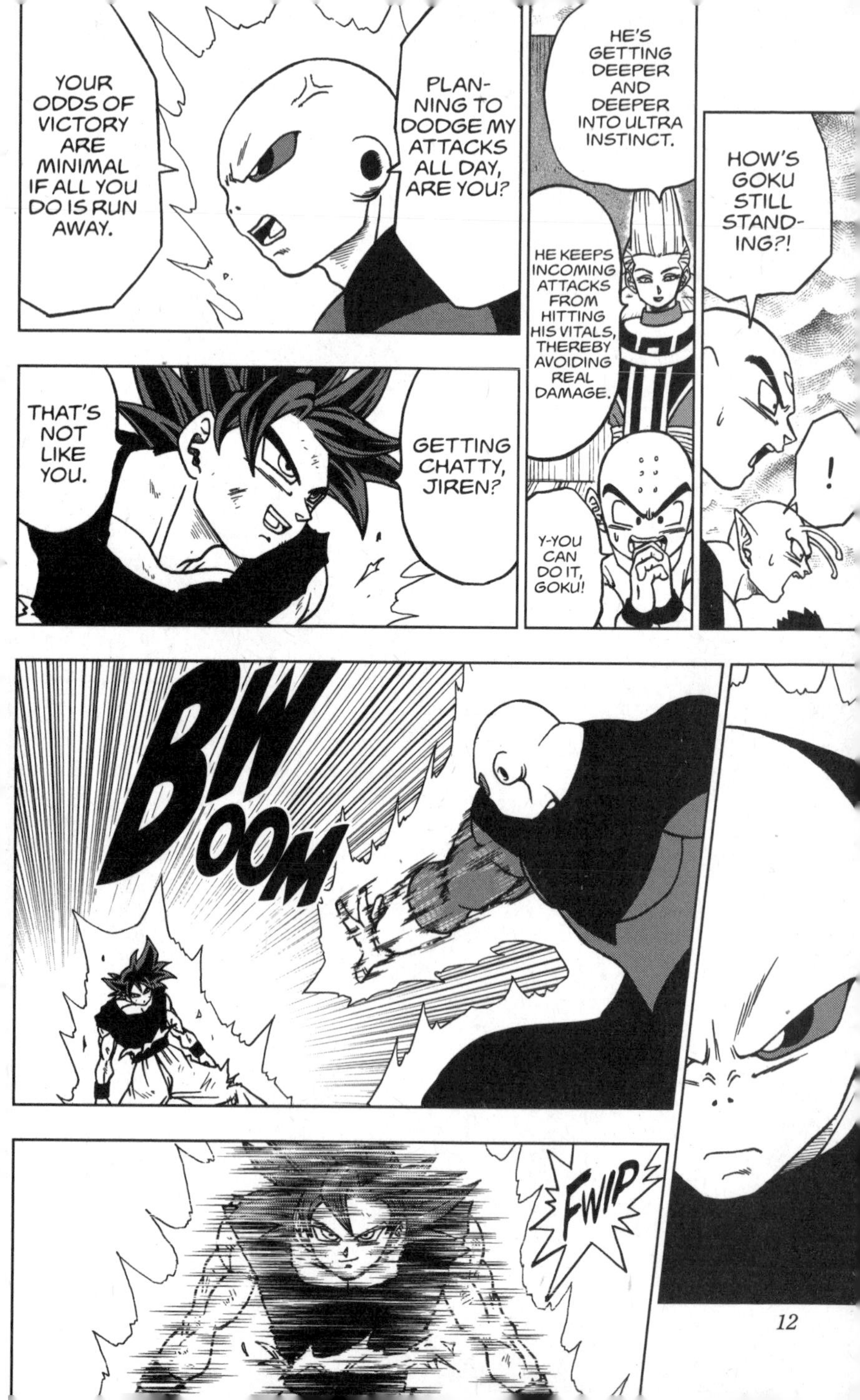
HOW'S GOKU STILL STANDING?!
!
HE'S GETTING DEEPER AND DEEPER INTO ULTRA INSTINCT.
HE KEEPS INCOMING ATTACKS FROM HITTING HIS VITALS, THEREBY AVOIDING REAL DAMAGE.
Y-YOU CAN DO IT, GOKU!
PLAN-NING TO DODGE MY ATTACKS ALL DAY, ARE YOU?
YOUR ODDS OF VICTORY ARE MINIMAL IF ALL YOU DO IS RUN AWAY.
GETTING CHATTY, JIREN?
THAT'S NOT LIKE YOU.
BWOOM
FWIP

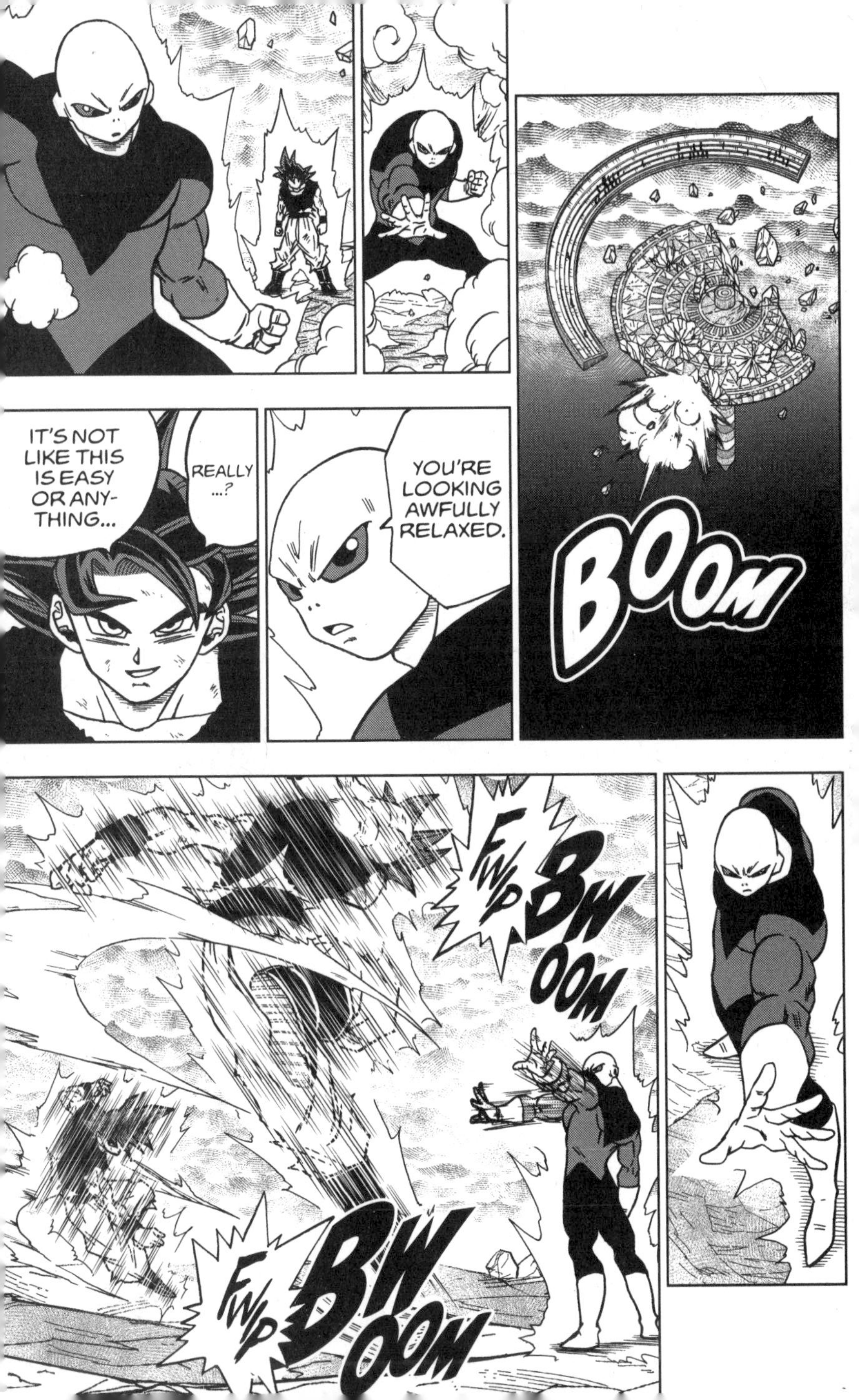
BOOM
YOU'RE LOOKING AWFULLY RELAXED.
REALLY ...?
IT'S NOT LIKE THIS IS EASY OR ANY-THING...
FWIP
BWOOM
FWIP
BWOOM

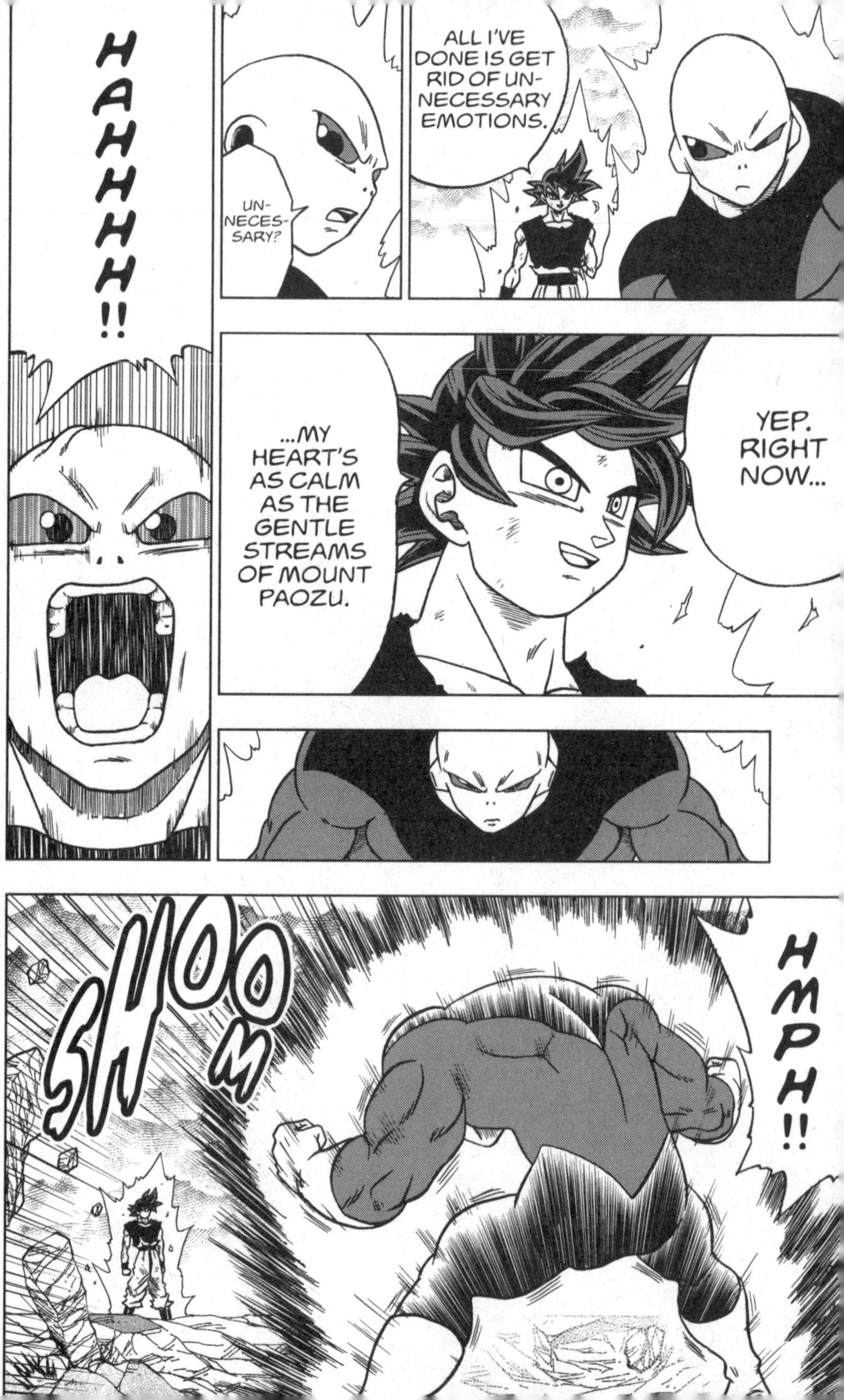
ALL I'VE DONE IS GET RID OF UN-NECESSARY EMOTIONS.
UN-NECES-SARY?
YEP. RIGHT NOW...
...MY HEART'S AS CALM AS THE GENTLE STREAMS OF MOUNT PAOZU.
HAHHHHH!!
HMPH!!
SHOOOM

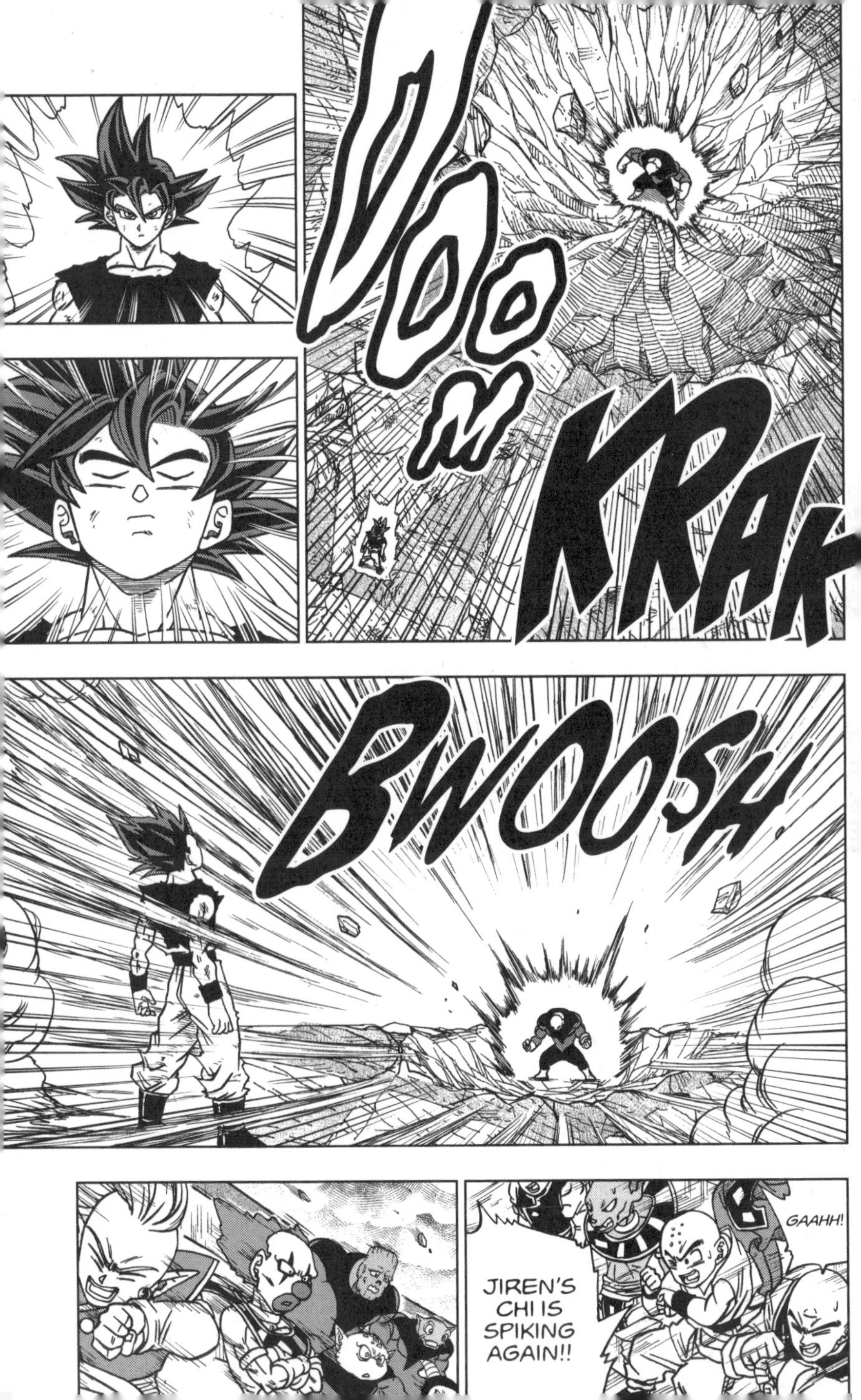
VOOOM
KRAK
BWOOSH
GAAHH!
JIREN'S CHI IS SPIKING AGAIN!!

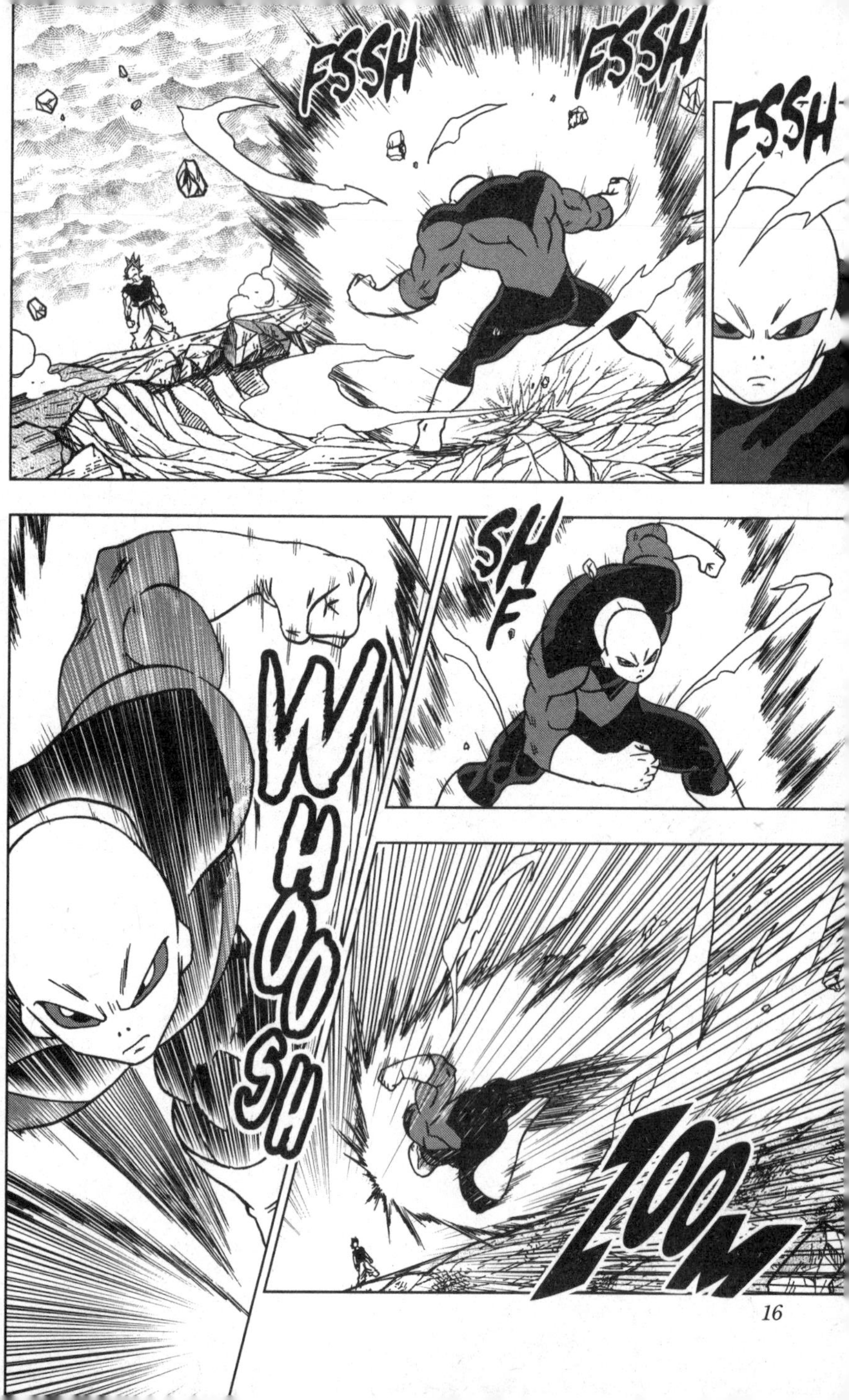
FSSH
FSSH
FSSH
SHF
ZOOM
WHOOSH

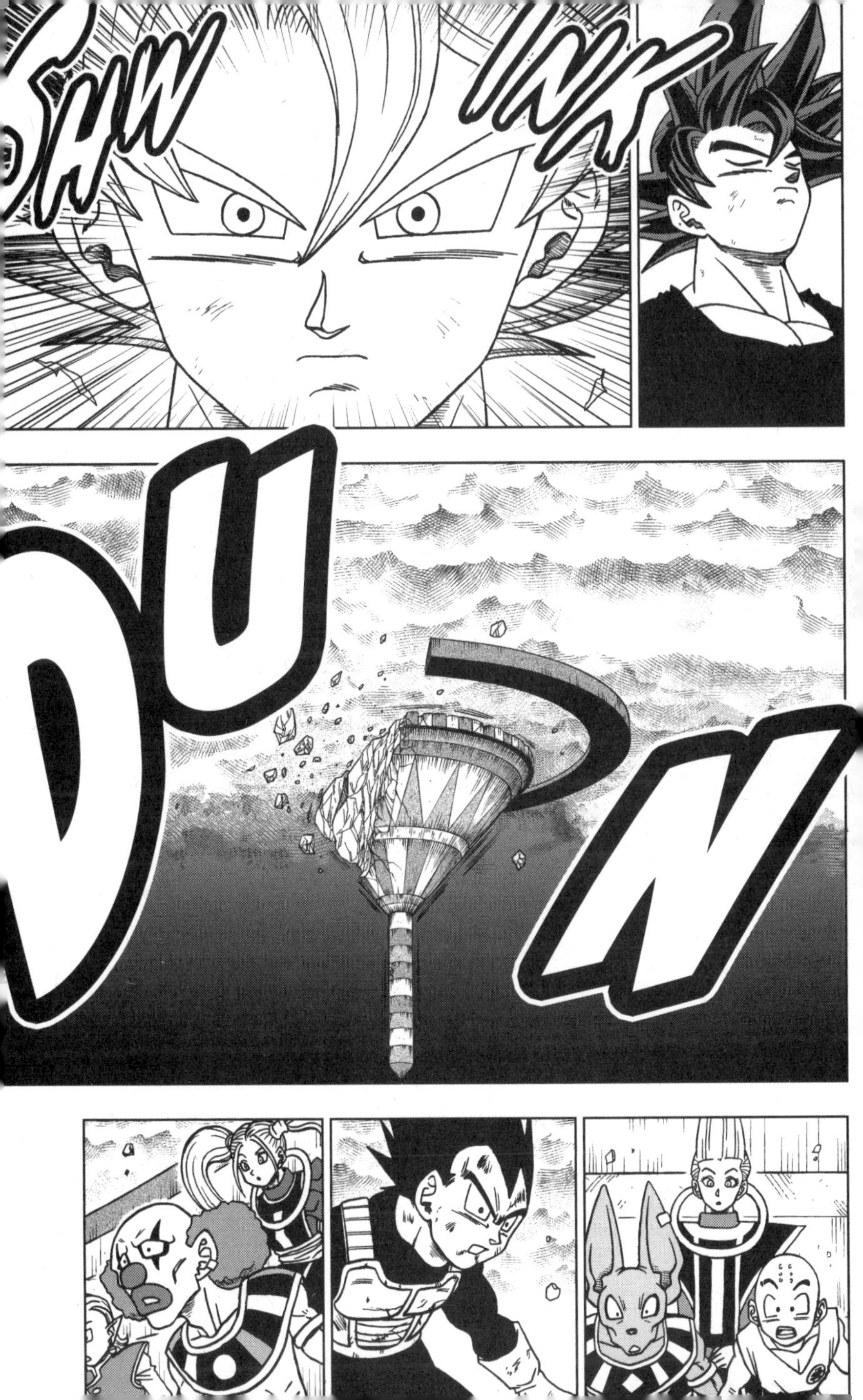

SHWINK
DUN

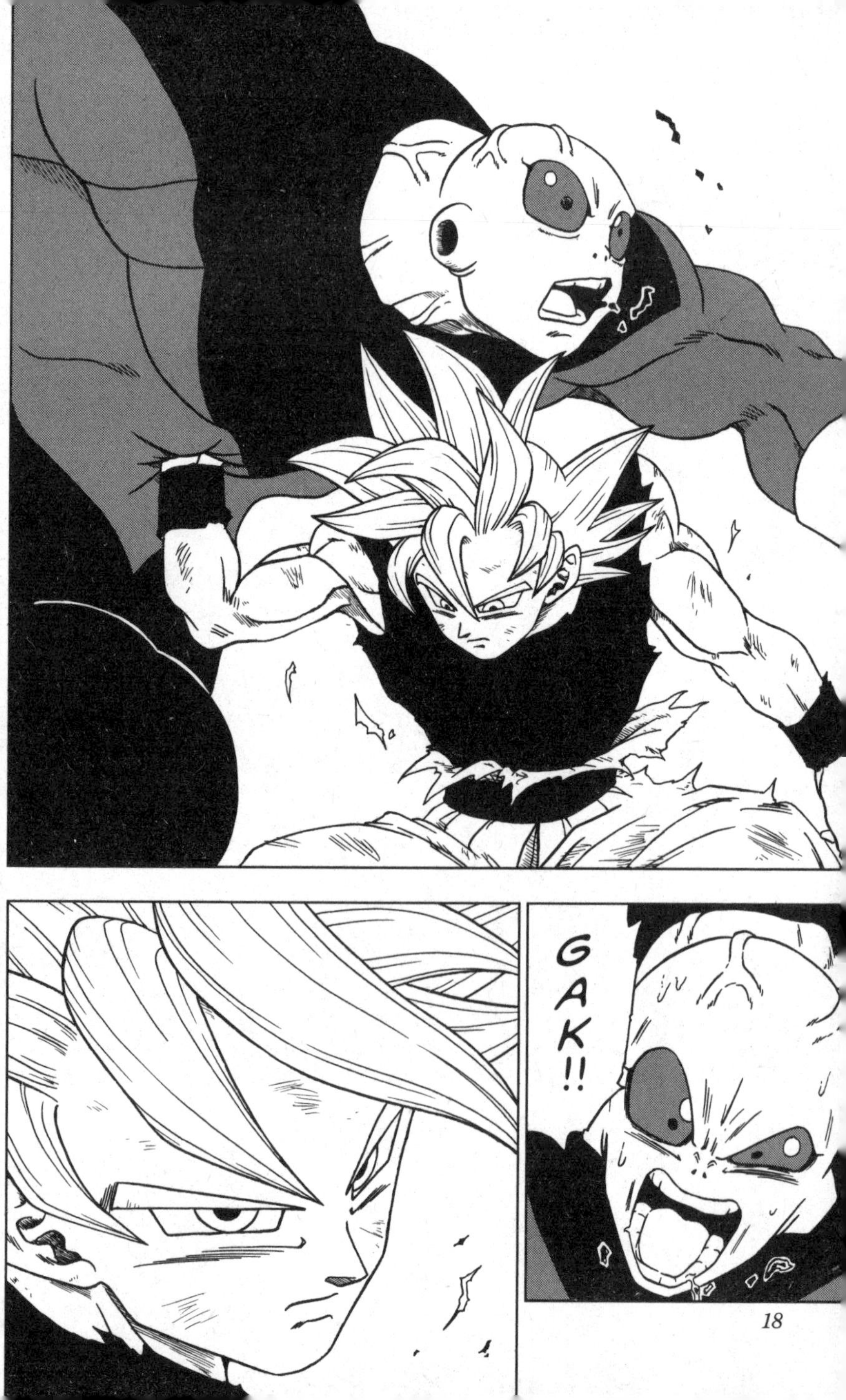
GAK!!

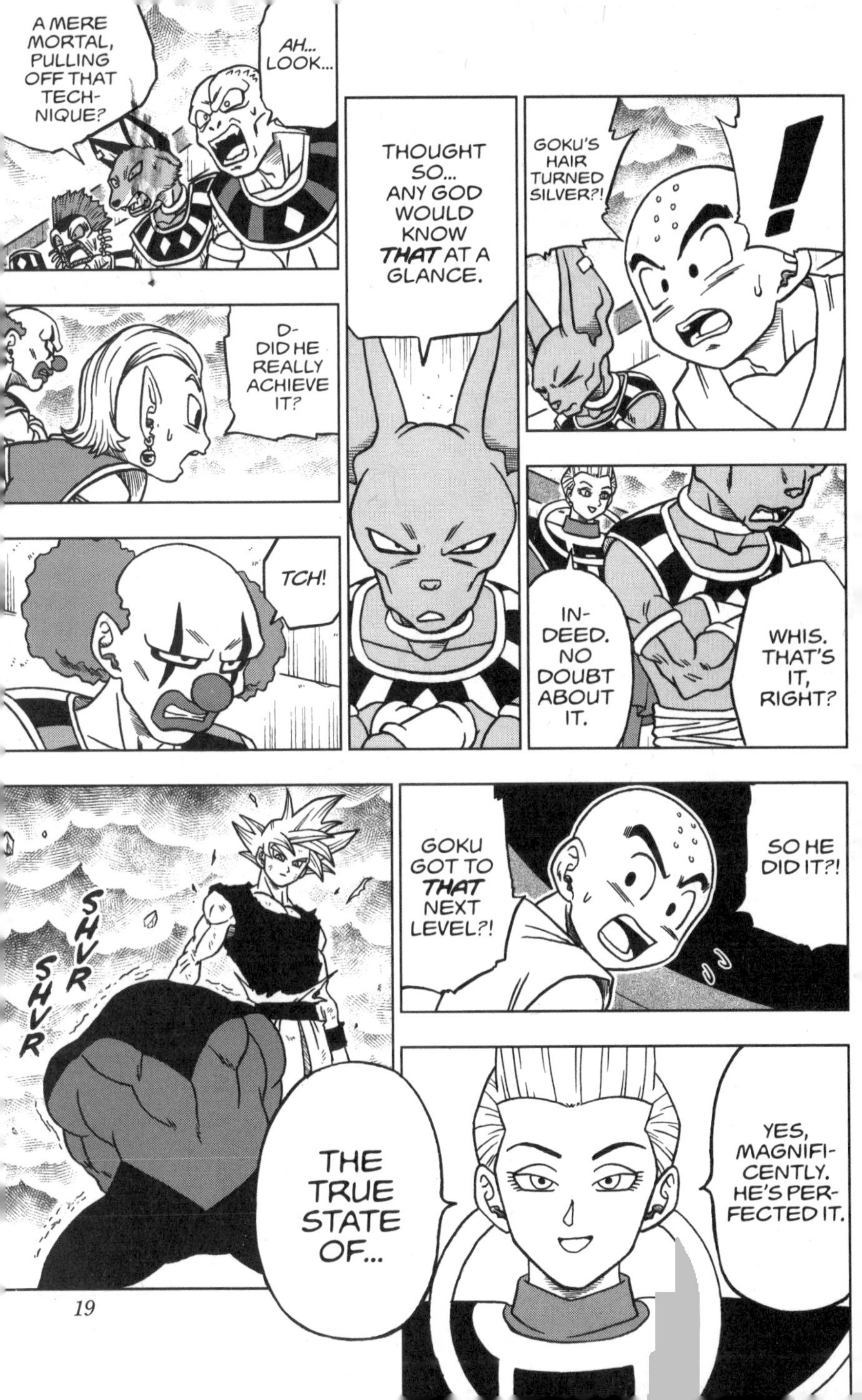

GOKU'S HAIR TURNED SILVER?!
!
WHIS. THAT'S IT, RIGHT?
IN-DEED. NO DOUBT ABOUT IT.
THOUGHT SO... ANY GOD WOULD KNOW *THAT* AT A GLANCE.
AH... LOOK...
A MERE MORTAL, PULLING OFF THAT TECH-NIQUE?
D-DID HE REALLY ACHIEVE IT?
TCH!
SO HE DID IT?!
GOKU GOT TO *THAT* NEXT LEVEL?!
YES, MAGNIFI-CENTLY. HE'S PER-FECTED IT.
THE TRUE STATE OF...
SHVR
SHVR

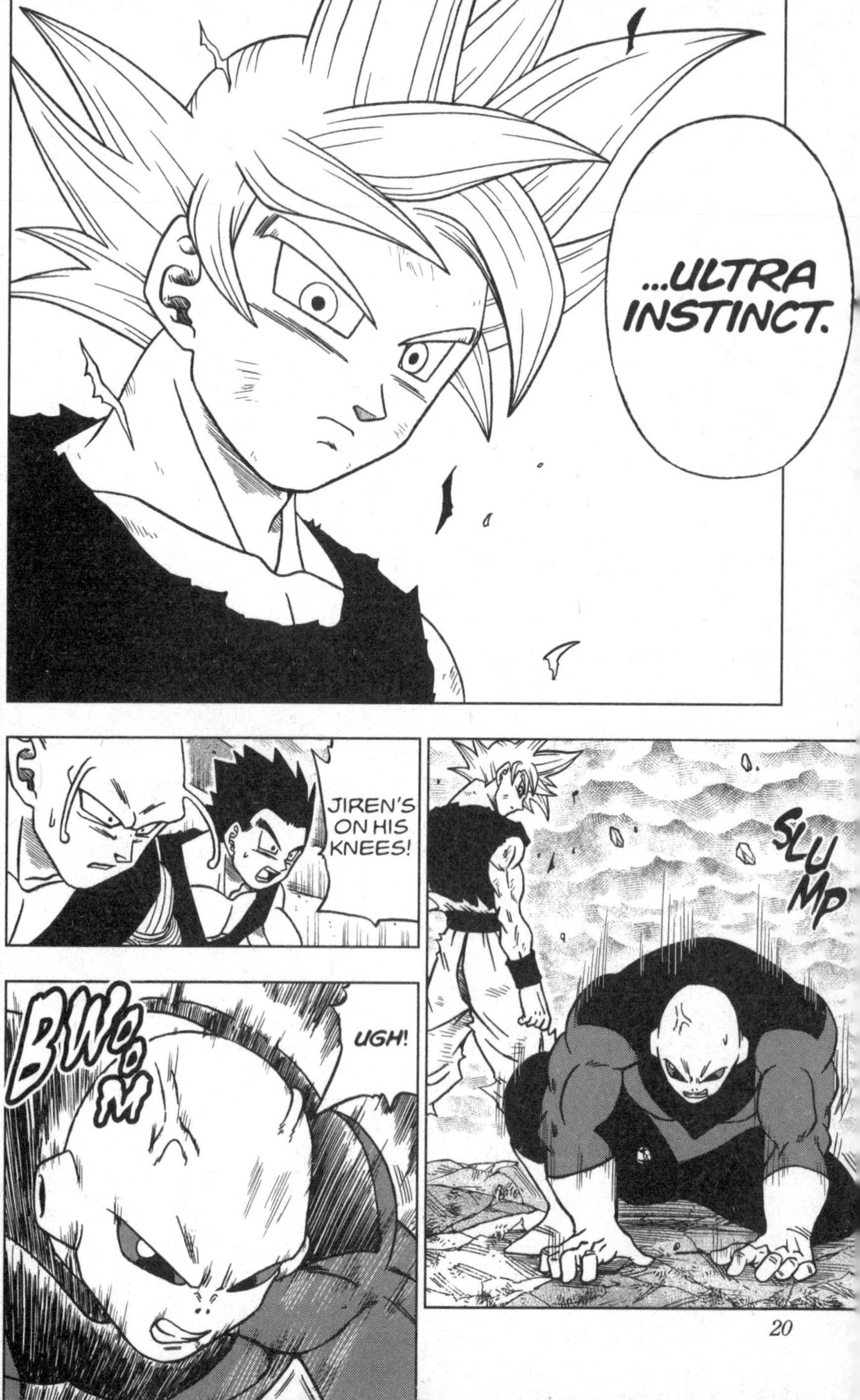
...ULTRA INSTINCT.
SLUMP
JIREN'S ON HIS KNEES!
UGH!
BWOOM

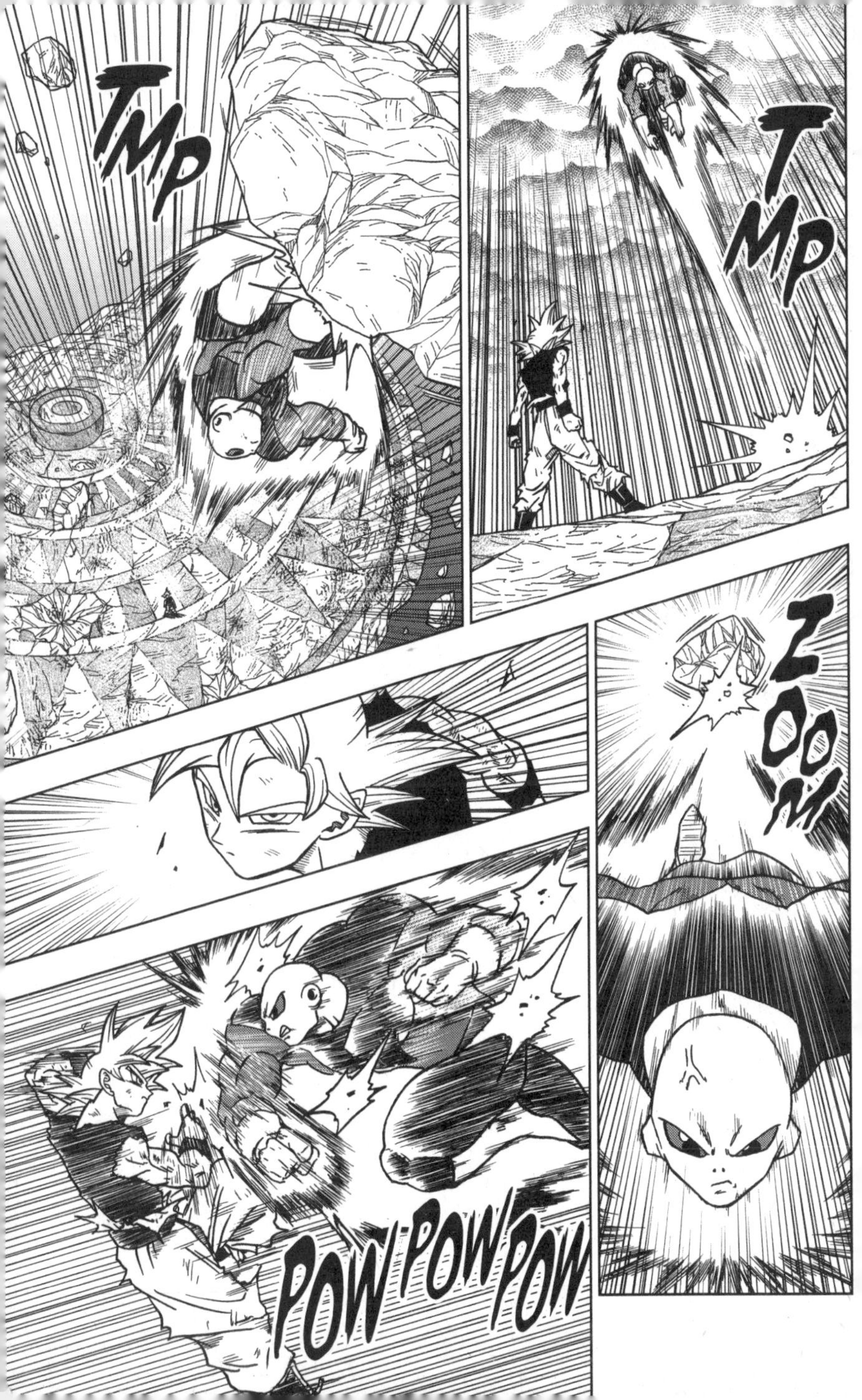
TMP
TMP
ZOOM
POW POW POW

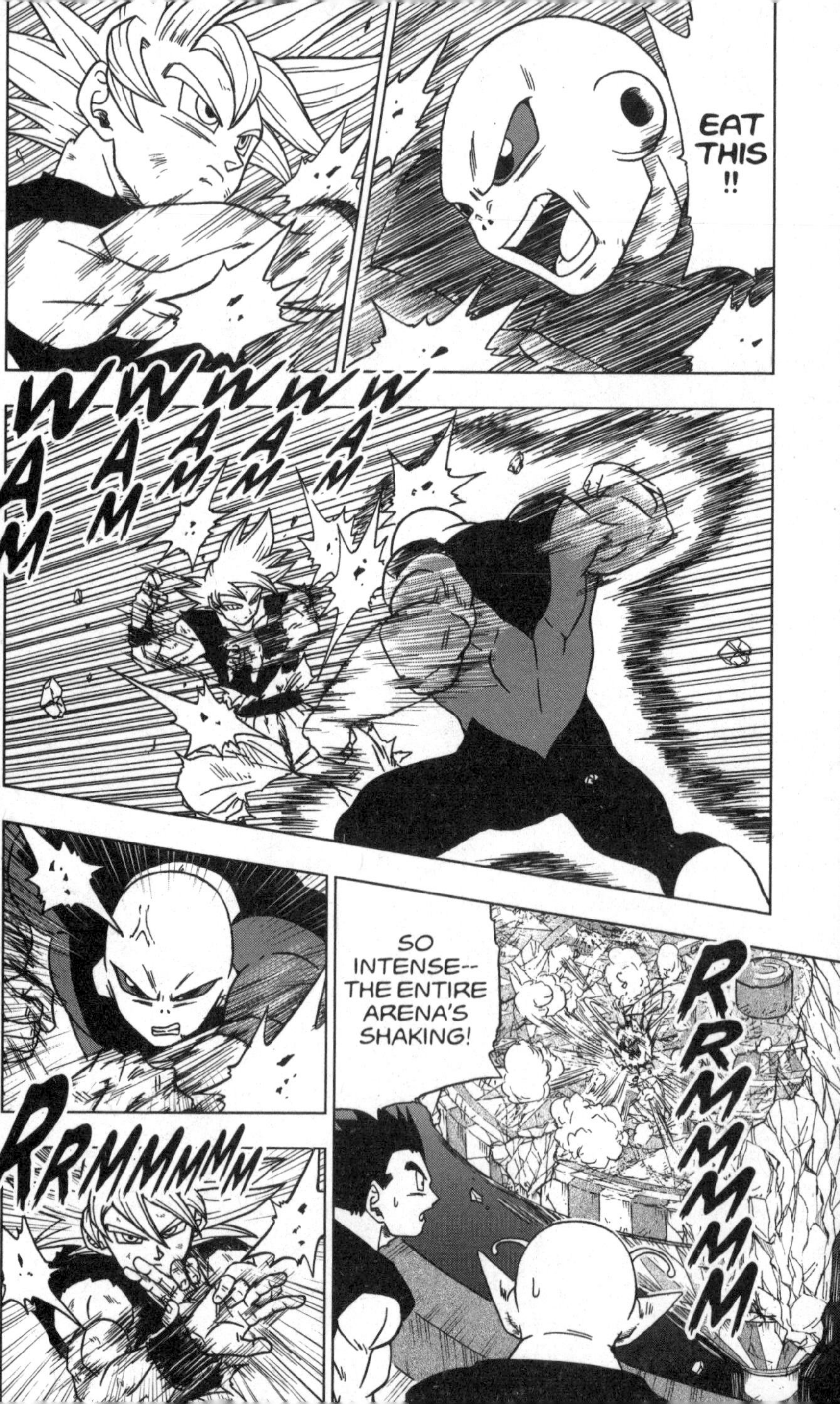
EAT THIS!!
WWWWWWWAAAAAAAMMMMMMM
SO INTENSE-- THE ENTIRE ARENA'S SHAKING!
RRMMMMMM
RRMMMMMM

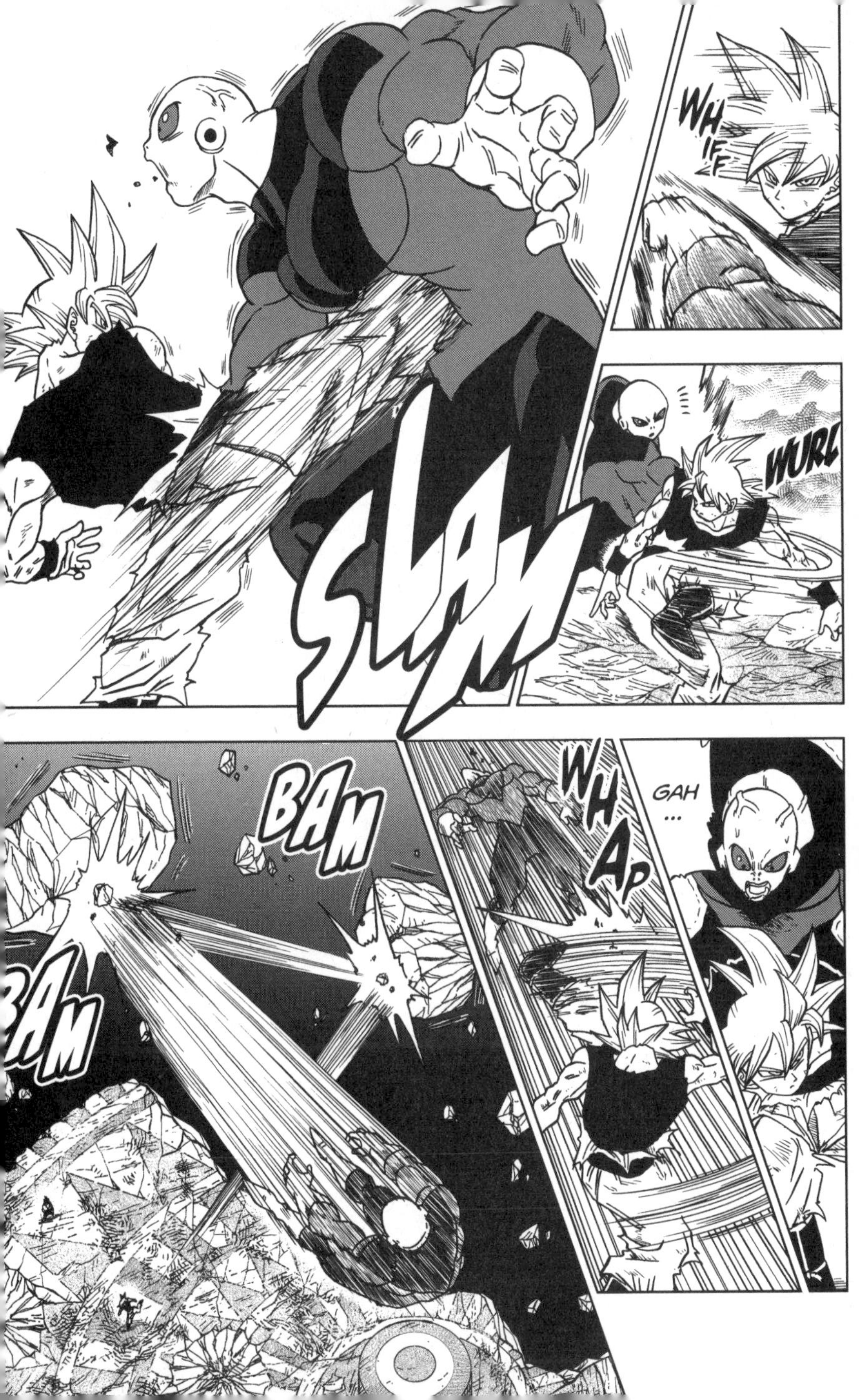

WHIFF
WURL
SLAM
GAH ...
WHAP
BAM
BAM

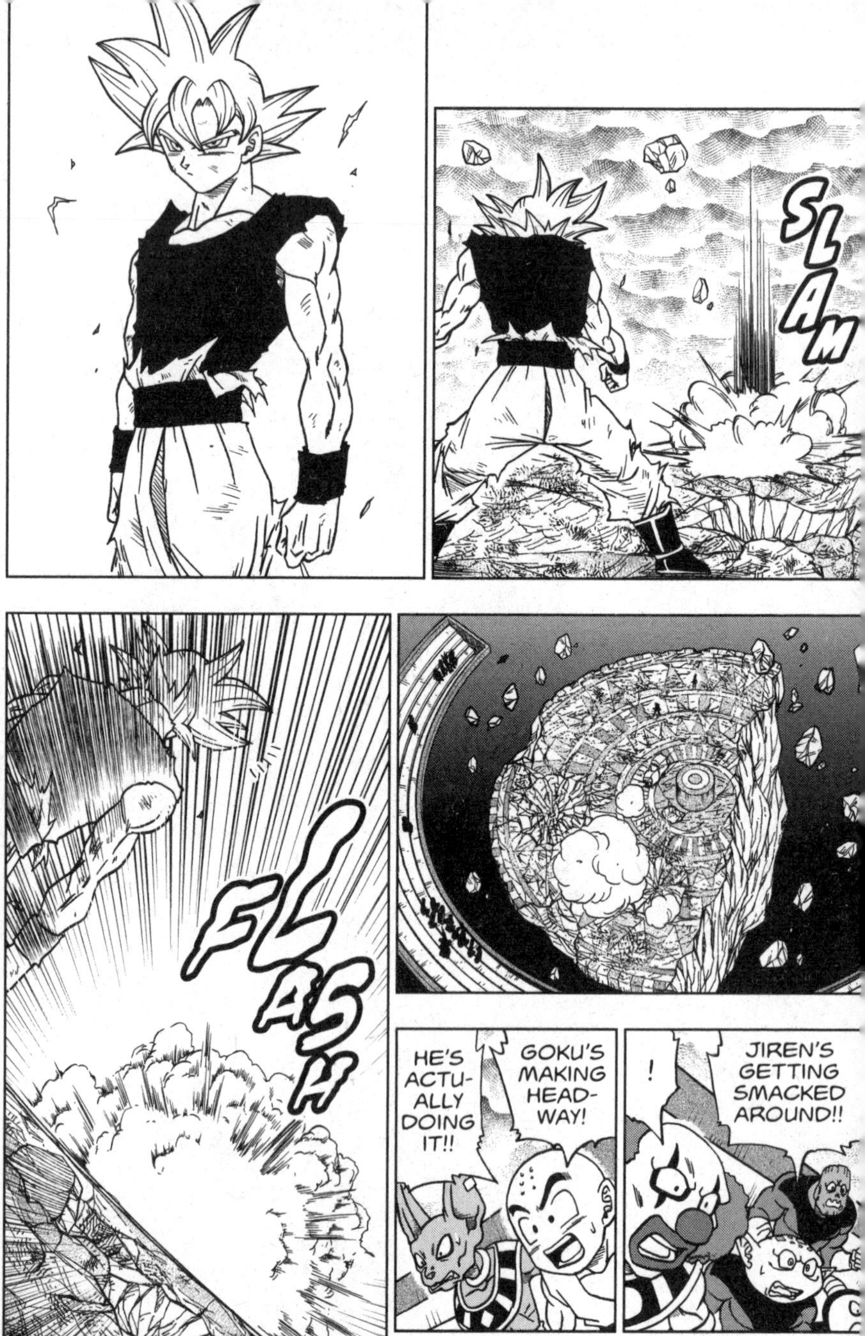
SLAM
JIREN'S GETTING SMACKED AROUND!!
!
GOKU'S MAKING HEAD-WAY!
HE'S ACTU-ALLY DOING IT!!
FLASH

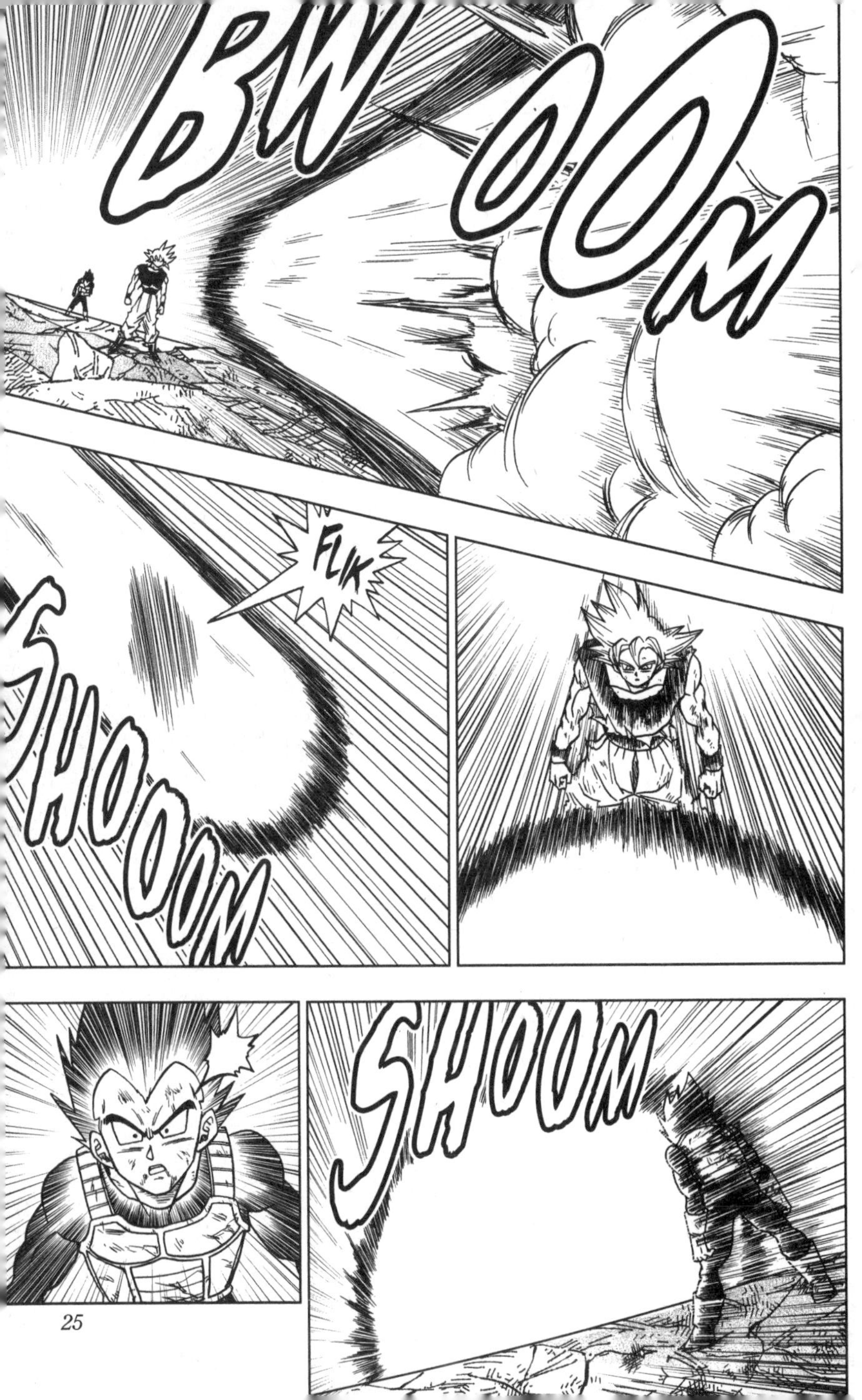
BWOOOM
FLIK
SHOOOOM
SHOOM

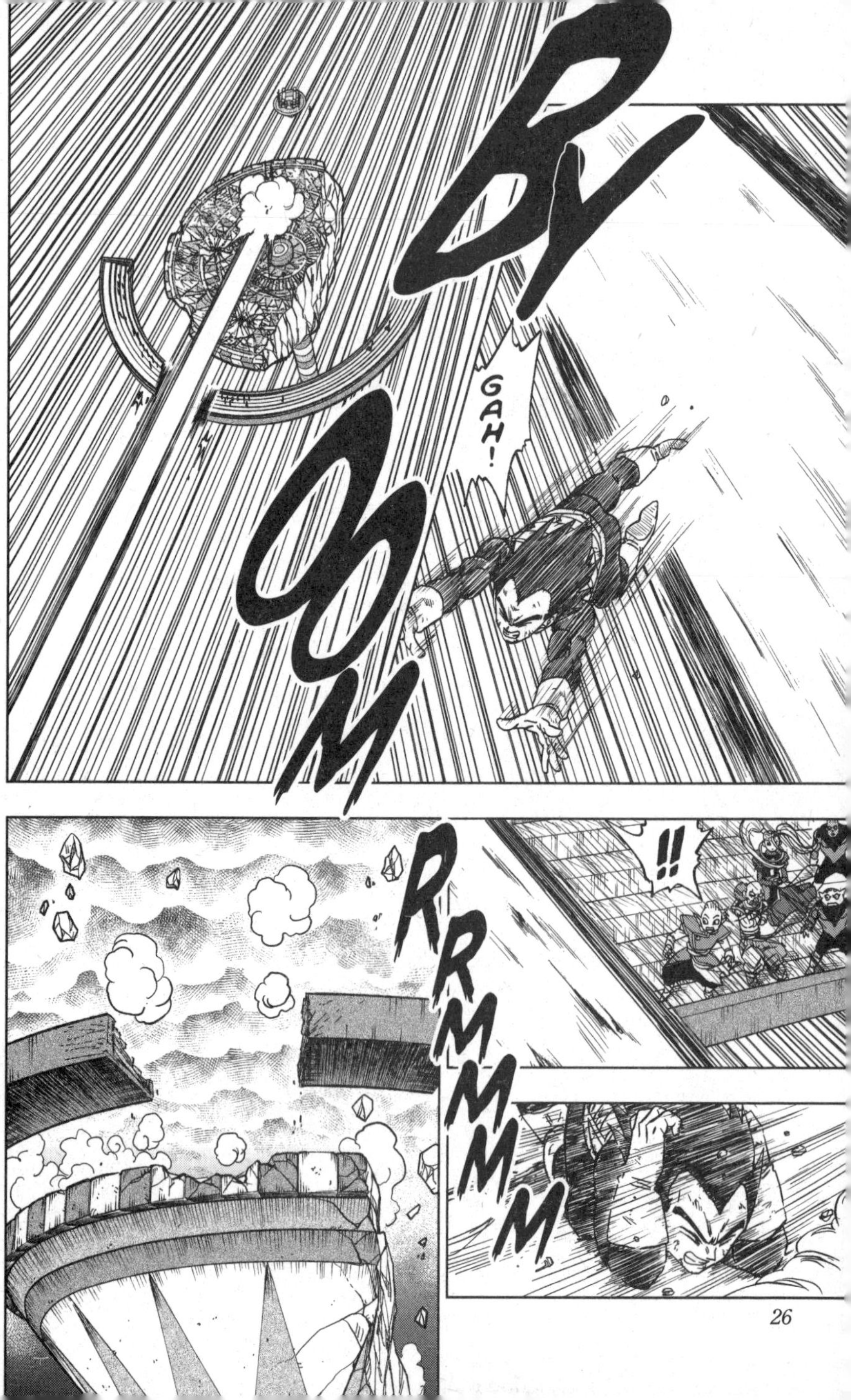
GAH!
!!
RRMMMM

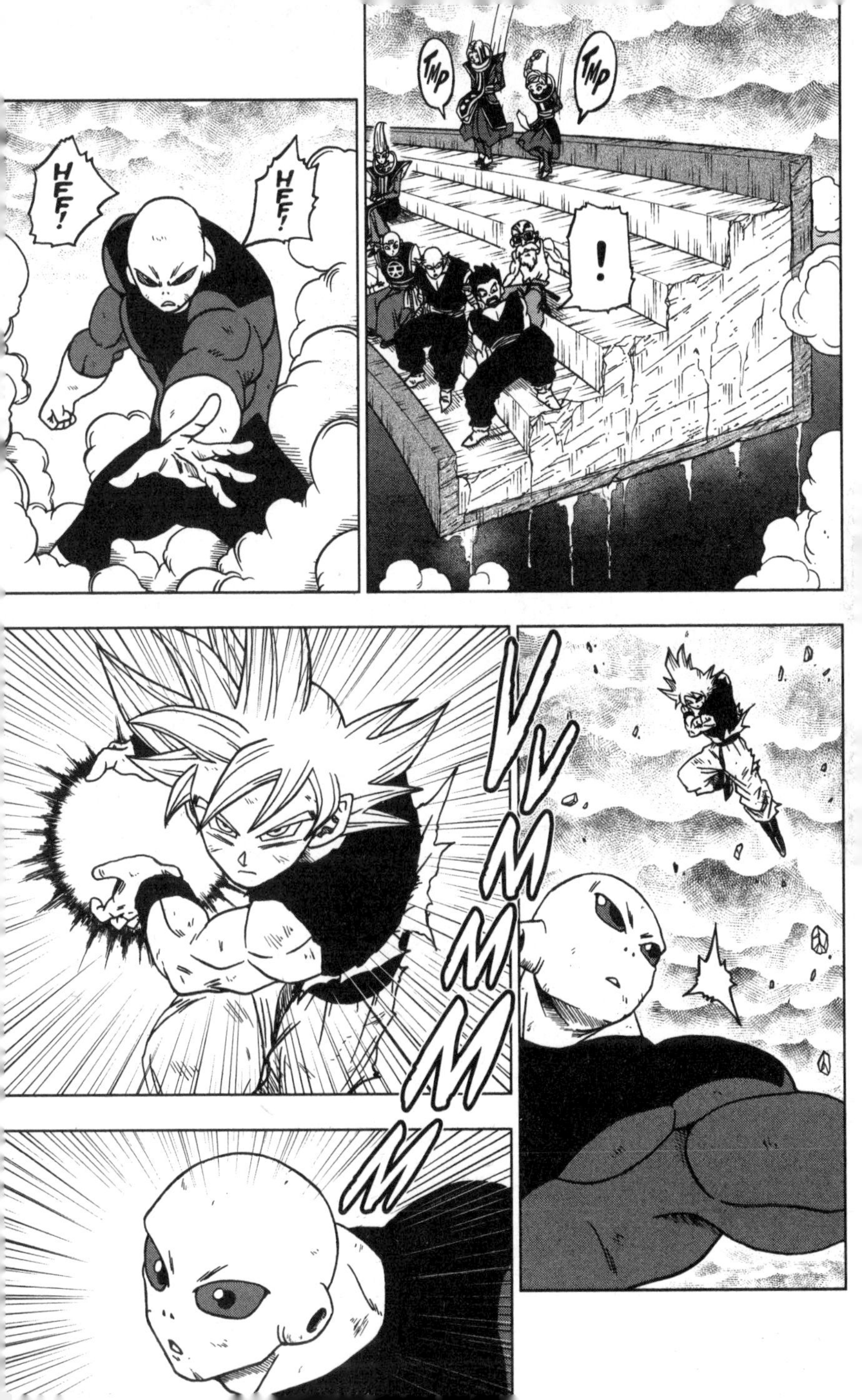
TMP
TMP
!
HEF!
HEF!
VVMMMMM

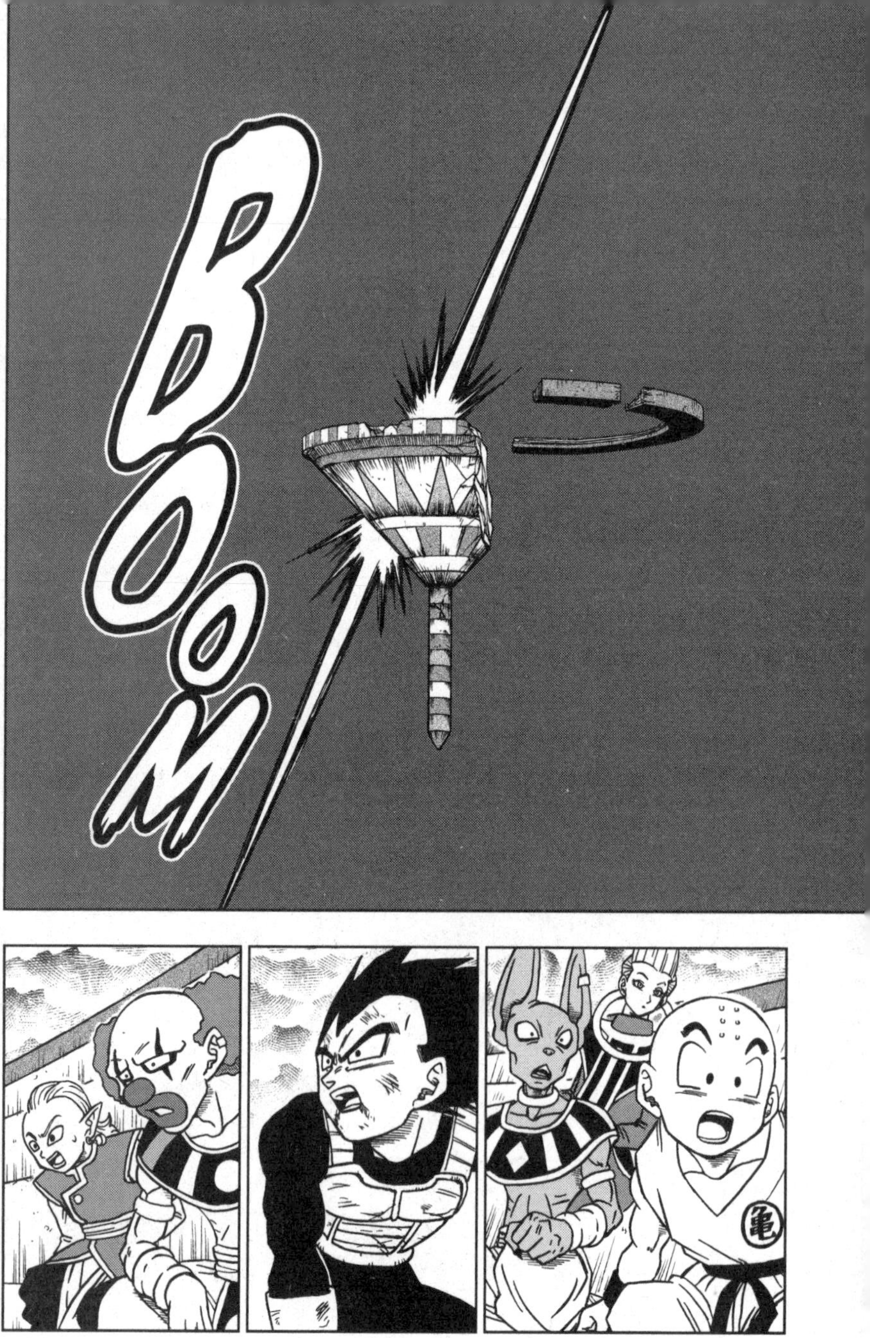
BOOM

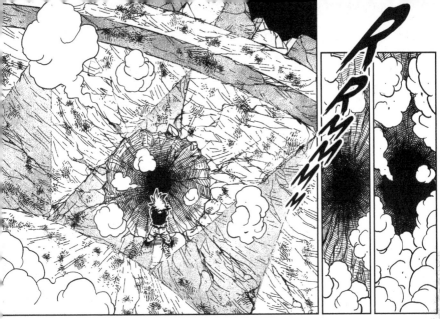

RRMMMM

DON'T WORRY.

IT CAN'T BE!!

DID HE FALL OFF?!

J-JIREN'S GONE!!

FSHHHHH

HE'S HANGING IN THERE.

LOOK...

HUH?

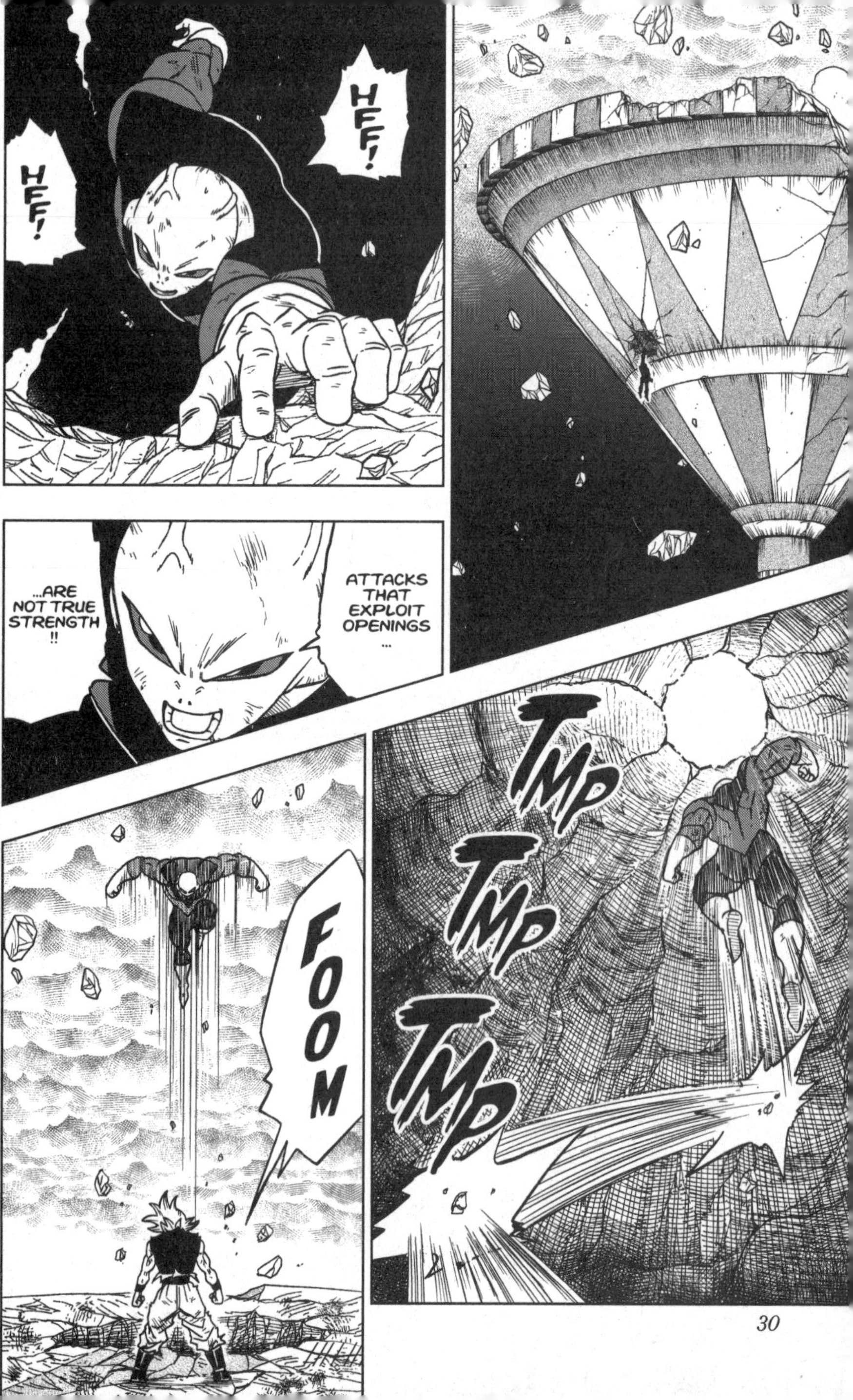
HFF!
HFF!
ATTACKS THAT EXPLOIT OPENINGS...
...ARE NOT TRUE STRENGTH!!
TMP TMP TMP
FOOM

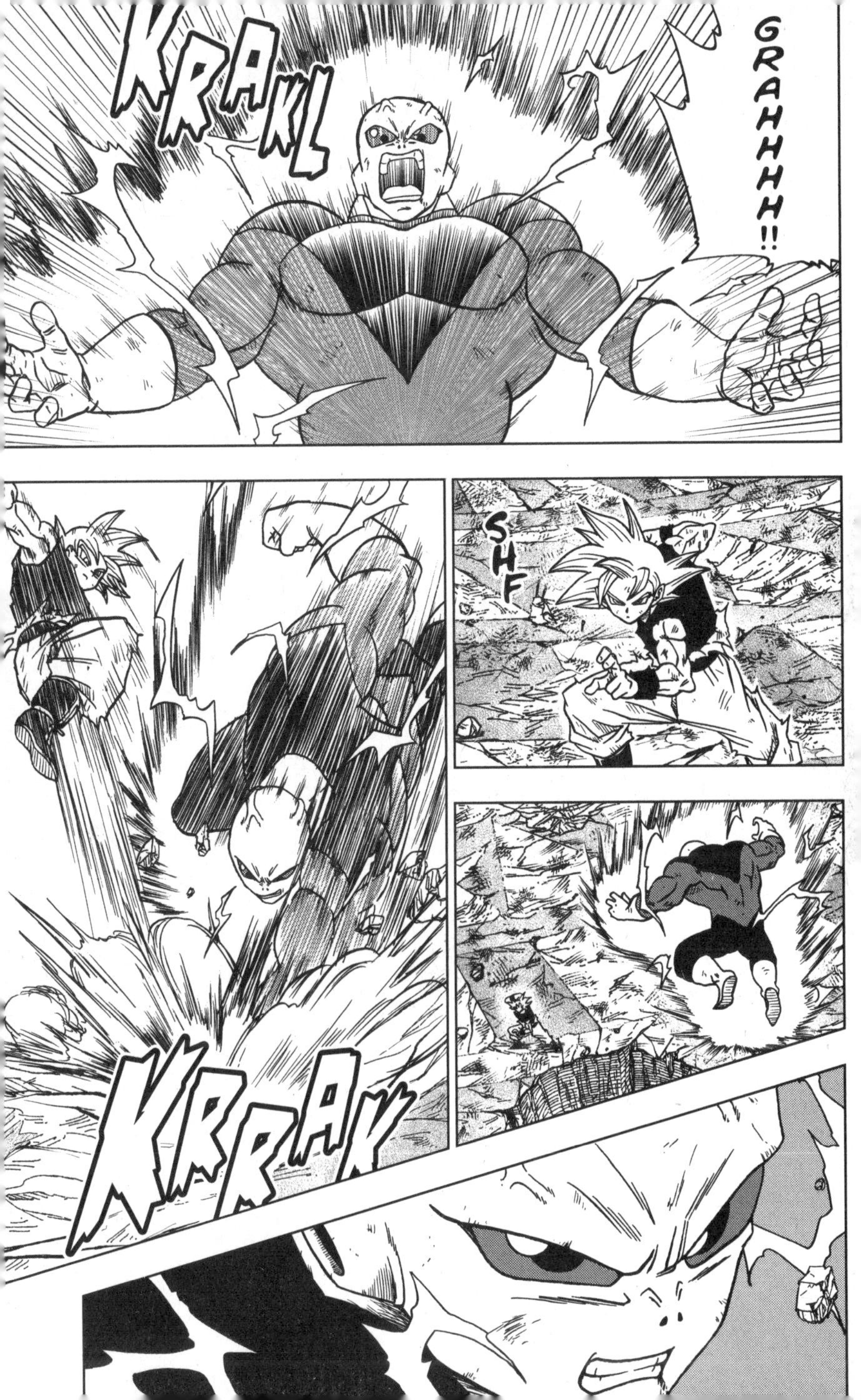
GRAHHHHH!!
KRAKL
SHF
KRRAK

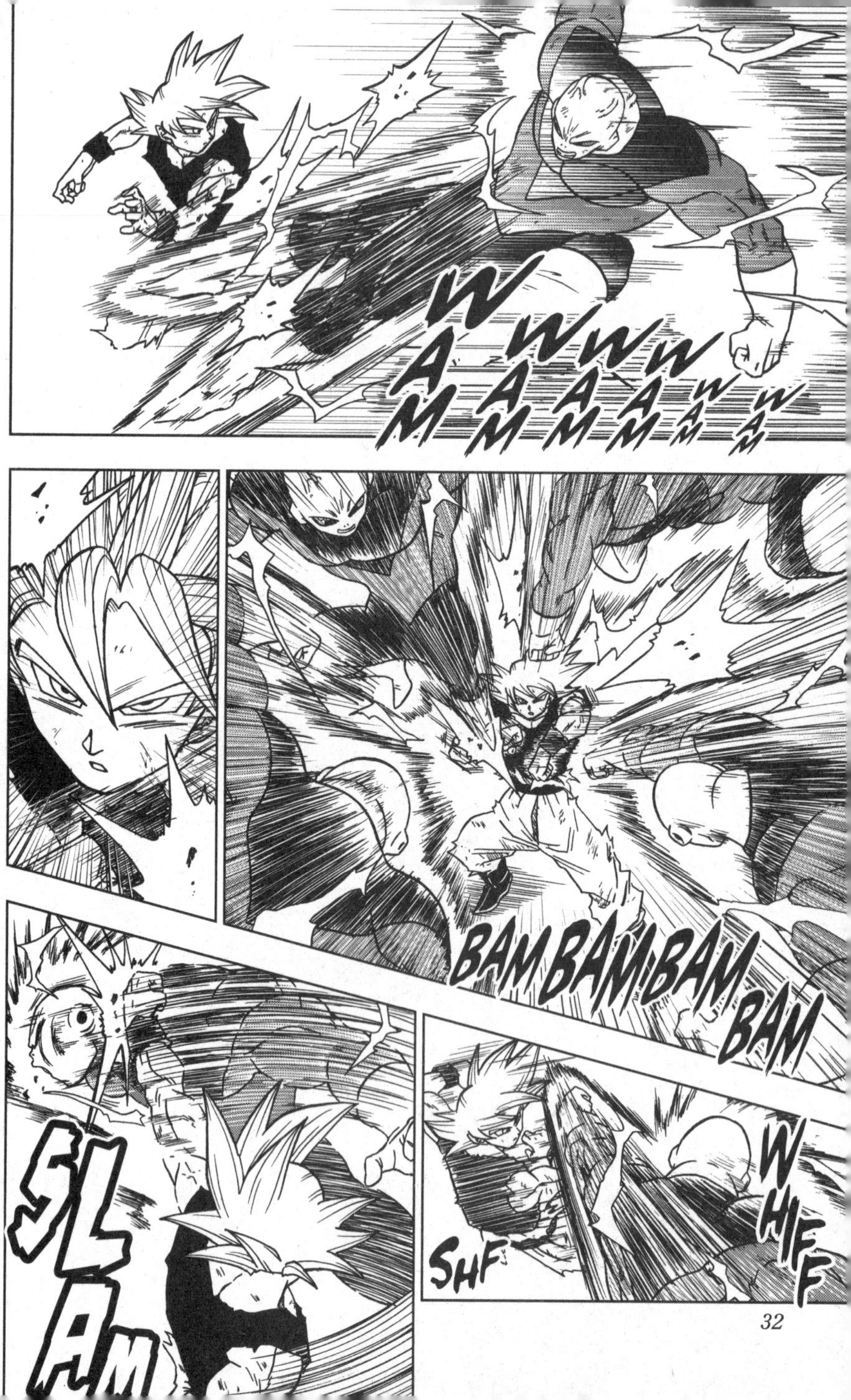
WAM WAM WAM WAM WAM WAM
BAM BAM BAM BAM BAM
WHIFF
SHF
SLAM

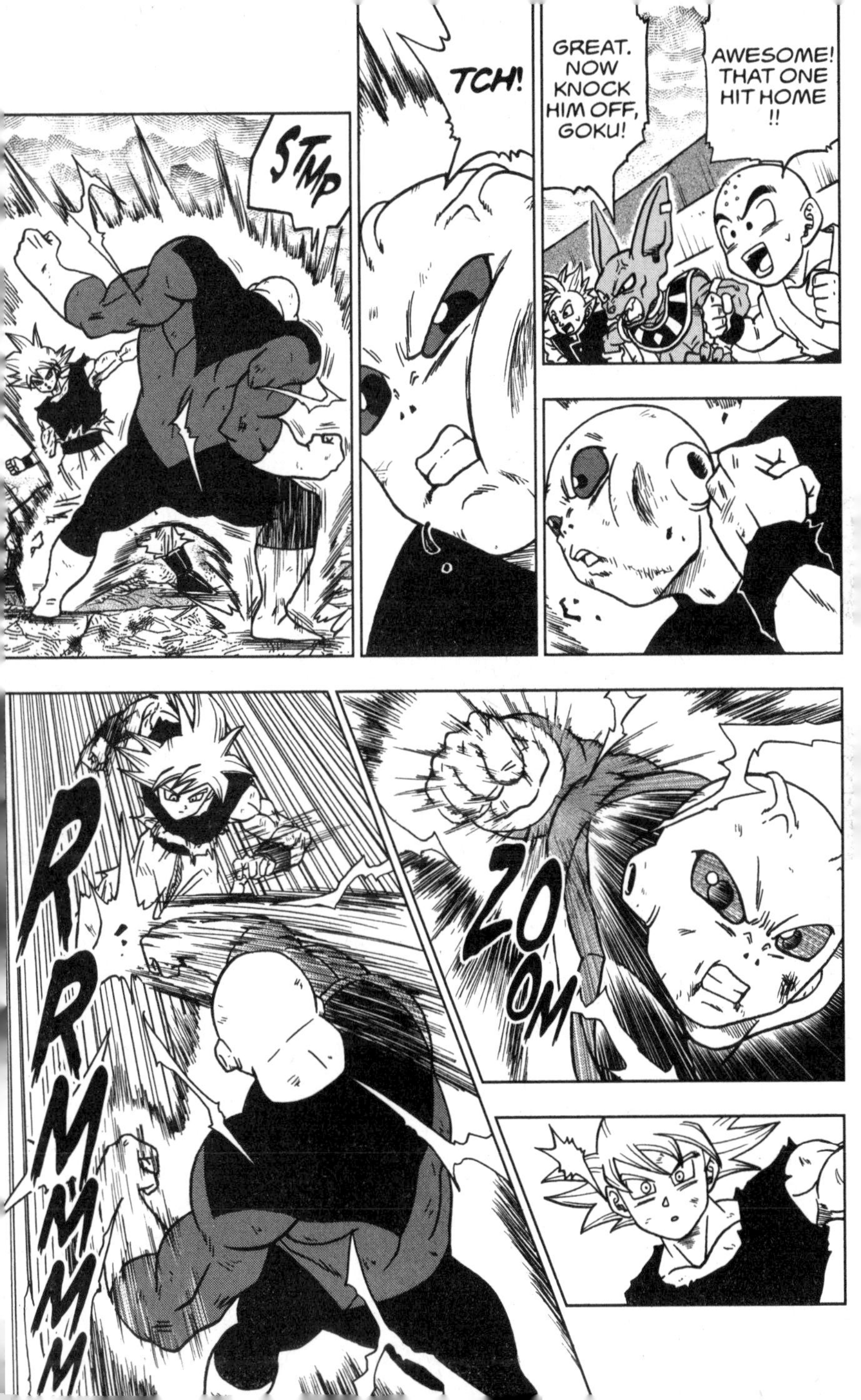
AWESOME! THAT ONE HIT HOME !!
GREAT. NOW KNOCK HIM OFF, GOKU!
TCH!
STMP
ZOOM
RRMMMMM

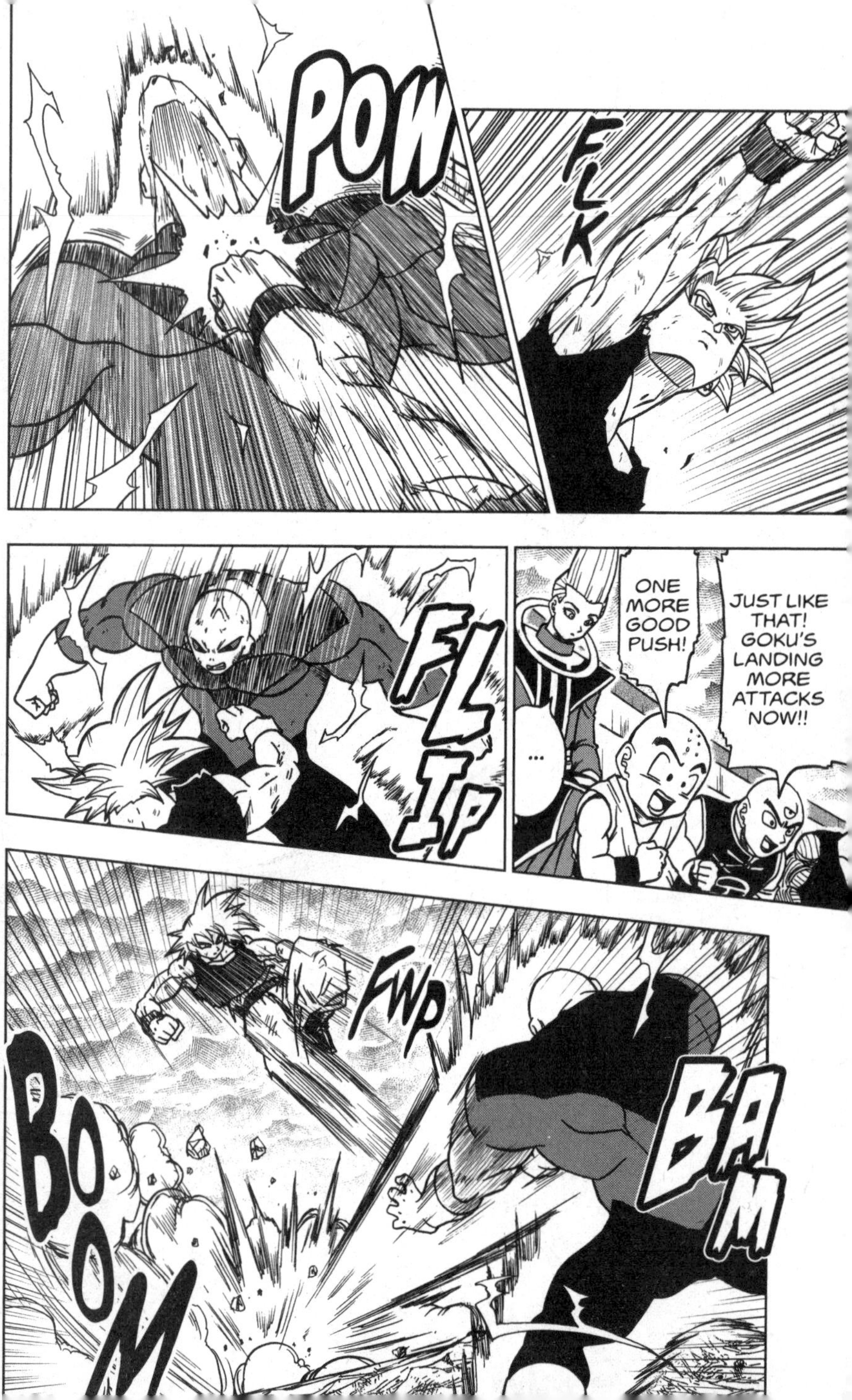
FLK
POW
JUST LIKE THAT! GOKU'S LANDING MORE ATTACKS NOW!!
ONE MORE GOOD PUSH!
...
FLIP
BAM
FWP
BOOM

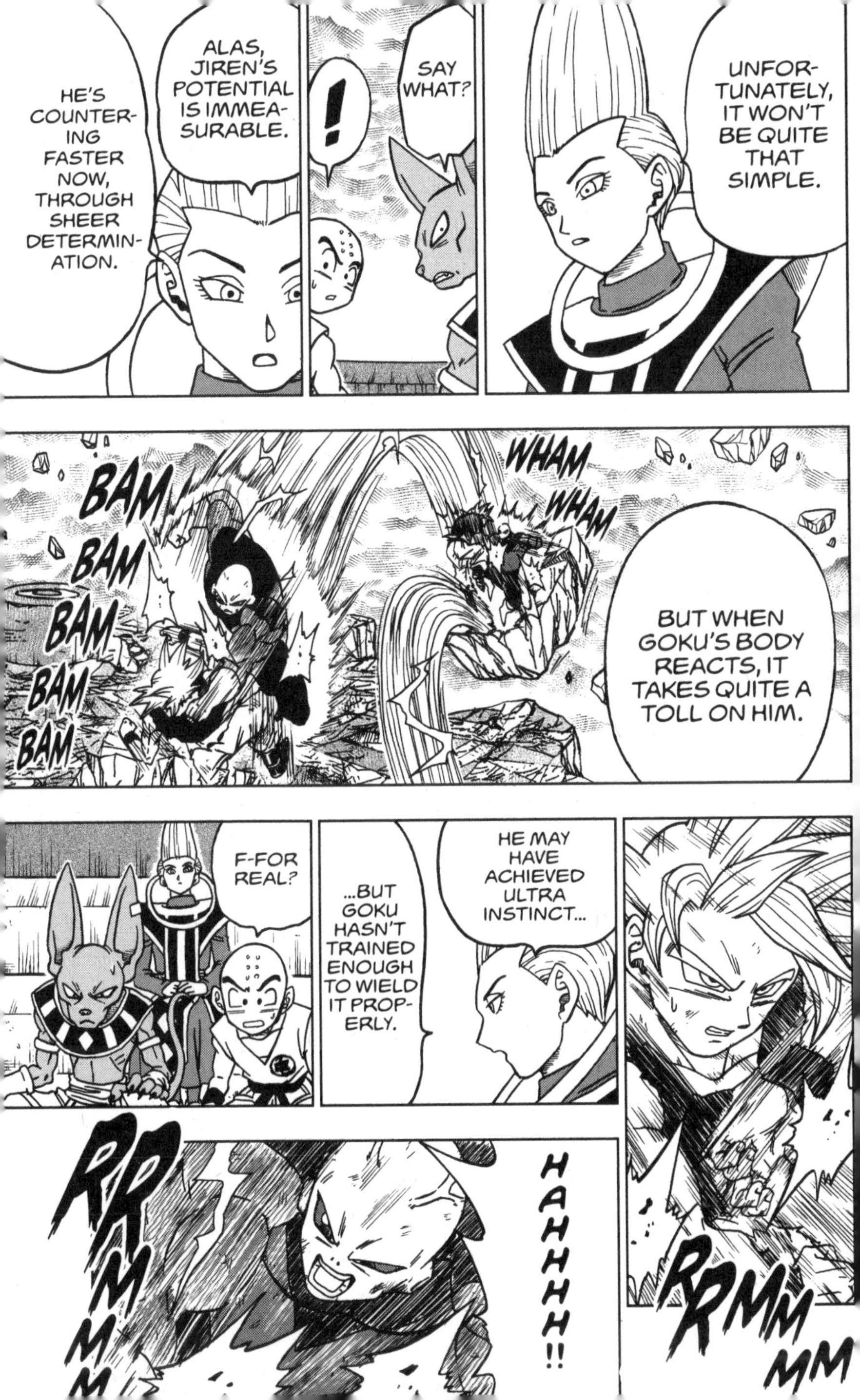
UNFORTUNATELY, IT WON'T BE QUITE THAT SIMPLE.
SAY WHAT?
!
ALAS, JIREN'S POTENTIAL IS IMMEASURABLE.
HE'S COUNTERING FASTER NOW, THROUGH SHEER DETERMINATION.
BUT WHEN GOKU'S BODY REACTS, IT TAKES QUITE A TOLL ON HIM.
WHAM WHAM
BAM BAM BAM BAM BAM BAM
RRMMMMM
HE MAY HAVE ACHIEVED ULTRA INSTINCT...
...BUT GOKU HASN'T TRAINED ENOUGH TO WIELD IT PROPERLY.
F-FOR REAL?
HAHHHHH!!
RRMMMM

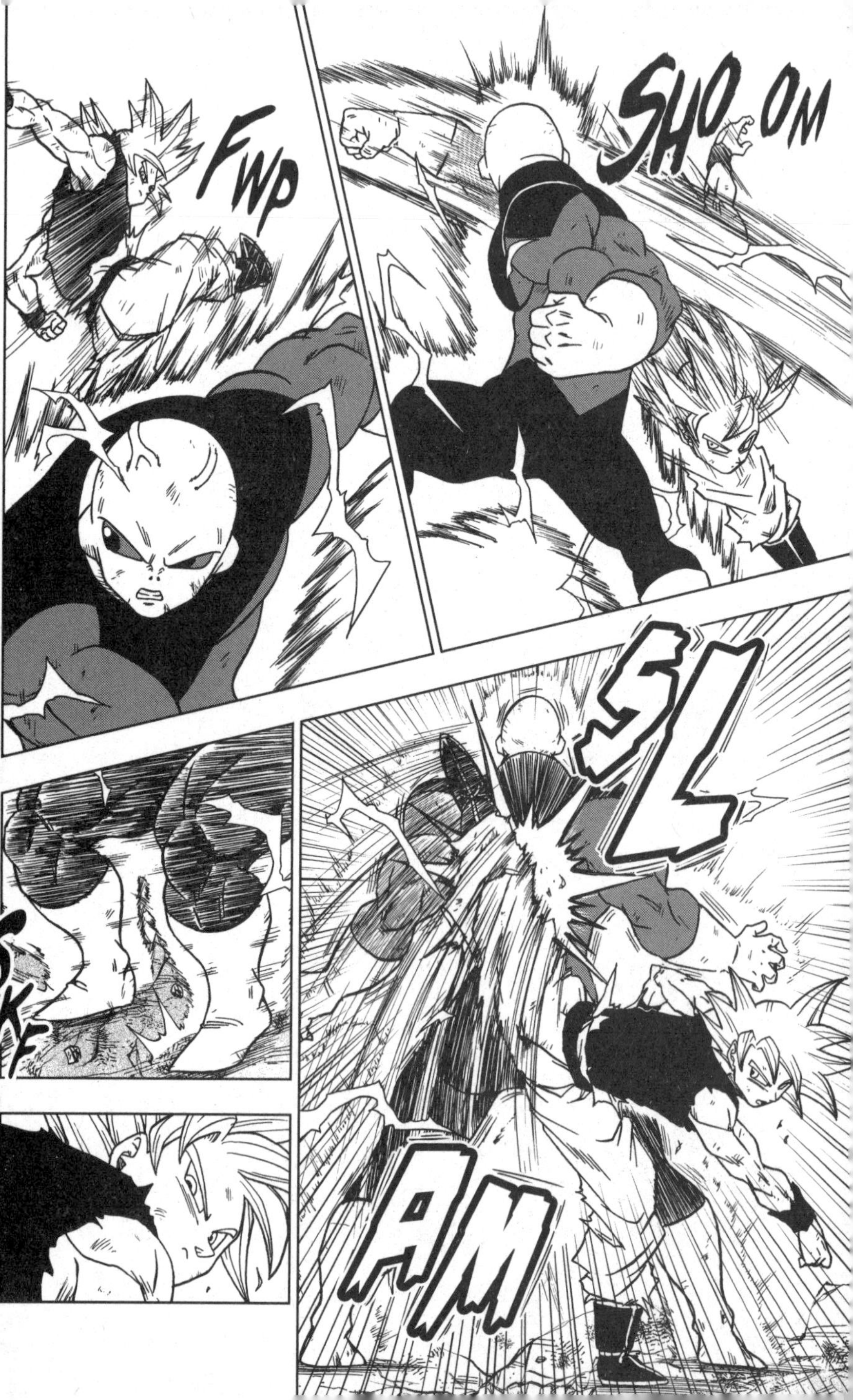
SHOOM
FWP
SLAM

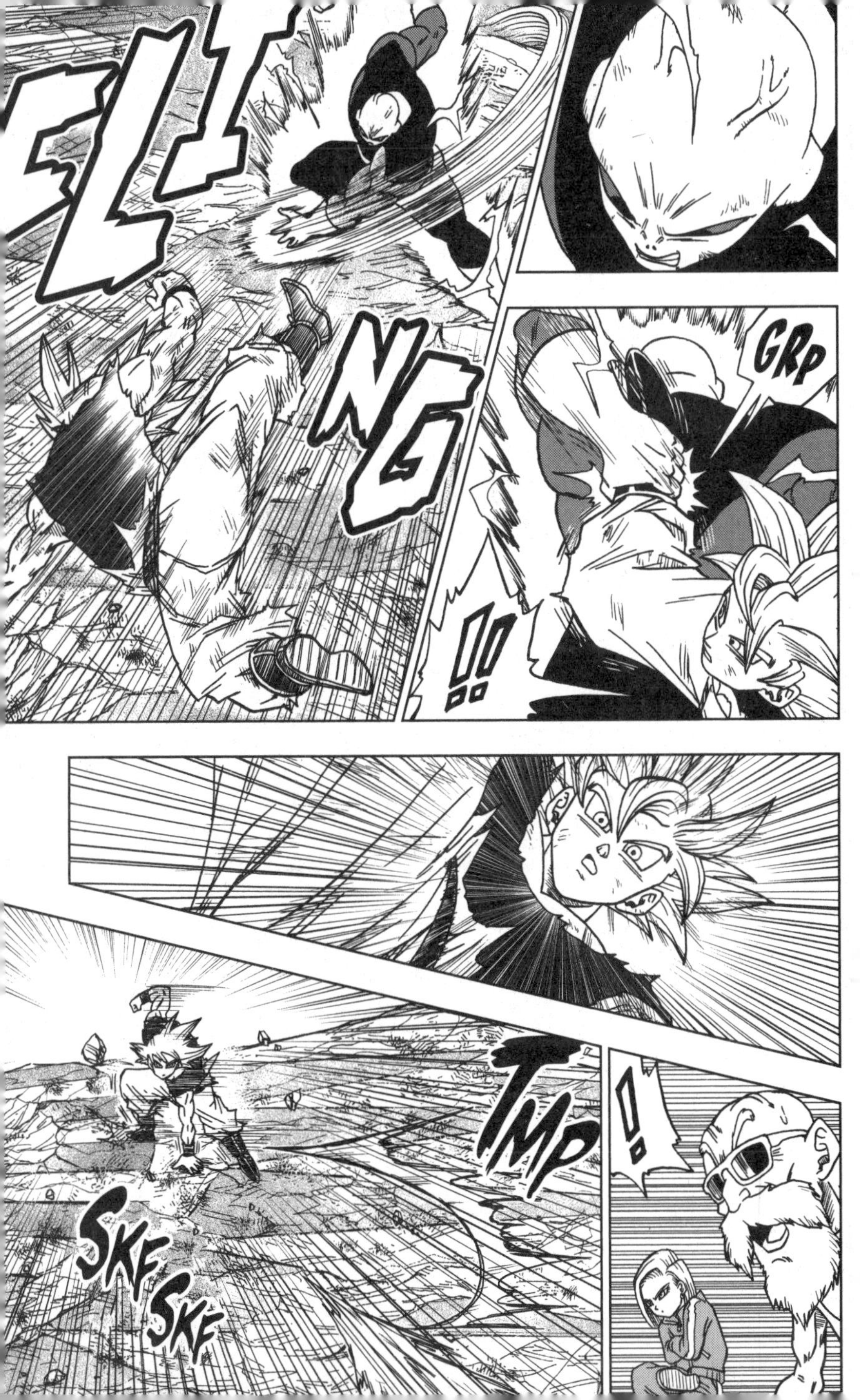
GRP
!!
!
TMP
SKF SKF

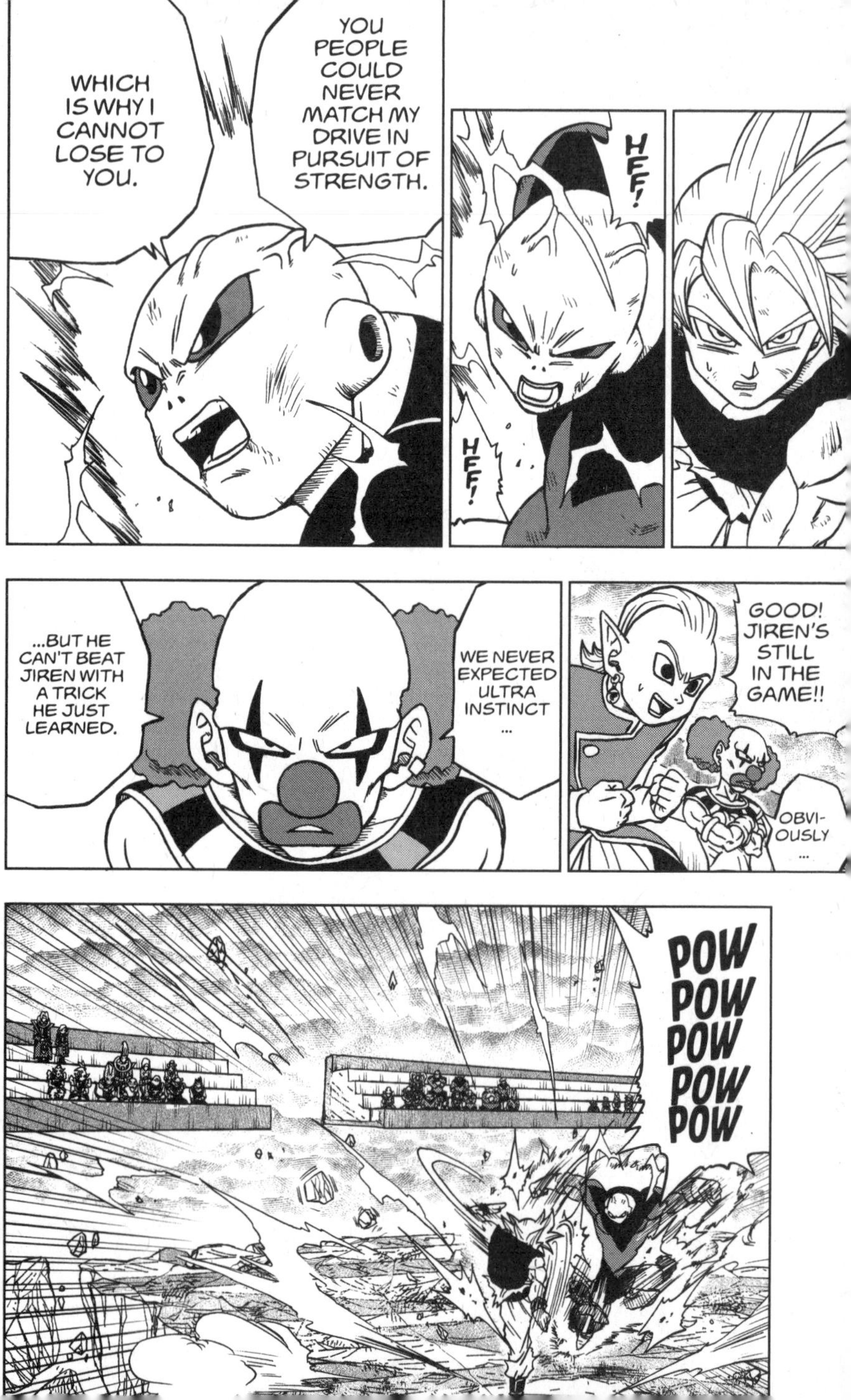
HEFF!
HEFF!
YOU PEOPLE COULD NEVER MATCH MY DRIVE IN PURSUIT OF STRENGTH.
WHICH IS WHY I CANNOT LOSE TO YOU.
GOOD! JIREN'S STILL IN THE GAME!!
OBVIOUSLY ...
WE NEVER EXPECTED ULTRA INSTINCT ...
...BUT HE CAN'T BEAT JIREN WITH A TRICK HE JUST LEARNED.
POW POW POW POW POW

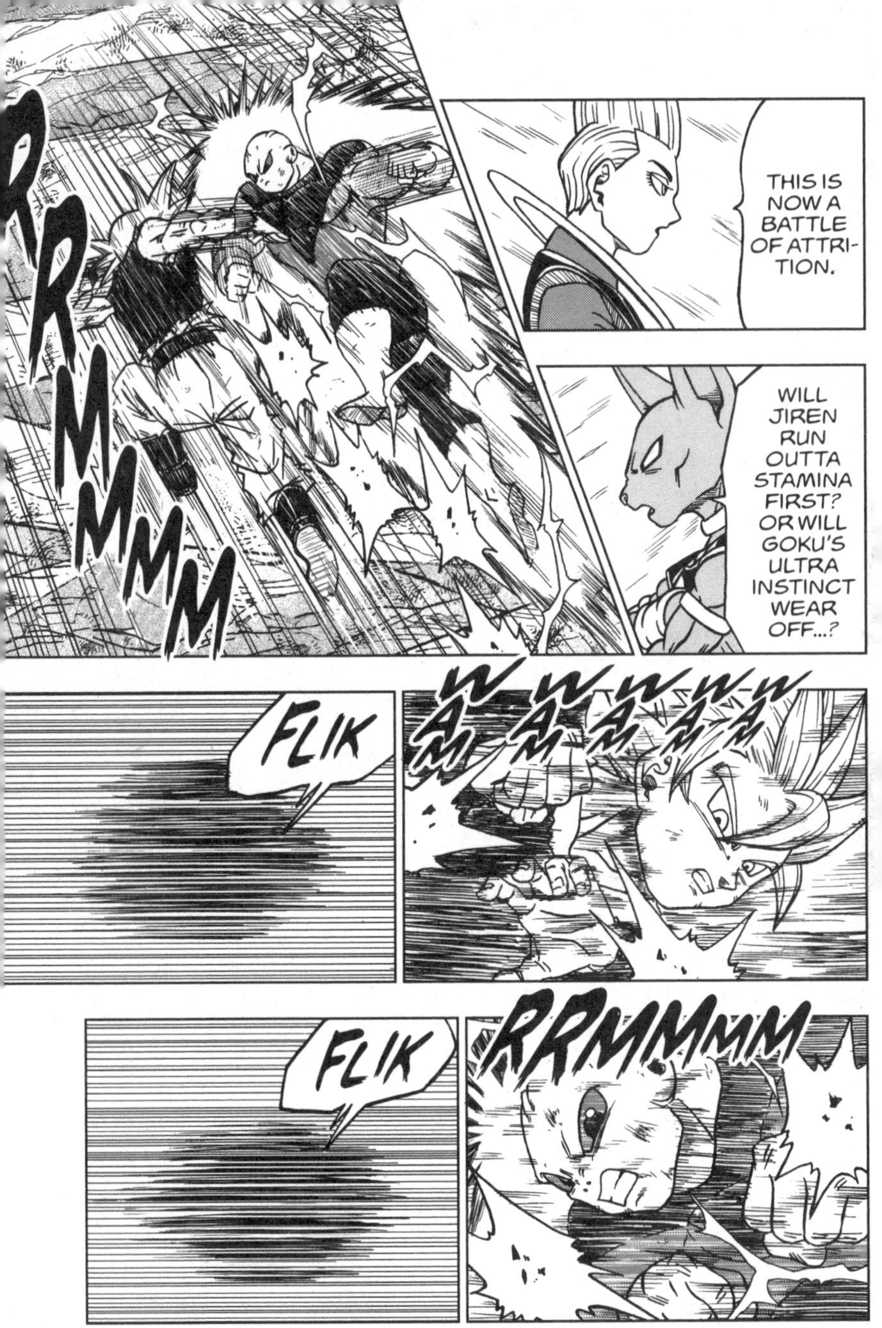
THIS IS NOW A BATTLE OF ATTRITION.
WILL JIREN RUN OUTTA STAMINA FIRST? OR WILL GOKU'S ULTRA INSTINCT WEAR OFF...?
RRMMMMMM
WAM WAM WAM WAM WAM
FLIK
RRMMMMM
FLIK

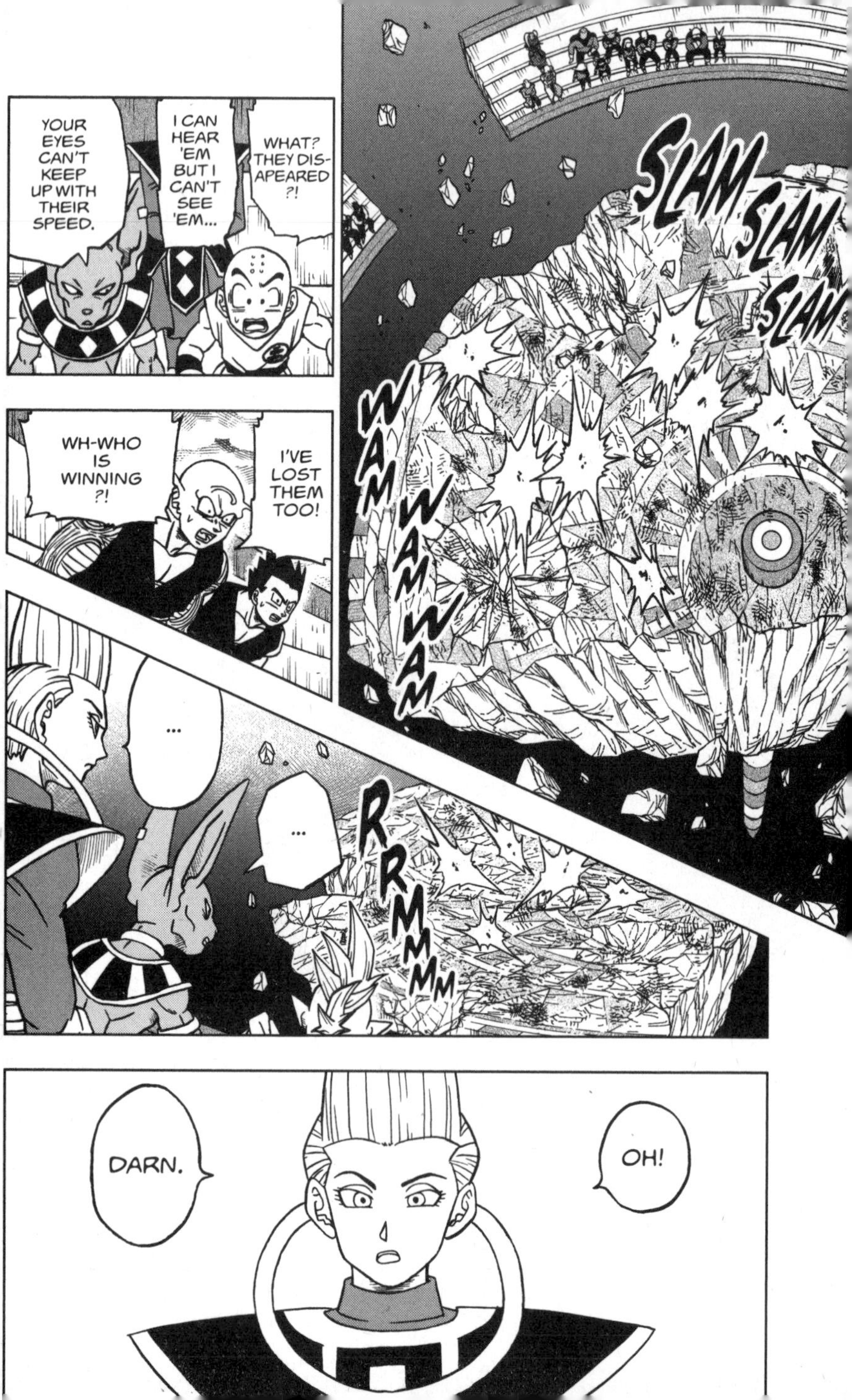
SLAM SLAM SLAM
WAM WAM WAM
WHAT? THEY DIS-APEARED?!
I CAN HEAR 'EM BUT I CAN'T SEE 'EM...
YOUR EYES CAN'T KEEP UP WITH THEIR SPEED.
I'VE LOST THEM TOO!
WH-WHO IS WINNING?!
...
...
RRRMMMM
OH!
DARN.

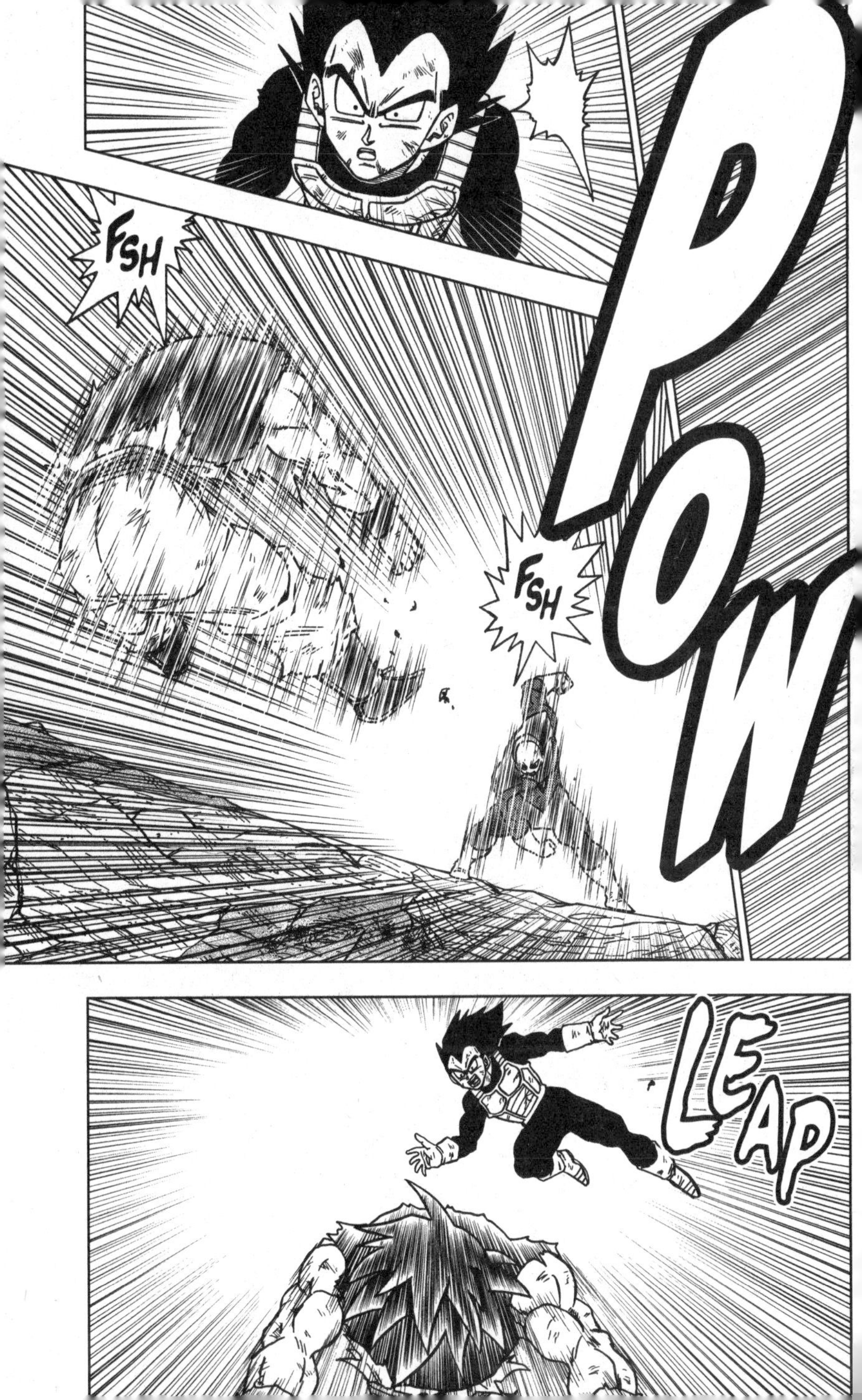
POW
FSH
FSH
LEAP

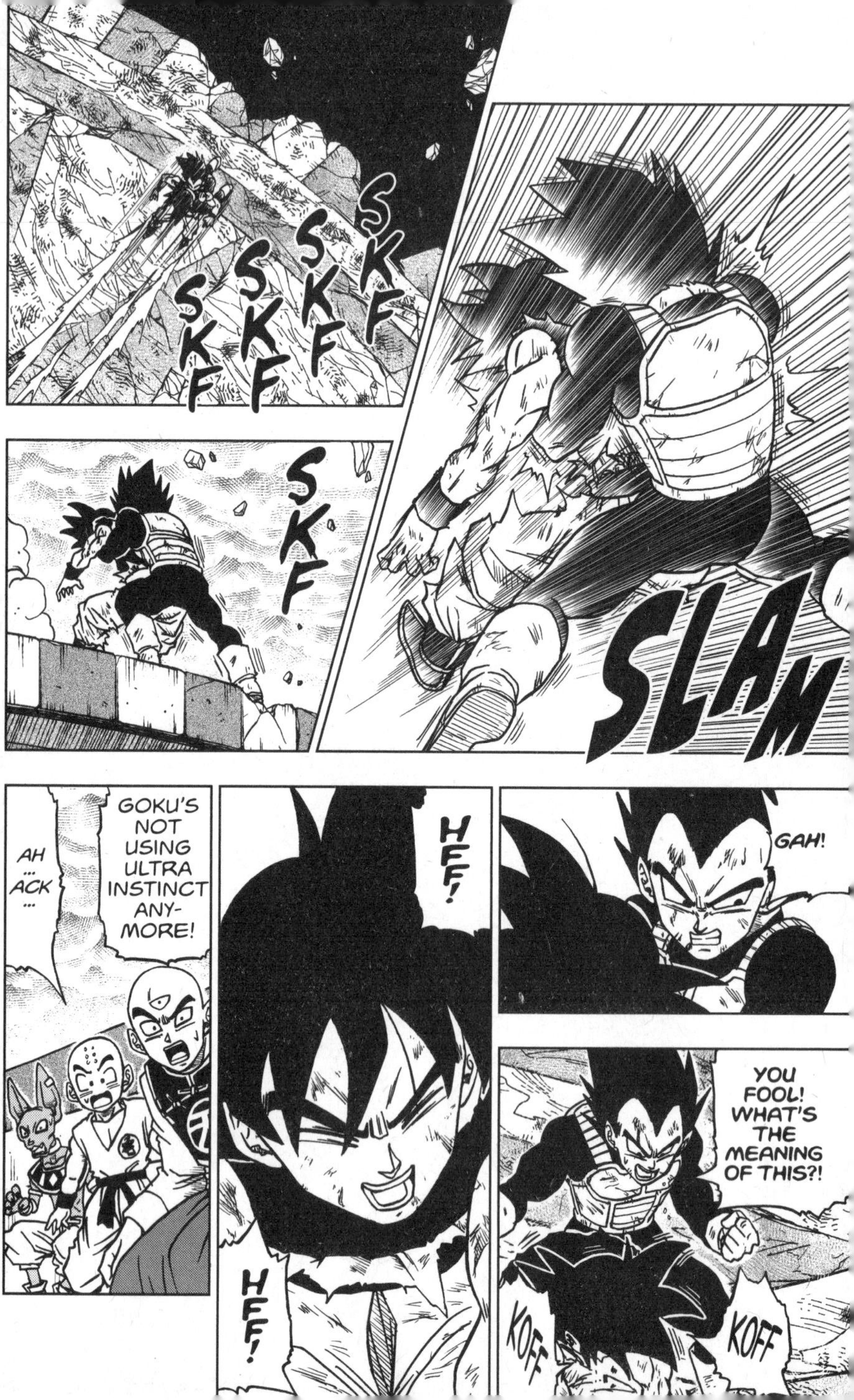
SLAM
SKF SKF SKF SKF
SKF
GAH!
YOU FOOL! WHAT'S THE MEANING OF THIS?!
KOFF KOFF
HFF! HFF!
GOKU'S NOT USING ULTRA INSTINCT ANYMORE!
AH ... ACK ...

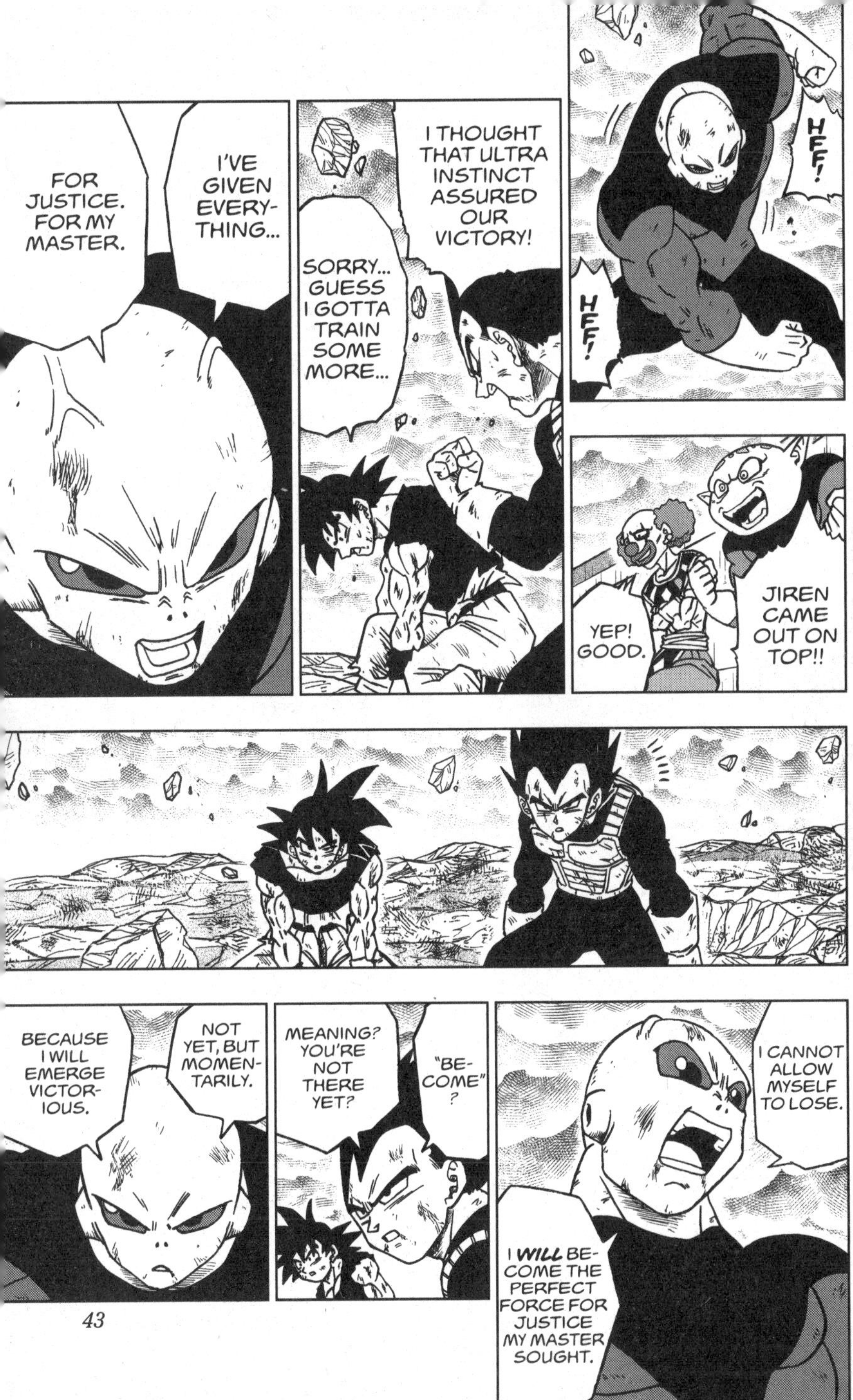
HEFF!
HEFF!
JIREN CAME OUT ON TOP!!
YEP! GOOD.
I THOUGHT THAT ULTRA INSTINCT ASSURED OUR VICTORY!
SORRY... GUESS I GOTTA TRAIN SOME MORE...
I'VE GIVEN EVERYTHING...
FOR JUSTICE. FOR MY MASTER.
I CANNOT ALLOW MYSELF TO LOSE.
I **WILL** BECOME THE PERFECT FORCE FOR JUSTICE MY MASTER SOUGHT.
"BECOME"?
MEANING? YOU'RE NOT THERE YET?
NOT YET, BUT MOMENTARILY.
BECAUSE I WILL EMERGE VICTORIOUS.

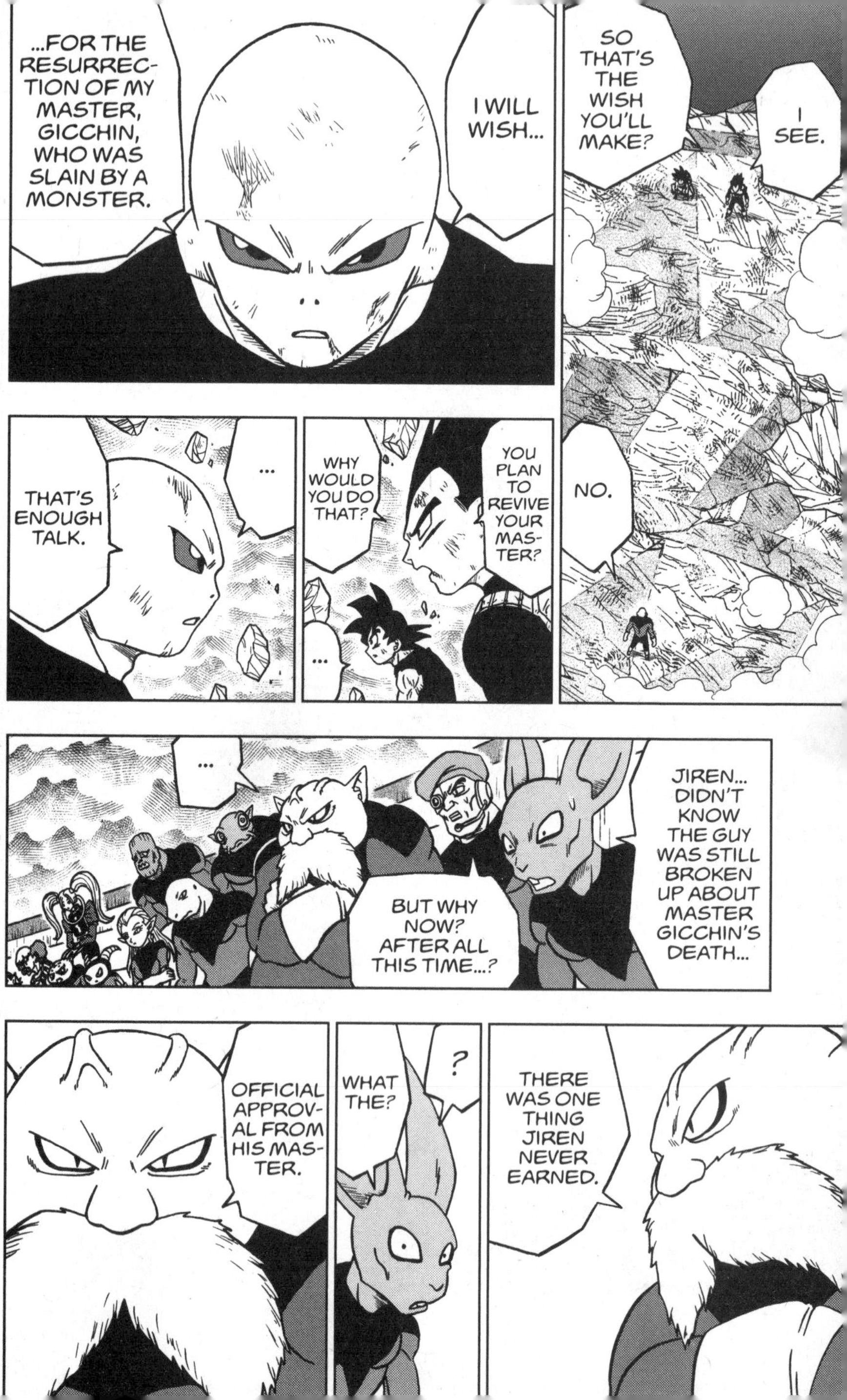
I SEE.
SO THAT'S THE WISH YOU'LL MAKE?
NO.
I WILL WISH...
...FOR THE RESURRECTION OF MY MASTER, GICCHIN, WHO WAS SLAIN BY A MONSTER.
YOU PLAN TO REVIVE YOUR MASTER?
WHY WOULD YOU DO THAT?
...
...
THAT'S ENOUGH TALK.
JIREN... DIDN'T KNOW THE GUY WAS STILL BROKEN UP ABOUT MASTER GICCHIN'S DEATH...
...
BUT WHY NOW? AFTER ALL THIS TIME...?
THERE WAS ONE THING JIREN NEVER EARNED.
?
WHAT THE?
OFFICIAL APPROVAL FROM HIS MASTER.

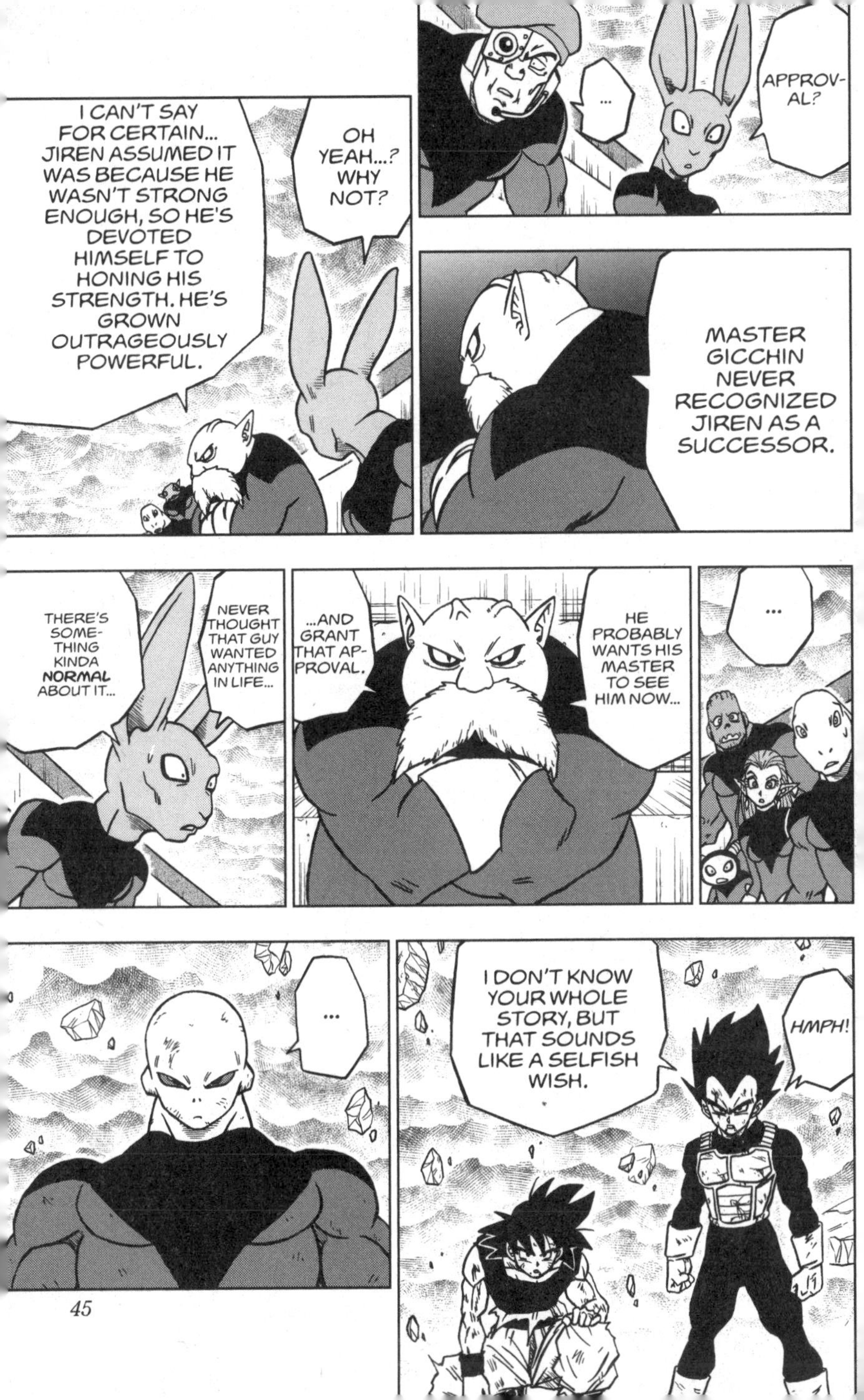
APPROV-AL?
...
MASTER GICCHIN NEVER RECOGNIZED JIREN AS A SUCCESSOR.
OH YEAH...? WHY NOT?
I CAN'T SAY FOR CERTAIN... JIREN ASSUMED IT WAS BECAUSE HE WASN'T STRONG ENOUGH, SO HE'S DEVOTED HIMSELF TO HONING HIS STRENGTH. HE'S GROWN OUTRAGEOUSLY POWERFUL.
...
HE PROBABLY WANTS HIS MASTER TO SEE HIM NOW...
...AND GRANT THAT AP-PROVAL.
NEVER THOUGHT THAT GUY WANTED ANYTHING IN LIFE...
THERE'S SOME-THING KINDA **NORMAL** ABOUT IT...
HMPH!
I DON'T KNOW YOUR WHOLE STORY, BUT THAT SOUNDS LIKE A SELFISH WISH.
...

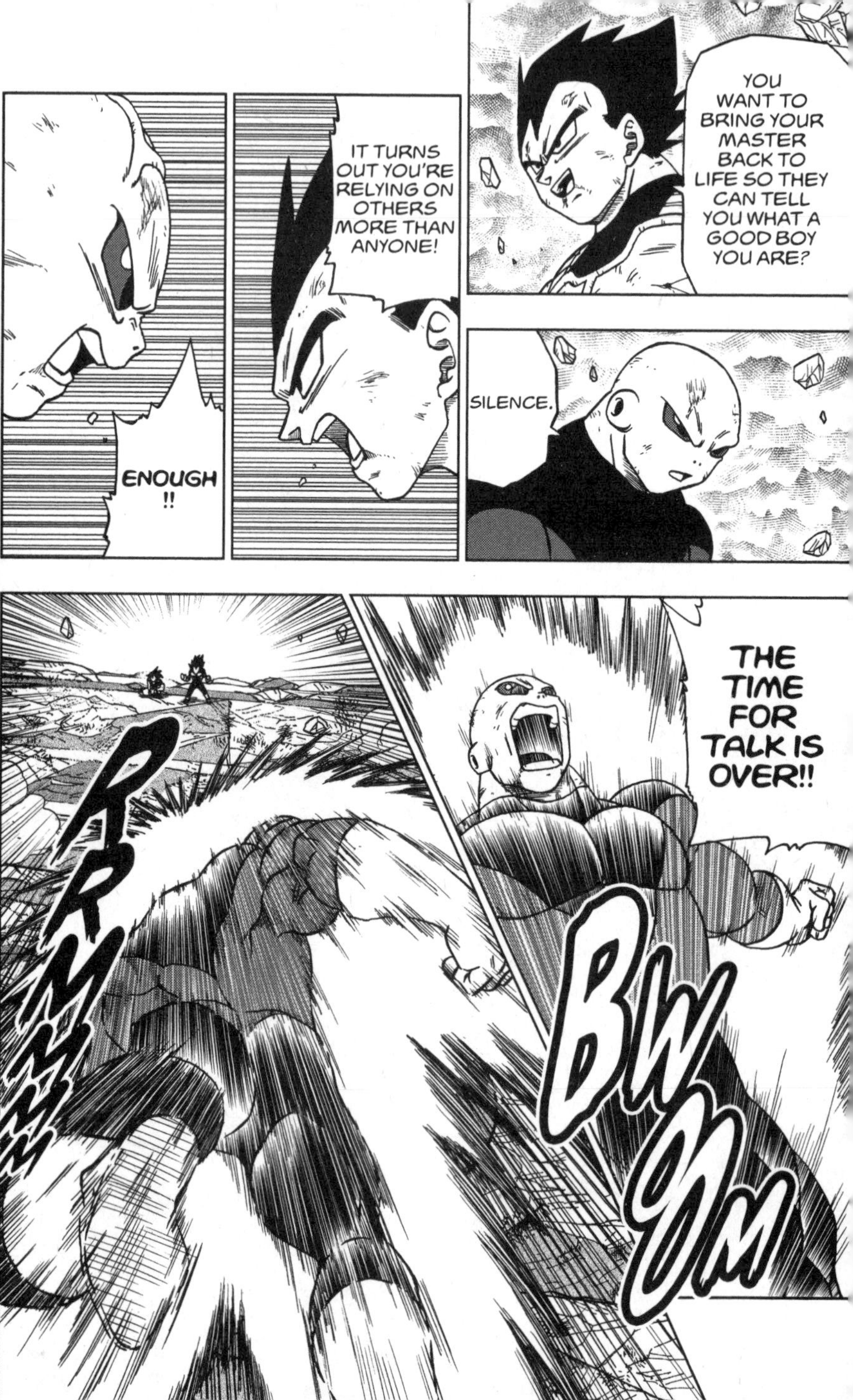
YOU WANT TO BRING YOUR MASTER BACK TO LIFE SO THEY CAN TELL YOU WHAT A GOOD BOY YOU ARE?
SILENCE.
IT TURNS OUT YOU'RE RELYING ON OTHERS MORE THAN ANYONE!
ENOUGH!!
THE TIME FOR TALK IS OVER!!

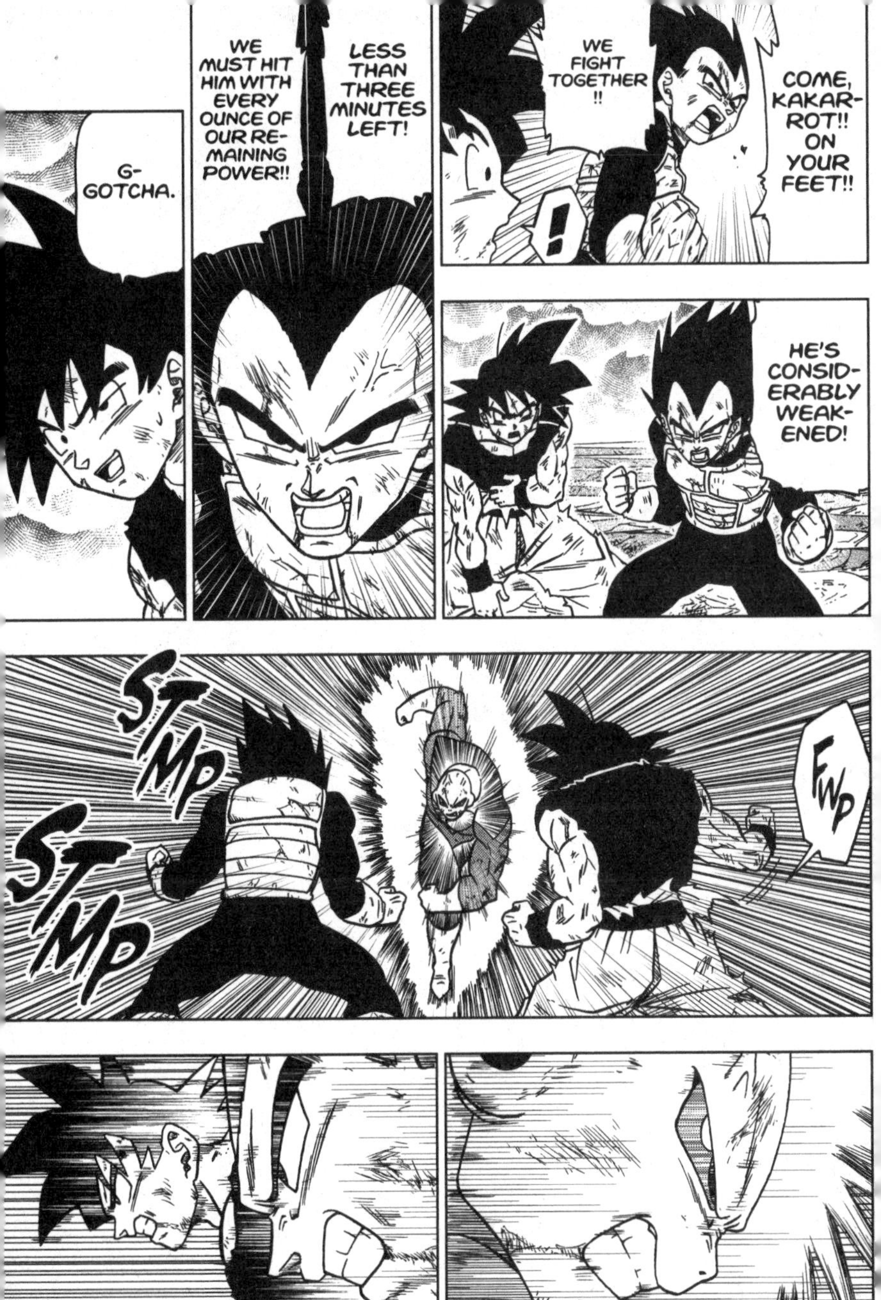
COME, KAKARROT!! ON YOUR FEET!!
WE FIGHT TOGETHER!!
!
HE'S CONSIDERABLY WEAKENED!
LESS THAN THREE MINUTES LEFT!
WE MUST HIT HIM WITH EVERY OUNCE OF OUR REMAINING POWER!!
G-GOTCHA.
FWP
STMP
STMP

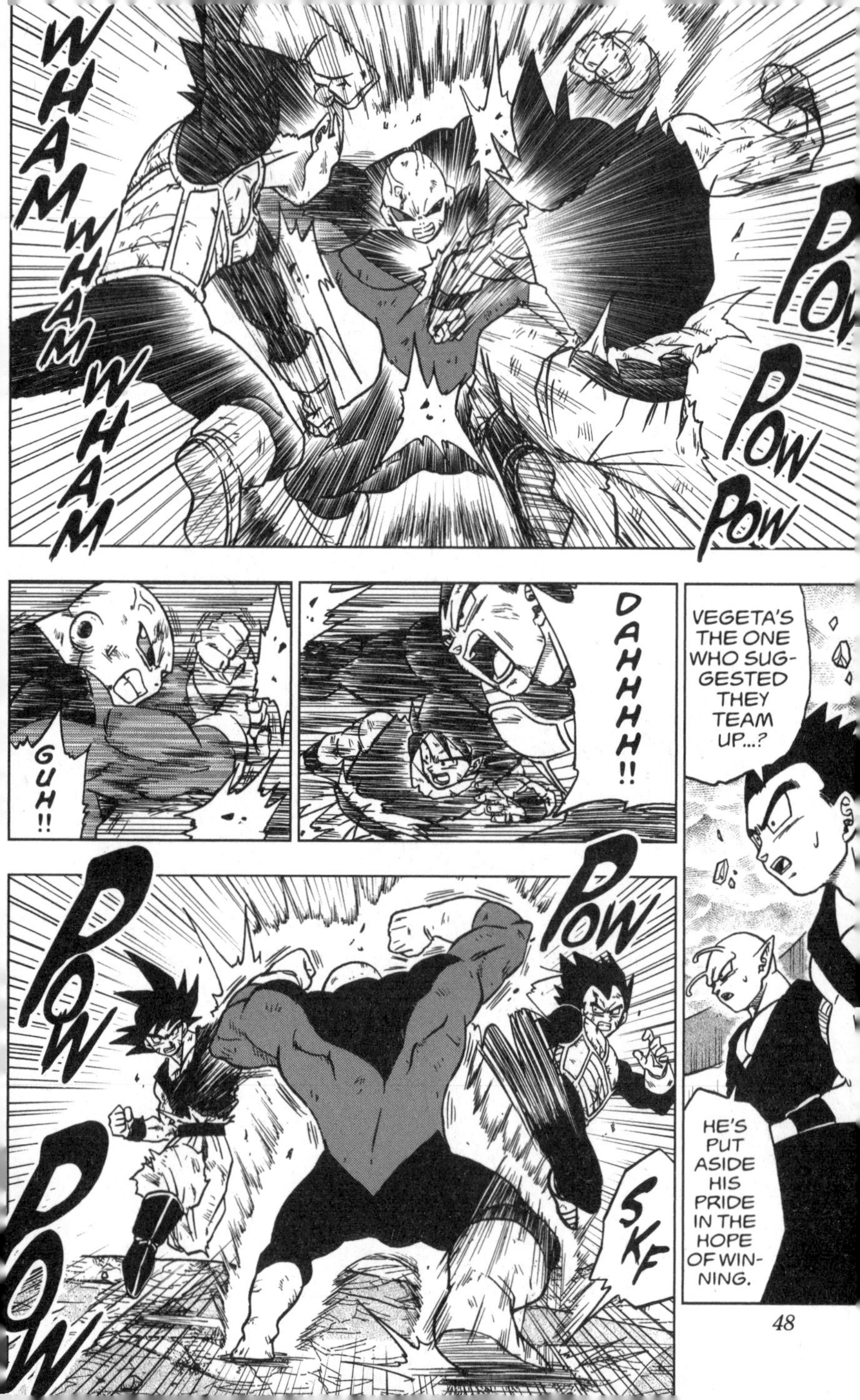

POW
POW
POW
WHAM
WHAM
WHAM
VEGETA'S THE ONE WHO SUG-GESTED THEY TEAM UP...?
HE'S PUT ASIDE HIS PRIDE IN THE HOPE OF WIN-NING.
DAHHHHH!!
GUH!!
POW
SKF
POW
POW

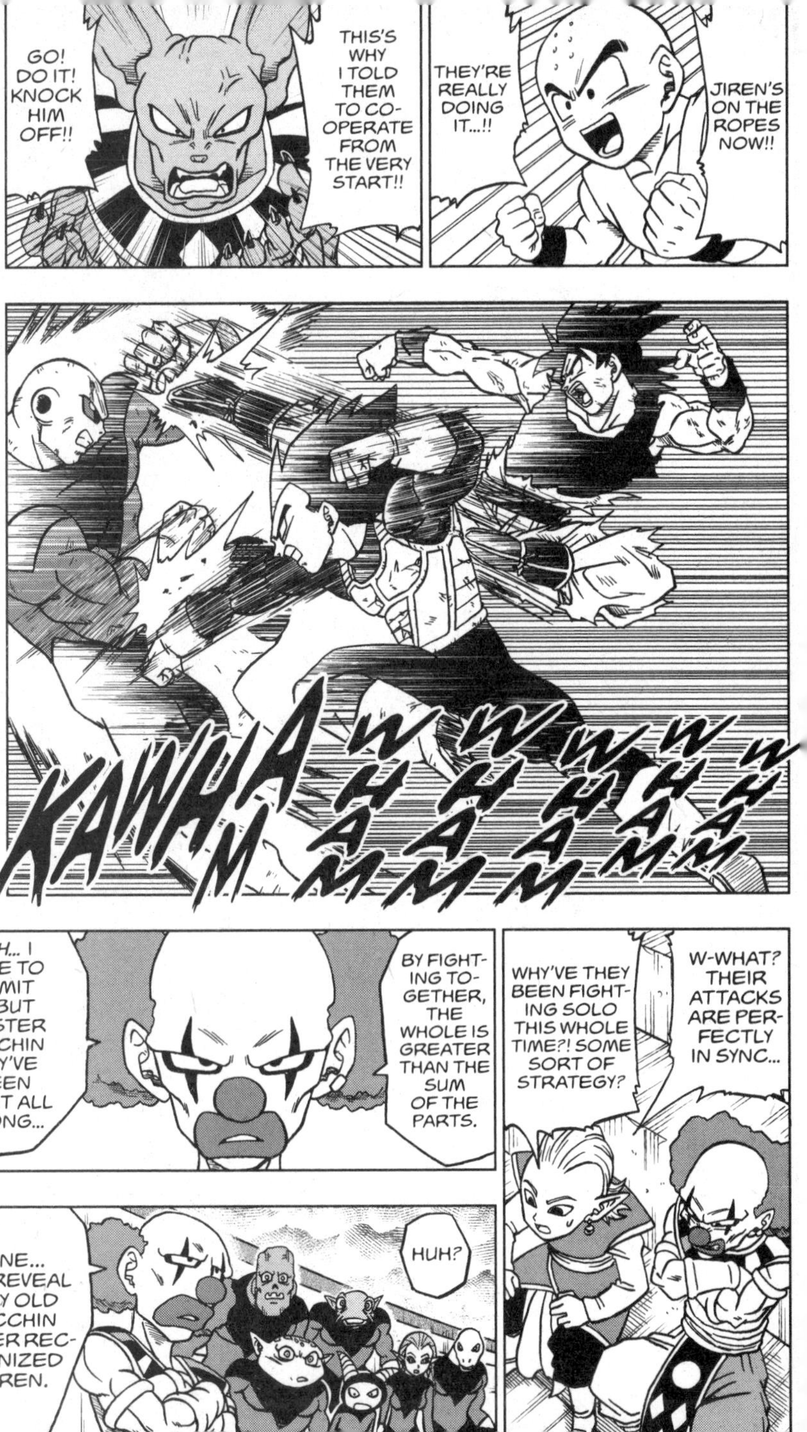
JIREN'S ON THE ROPES NOW!!
THEY'RE REALLY DOING IT...!!
THIS'S WHY I TOLD THEM TO CO-OPERATE FROM THE VERY START!!
GO! DO IT! KNOCK HIM OFF!!
KAWHAM WHAM WHAM WHAM WHAM WHAM WHAM
W-WHAT? THEIR ATTACKS ARE PERFECTLY IN SYNC...
WHY'VE THEY BEEN FIGHTING SOLO THIS WHOLE TIME?! SOME SORT OF STRATEGY?
BY FIGHTING TOGETHER, THE WHOLE IS GREATER THAN THE SUM OF THE PARTS.
TCH... I HATE TO ADMIT IT, BUT MASTER GICCHIN MAY'VE BEEN RIGHT ALL ALONG...
HUH?
FINE... I'LL REVEAL WHY OLD GICCHIN NEVER RECOGNIZED JIREN.

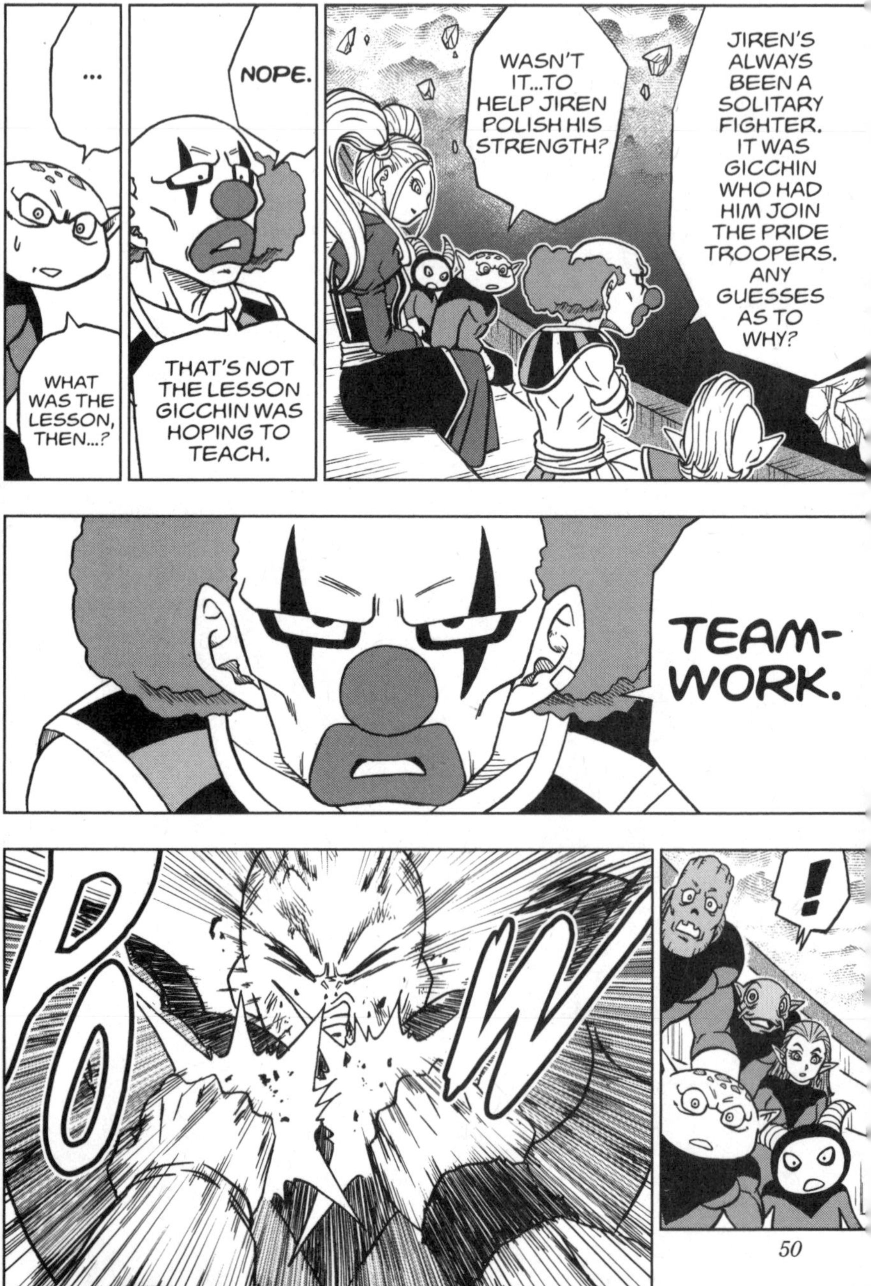
JIREN'S ALWAYS BEEN A SOLITARY FIGHTER. IT WAS GICCHIN WHO HAD HIM JOIN THE PRIDE TROOPERS. ANY GUESSES AS TO WHY?
WASN'T IT...TO HELP JIREN POLISH HIS STRENGTH?
NOPE.
THAT'S NOT THE LESSON GICCHIN WAS HOPING TO TEACH.
...
WHAT WAS THE LESSON, THEN...?
TEAM-WORK.
!
BOW

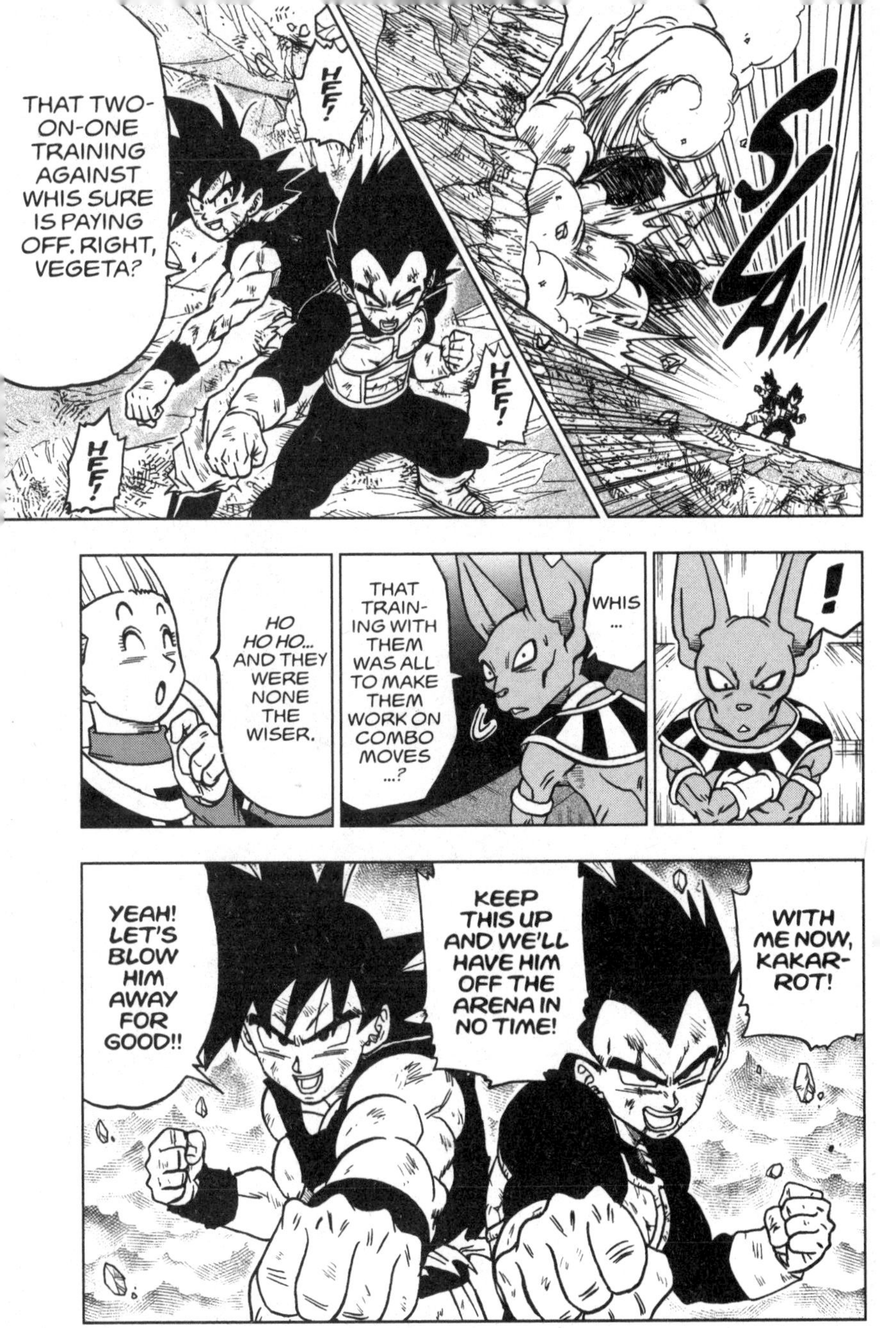
SLAM
HEF!
THAT TWO-ON-ONE TRAINING AGAINST WHIS SURE IS PAYING OFF. RIGHT, VEGETA?
HEF!
HEF!
!
WHIS ...
THAT TRAINING WITH THEM WAS ALL TO MAKE THEM WORK ON COMBO MOVES ...?
HO HO HO... AND THEY WERE NONE THE WISER.
WITH ME NOW, KAKARROT!
KEEP THIS UP AND WE'LL HAVE HIM OFF THE ARENA IN NO TIME!
YEAH! LET'S BLOW HIM AWAY FOR GOOD!!

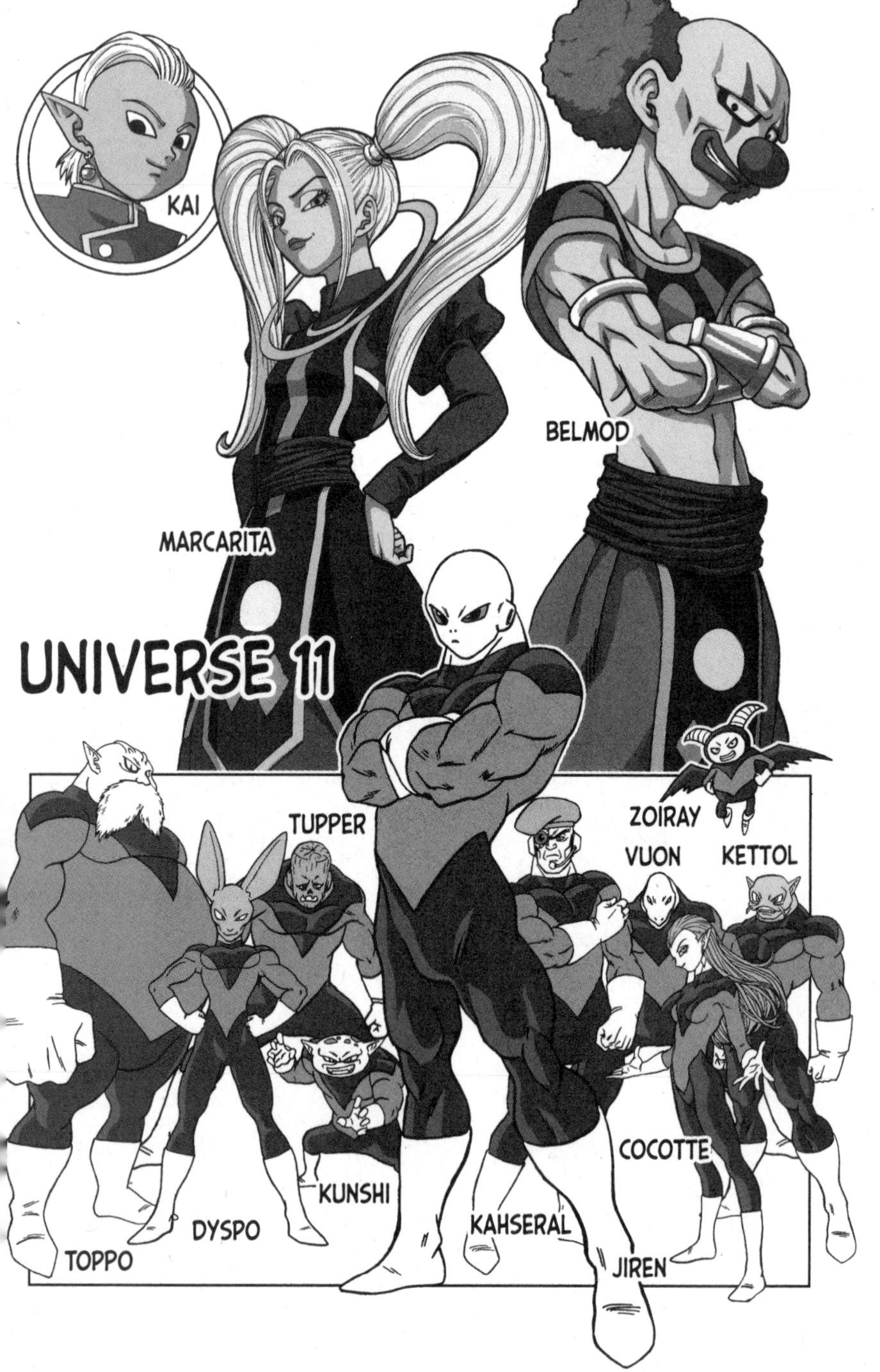
KAI
BELMOD
MARCARITA
UNIVERSE 11
ZOIRAY
TUPPER
VUON
KETTOL
COCOTTE
KUNSHI
DYSPO
KAHSERAL
TOPPO
JIREN

DRAGON BALL SUPER

CHAPTER 42: BATTLE'S END AND AFTERMATH

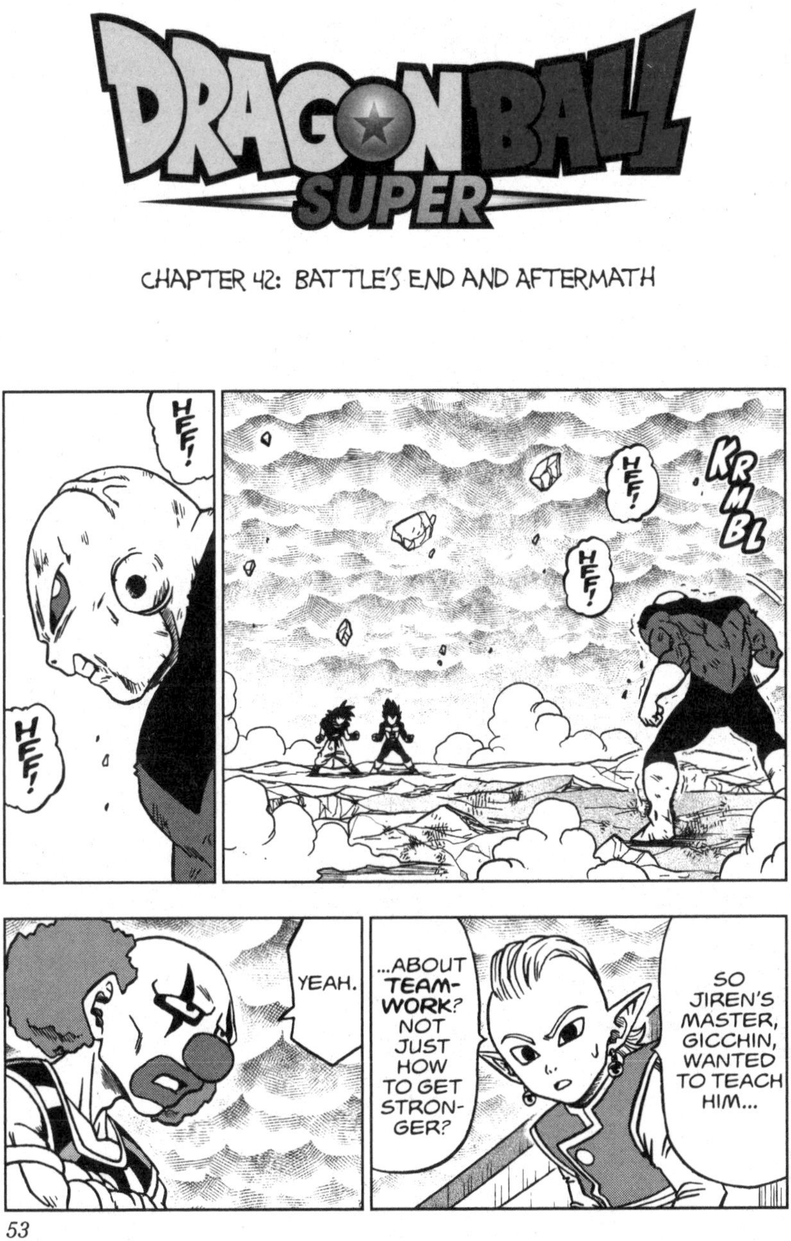
KRMBL
HEF!
HEF!
HEF!
HEF!
SO JIREN'S MASTER, GICCHIN, WANTED TO TEACH HIM...
...ABOUT TEAMWORK? NOT JUST HOW TO GET STRONGER?
YEAH.

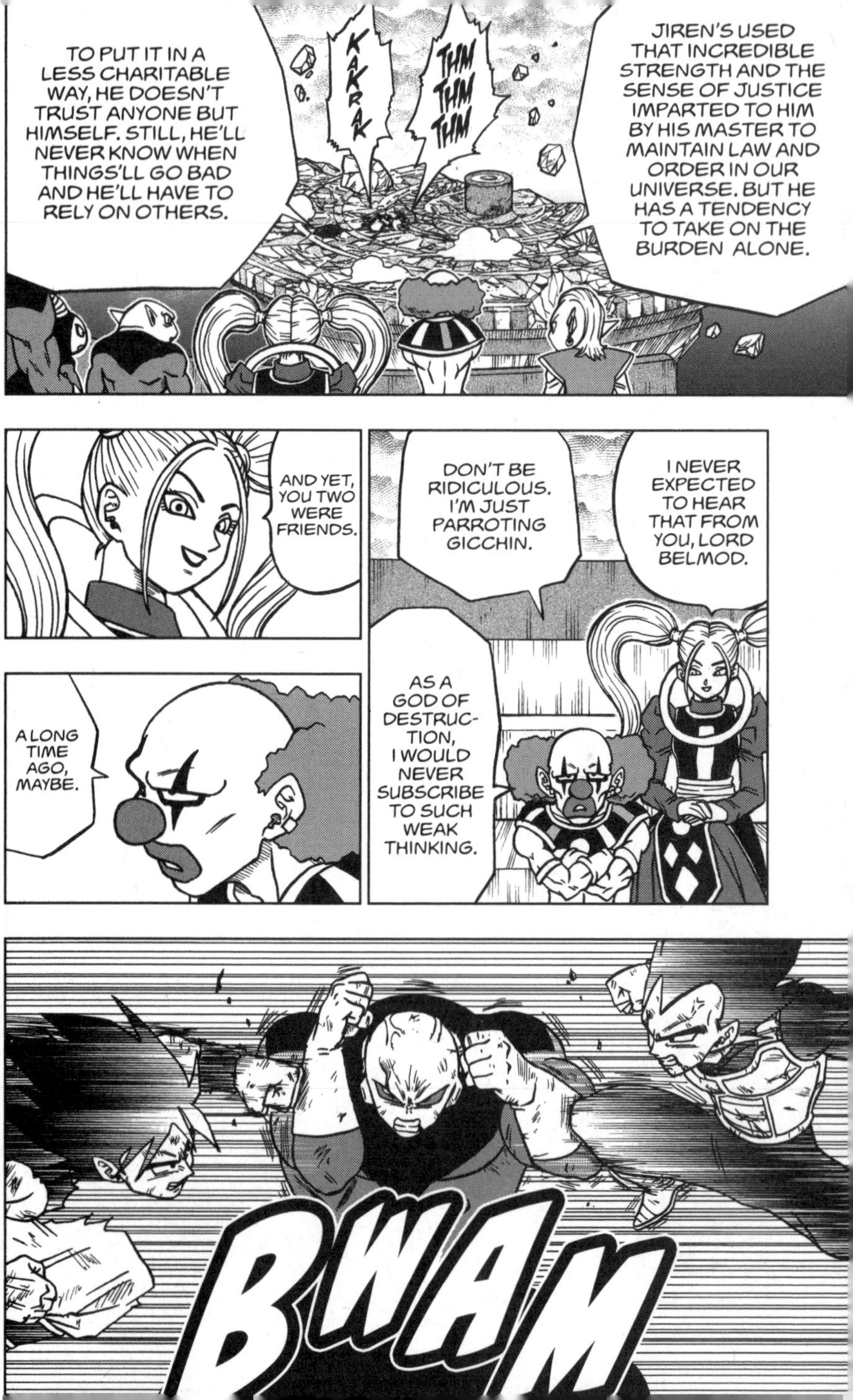
JIREN'S USED THAT INCREDIBLE STRENGTH AND THE SENSE OF JUSTICE IMPARTED TO HIM BY HIS MASTER TO MAINTAIN LAW AND ORDER IN OUR UNIVERSE. BUT HE HAS A TENDENCY TO TAKE ON THE BURDEN ALONE.
THM THM THM
KAKRAK
TO PUT IT IN A LESS CHARITABLE WAY, HE DOESN'T TRUST ANYONE BUT HIMSELF. STILL, HE'LL NEVER KNOW WHEN THINGS'LL GO BAD AND HE'LL HAVE TO RELY ON OTHERS.
I NEVER EXPECTED TO HEAR THAT FROM YOU, LORD BELMOD.
DON'T BE RIDICULOUS. I'M JUST PARROTING GICCHIN.
AS A GOD OF DESTRUC-TION, I WOULD NEVER SUBSCRIBE TO SUCH WEAK THINKING.
AND YET, YOU TWO WERE FRIENDS.
A LONG TIME AGO, MAYBE.
BWAM

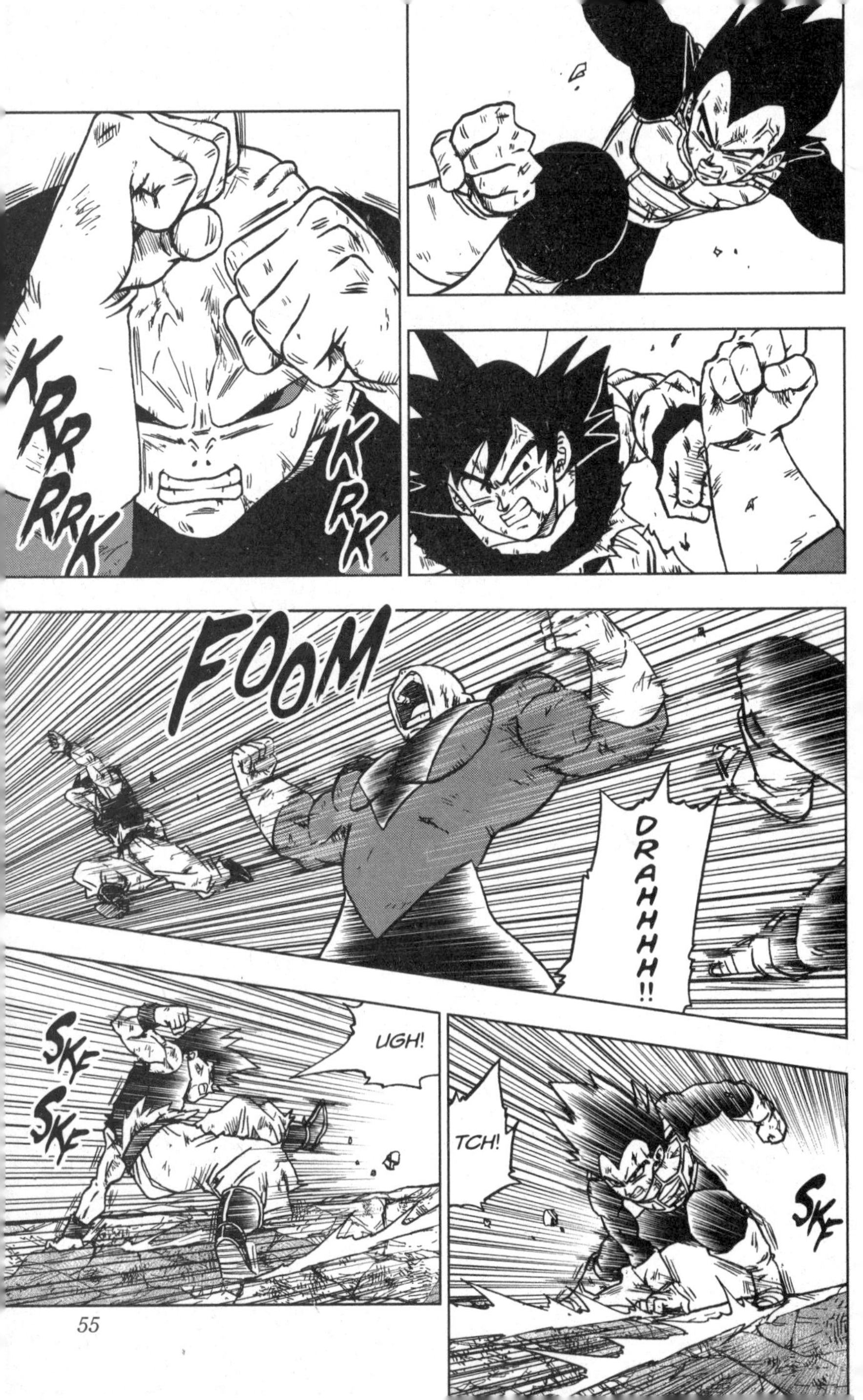

KRK
KRRRRK
DRAHHHHH!!
FOOM
TCH!
SKF
UGH!
SKF SKF

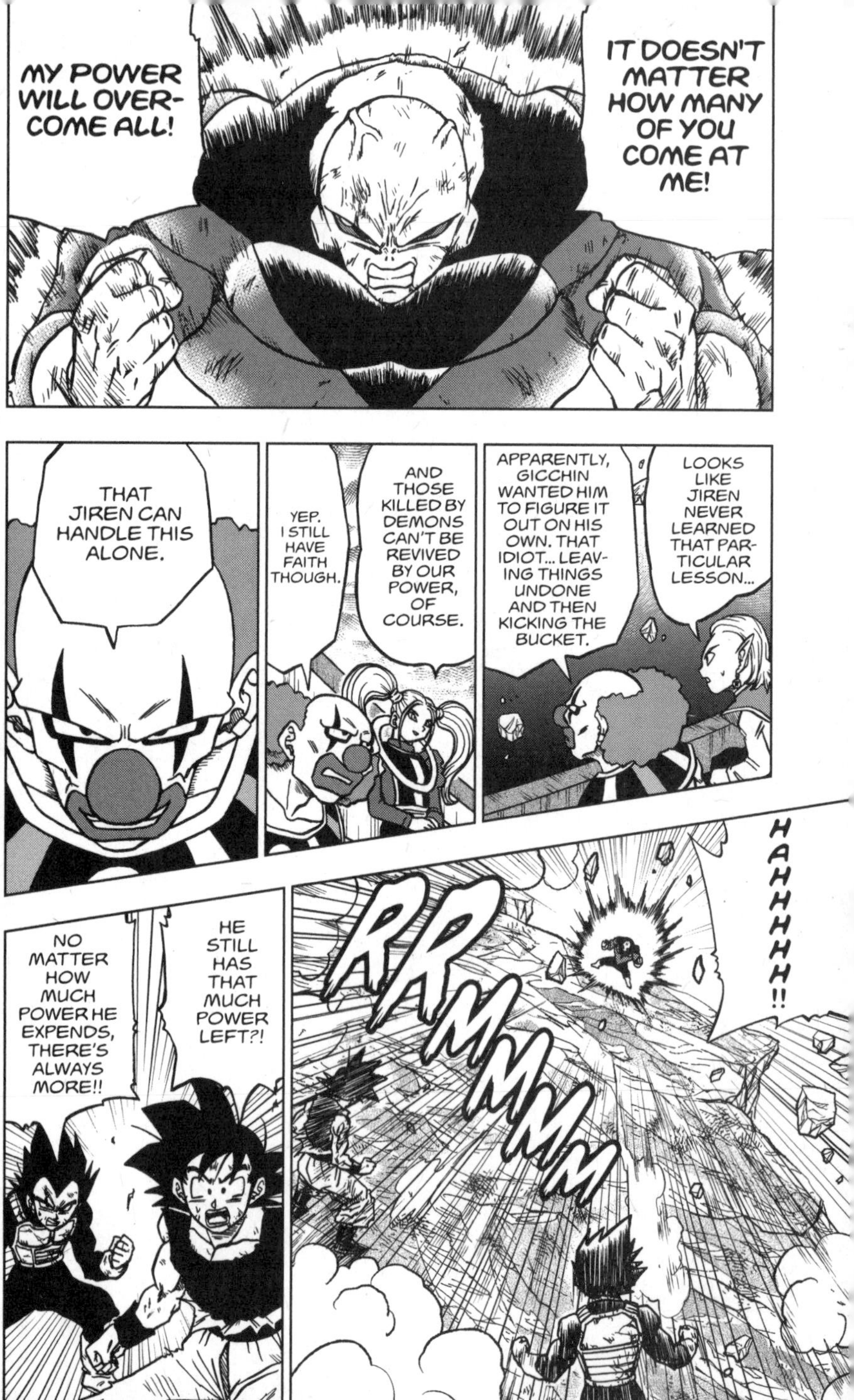
IT DOESN'T MATTER HOW MANY OF YOU COME AT ME!
MY POWER WILL OVERCOME ALL!
LOOKS LIKE JIREN NEVER LEARNED THAT PARTICULAR LESSON...
APPARENTLY, GICCHIN WANTED HIM TO FIGURE IT OUT ON HIS OWN. THAT IDIOT... LEAVING THINGS UNDONE AND THEN KICKING THE BUCKET.
AND THOSE KILLED BY DEMONS CAN'T BE REVIVED BY OUR POWER, OF COURSE.
YEP. I STILL HAVE FAITH THOUGH.
THAT JIREN CAN HANDLE THIS ALONE.
HAHHHHHH!!
RRMMMMM
HE STILL HAS THAT MUCH POWER LEFT?!
NO MATTER HOW MUCH POWER HE EXPENDS, THERE'S ALWAYS MORE!!

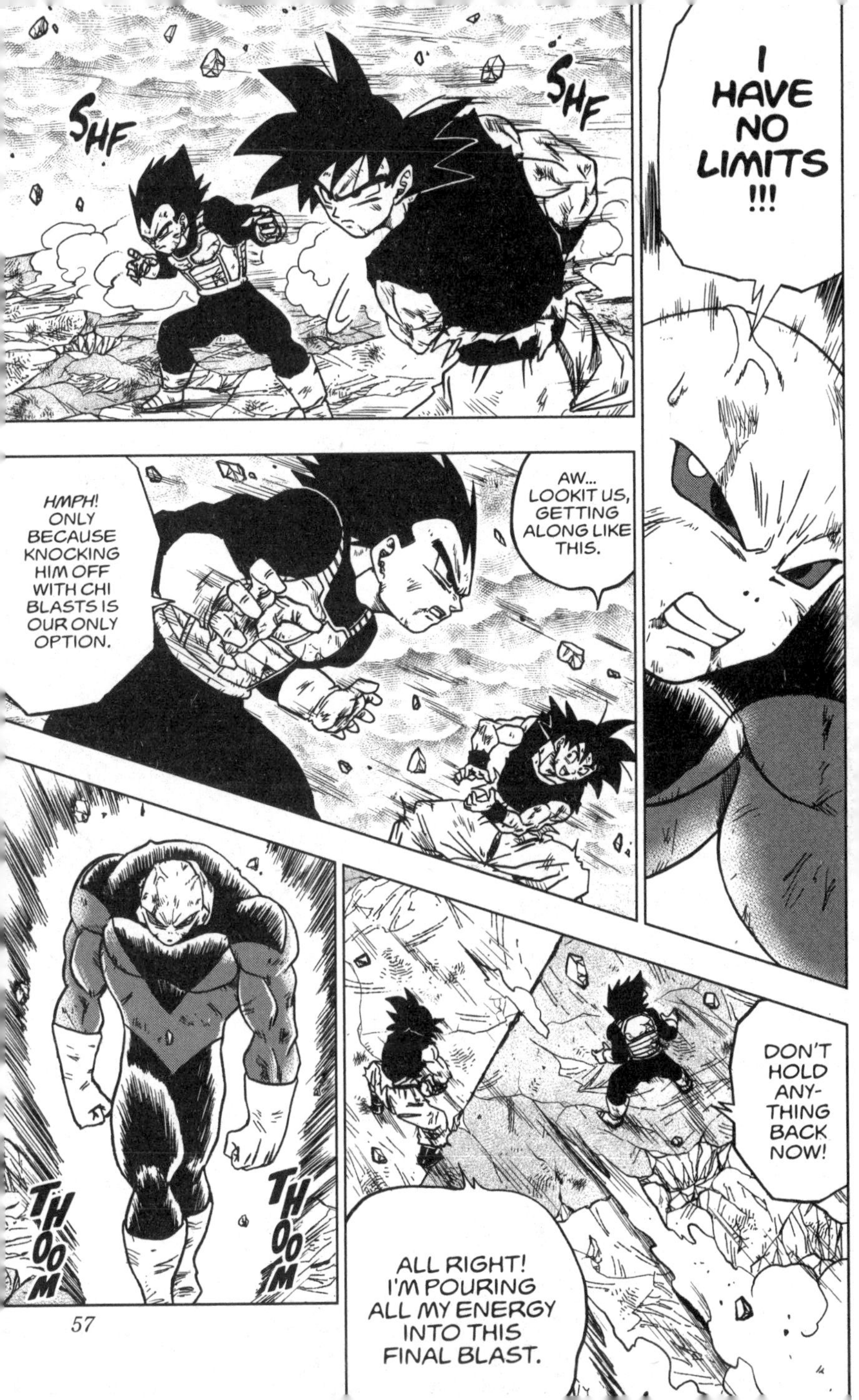
I HAVE NO LIMITS!!!
SHF
SHF
AW... LOOKIT US, GETTING ALONG LIKE THIS.
HMPH! ONLY BECAUSE KNOCKING HIM OFF WITH CHI BLASTS IS OUR ONLY OPTION.
DON'T HOLD ANY-THING BACK NOW!
ALL RIGHT! I'M POURING ALL MY ENERGY INTO THIS FINAL BLAST.
THOOM
THOOM

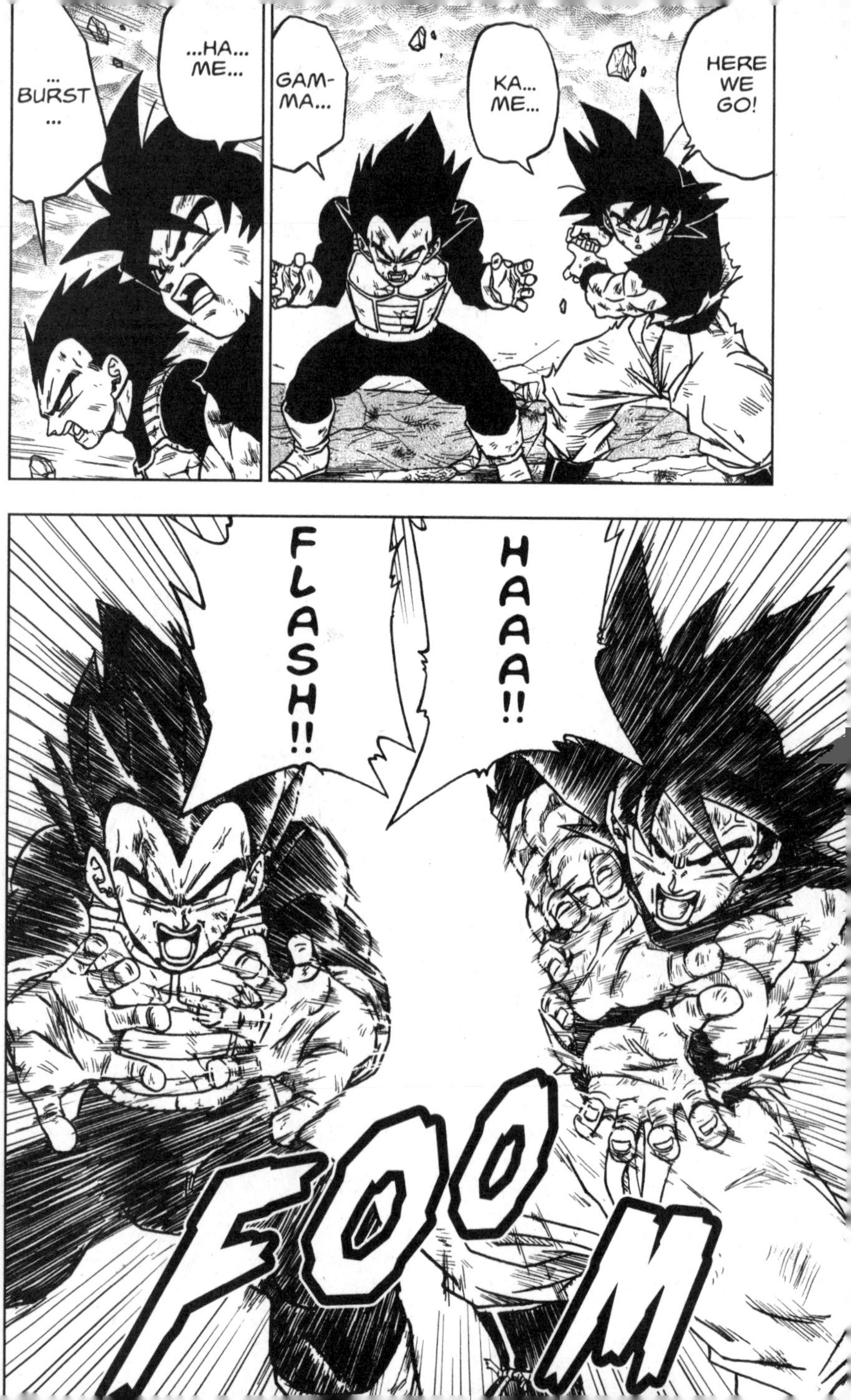
HERE WE GO!
KA... ME...
GAM-MA...
...HA... ME...
... BURST ...
HAAAA!!
FLASH!!
FOOM

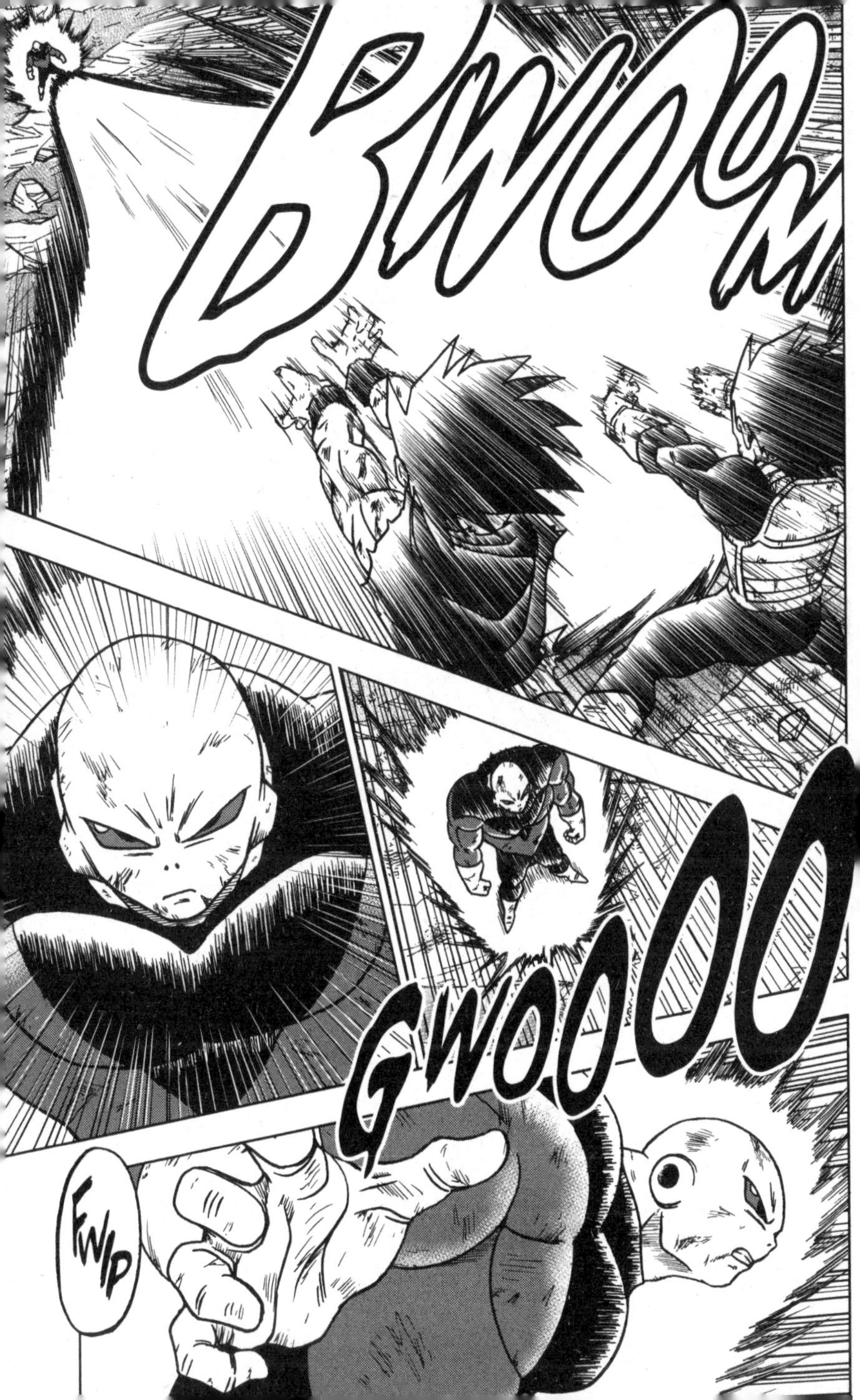
BWOOM
GWOOOO
FWIP

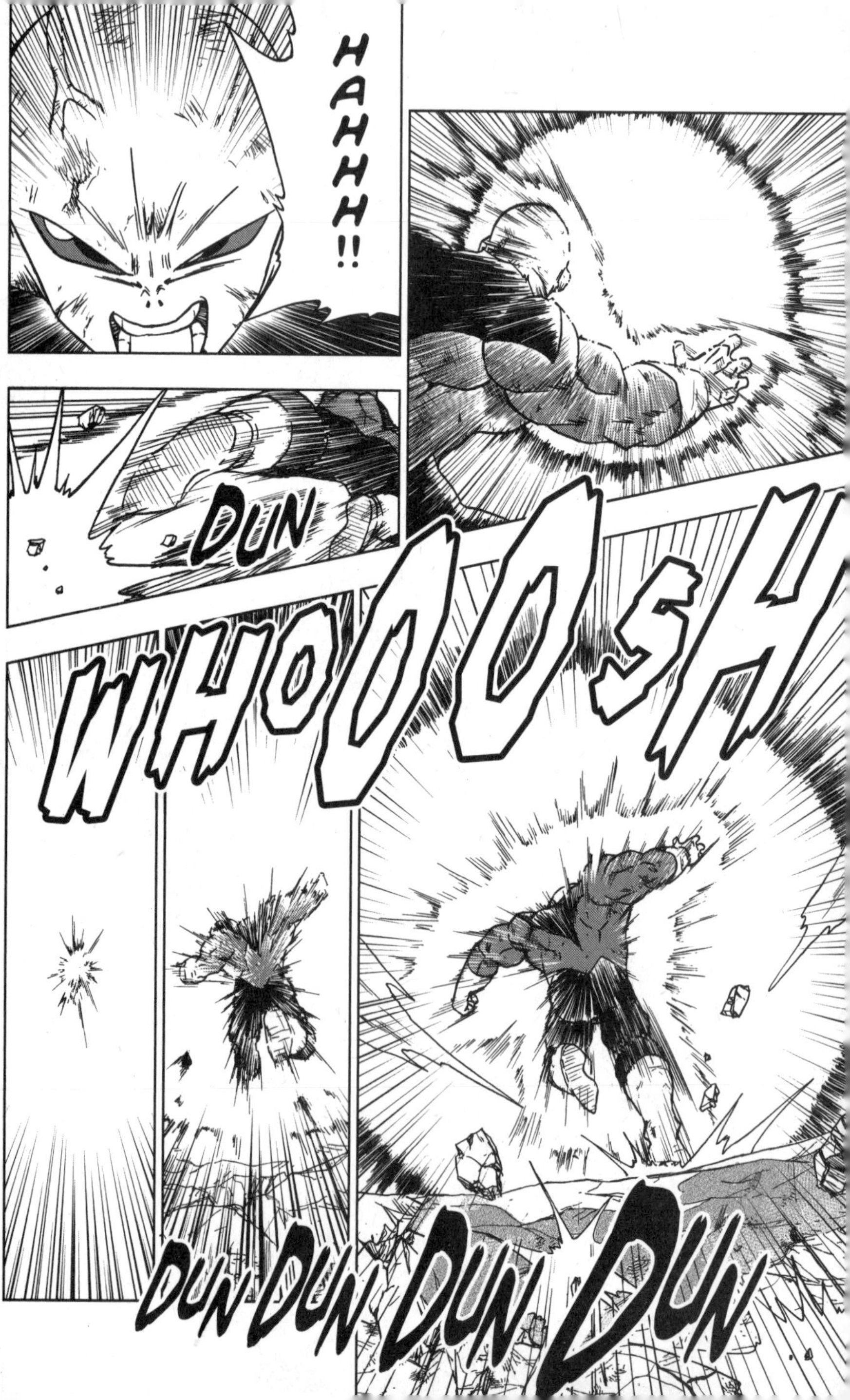
HAHHHH!!
DUN
WHOOOSH
DUN DUN DUN DUN

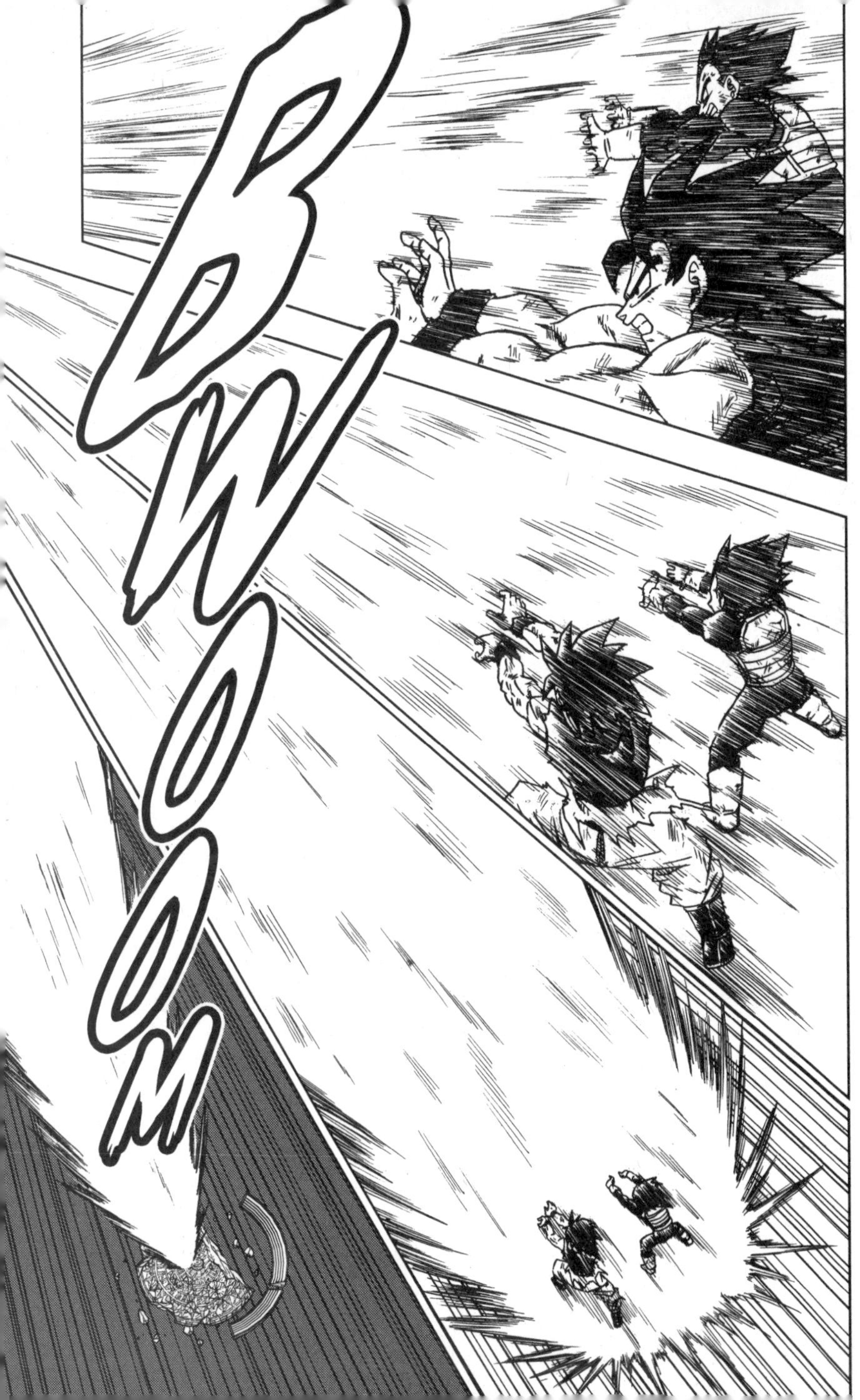
BWOOOOM

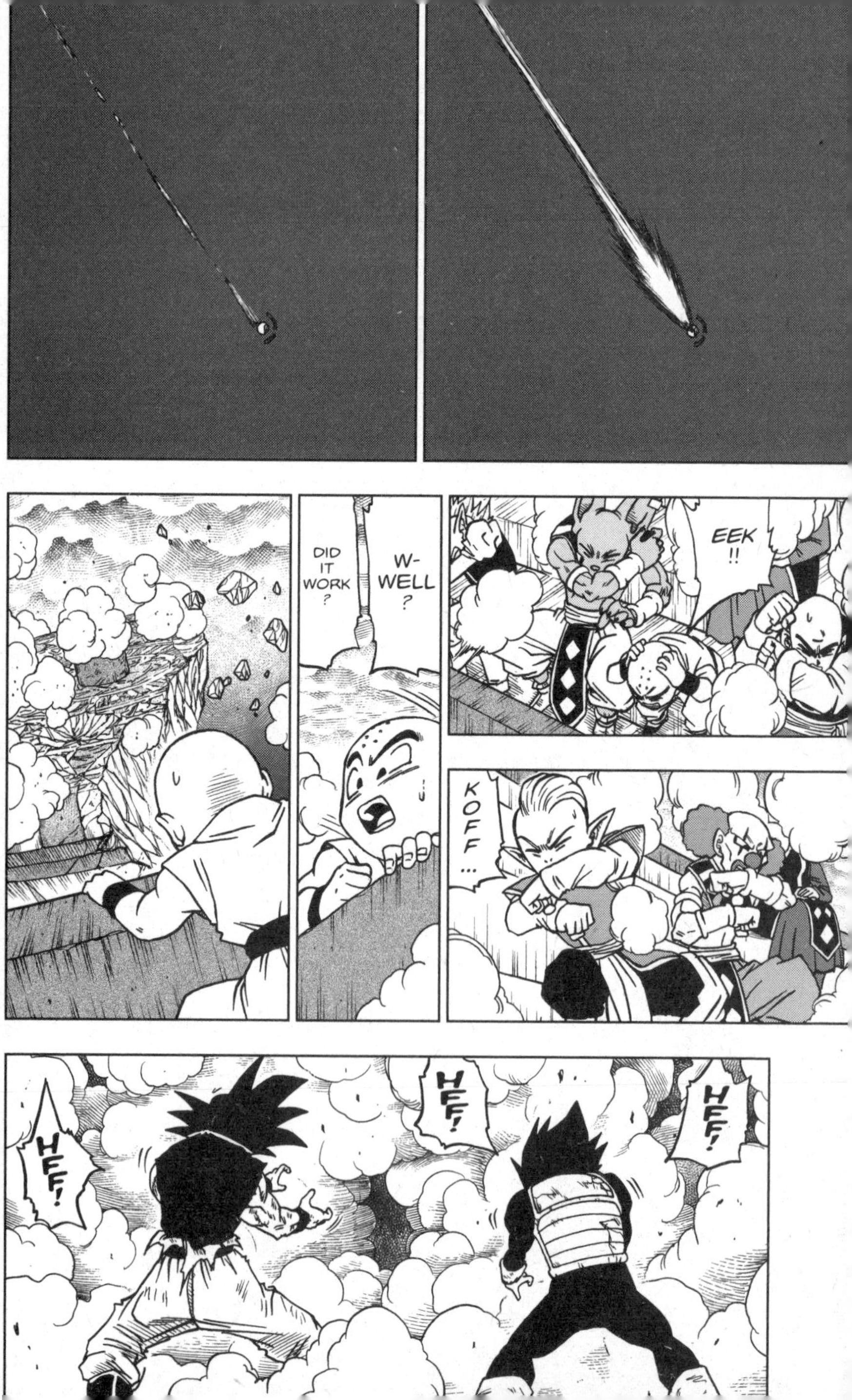
EEK !!
KOFF ...
W-WELL ?
DID IT WORK ?
HEF!
HEF!
HEF!

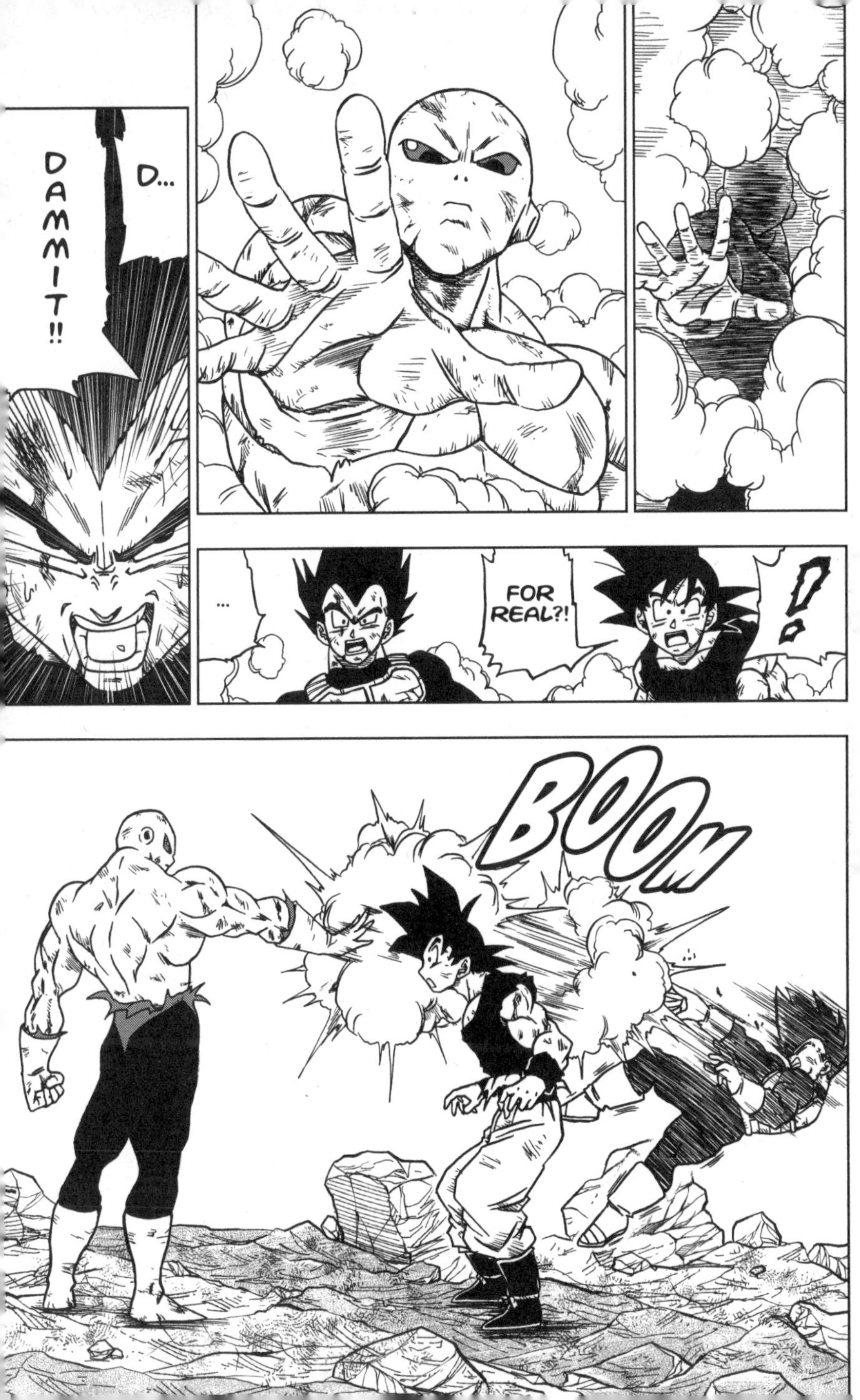
!!
FOR REAL?!
...
D...
DAMMIT!!
BOOM

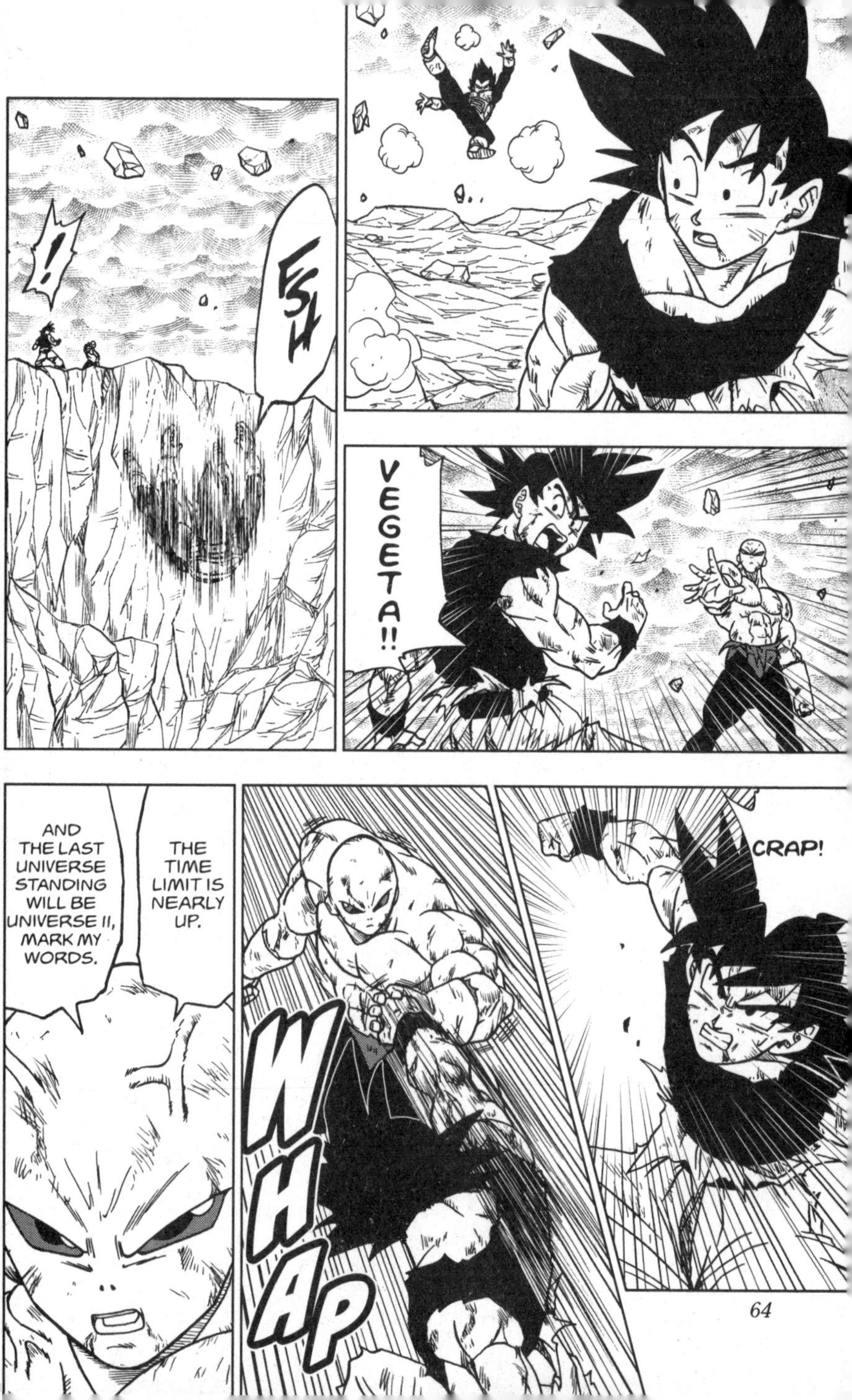
VEGETA!!
!
FSH
CRAP!
WHAP
THE TIME LIMIT IS NEARLY UP.
AND THE LAST UNIVERSE STANDING WILL BE UNIVERSE 11, MARK MY WORDS.

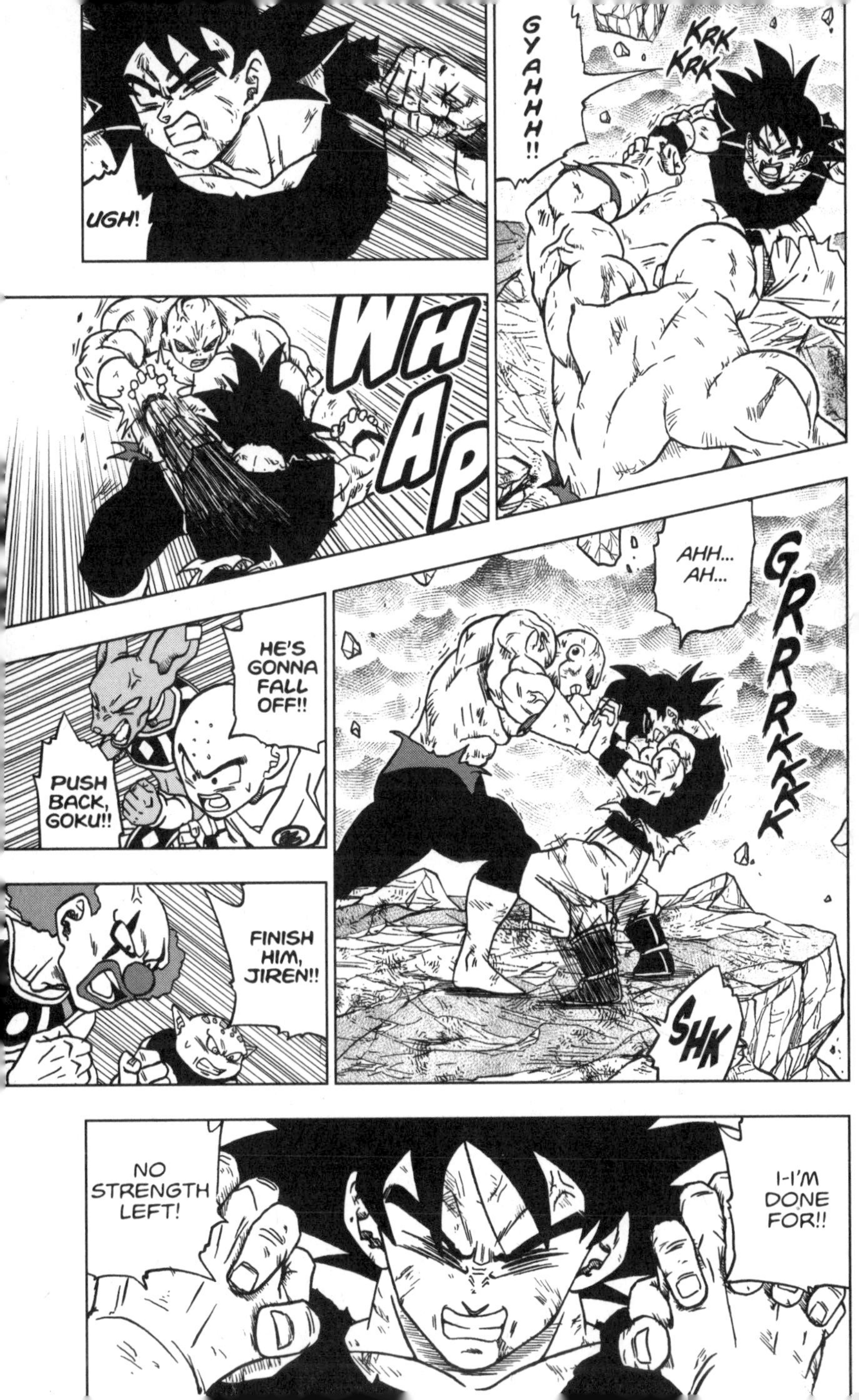
GYAHHH!!
KRK KRK
UGH!
WHAP
AHH... AH...
GRRRKKK
SHK
HE'S GONNA FALL OFF!!
PUSH BACK, GOKU!!
FINISH HIM, JIREN!!
I-I'M DONE FOR!!
NO STRENGTH LEFT!

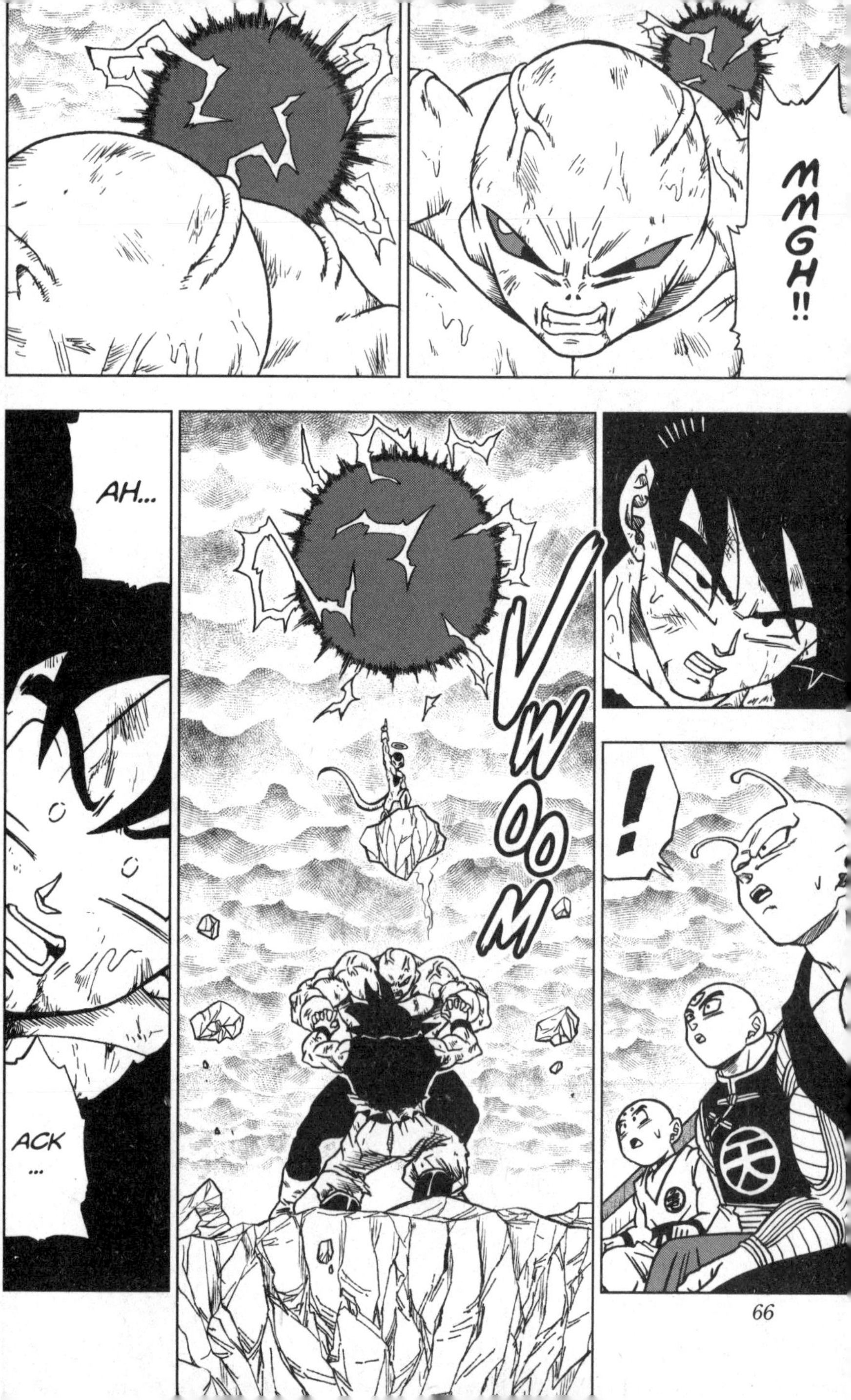
MMGH!!
!
VWOOM
AH...
ACK ...

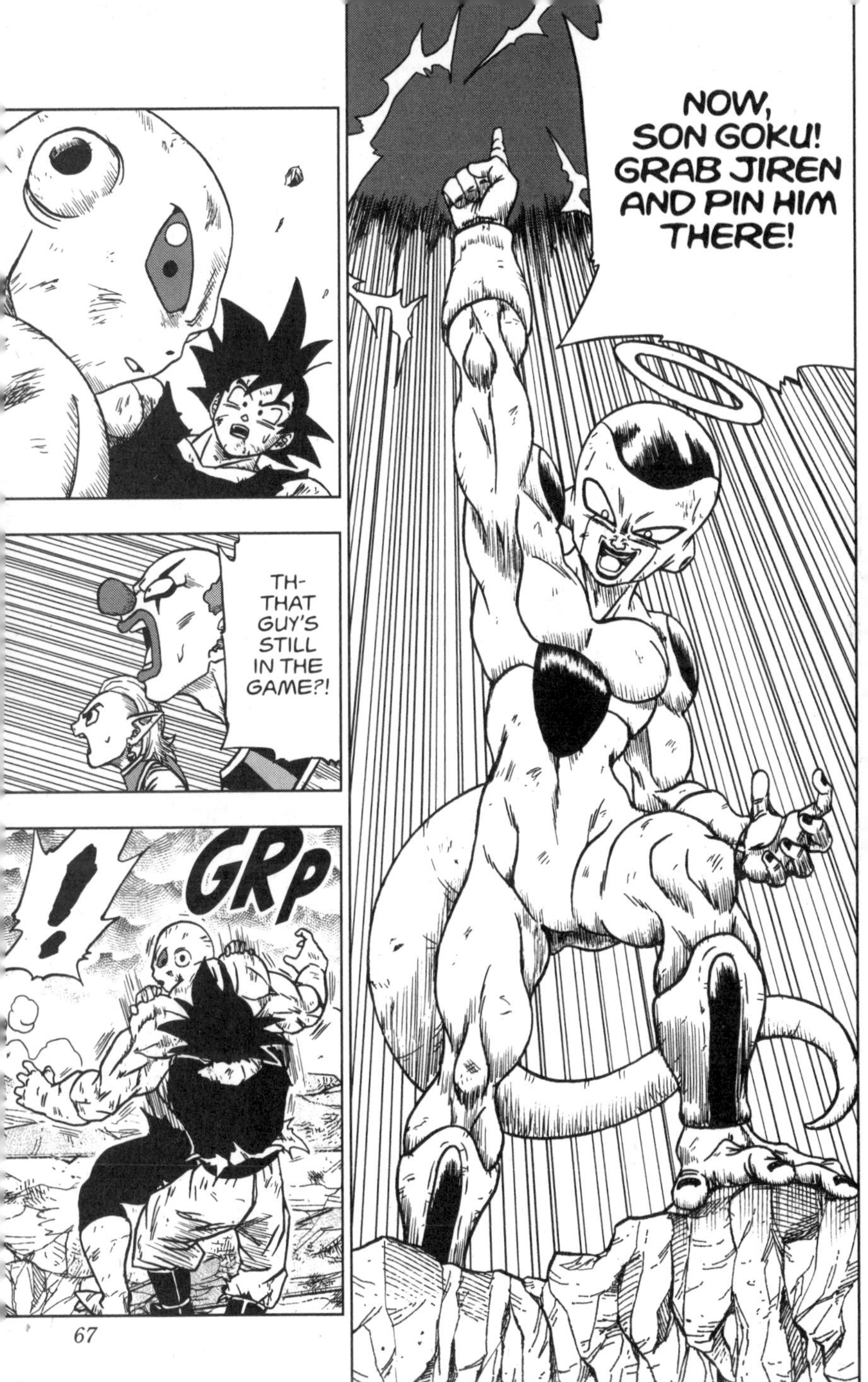
NOW, SON GOKU! GRAB JIREN AND PIN HIM THERE!
TH-THAT GUY'S STILL IN THE GAME?!
!
GRP

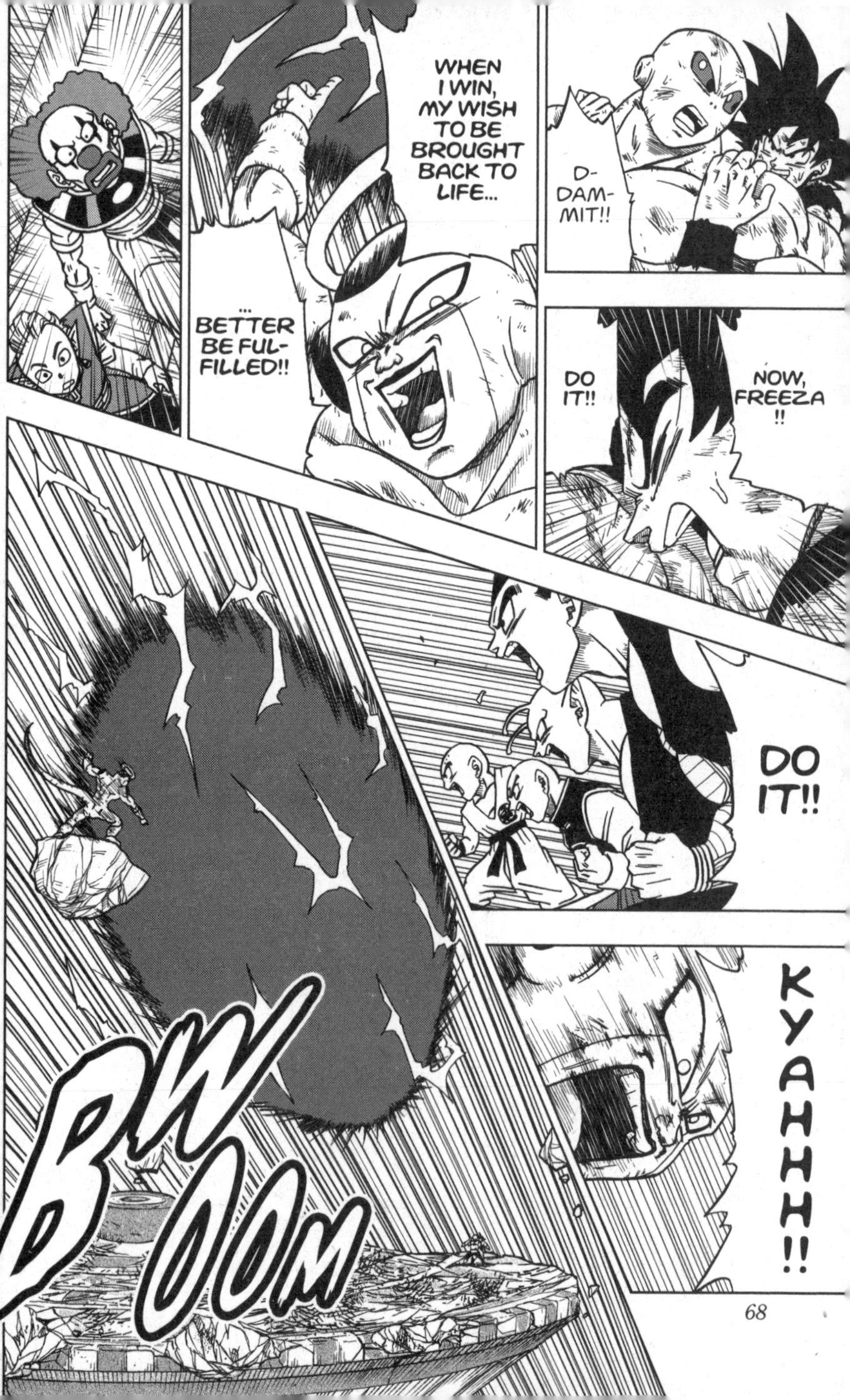
D-DAMMIT!!
NOW, FREEZA!!
DO IT!!
WHEN I WIN, MY WISH TO BE BROUGHT BACK TO LIFE...
...BETTER BE FULFILLED!!
DO IT!!
KYAHHH!!
BWOOM

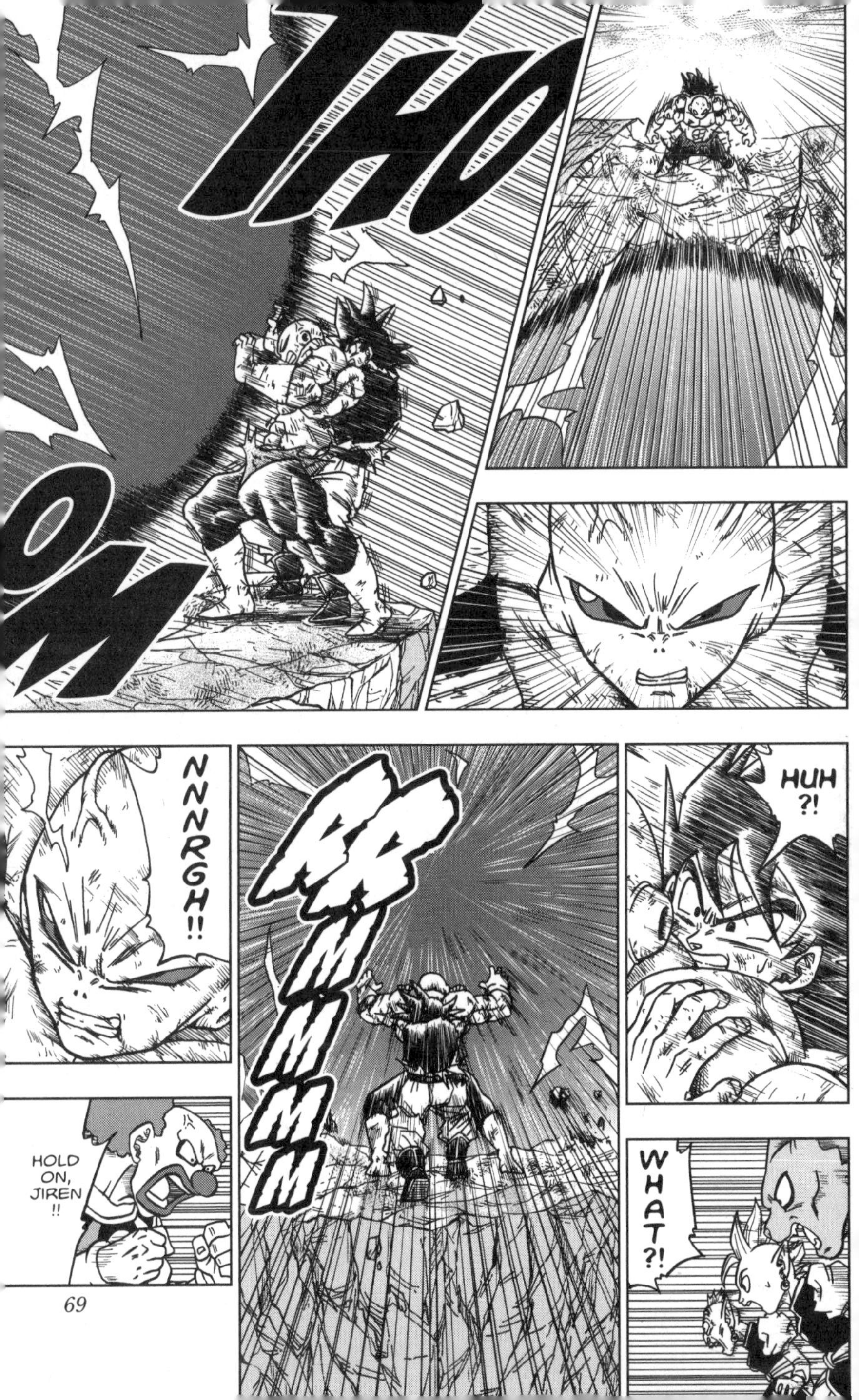
HUH ?!
WHAT?!
NNNRGH!!
HOLD ON, JIREN !!

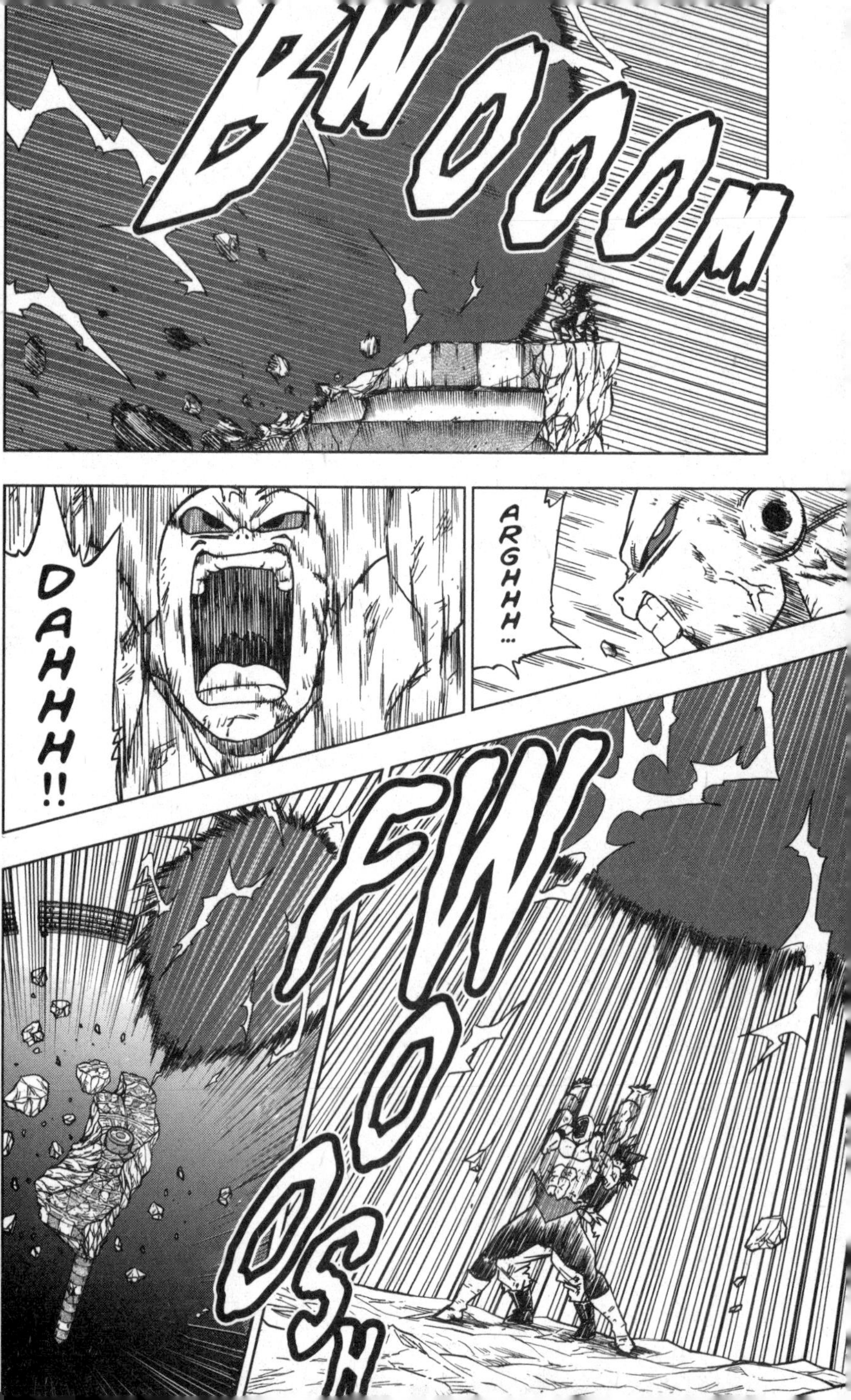
BWOOOOM
ARGHHH...
DAHHHH!!
FWOOSH

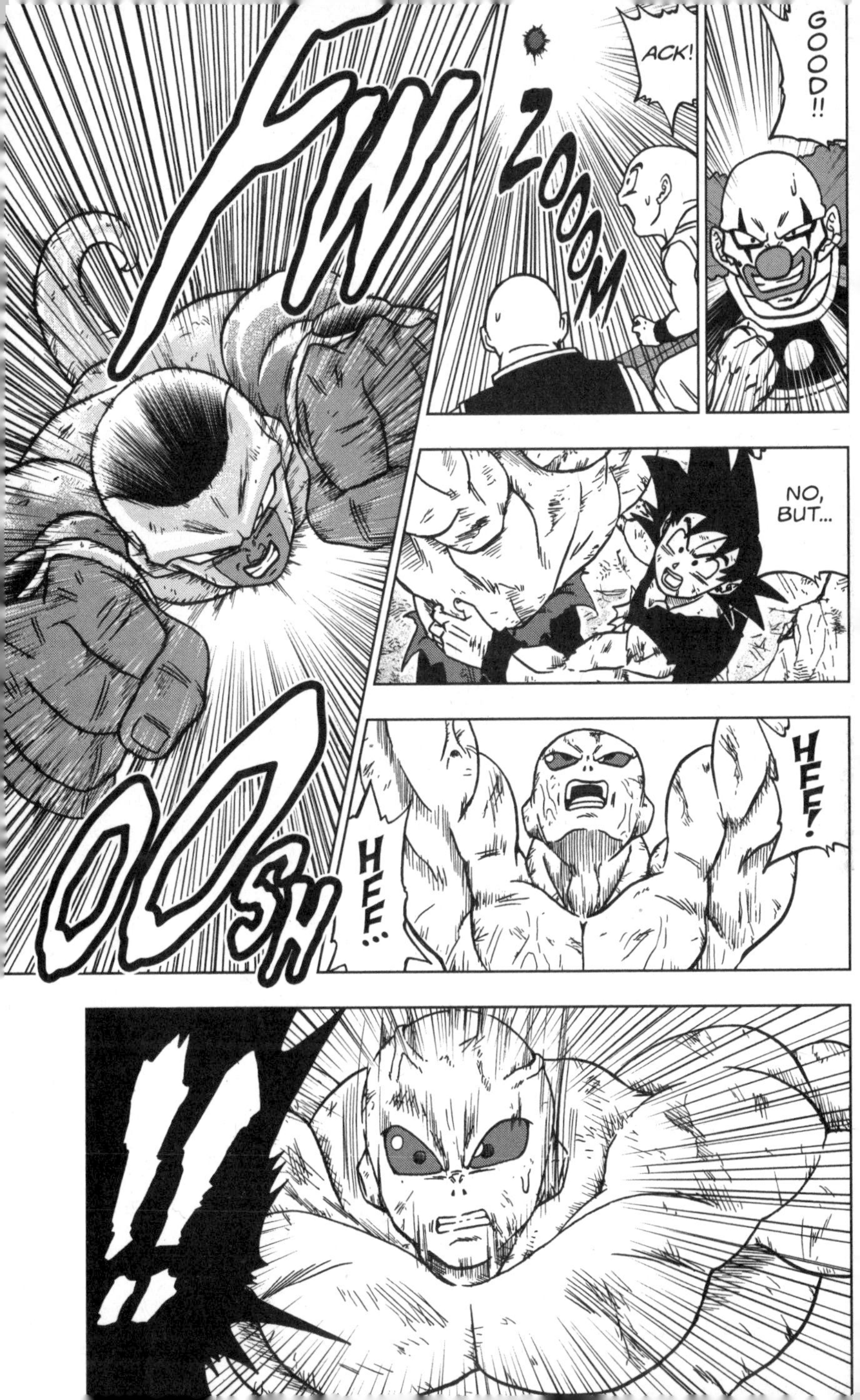
GOOD!!
ACK!
ZOOOM
NO, BUT...
HEFF!
HEFF..
FWW
OOSH
!!

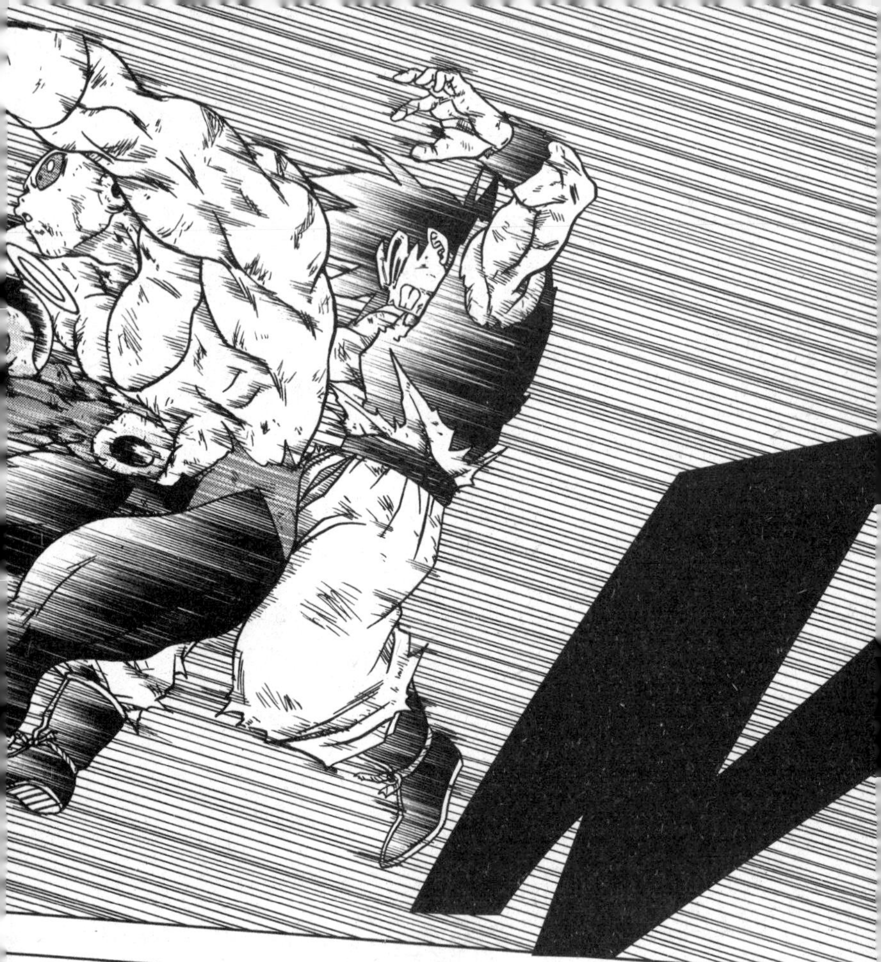
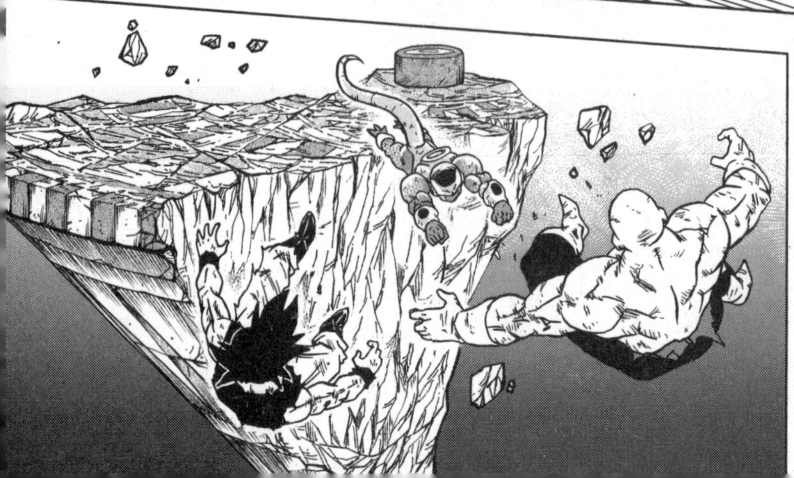

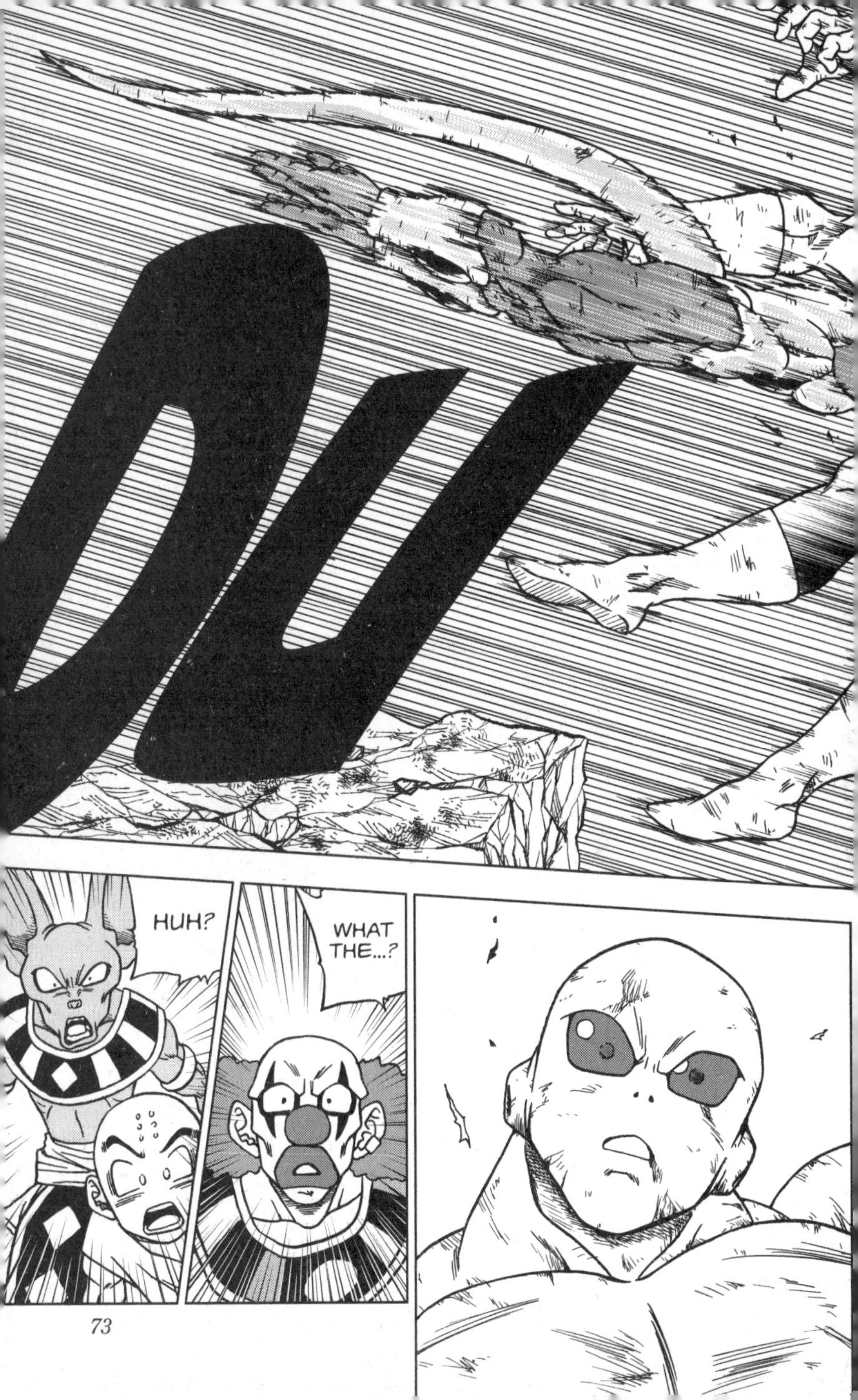
WHAT THE...?
HUH?

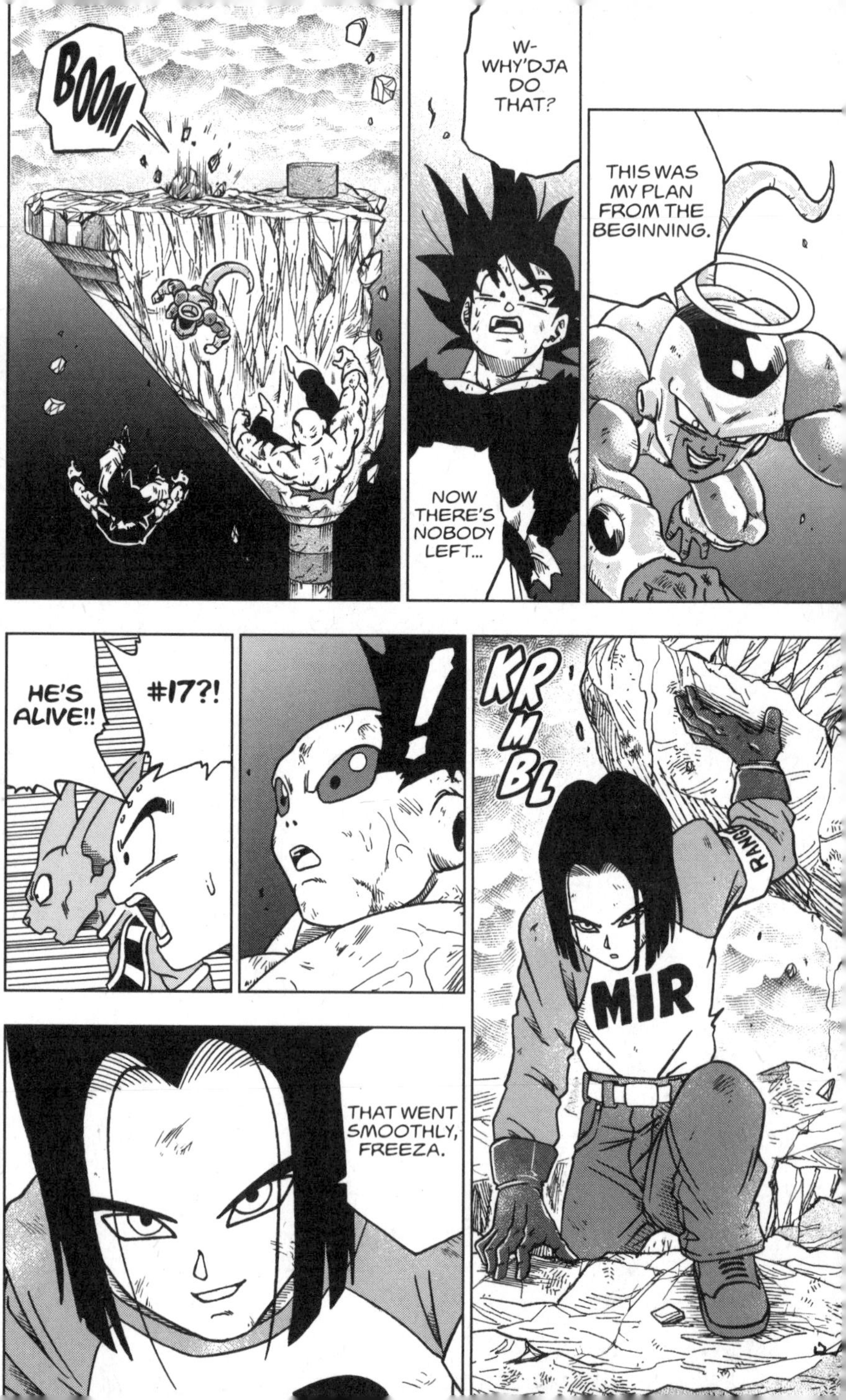
THIS WAS MY PLAN FROM THE BEGINNING.
W- WHY'DJA DO THAT?
NOW THERE'S NOBODY LEFT...
BOOM
KRMBL
MIR
!
#17?!
HE'S ALIVE!!
THAT WENT SMOOTHLY, FREEZA.

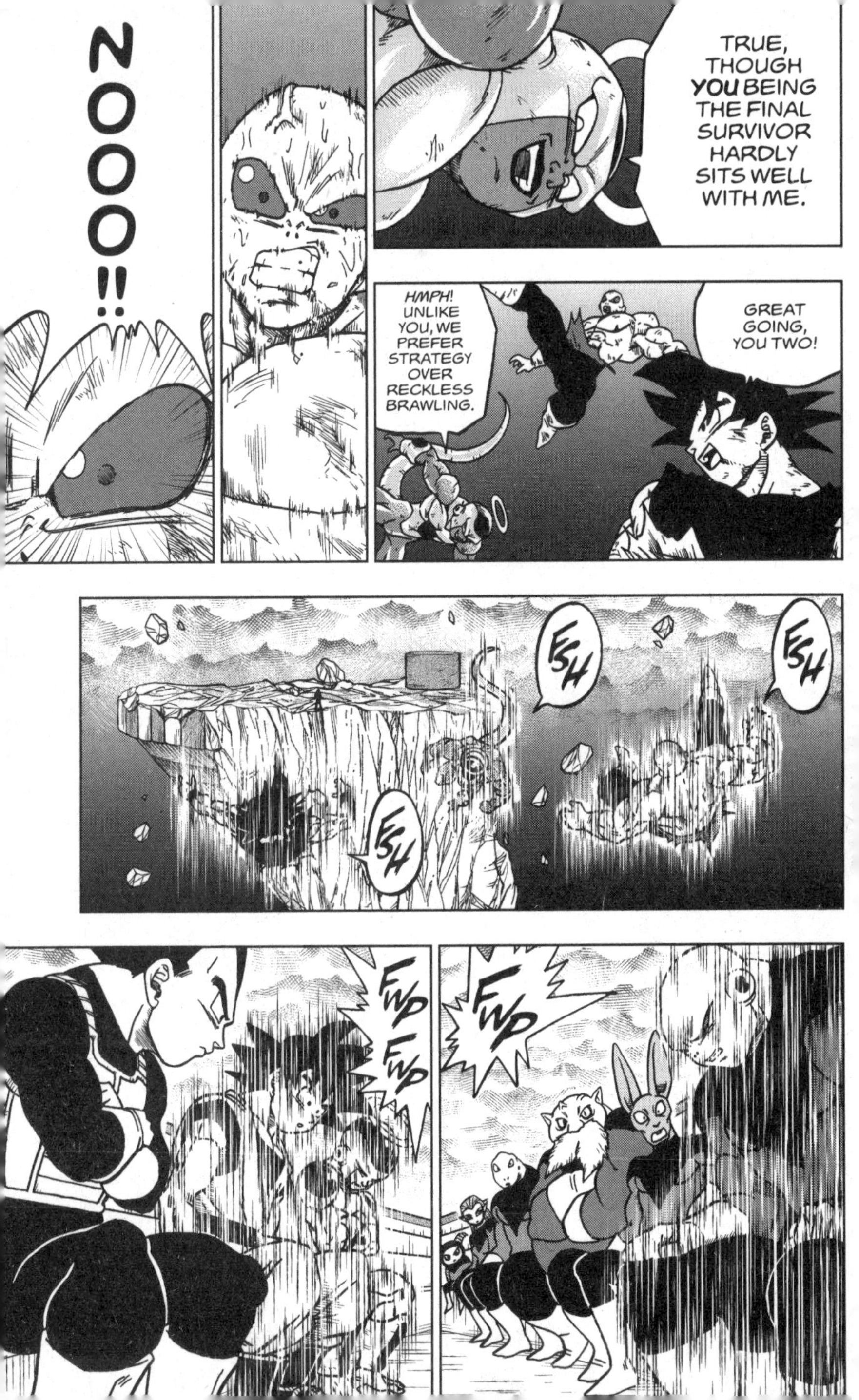
TRUE, THOUGH **YOU** BEING THE FINAL SURVIVOR HARDLY SITS WELL WITH ME.
GREAT GOING, YOU TWO!
HMPH! UNLIKE YOU, WE PREFER STRATEGY OVER RECKLESS BRAWLING.
NOOOO!!
FSH
FSH
FSH
FWP
FWP
FWP
FWP

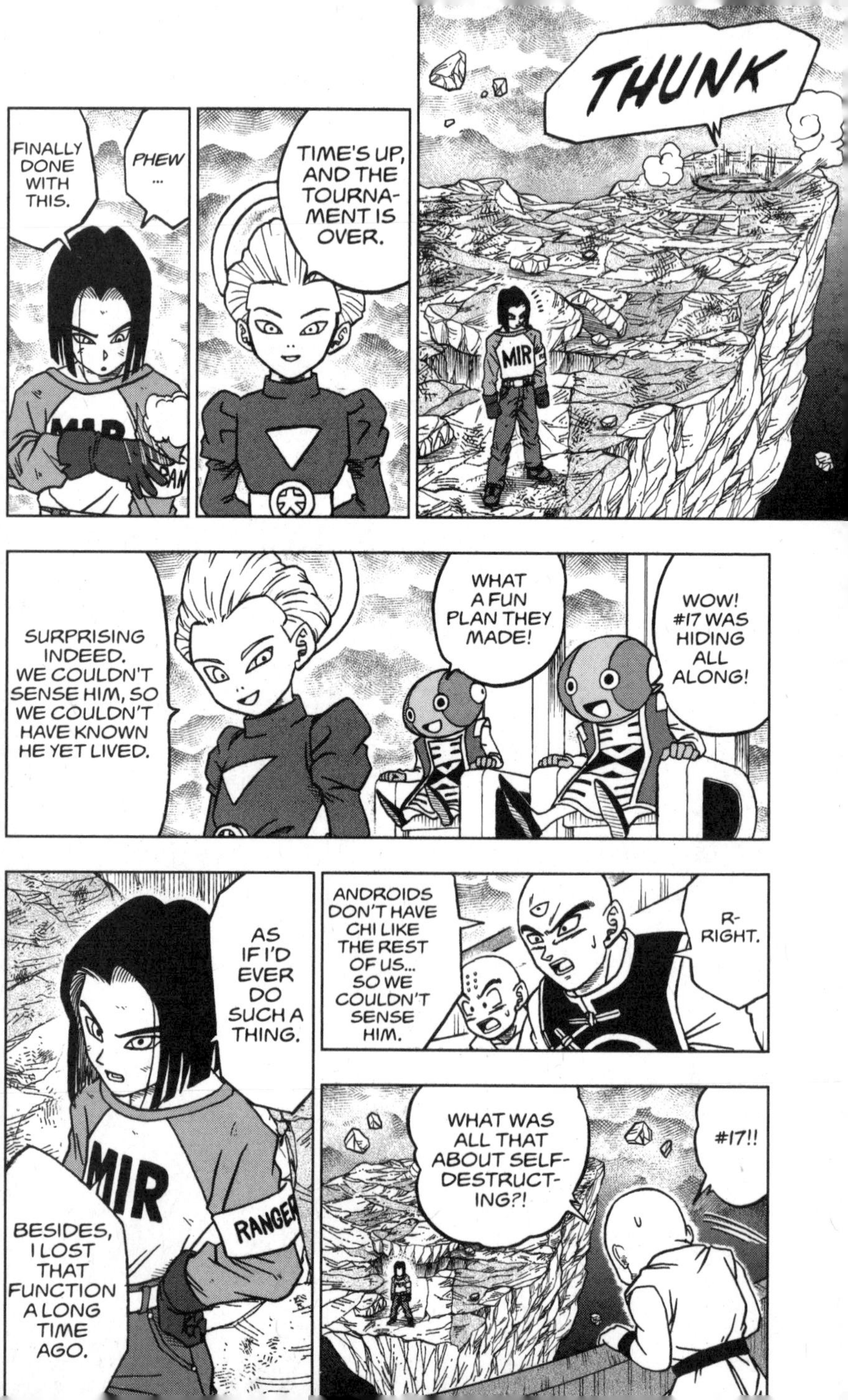
THUNK
TIME'S UP, AND THE TOURNAMENT IS OVER.
PHEW...
FINALLY DONE WITH THIS.
WOW! #17 WAS HIDING ALL ALONG!
WHAT A FUN PLAN THEY MADE!
SURPRISING INDEED. WE COULDN'T SENSE HIM, SO WE COULDN'T HAVE KNOWN HE YET LIVED.
R-RIGHT.
ANDROIDS DON'T HAVE CHI LIKE THE REST OF US... SO WE COULDN'T SENSE HIM.
#17!!
WHAT WAS ALL THAT ABOUT SELF-DESTRUCTING?!
AS IF I'D EVER DO SUCH A THING.
BESIDES, I LOST THAT FUNCTION A LONG TIME AGO.

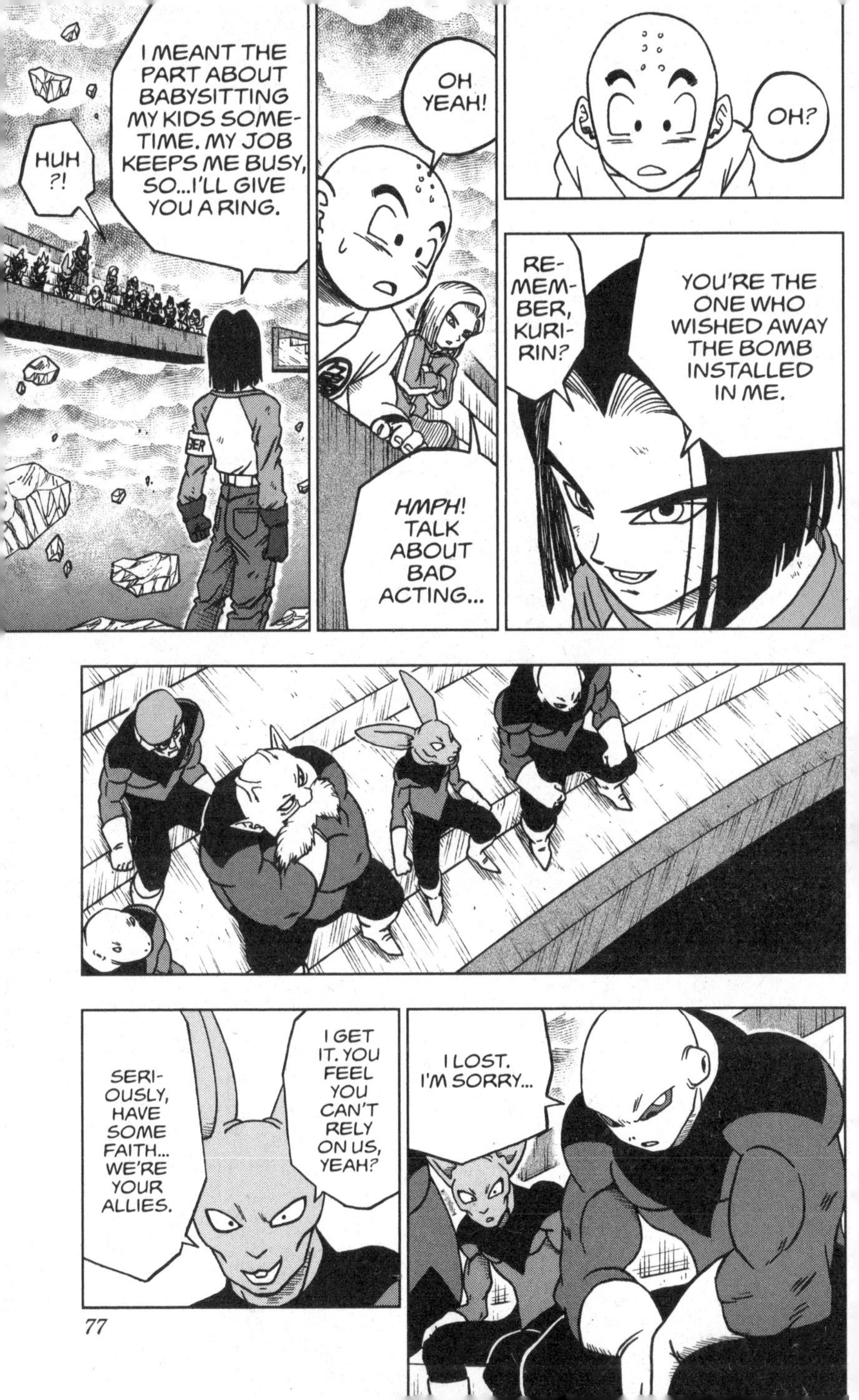
OH?
RE-MEM-BER, KURI-RIN?
YOU'RE THE ONE WHO WISHED AWAY THE BOMB INSTALLED IN ME.
OH YEAH!
HMPH! TALK ABOUT BAD ACTING...
I MEANT THE PART ABOUT BABYSITTING MY KIDS SOME-TIME. MY JOB KEEPS ME BUSY, SO...I'LL GIVE YOU A RING.
HUH ?!
I LOST. I'M SORRY...
I GET IT. YOU FEEL YOU CAN'T RELY ON US, YEAH?
SERI-OUSLY, HAVE SOME FAITH... WE'RE YOUR ALLIES.

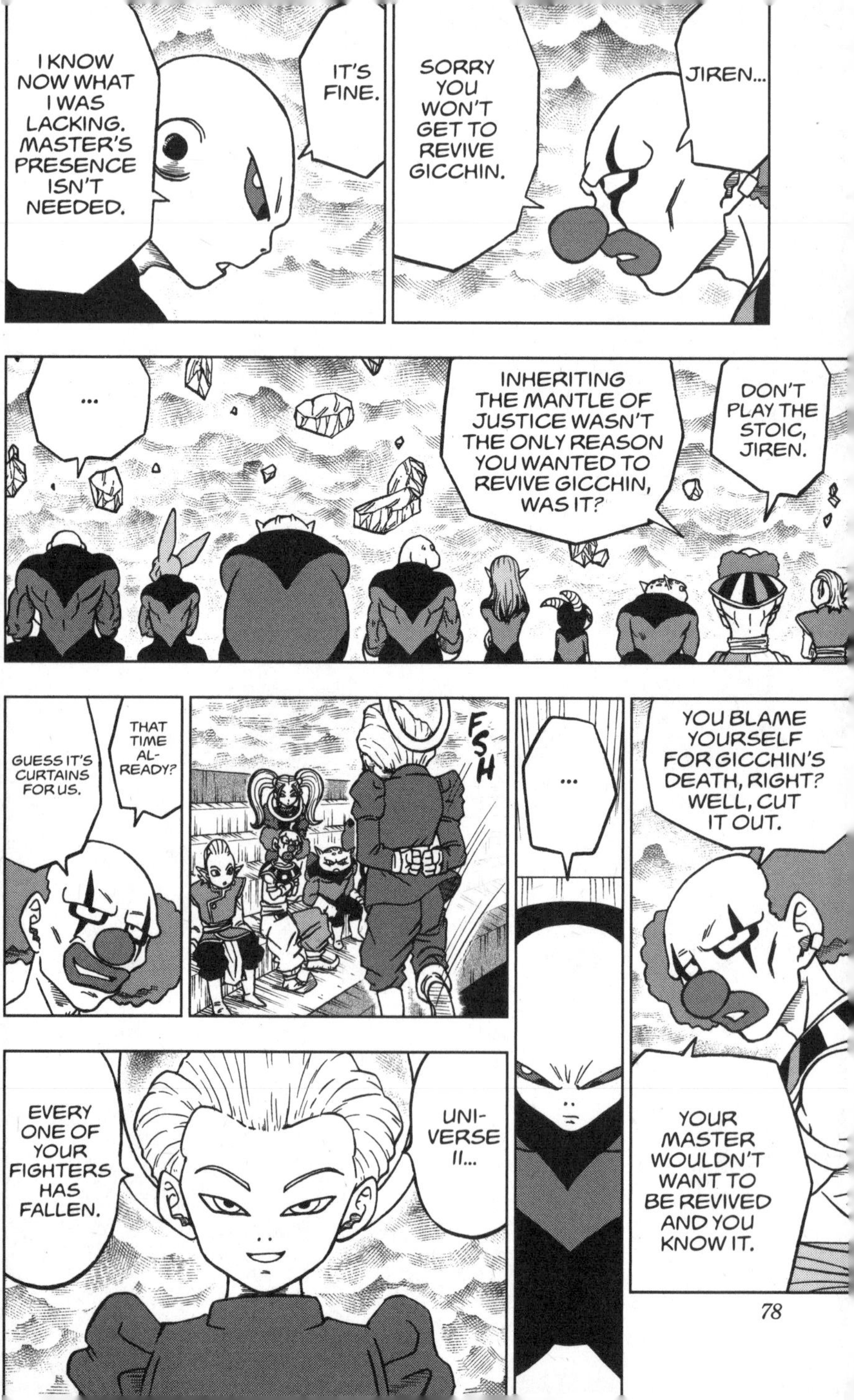
JIREN...
SORRY YOU WON'T GET TO REVIVE GICCHIN.
IT'S FINE.
I KNOW NOW WHAT I WAS LACKING. MASTER'S PRESENCE ISN'T NEEDED.
DON'T PLAY THE STOIC, JIREN.
INHERITING THE MANTLE OF JUSTICE WASN'T THE ONLY REASON YOU WANTED TO REVIVE GICCHIN, WAS IT?
...
YOU BLAME YOURSELF FOR GICCHIN'S DEATH, RIGHT? WELL, CUT IT OUT.
YOUR MASTER WOULDN'T WANT TO BE REVIVED AND YOU KNOW IT.
...
FSH
THAT TIME AL-READY?
GUESS IT'S CURTAINS FOR US.
UNI-VERSE 11...
EVERY ONE OF YOUR FIGHTERS HAS FALLEN.

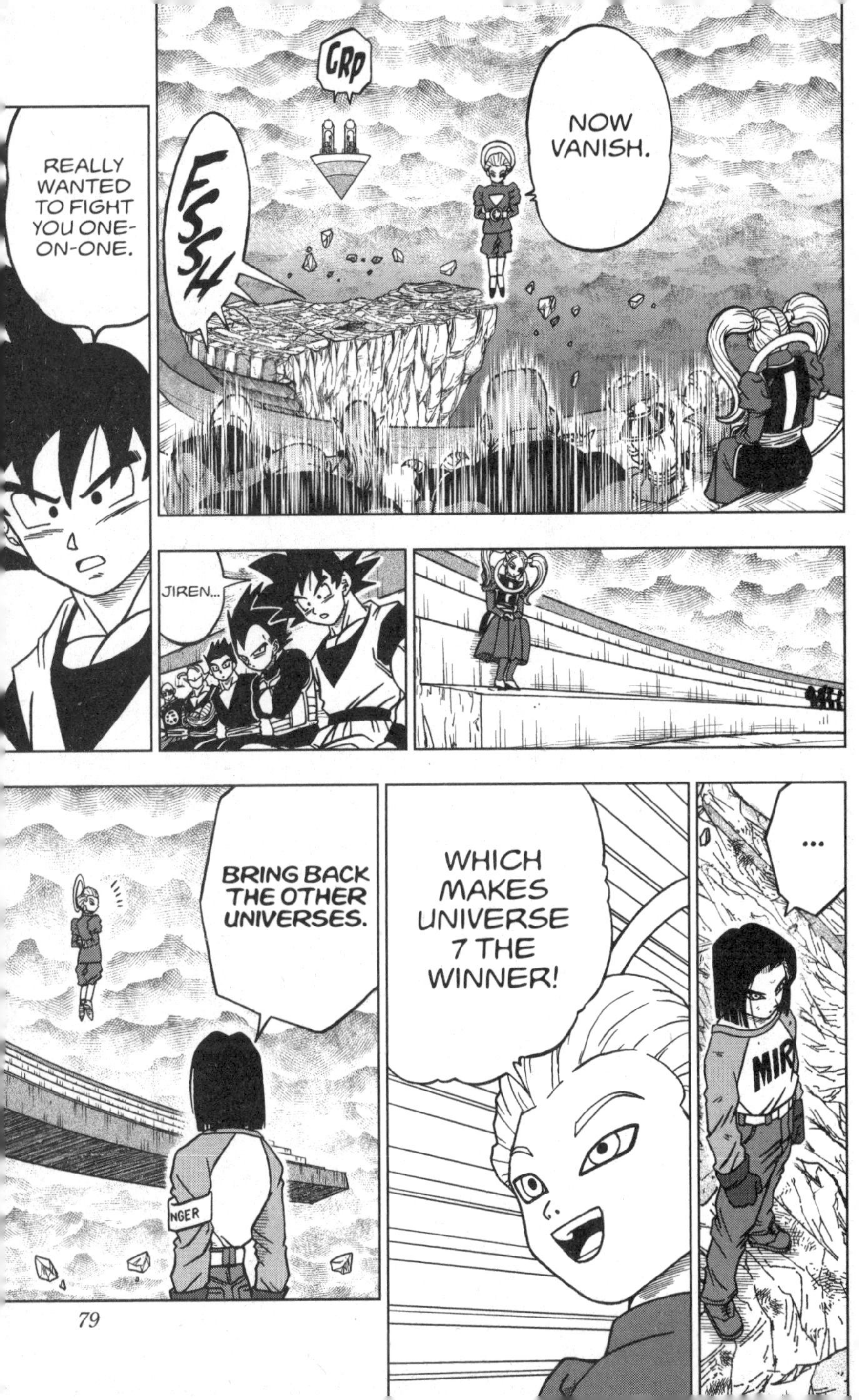
NOW VANISH.
GRP
FSSH
JIREN...
REALLY WANTED TO FIGHT YOU ONE-ON-ONE.
...
WHICH MAKES UNIVERSE 7 THE WINNER!
BRING BACK THE OTHER UNIVERSES.
NGER
MIR

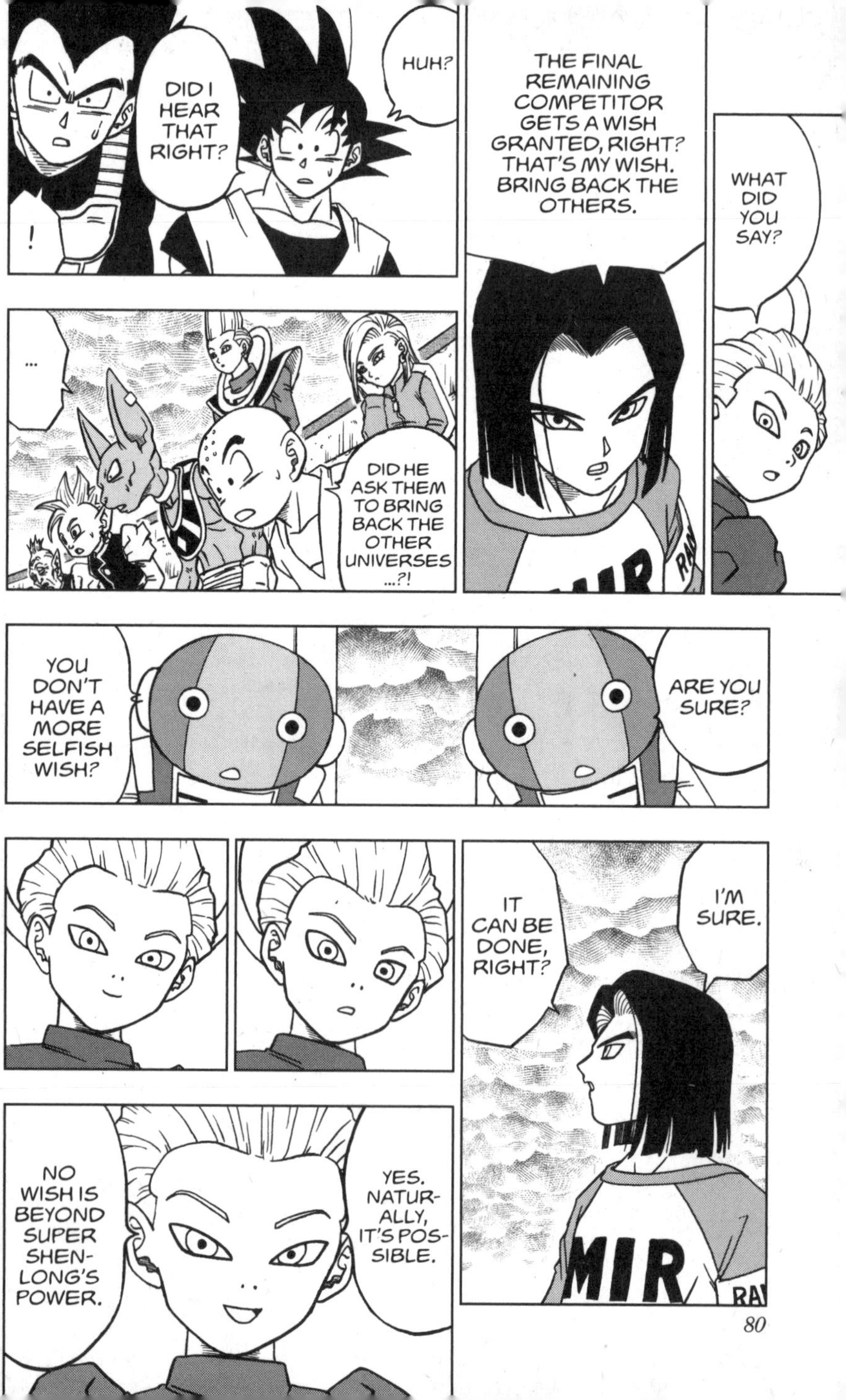
WHAT DID YOU SAY?
THE FINAL REMAINING COMPETITOR GETS A WISH GRANTED, RIGHT? THAT'S MY WISH. BRING BACK THE OTHERS.
HUH?
DID I HEAR THAT RIGHT?
!
DID HE ASK THEM TO BRING BACK THE OTHER UNIVERSES ...?!
...
ARE YOU SURE?
YOU DON'T HAVE A MORE SELFISH WISH?
I'M SURE.
IT CAN BE DONE, RIGHT?
YES. NATUR-ALLY, IT'S POS-SIBLE.
NO WISH IS BEYOND SUPER SHEN-LONG'S POWER.

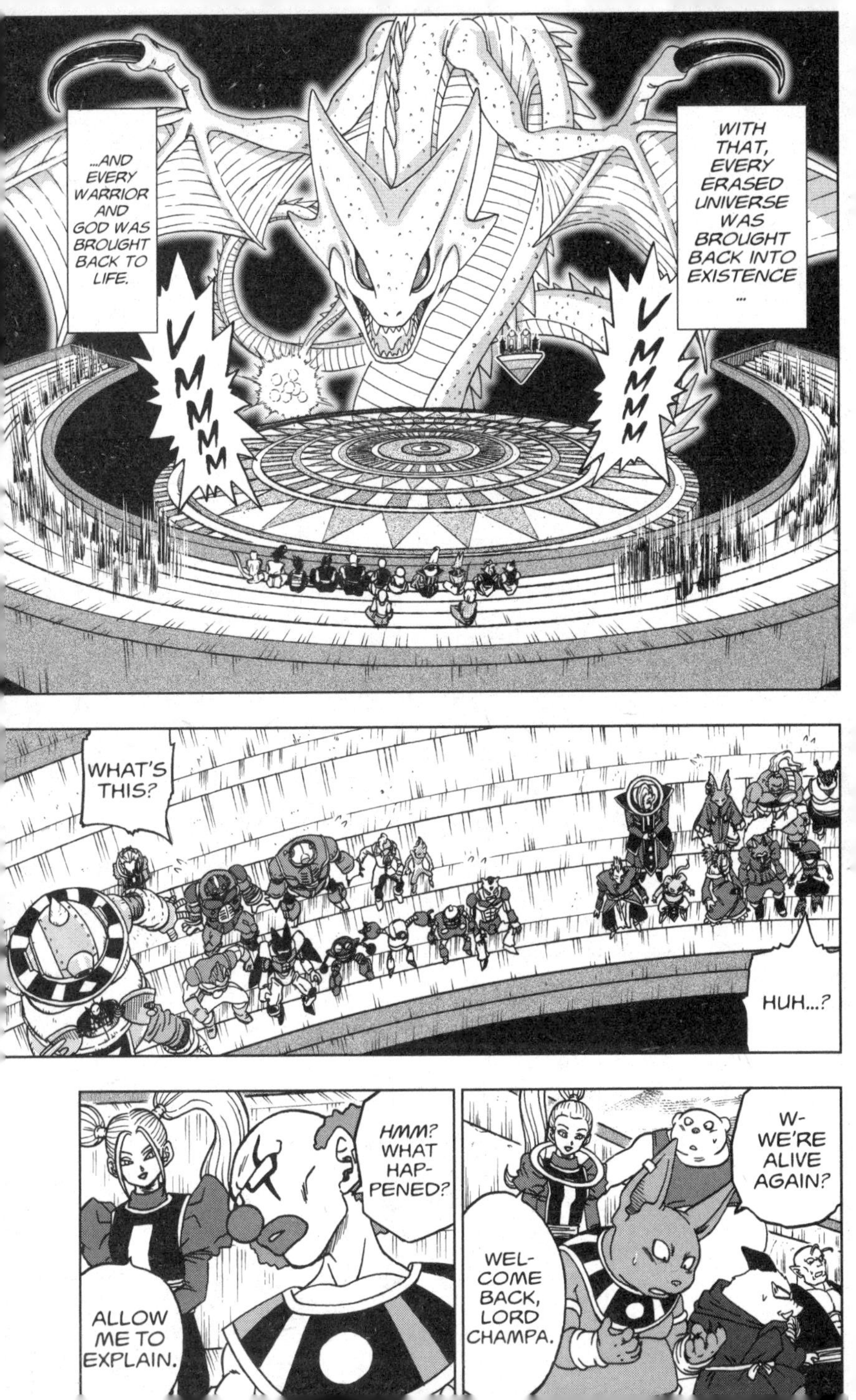
WITH THAT, EVERY ERASED UNIVERSE WAS BROUGHT BACK INTO EXISTENCE ...
VMMMMM
...AND EVERY WARRIOR AND GOD WAS BROUGHT BACK TO LIFE.
VMMMM
HUH...?
WHAT'S THIS?
W- WE'RE ALIVE AGAIN?
WEL- COME BACK, LORD CHAMPA.
HMM? WHAT HAP- PENED?
ALLOW ME TO EXPLAIN.

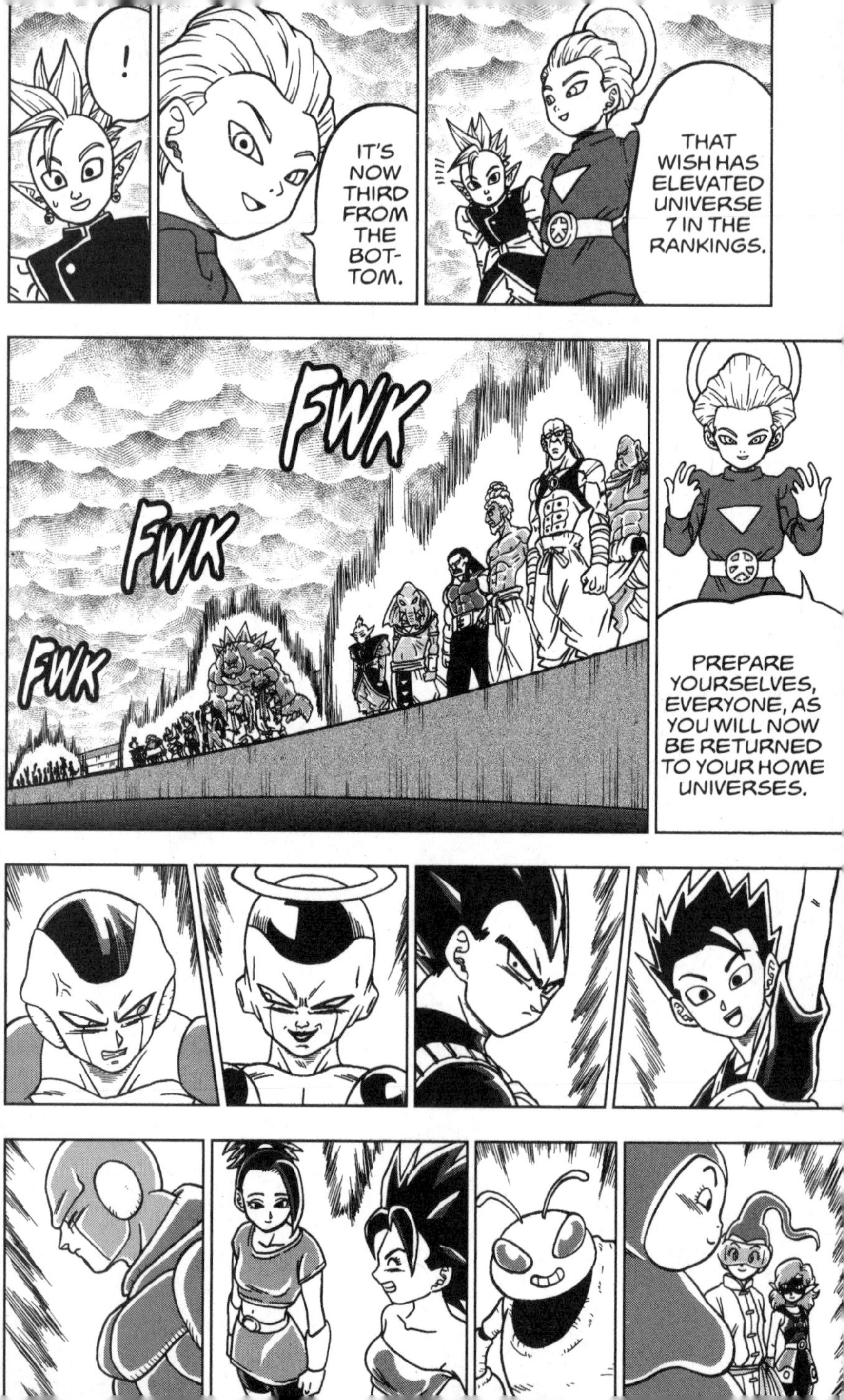
THAT WISH HAS ELEVATED UNIVERSE 7 IN THE RANKINGS.
IT'S NOW THIRD FROM THE BOT-TOM.
!
PREPARE YOURSELVES, EVERYONE, AS YOU WILL NOW BE RETURNED TO YOUR HOME UNIVERSES.
FWK
FWK
FWK

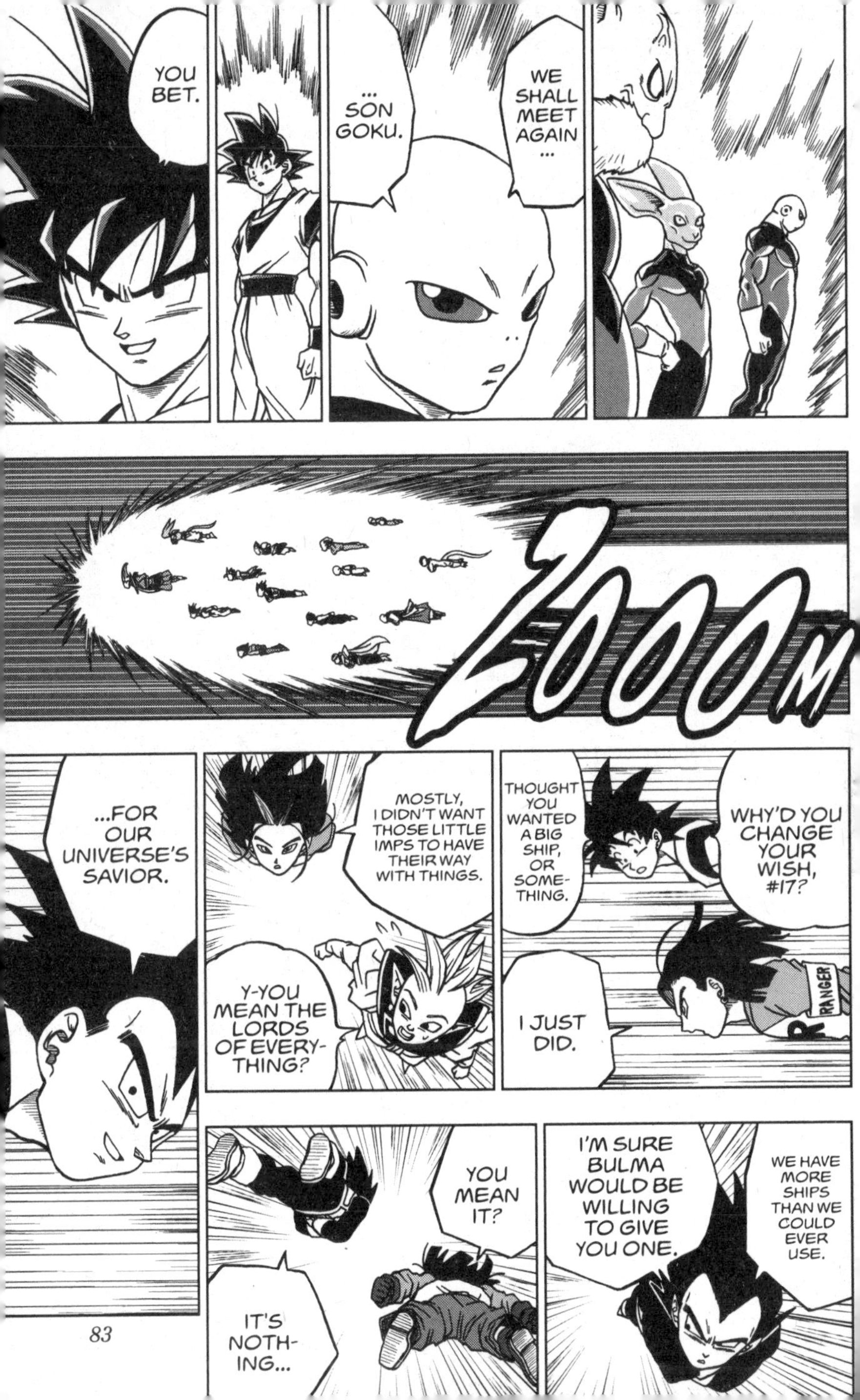
WE SHALL MEET AGAIN ...
... SON GOKU.
YOU BET.
ZOOOM
WHY'D YOU CHANGE YOUR WISH, #17?
THOUGHT YOU WANTED A BIG SHIP, OR SOMETHING.
I JUST DID.
MOSTLY, I DIDN'T WANT THOSE LITTLE IMPS TO HAVE THEIR WAY WITH THINGS.
Y-YOU MEAN THE LORDS OF EVERYTHING?
RANGER
WE HAVE MORE SHIPS THAN WE COULD EVER USE.
I'M SURE BULMA WOULD BE WILLING TO GIVE YOU ONE.
YOU MEAN IT?
IT'S NOTH-ING...
...FOR OUR UNIVERSE'S SAVIOR.

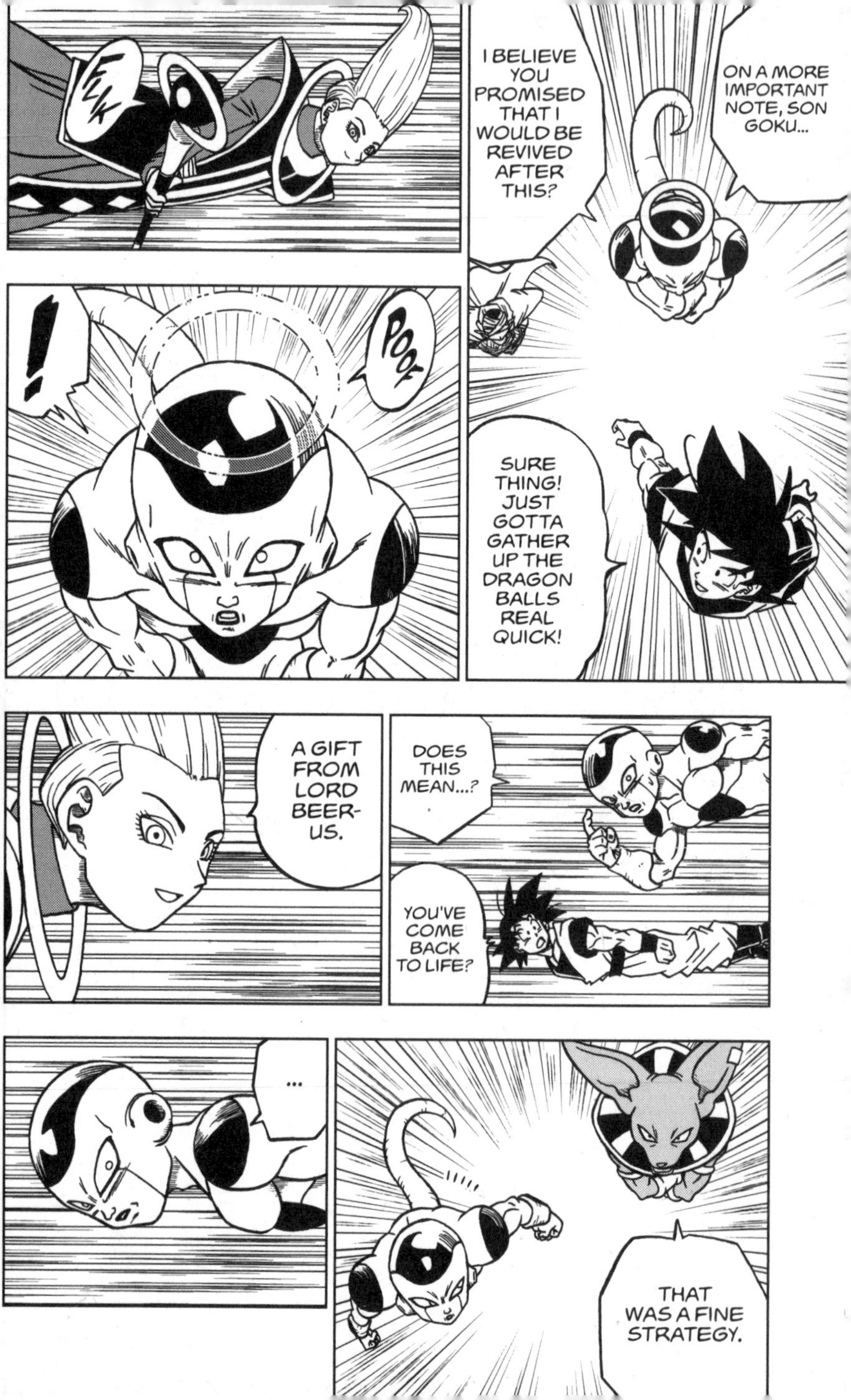
ON A MORE IMPORTANT NOTE, SON GOKU...
I BELIEVE YOU PROMISED THAT I WOULD BE REVIVED AFTER THIS?
SURE THING! JUST GOTTA GATHER UP THE DRAGON BALLS REAL QUICK!
FLIK
POOF
!
DOES THIS MEAN...?
YOU'VE COME BACK TO LIFE?
A GIFT FROM LORD BEER-US.
THAT WAS A FINE STRATEGY.
...

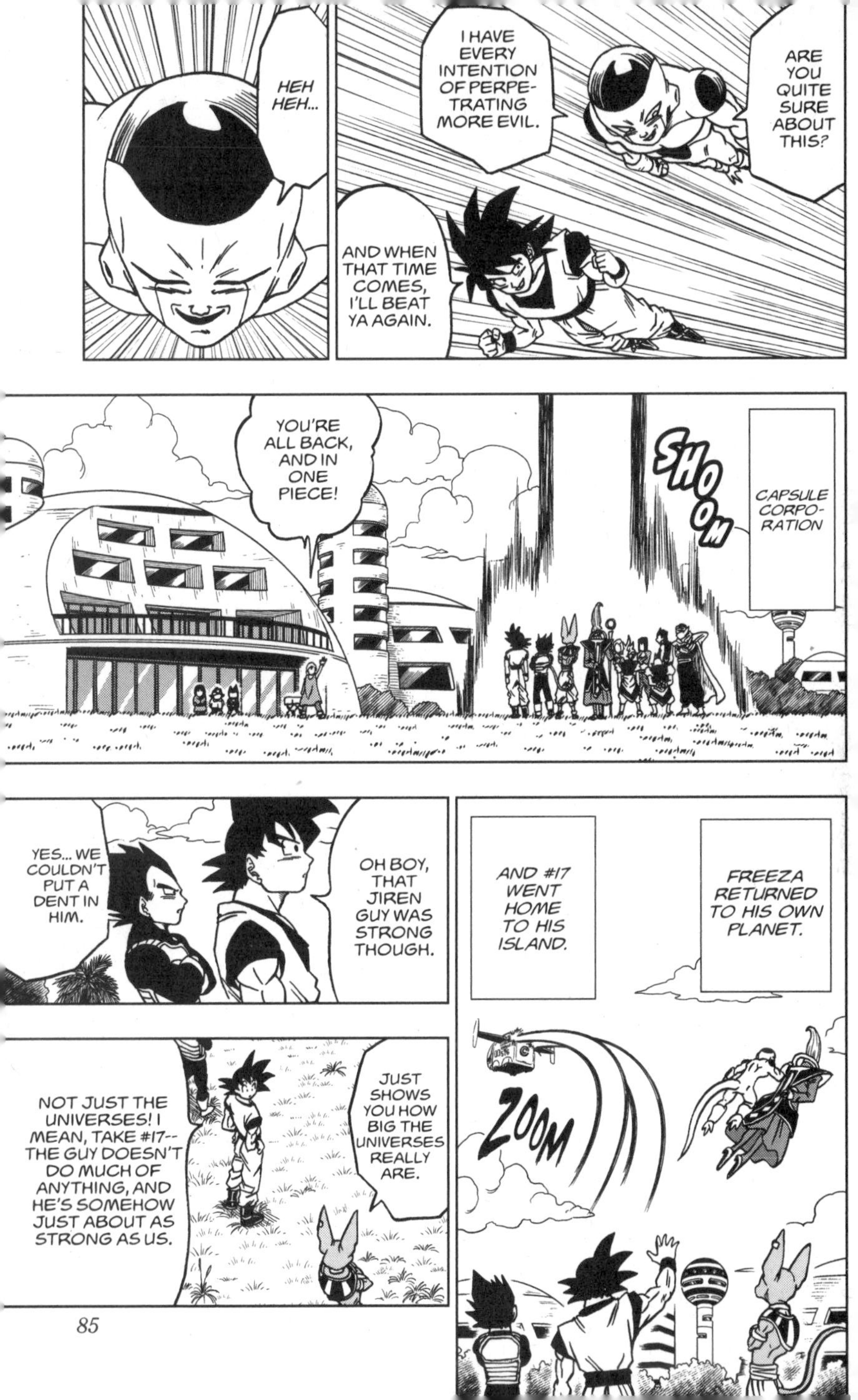
ARE YOU QUITE SURE ABOUT THIS?
I HAVE EVERY INTENTION OF PERPE-TRATING MORE EVIL.
AND WHEN THAT TIME COMES, I'LL BEAT YA AGAIN.
HEH HEH...
CAPSULE CORPO-RATION
SHOOM
YOU'RE ALL BACK, AND IN ONE PIECE!
FREEZA RETURNED TO HIS OWN PLANET.
AND #17 WENT HOME TO HIS ISLAND.
ZOOM
OH BOY, THAT JIREN GUY WAS STRONG THOUGH.
YES... WE COULDN'T PUT A DENT IN HIM.
JUST SHOWS YOU HOW BIG THE UNIVERSES REALLY ARE.
NOT JUST THE UNIVERSES! I MEAN, TAKE #17-- THE GUY DOESN'T DO MUCH OF ANYTHING, AND HE'S SOMEHOW JUST ABOUT AS STRONG AS US.

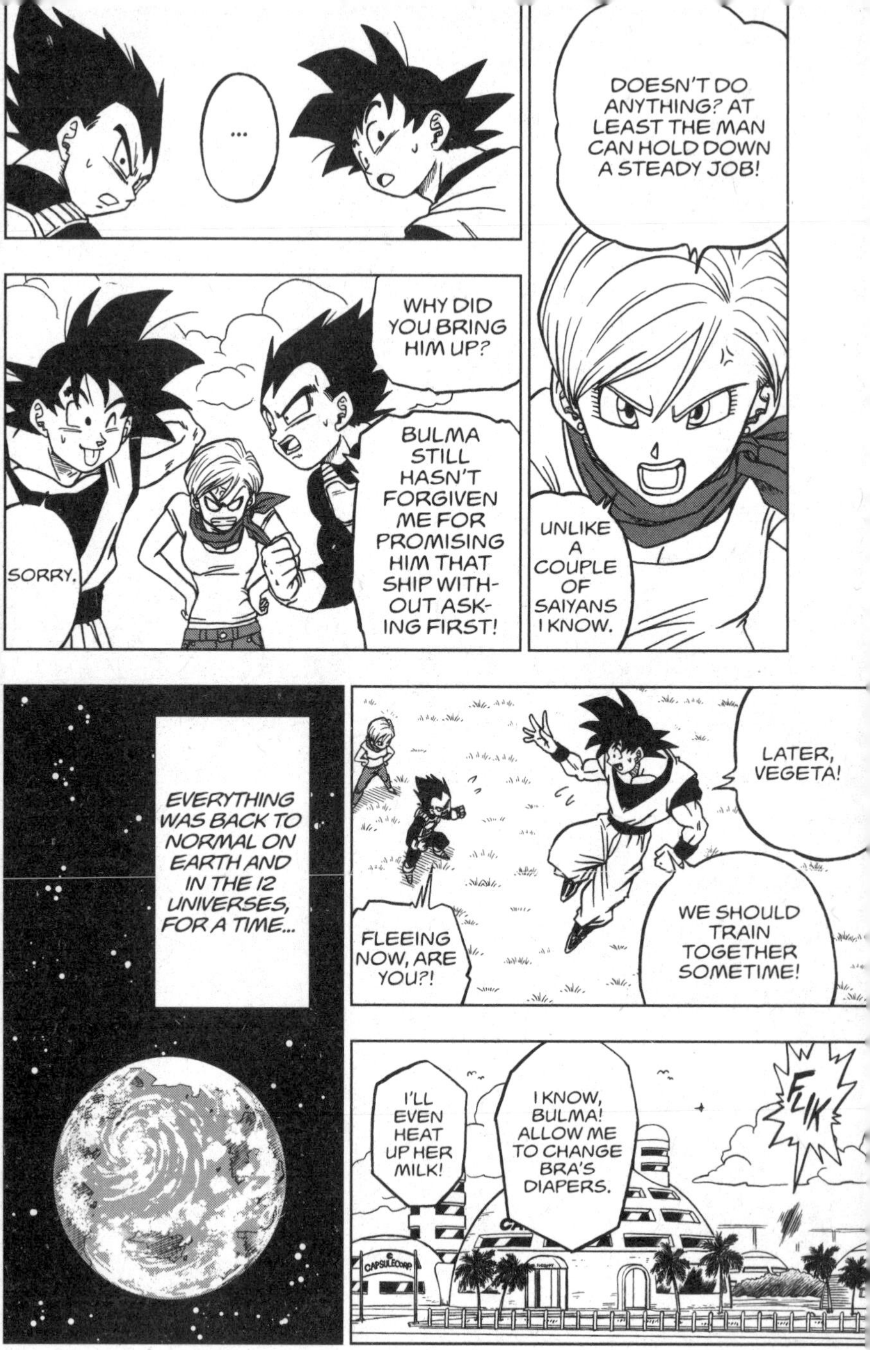
DOESN'T DO ANYTHING? AT LEAST THE MAN CAN HOLD DOWN A STEADY JOB!
UNLIKE A COUPLE OF SAIYANS I KNOW.
...
WHY DID YOU BRING HIM UP?
BULMA STILL HASN'T FORGIVEN ME FOR PROMISING HIM THAT SHIP WITH-OUT ASK-ING FIRST!
SORRY.
LATER, VEGETA!
WE SHOULD TRAIN TOGETHER SOMETIME!
FLEEING NOW, ARE YOU?!
FLIK
I KNOW, BULMA! ALLOW ME TO CHANGE BRA'S DIAPERS.
I'LL EVEN HEAT UP HER MILK!
CAPSULE CORP.
EVERYTHING WAS BACK TO NORMAL ON EARTH AND IN THE 12 UNIVERSES, FOR A TIME...

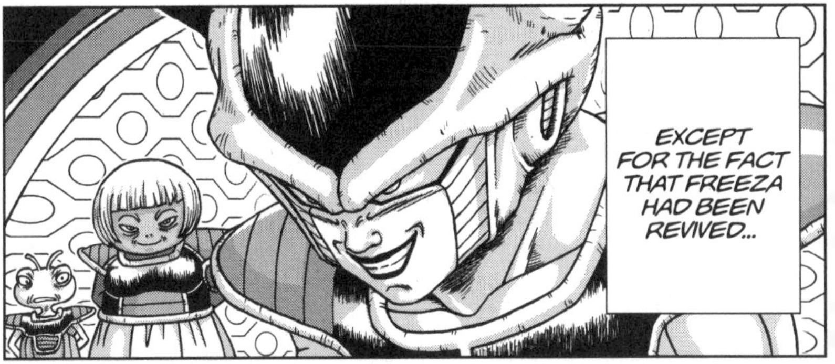
EXCEPT FOR THE FACT THAT FREEZA HAD BEEN REVIVED...

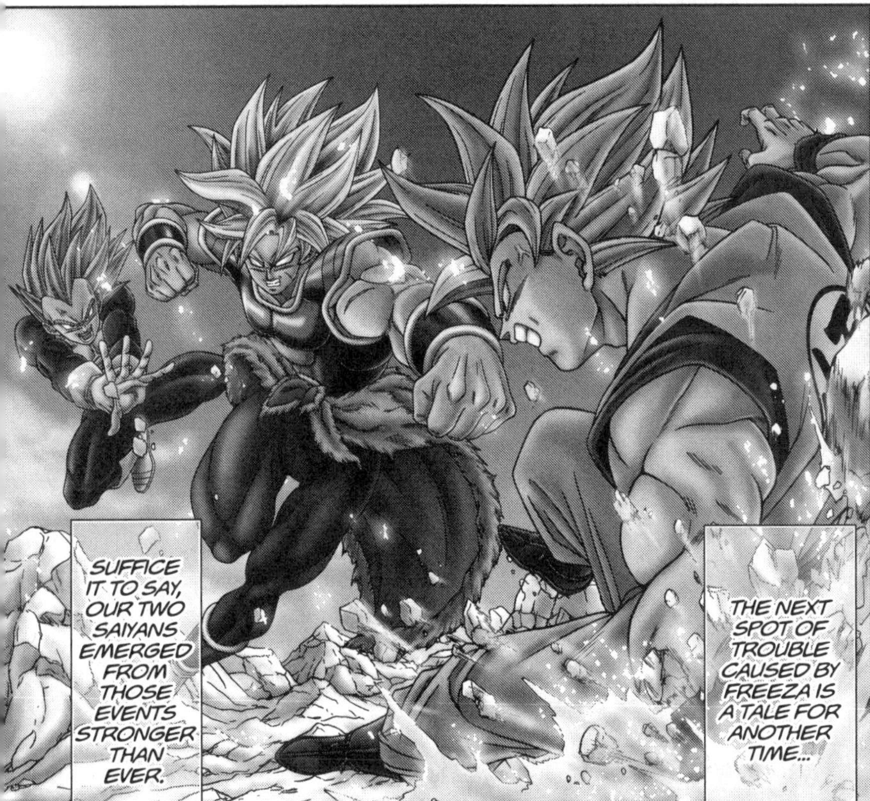
THE NEXT SPOT OF TROUBLE CAUSED BY FREEZA IS A TALE FOR ANOTHER TIME...
SUFFICE IT TO SAY, OUR TWO SAIYANS EMERGED FROM THOSE EVENTS STRONGER THAN EVER.

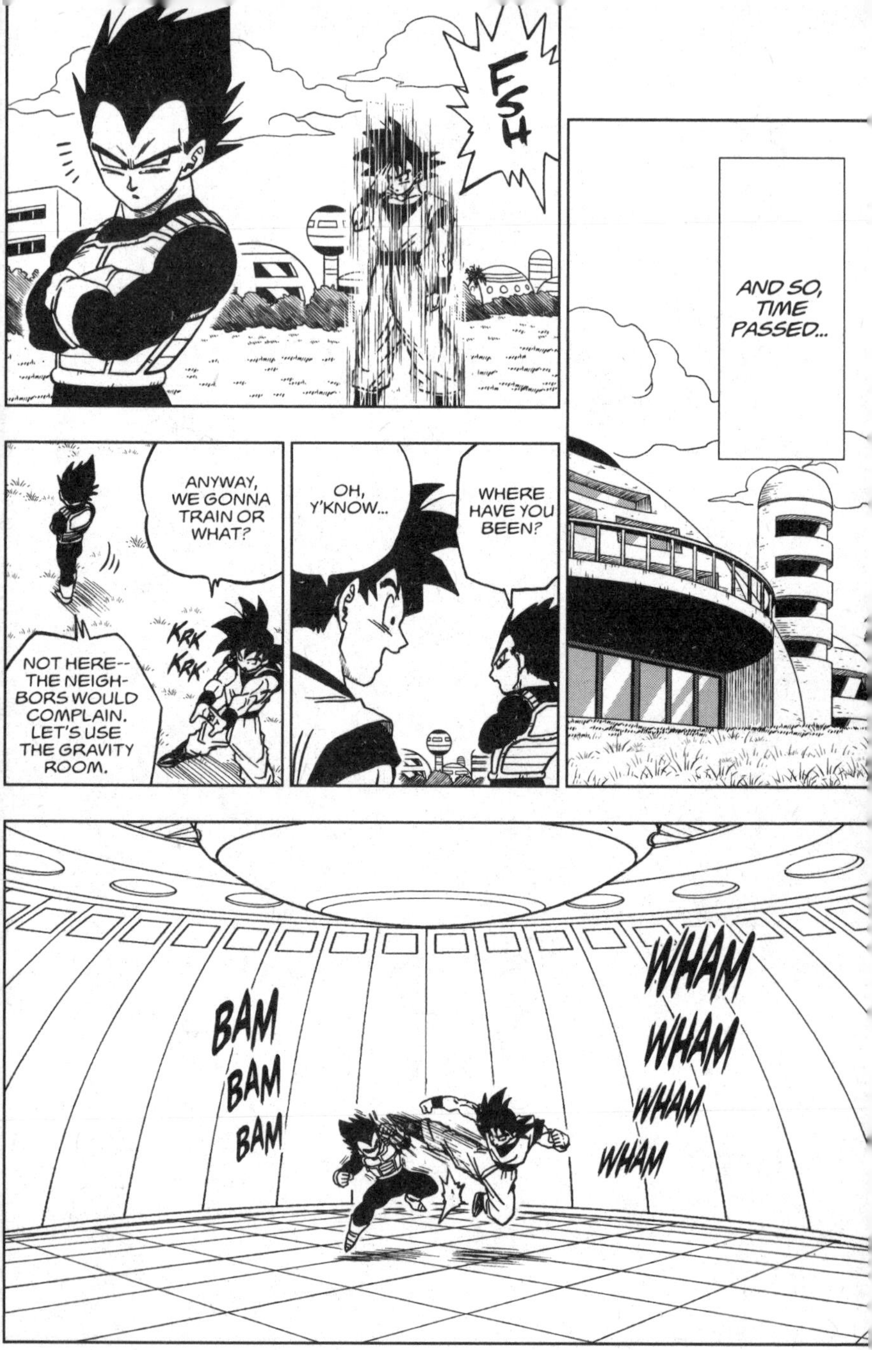
AND SO, TIME PASSED...
FSH
WHERE HAVE YOU BEEN?
OH, Y'KNOW...
ANYWAY, WE GONNA TRAIN OR WHAT?
KRK KRK
NOT HERE--THE NEIGHBORS WOULD COMPLAIN. LET'S USE THE GRAVITY ROOM.
WHAM WHAM WHAM WHAM
BAM BAM BAM

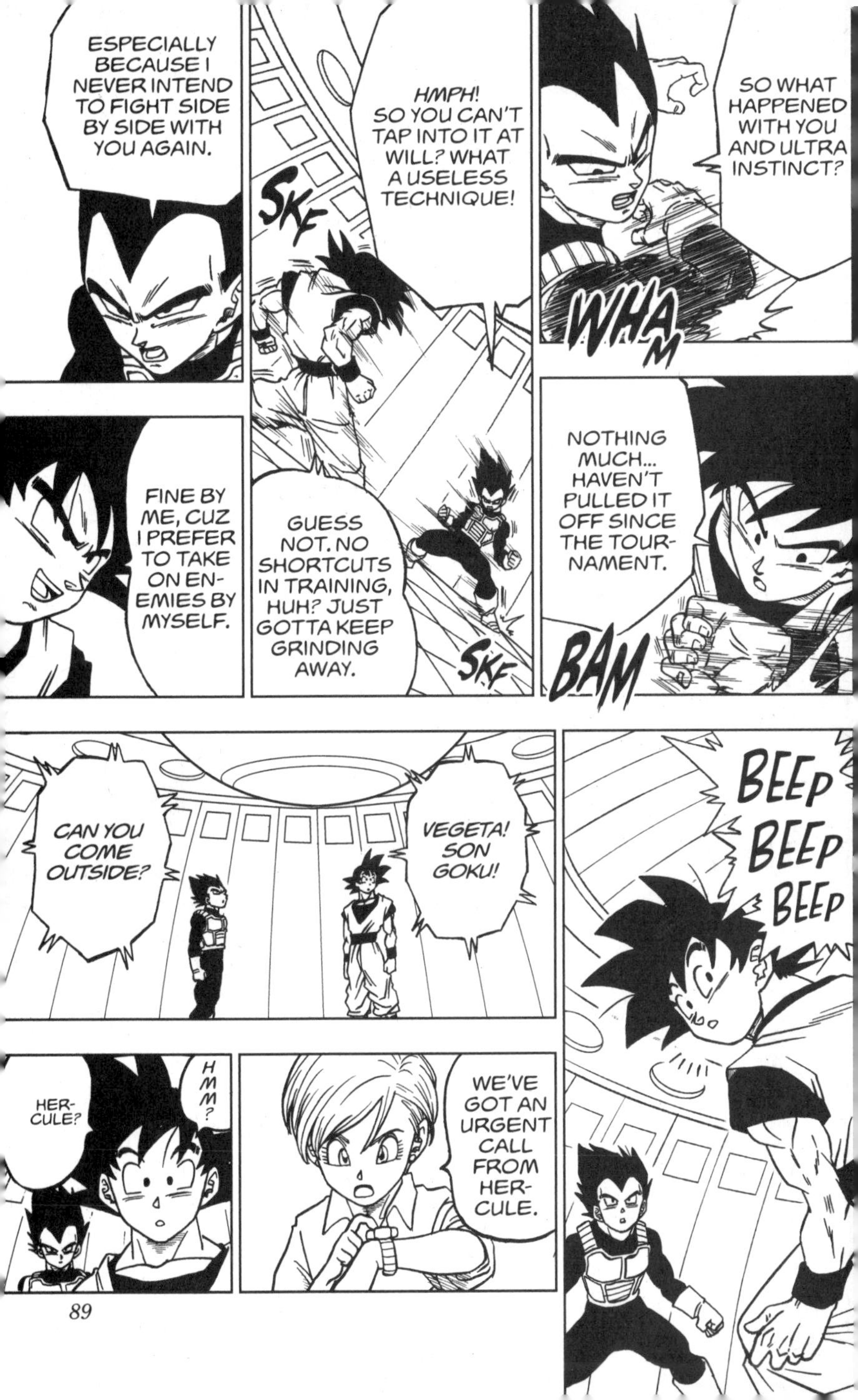
SO WHAT HAPPENED WITH YOU AND ULTRA INSTINCT?
WHAM
NOTHING MUCH... HAVEN'T PULLED IT OFF SINCE THE TOUR-NAMENT.
BAM
SKF
HMPH! SO YOU CAN'T TAP INTO IT AT WILL? WHAT A USELESS TECHNIQUE!
GUESS NOT. NO SHORTCUTS IN TRAINING, HUH? JUST GOTTA KEEP GRINDING AWAY.
SKF
ESPECIALLY BECAUSE I NEVER INTEND TO FIGHT SIDE BY SIDE WITH YOU AGAIN.
FINE BY ME, CUZ I PREFER TO TAKE ON EN-EMIES BY MYSELF.
BEEP
BEEP
BEEP
VEGETA! SON GOKU!
CAN YOU COME OUTSIDE?
WE'VE GOT AN URGENT CALL FROM HER-CULE.
HMM?
HER-CULE?

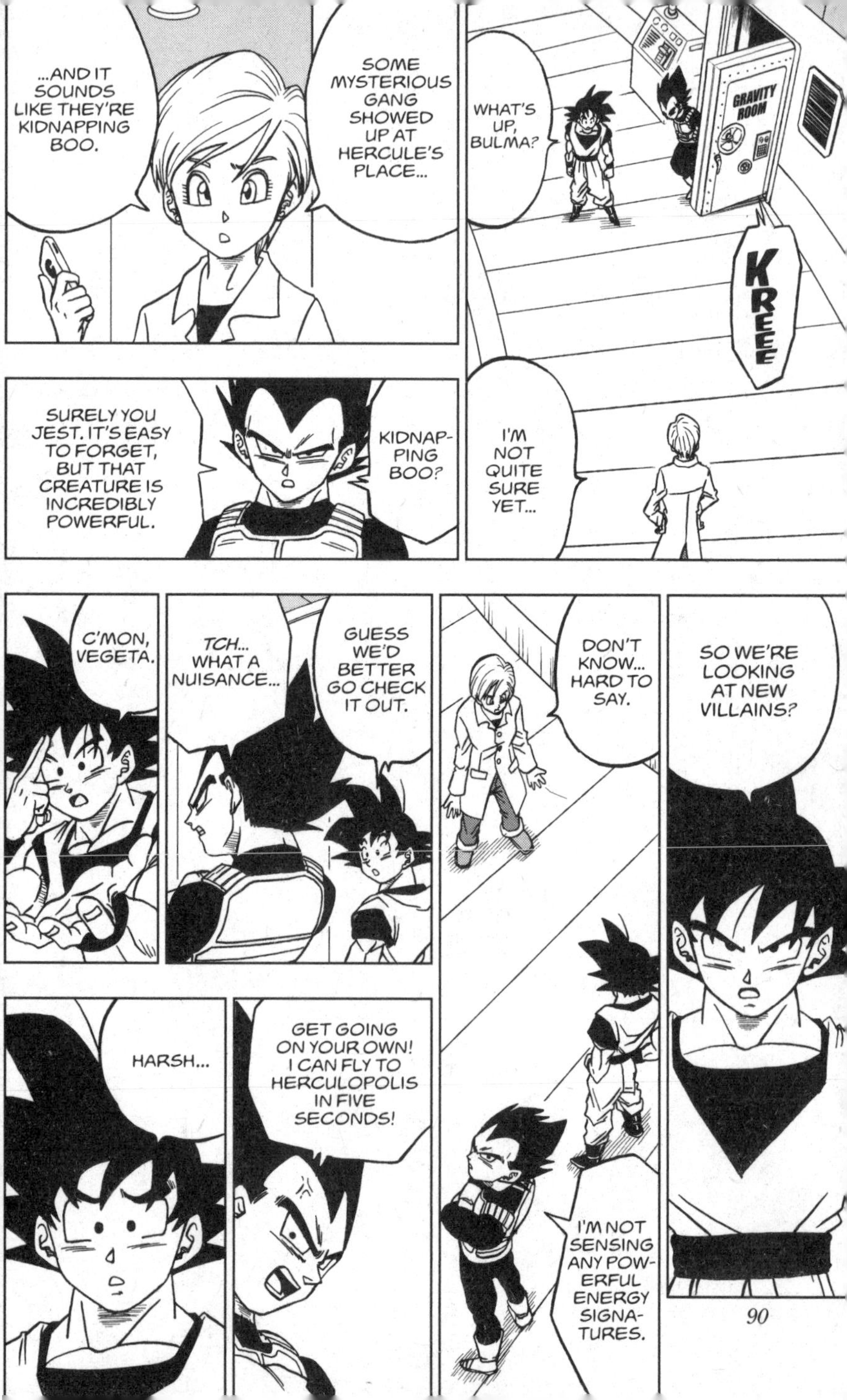
WHAT'S UP, BULMA?
KREEE
SOME MYSTERIOUS GANG SHOWED UP AT HERCULE'S PLACE...
...AND IT SOUNDS LIKE THEY'RE KIDNAPPING BOO.
I'M NOT QUITE SURE YET...
KIDNAP-PING BOO?
SURELY YOU JEST. IT'S EASY TO FORGET, BUT THAT CREATURE IS INCREDIBLY POWERFUL.
SO WE'RE LOOKING AT NEW VILLAINS?
DON'T KNOW... HARD TO SAY.
I'M NOT SENSING ANY POW-ERFUL ENERGY SIGNA-TURES.
GUESS WE'D BETTER GO CHECK IT OUT.
TCH... WHAT A NUISANCE...
C'MON, VEGETA.
GET GOING ON YOUR OWN! I CAN FLY TO HERCULOPOLIS IN FIVE SECONDS!
HARSH...

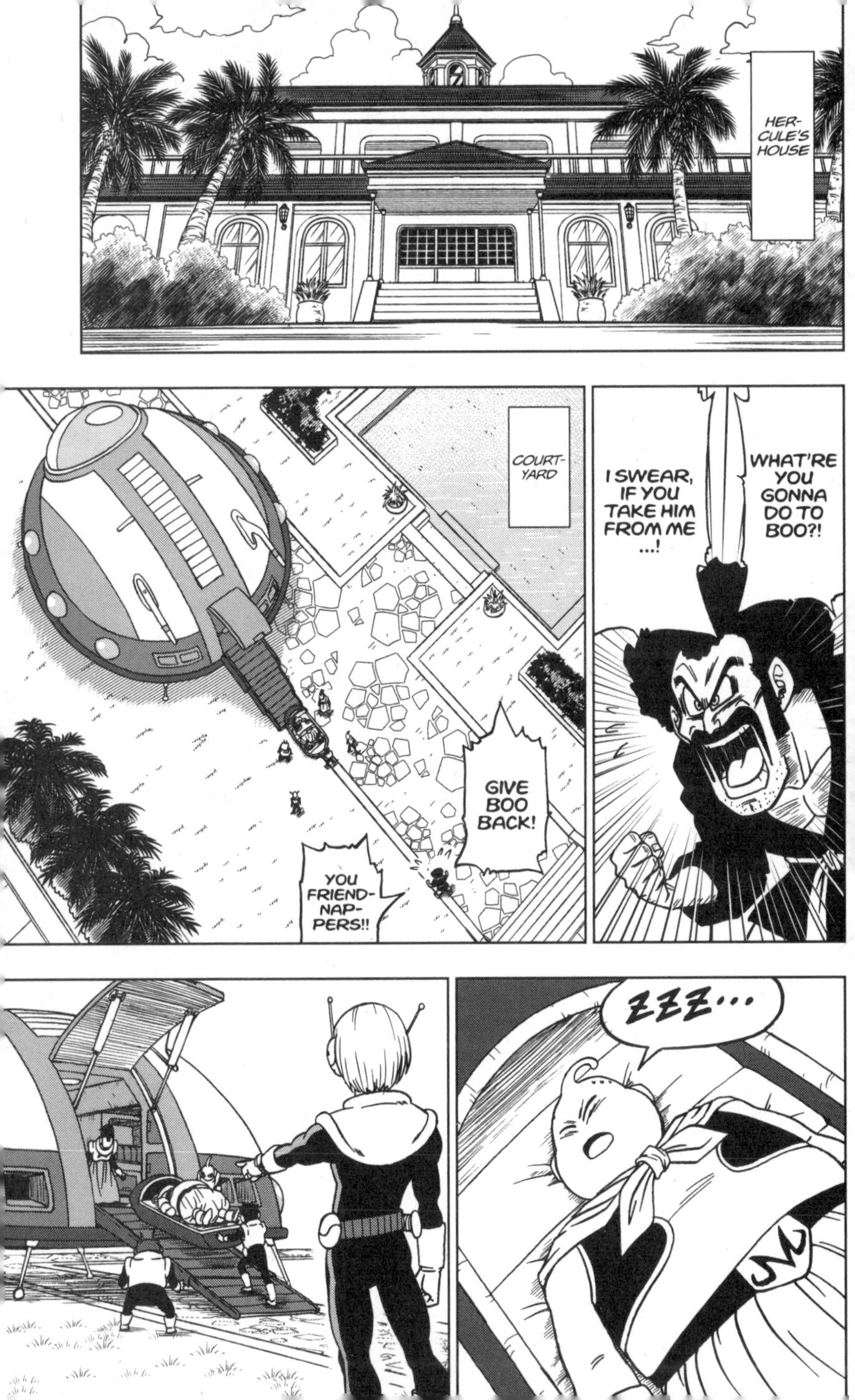
HER-
CULE'S
HOUSE
WHAT'RE YOU GONNA DO TO BOO?!
I SWEAR, IF YOU TAKE HIM FROM ME ...!
COURT-
YARD
GIVE BOO BACK!
YOU FRIEND-NAP-PERS!!
ZZZ...

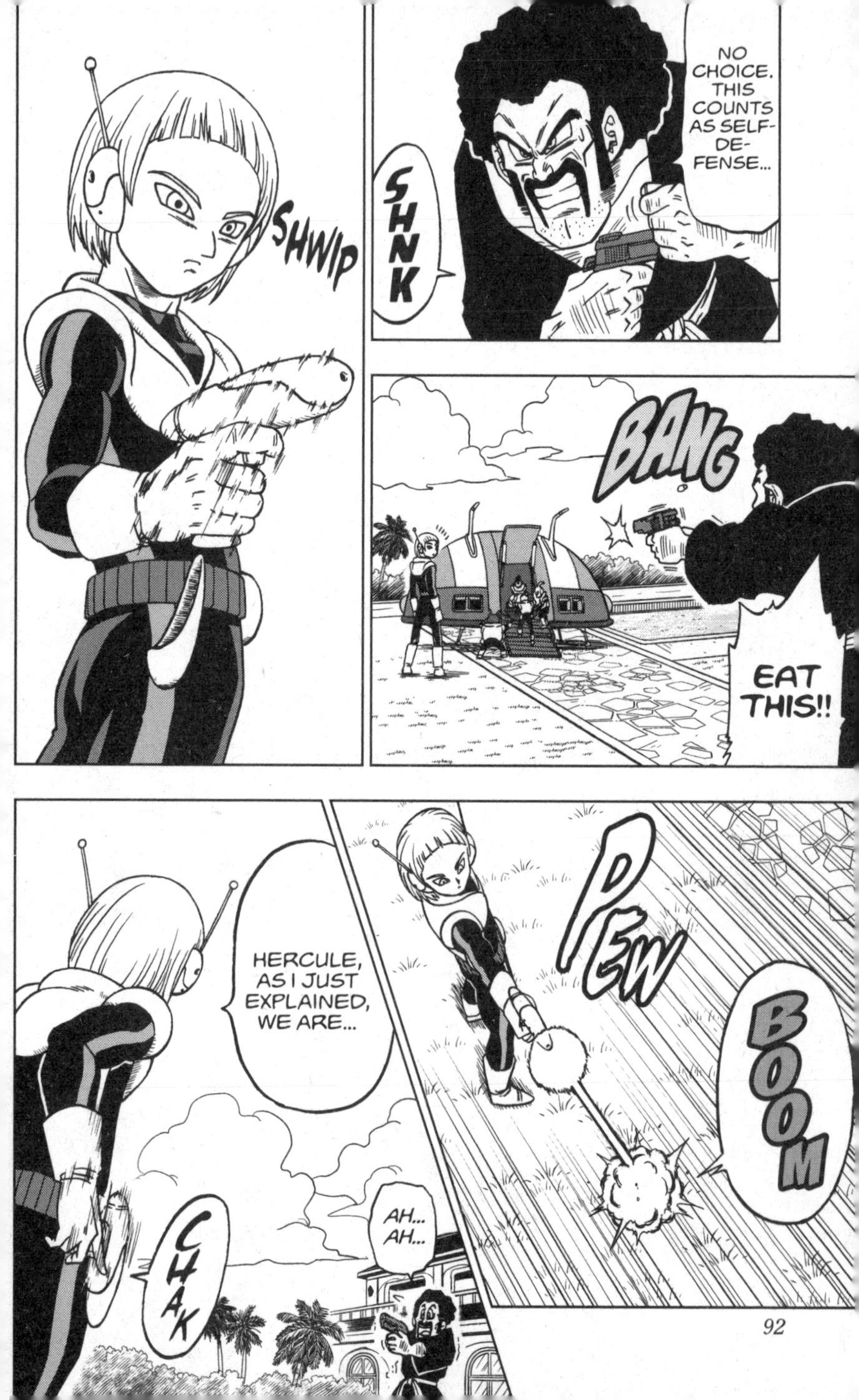

NO CHOICE. THIS COUNTS AS SELF-DEFENSE...
SHNK
BANG
EAT THIS!!
SHWIP
PEW
BOOM
HERCULE, AS I JUST EXPLAINED, WE ARE...
CHAK
AH... AH...

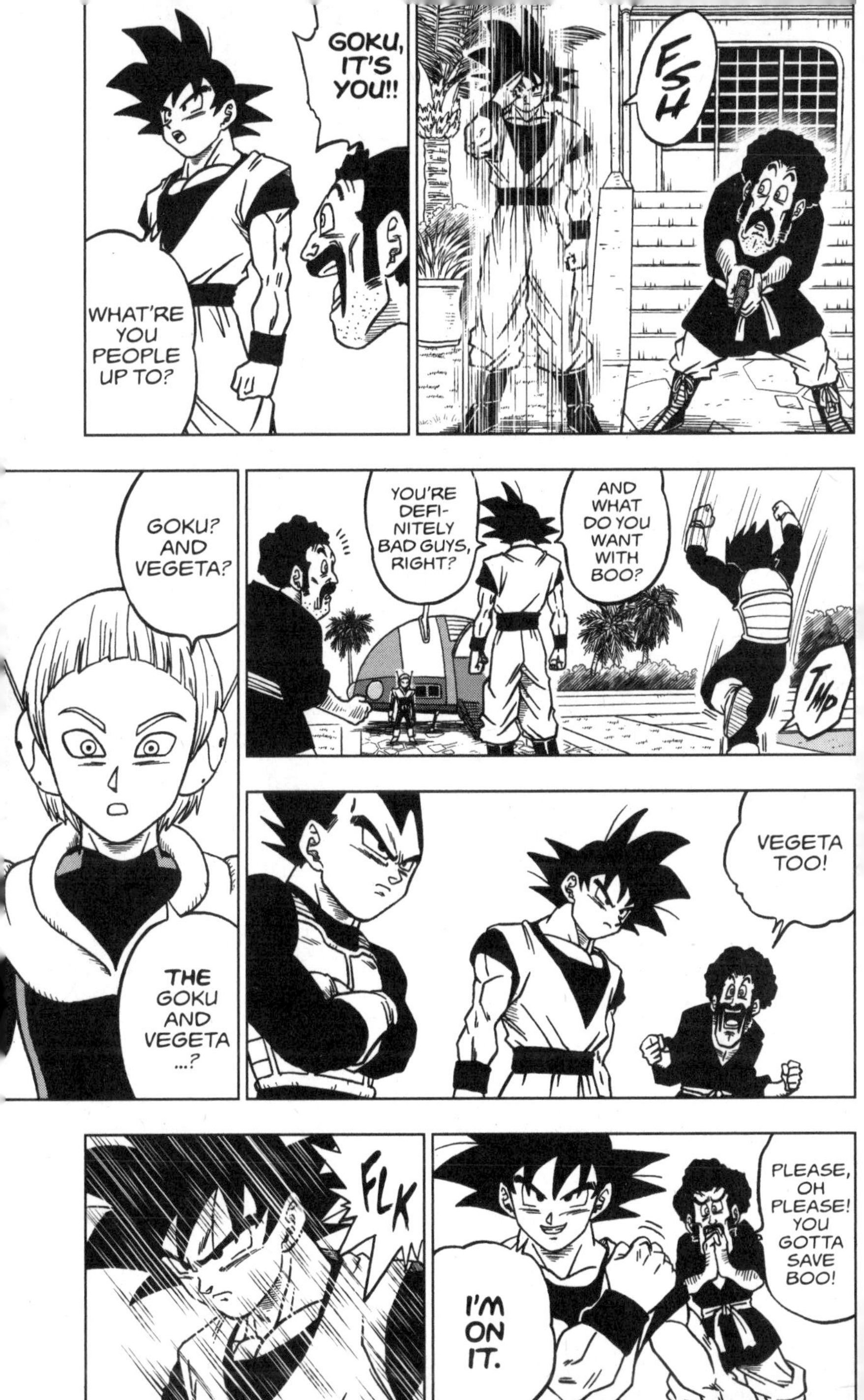
FSH
GOKU, IT'S YOU!!
WHAT'RE YOU PEOPLE UP TO?
AND WHAT DO YOU WANT WITH BOO?
YOU'RE DEFI-NITELY BAD GUYS, RIGHT?
TMP
VEGETA TOO!
GOKU? AND VEGETA?
THE GOKU AND VEGETA ...?
PLEASE, OH PLEASE! YOU GOTTA SAVE BOO!
I'M ON IT.
FLK

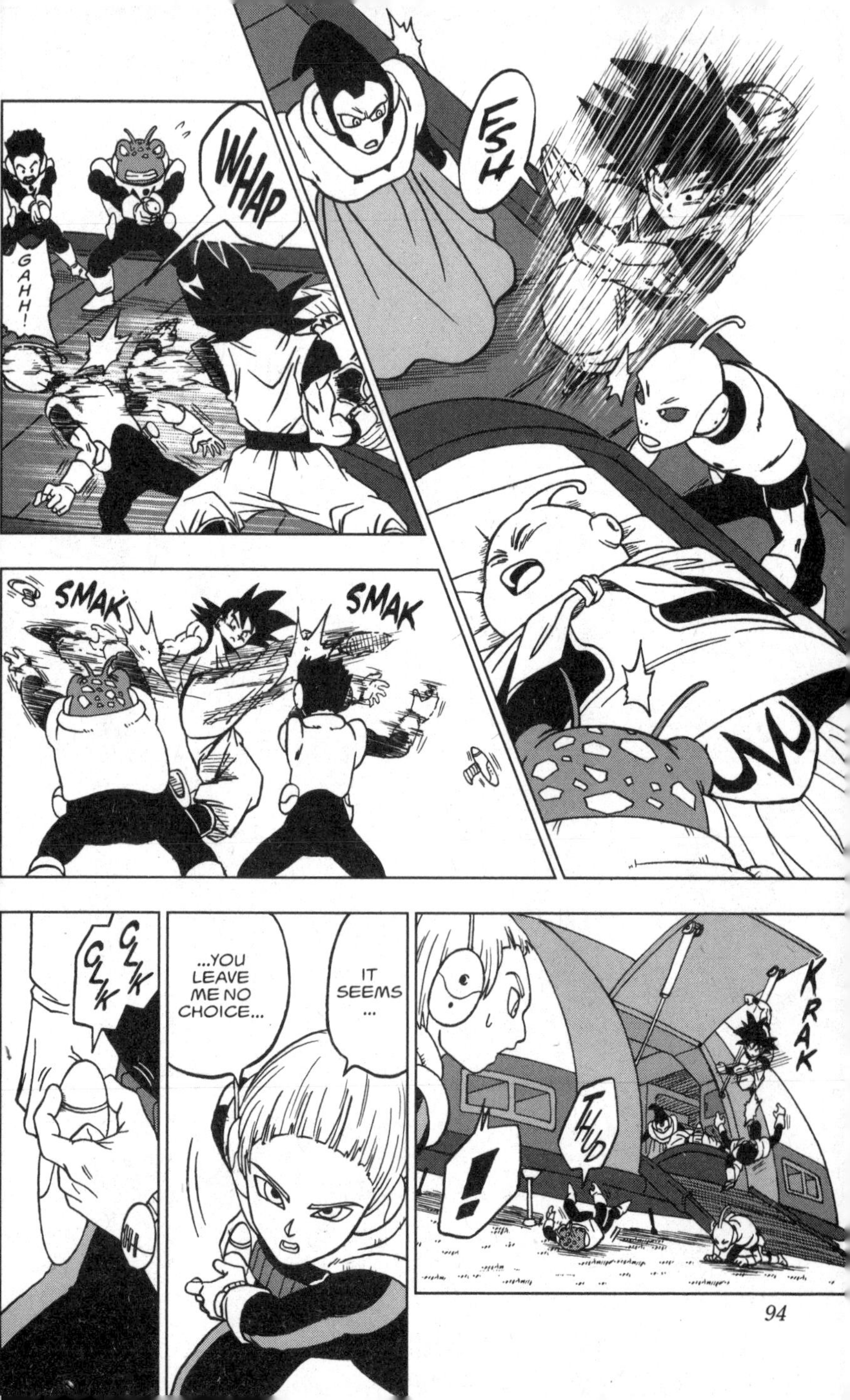
FSH
WHAP
GAHHH!
SMAK
SMAK
KRAK
THUD
!
IT SEEMS...
...YOU LEAVE ME NO CHOICE...
CLIK
CLIK

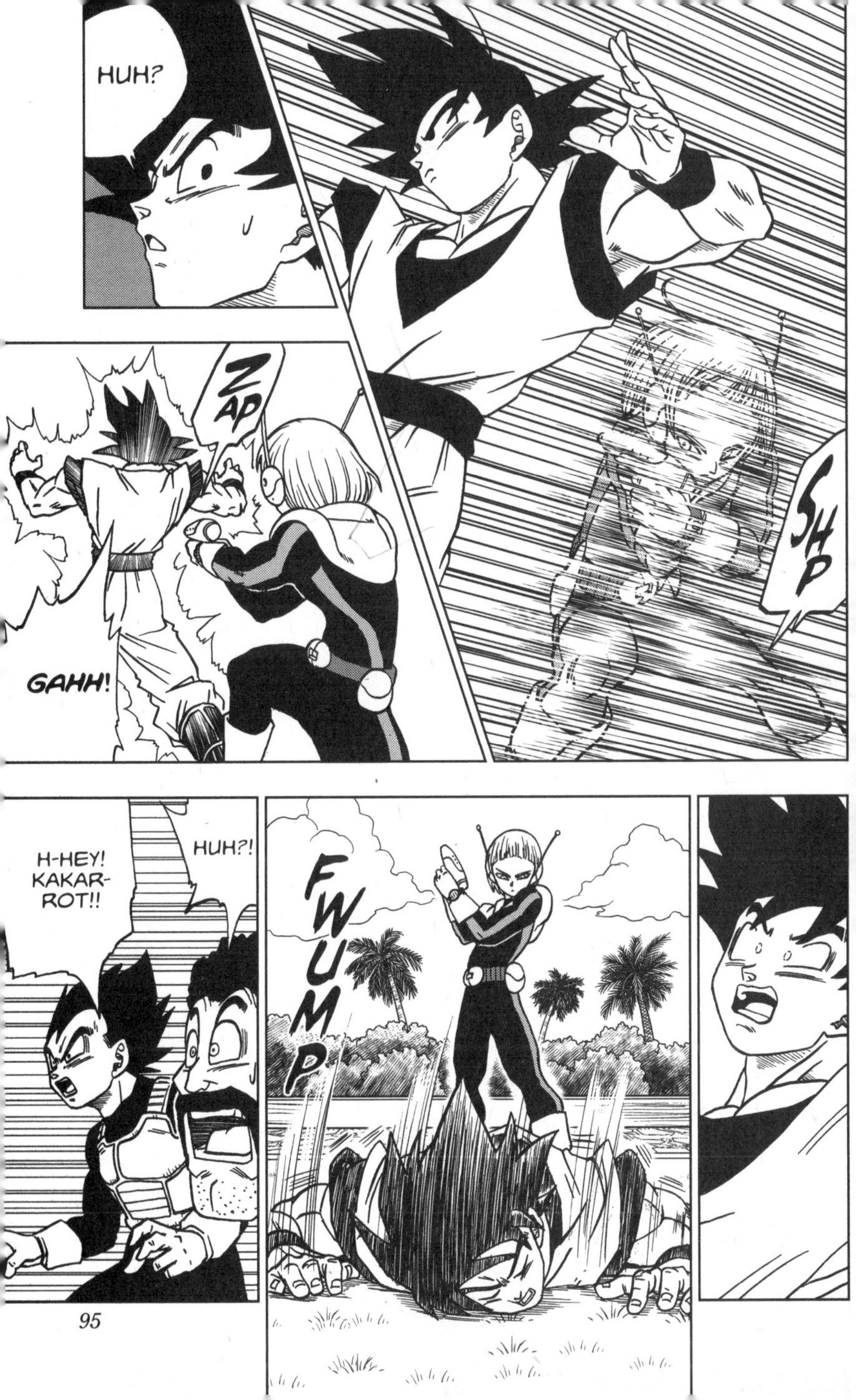
SHP
HUH?
ZAP
GAHH!
FWUMP
HUH?!
H-HEY! KAKAR-ROT!!

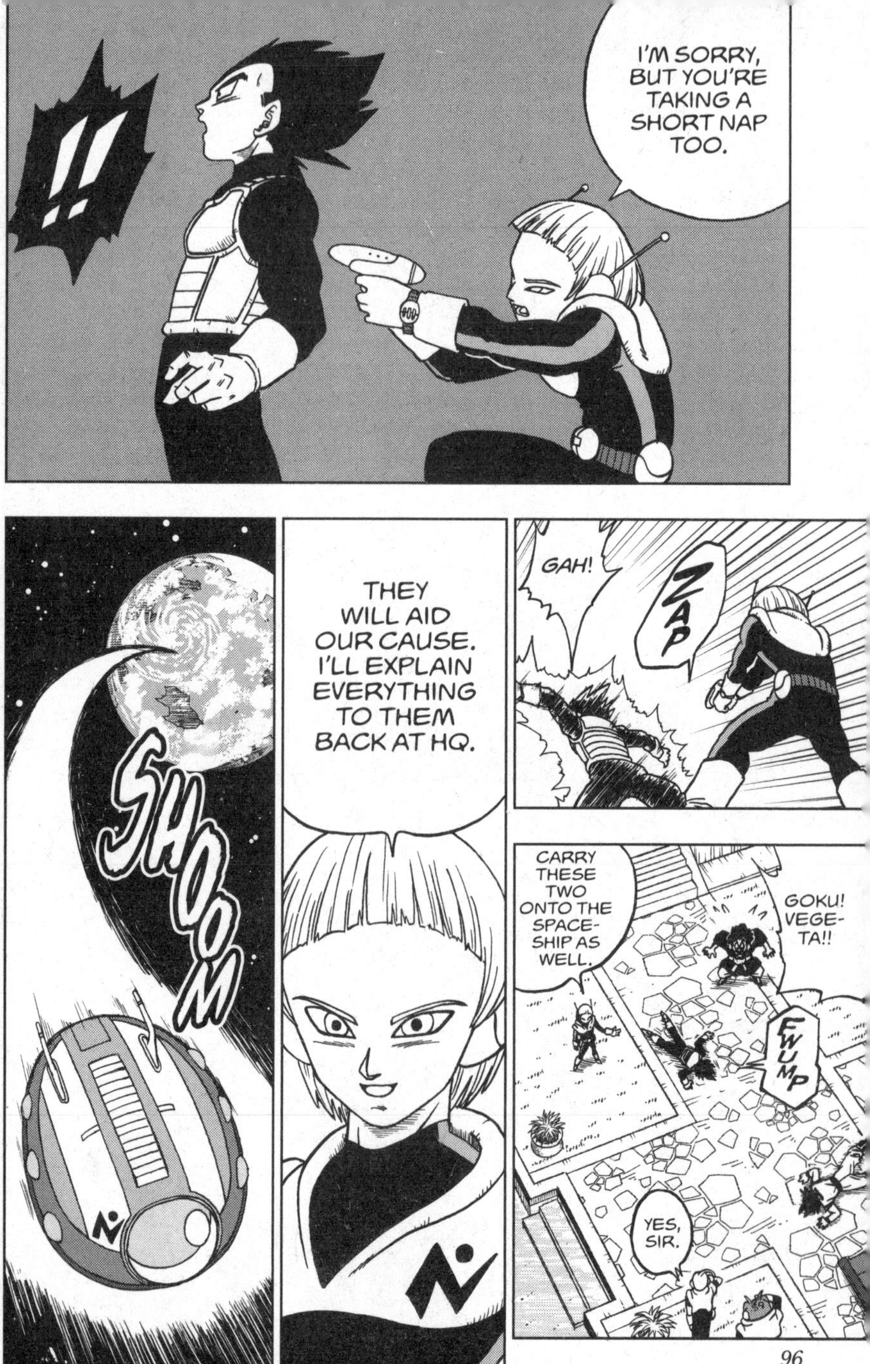
I'M SORRY, BUT YOU'RE TAKING A SHORT NAP TOO.
!!
ZAP
GAH!
GOKU! VEGE-TA!!
CARRY THESE TWO ONTO THE SPACE-SHIP AS WELL.
FWUMP
YES, SIR.
THEY WILL AID OUR CAUSE. I'LL EXPLAIN EVERYTHING TO THEM BACK AT HQ.
SHOOM

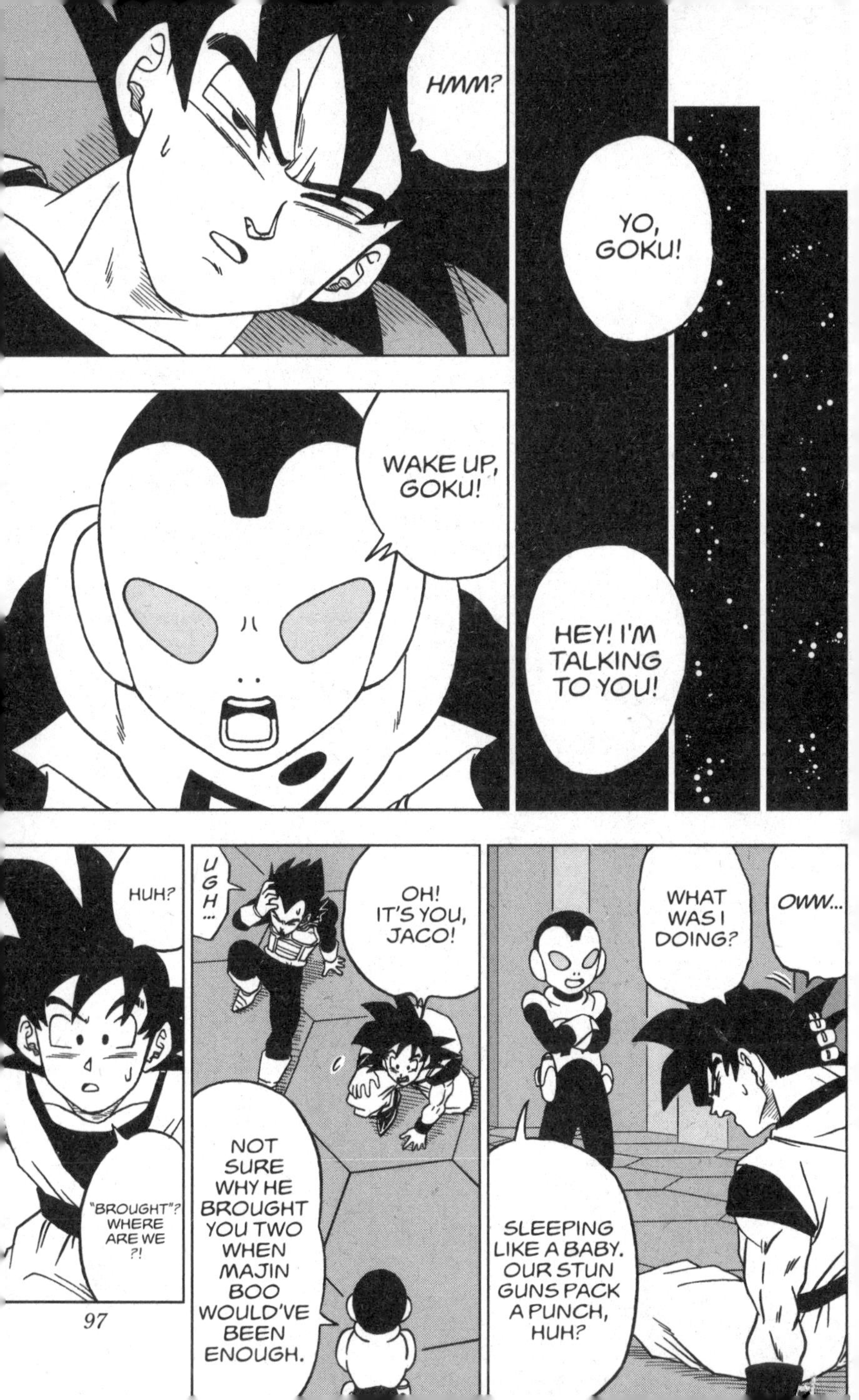
YO, GOKU!
HEY! I'M TALKING TO YOU!
HMM?
WAKE UP, GOKU!
OWW...
WHAT WAS I DOING?
SLEEPING LIKE A BABY. OUR STUN GUNS PACK A PUNCH, HUH?
OH! IT'S YOU, JACO!
UGH...
NOT SURE WHY HE BROUGHT YOU TWO WHEN MAJIN BOO WOULD'VE BEEN ENOUGH.
HUH?
"BROUGHT"? WHERE ARE WE ?!

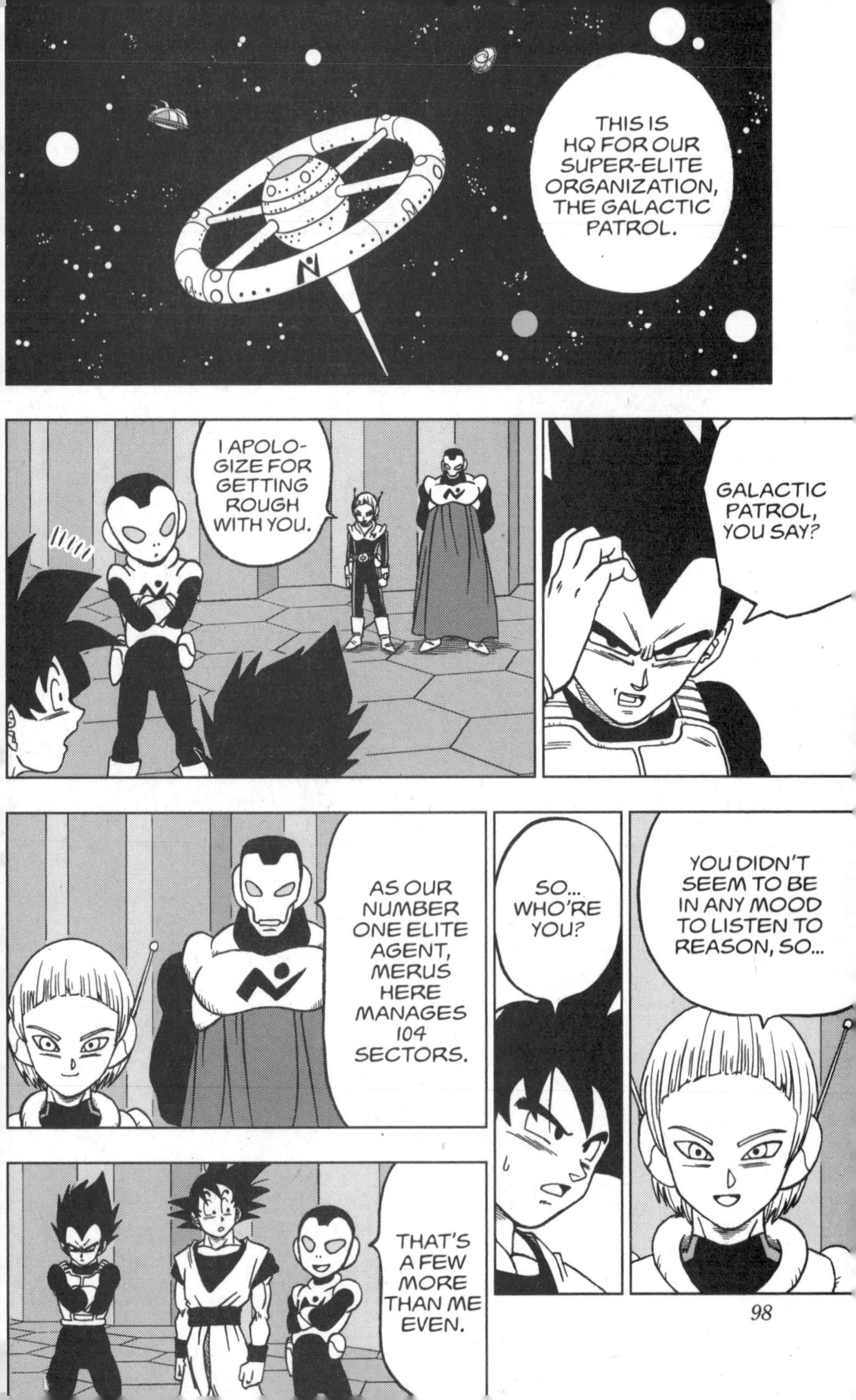
THIS IS HQ FOR OUR SUPER-ELITE ORGANIZATION, THE GALACTIC PATROL.
GALACTIC PATROL, YOU SAY?
I APOLOGIZE FOR GETTING ROUGH WITH YOU.
YOU DIDN'T SEEM TO BE IN ANY MOOD TO LISTEN TO REASON, SO...
SO... WHO'RE YOU?
AS OUR NUMBER ONE ELITE AGENT, MERUS HERE MANAGES 104 SECTORS.
THAT'S A FEW MORE THAN ME EVEN.

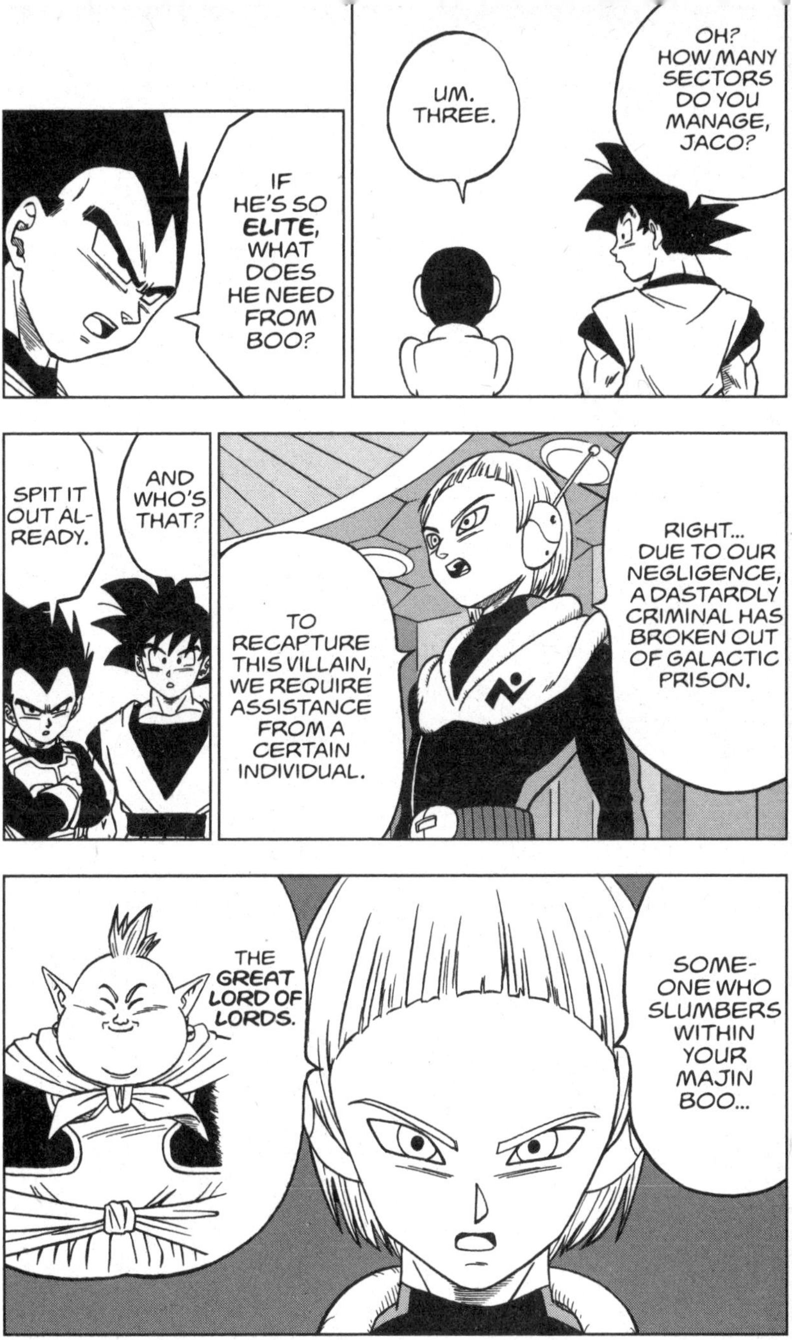
OH? HOW MANY SECTORS DO YOU MANAGE, JACO?
UM. THREE.
IF HE'S SO **ELITE**, WHAT DOES HE NEED FROM BOO?
RIGHT... DUE TO OUR NEGLIGENCE, A DASTARDLY CRIMINAL HAS BROKEN OUT OF GALACTIC PRISON.
TO RECAPTURE THIS VILLAIN, WE REQUIRE ASSISTANCE FROM A CERTAIN INDIVIDUAL.
AND WHO'S THAT?
SPIT IT OUT AL-READY.
SOME-ONE WHO SLUMBERS WITHIN YOUR MAJIN BOO...
THE **GREAT LORD OF LORDS.**

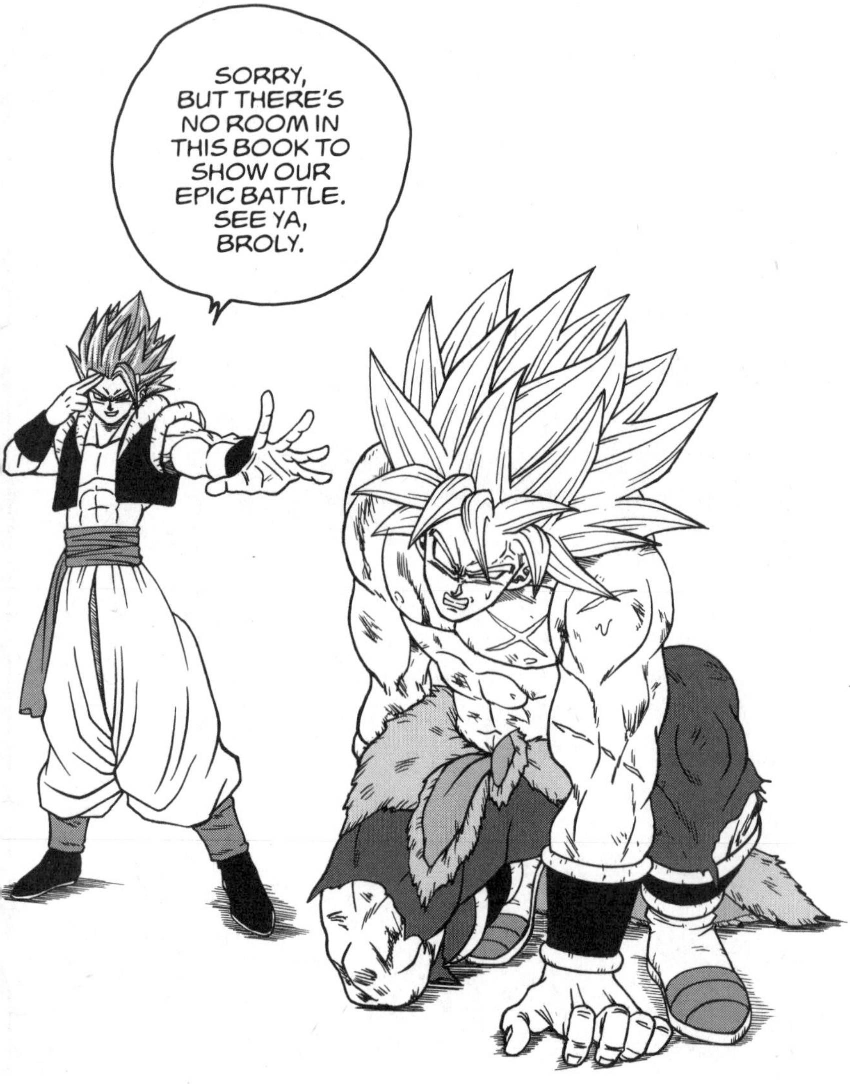
SORRY, BUT THERE'S NO ROOM IN THIS BOOK TO SHOW OUR EPIC BATTLE. SEE YA, BROLY.

DRAGON BALL SUPER

CHAPTER 43: JOINING THE GALACTIC PATROL!

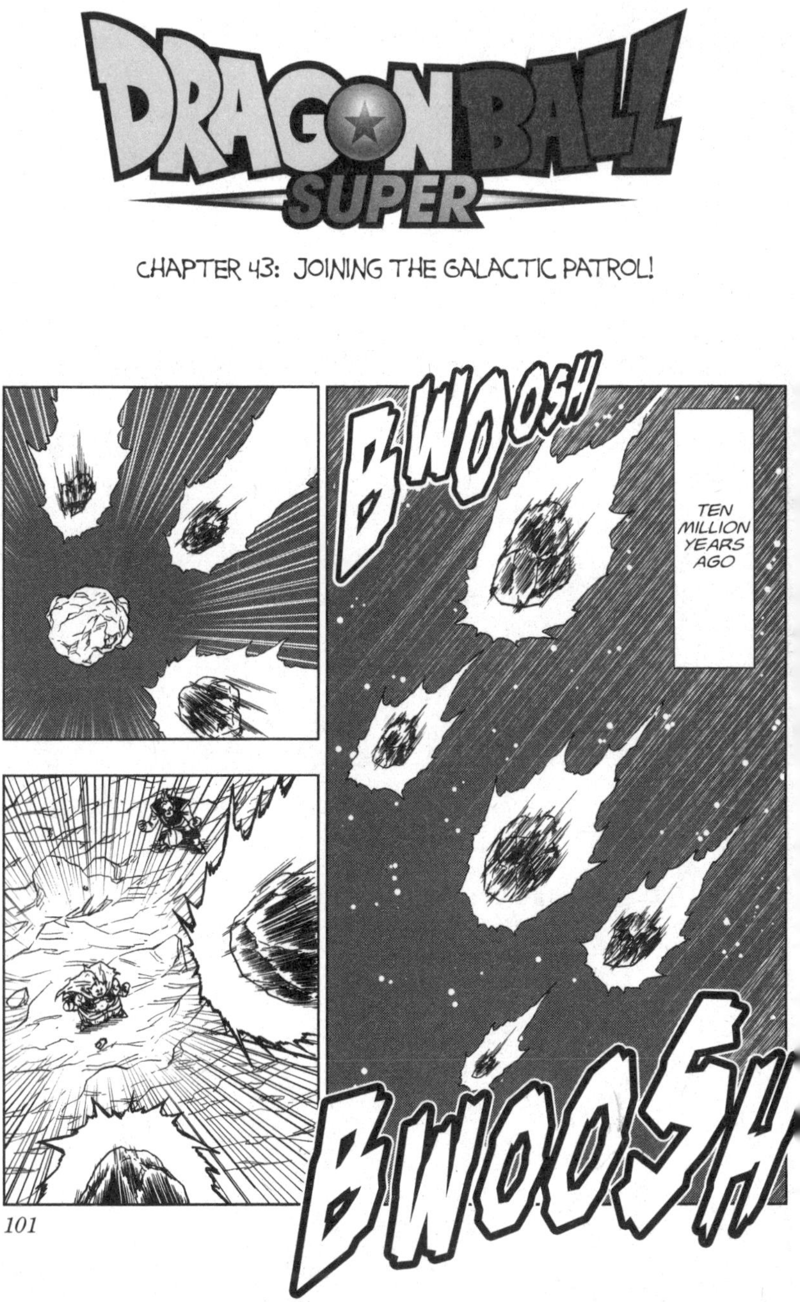
BWOOSH
TEN MILLION YEARS AGO
BWOOSH

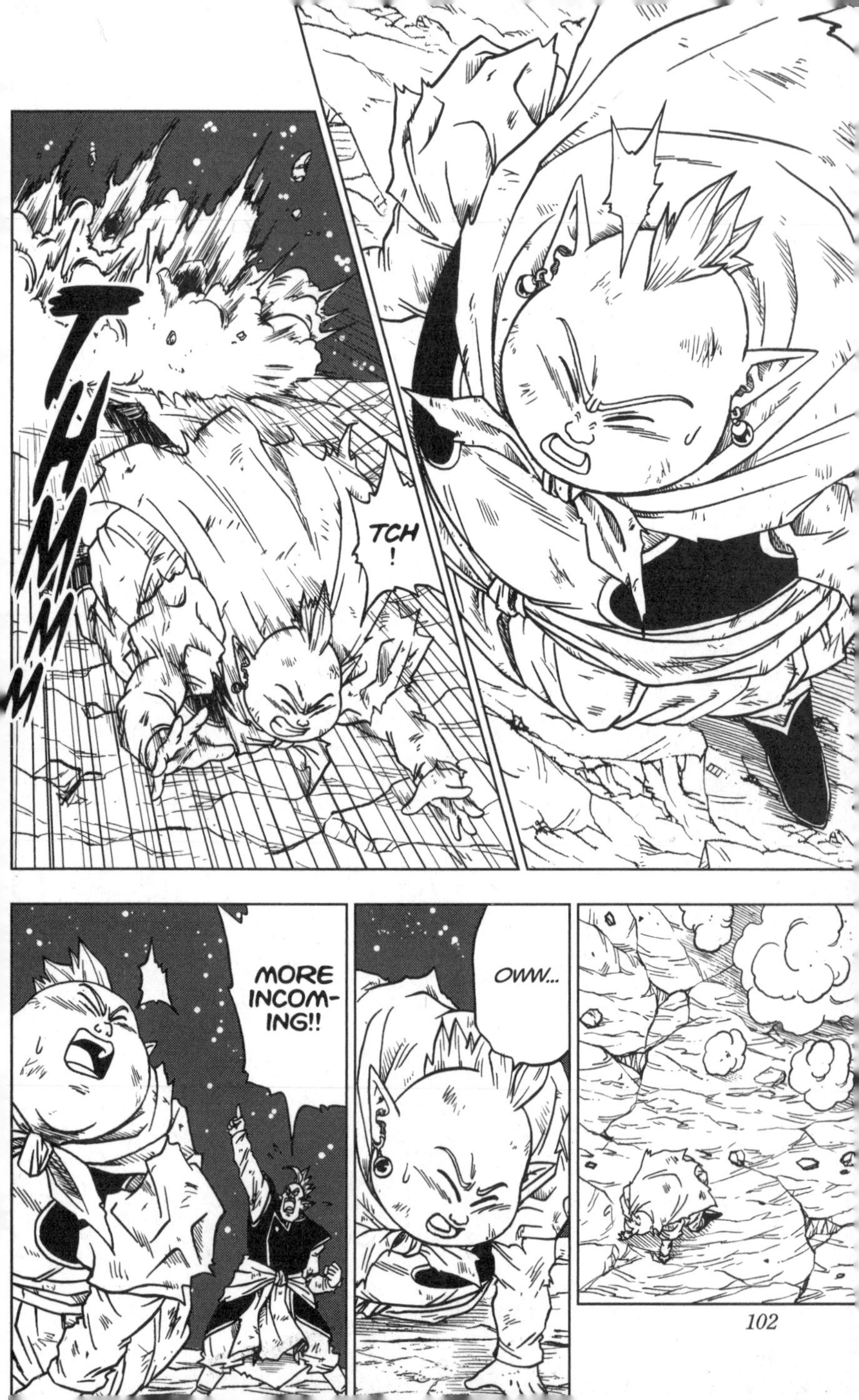
TCH!
THMMMM
OWW...
MORE INCOM-ING!!

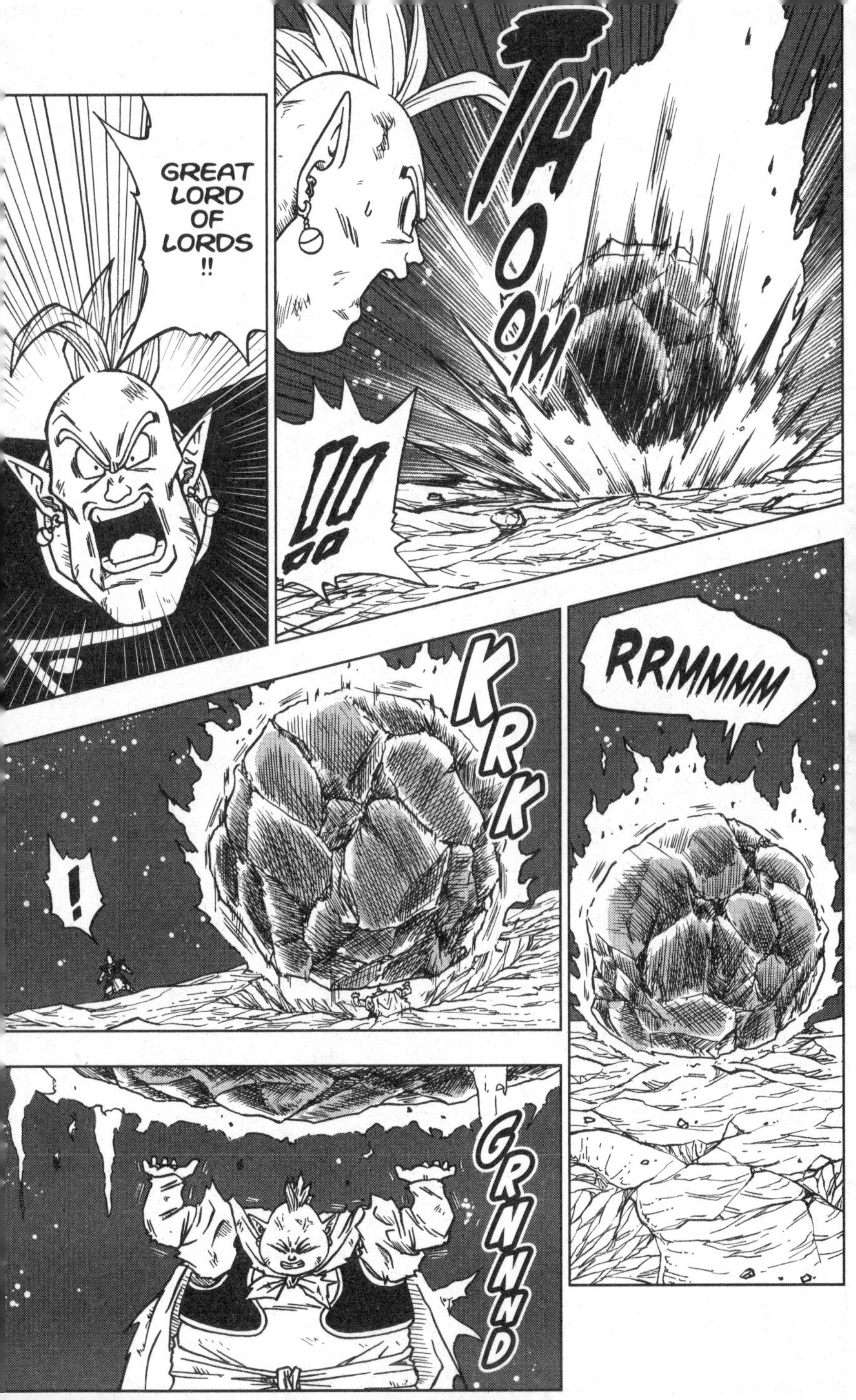
THOOM
!!
GREAT LORD OF LORDS !!
RRMMMM
KRK
!
GRNNND

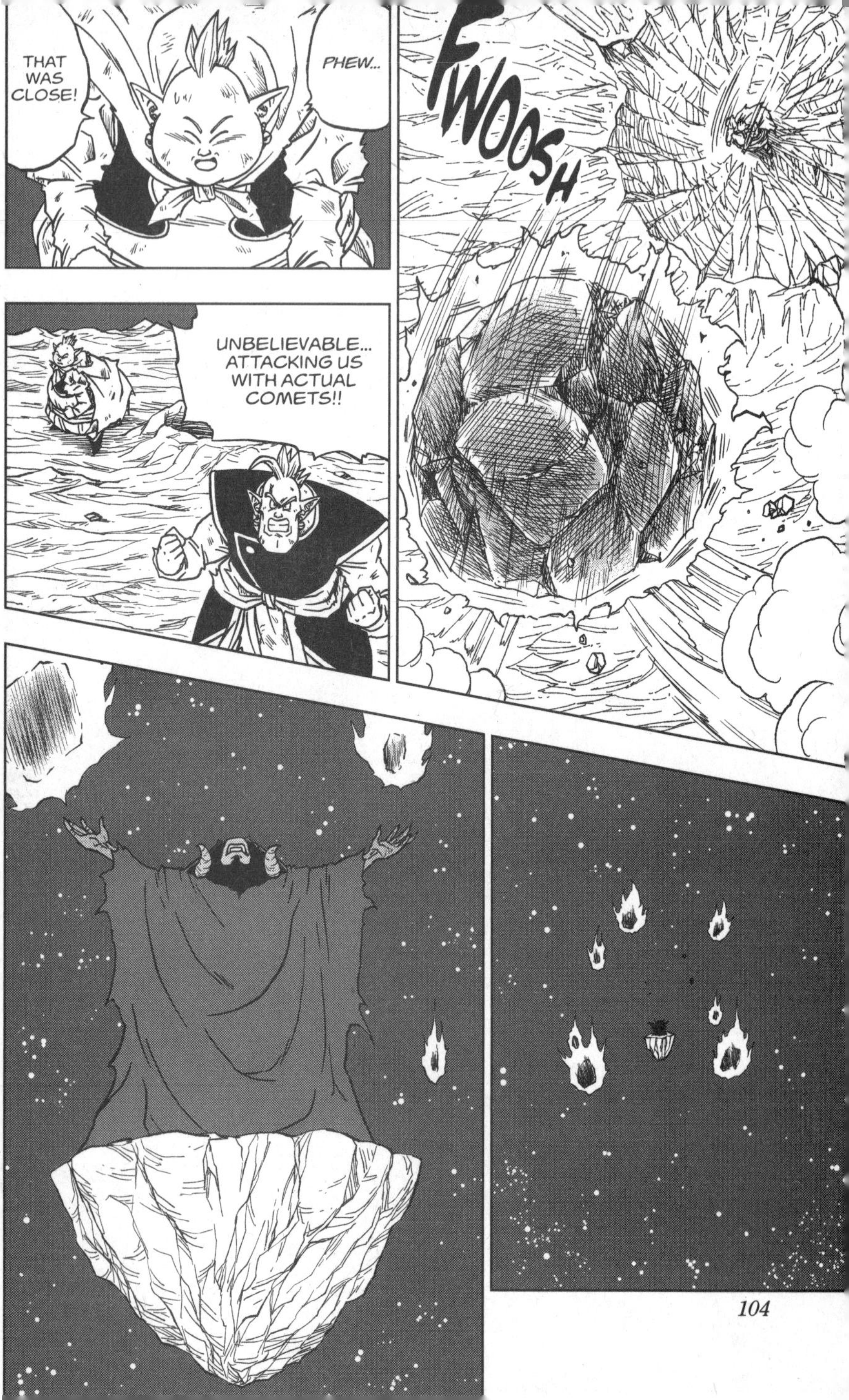
FWOOSH
PHEW...
THAT WAS CLOSE!
UNBELIEVABLE... ATTACKING US WITH ACTUAL COMETS!!

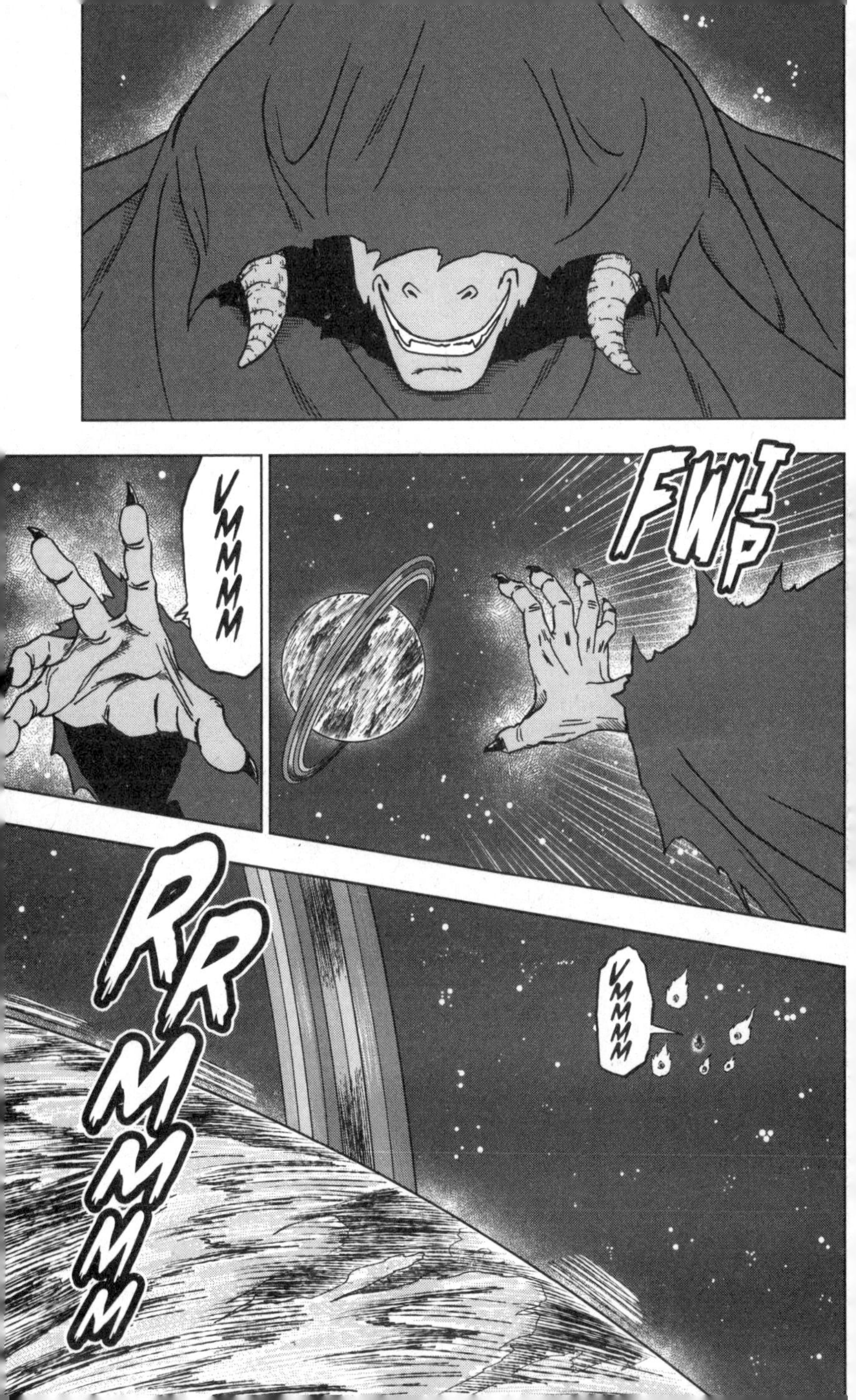
FWIP
VMMMM
VMMMM
RRMMMM

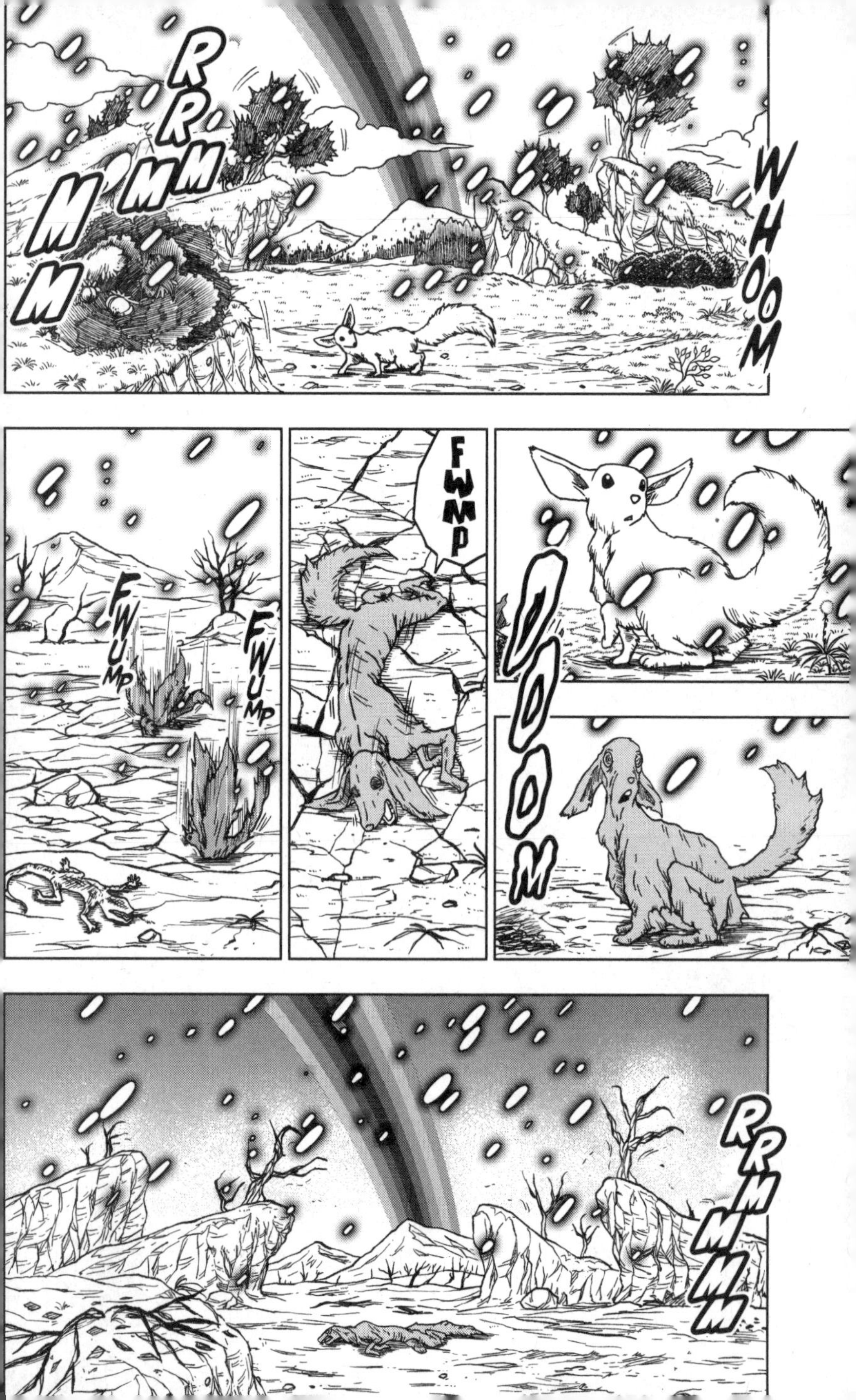
WHOOM
RRMMMMM
OOOM
FWMP
FWUMP
FWUMP
RRMMMMMM

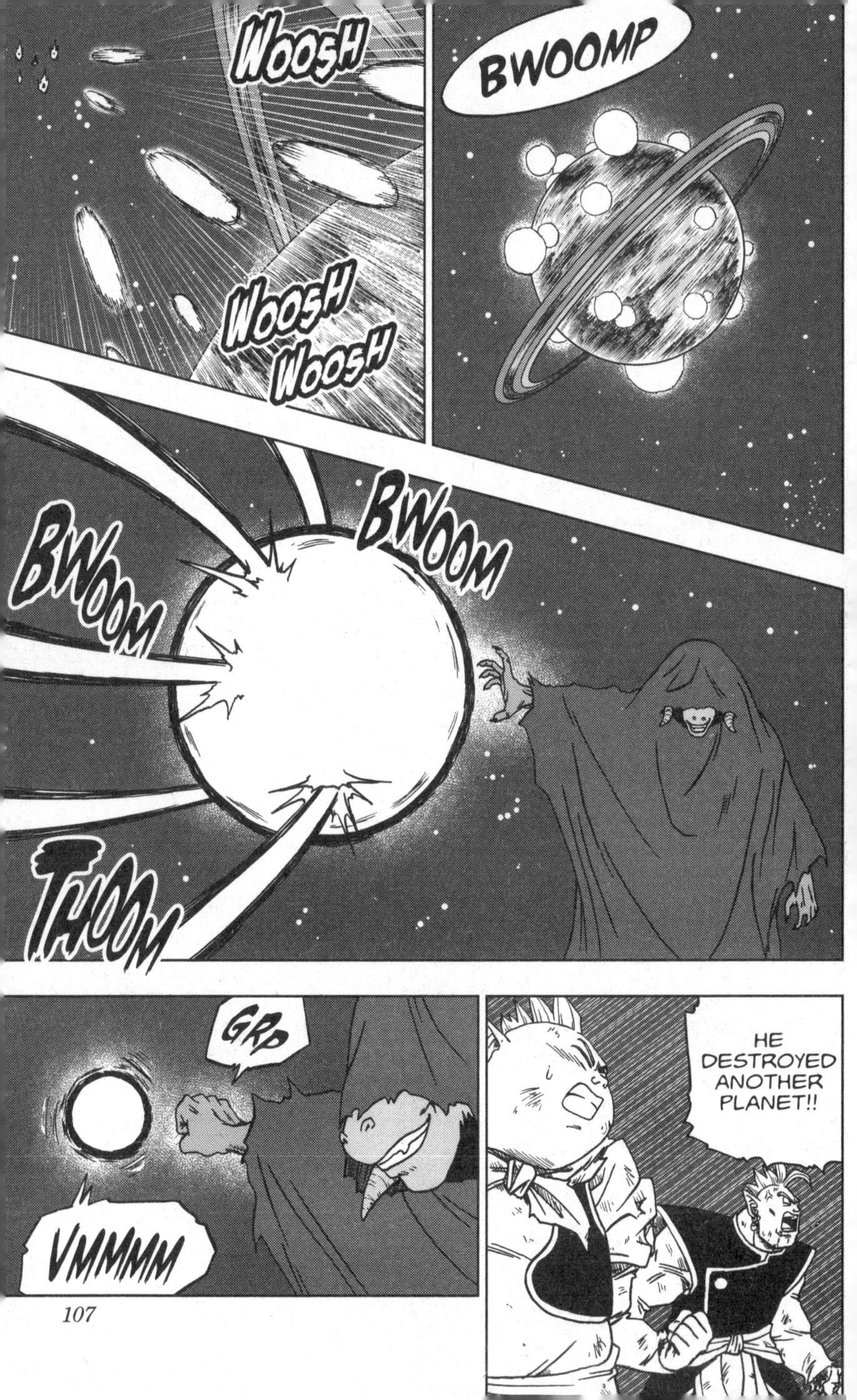
BWOOMP
WOOSH
WOOSH WOOSH
BWOOM
BWOOM
THOOM
HE DESTROYED ANOTHER PLANET!!
GRP
VMMMM

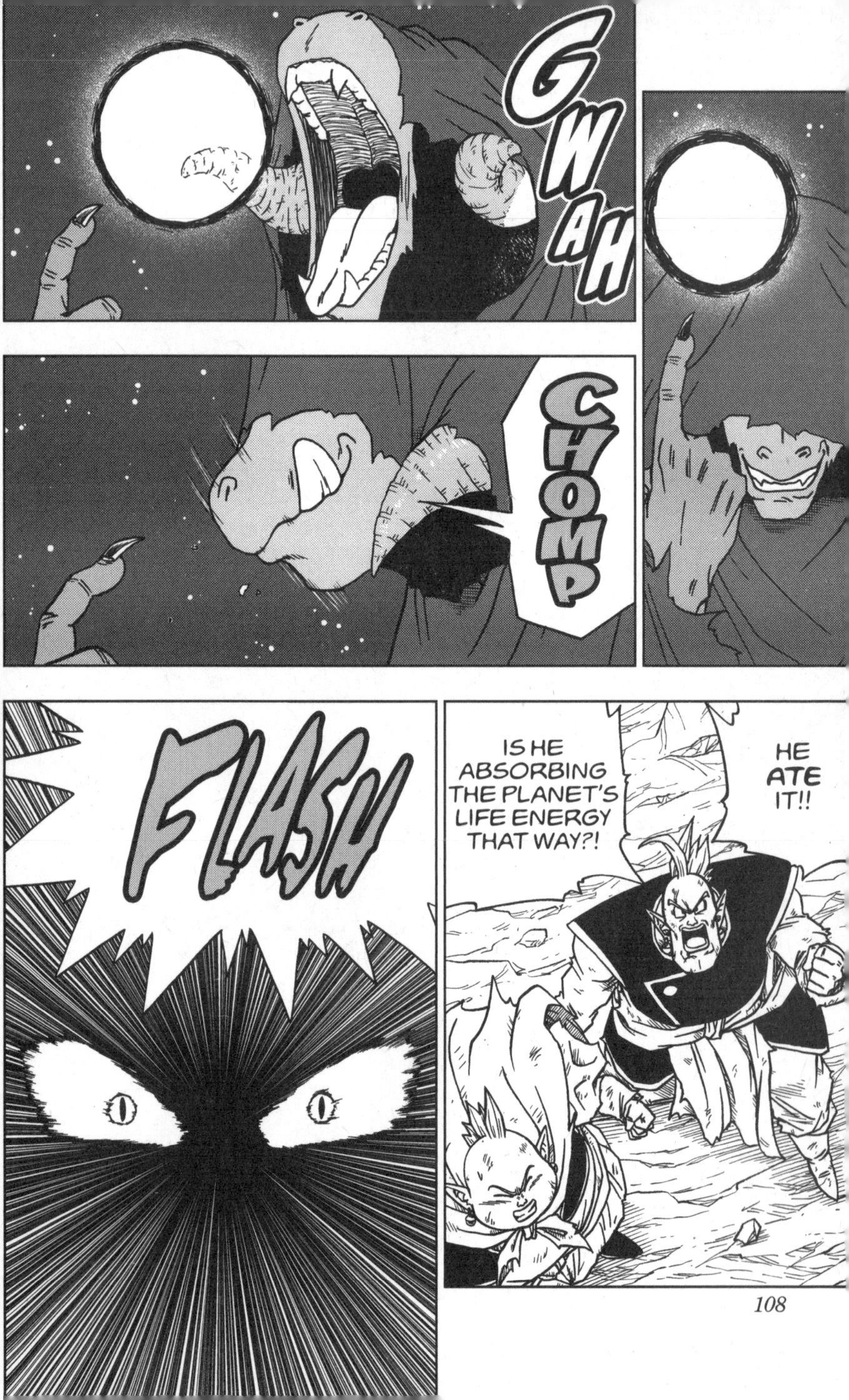
GWAH
CHOMP
HE ATE IT!!
IS HE ABSORBING THE PLANET'S LIFE ENERGY THAT WAY?!
FLASH

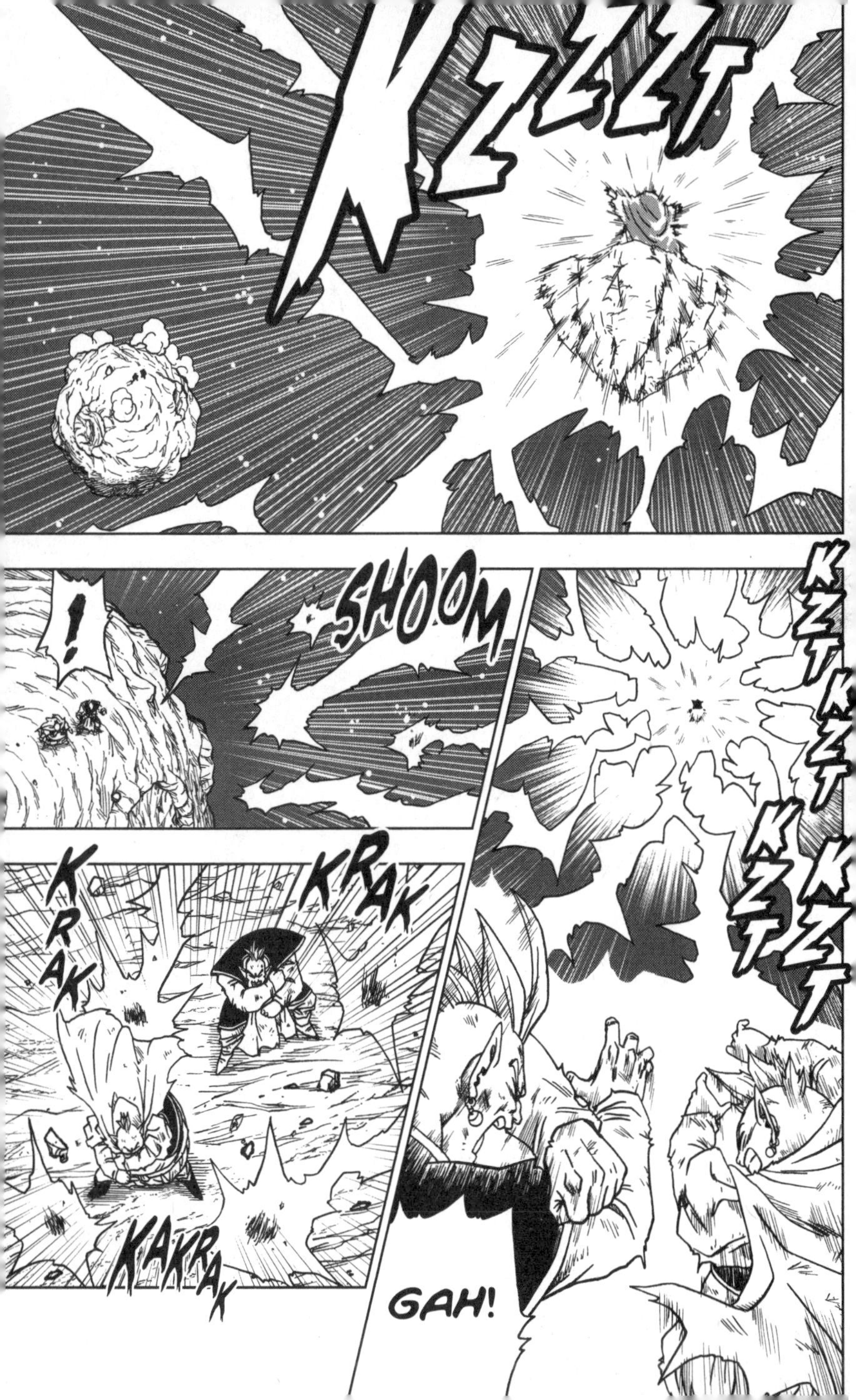
KZZZT
KZT
KZT
KZT
KZT
GAH!
SHOOM
!
KRAK
KRAK
KAKRAK

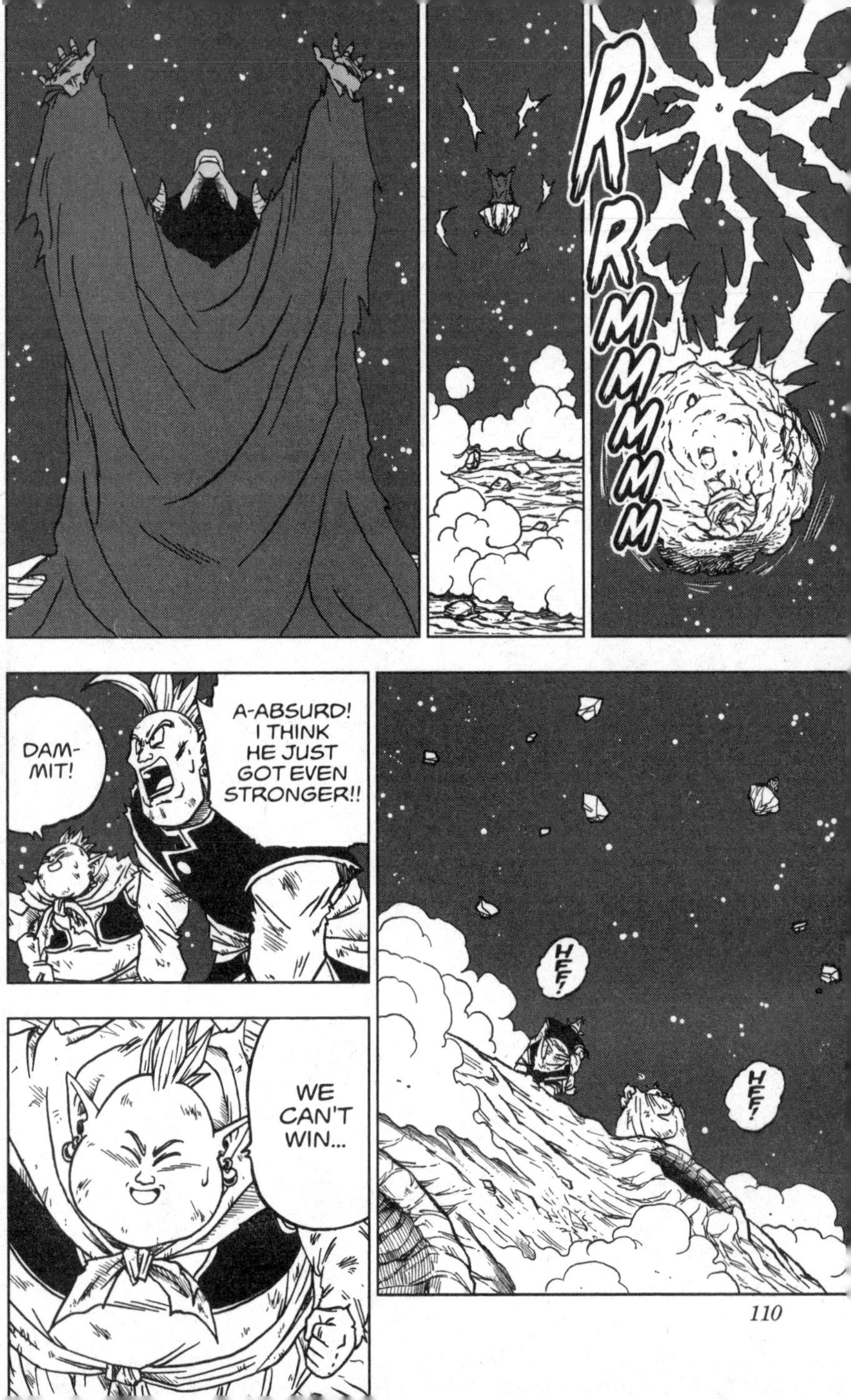
RRMMMMMM
HEF!
HEF!
A-ABSURD! I THINK HE JUST GOT EVEN STRONGER!!
DAM-MIT!
WE CAN'T WIN...

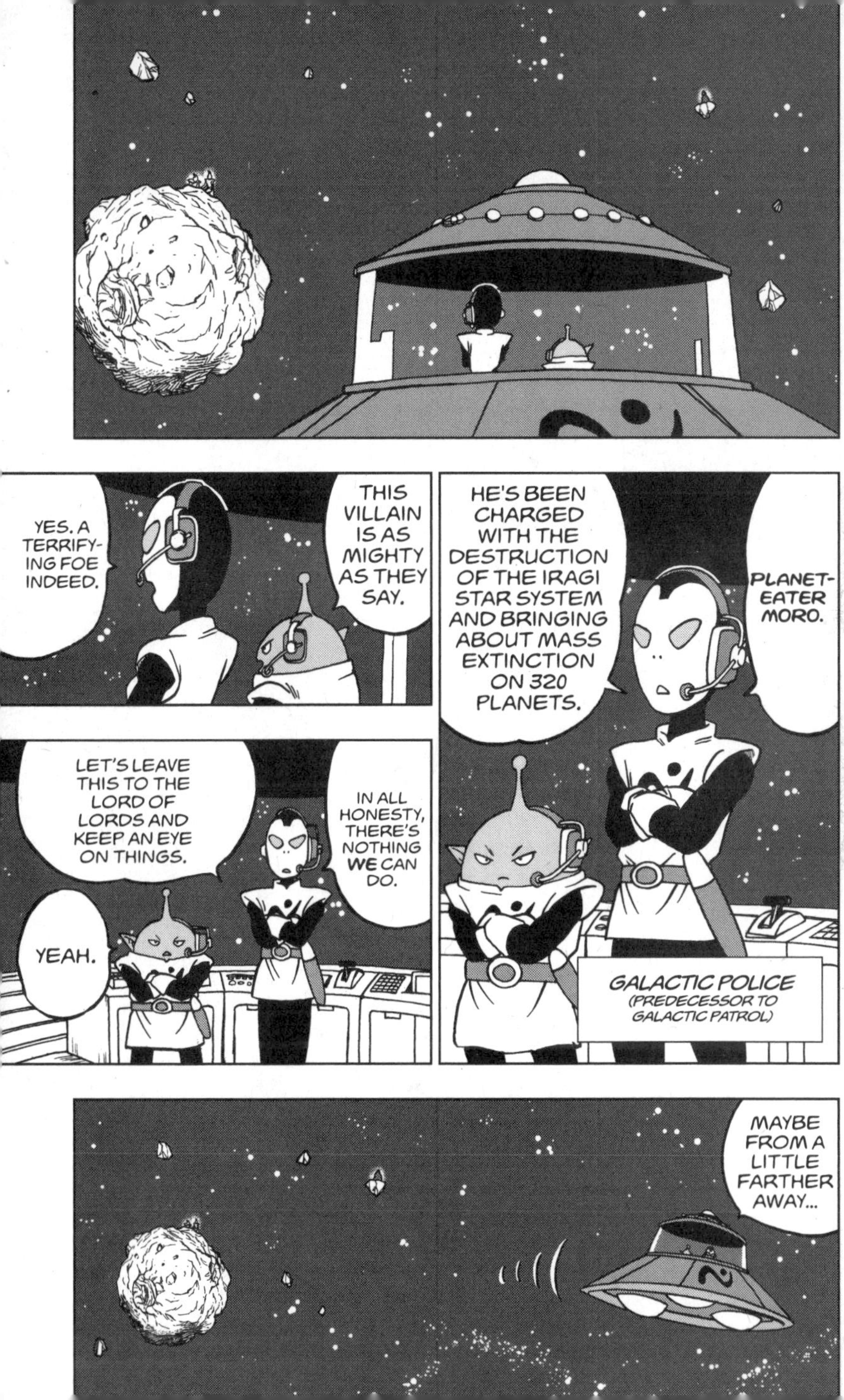
PLANET-EATER MORO.
HE'S BEEN CHARGED WITH THE DESTRUCTION OF THE IRAGI STAR SYSTEM AND BRINGING ABOUT MASS EXTINCTION ON 320 PLANETS.
GALACTIC POLICE (PREDECESSOR TO GALACTIC PATROL)
THIS VILLAIN IS AS MIGHTY AS THEY SAY.
YES. A TERRIFYING FOE INDEED.
IN ALL HONESTY, THERE'S NOTHING **WE** CAN DO.
LET'S LEAVE THIS TO THE LORD OF LORDS AND KEEP AN EYE ON THINGS.
YEAH.
MAYBE FROM A LITTLE FARTHER AWAY...

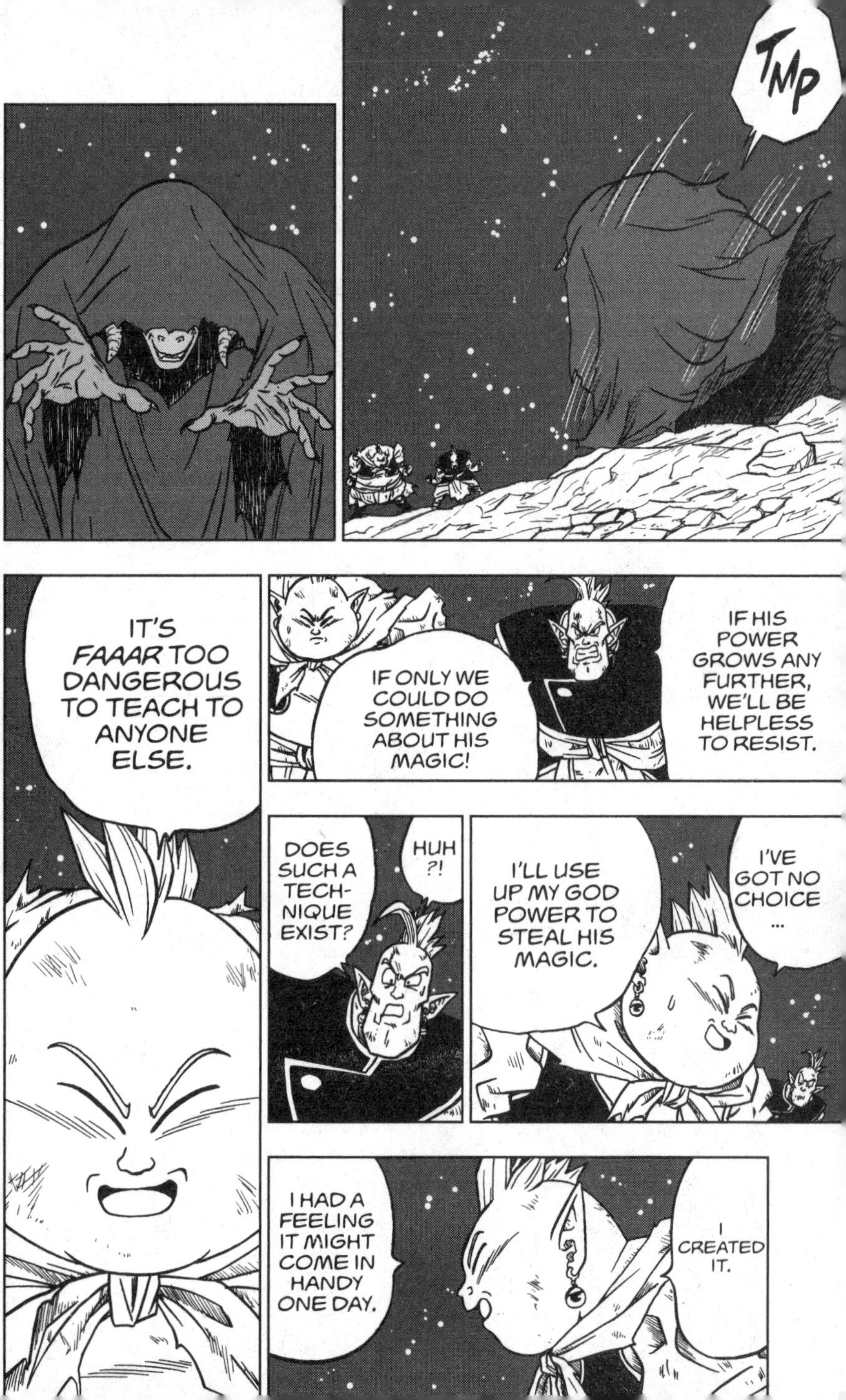
TMP
IF HIS POWER GROWS ANY FURTHER, WE'LL BE HELPLESS TO RESIST.
IF ONLY WE COULD DO SOMETHING ABOUT HIS MAGIC!
I'VE GOT NO CHOICE...
I'LL USE UP MY GOD POWER TO STEAL HIS MAGIC.
HUH ?!
DOES SUCH A TECH-NIQUE EXIST?
I CREATED IT.
I HAD A FEELING IT MIGHT COME IN HANDY ONE DAY.
IT'S *FAAAR* TOO DANGEROUS TO TEACH TO ANYONE ELSE.

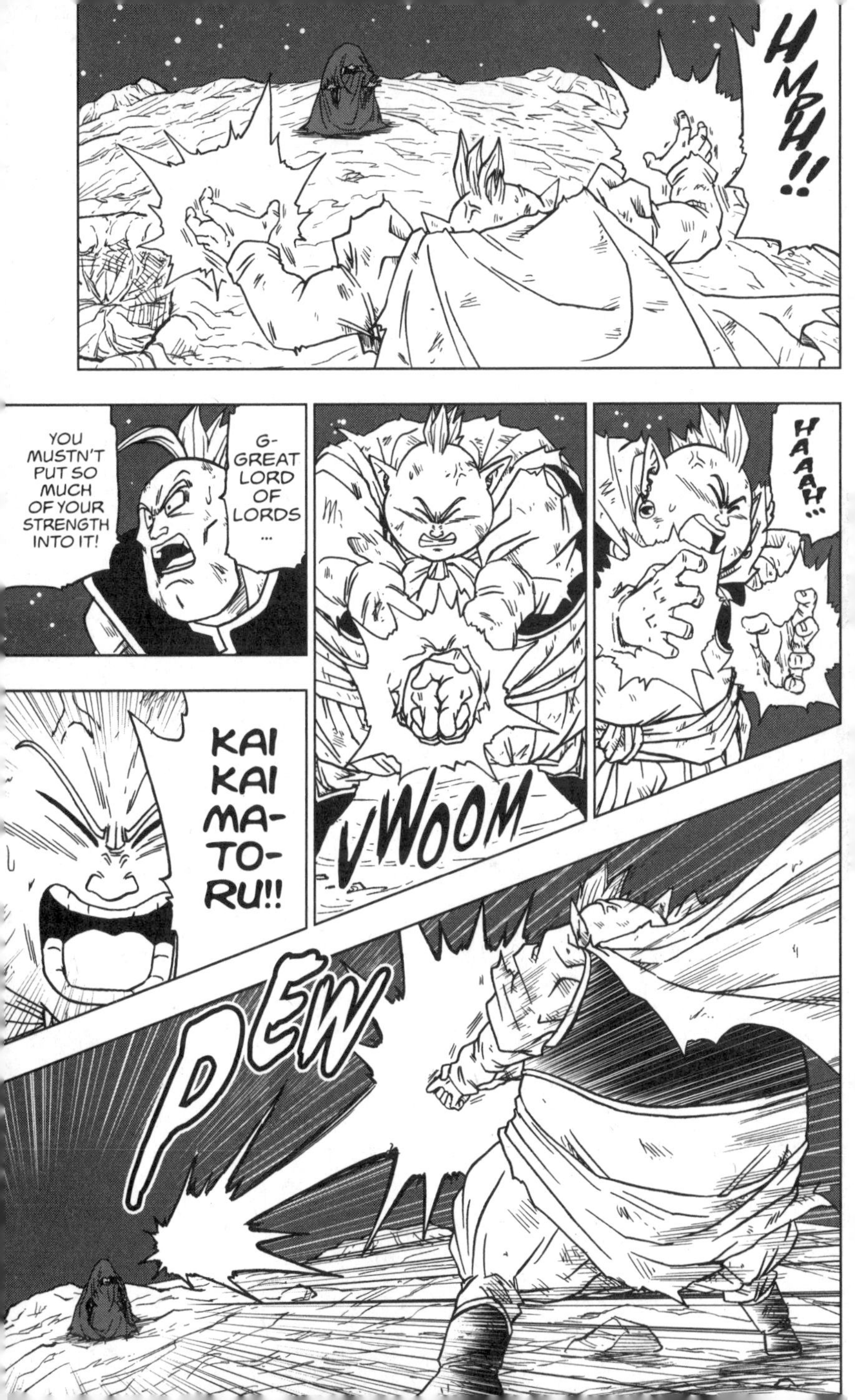
HMPH!!
HAAAH...
VWOOM
G-GREAT LORD OF LORDS...
YOU MUSTN'T PUT SO MUCH OF YOUR STRENGTH INTO IT!
KAI KAI MA-TO-RU!!
PEW

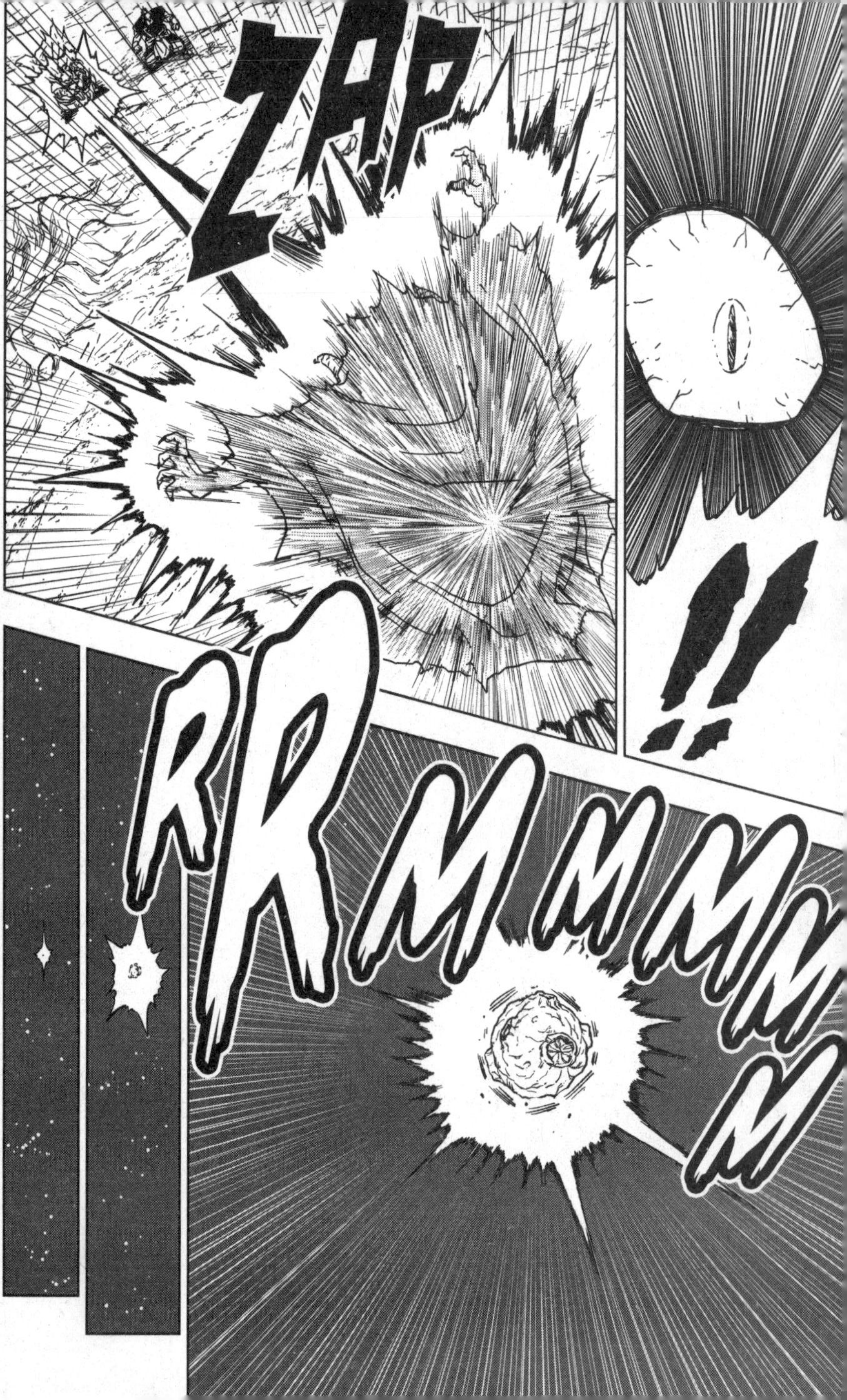

ZAP
!!
RRMMMMMM

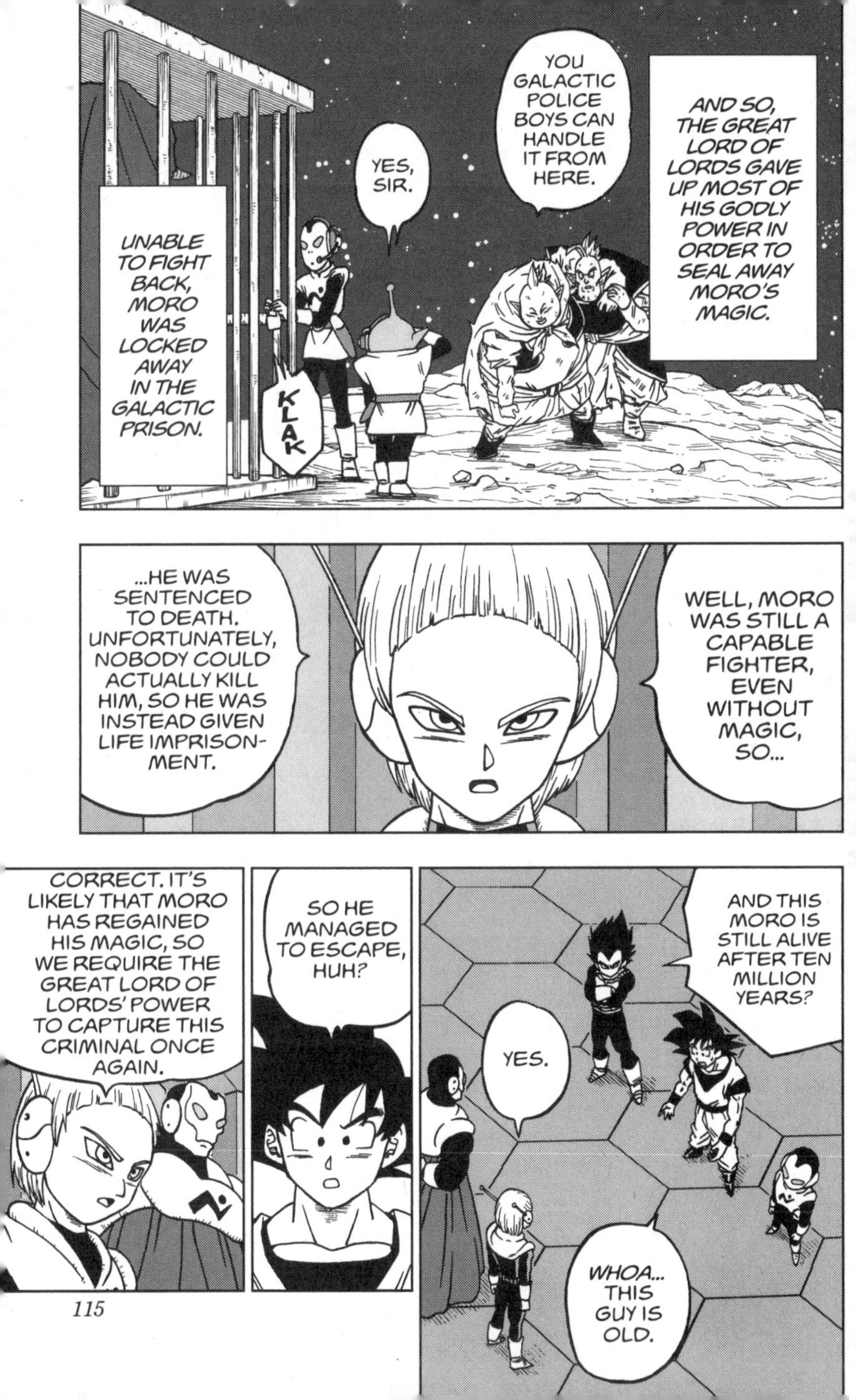
AND SO, THE GREAT LORD OF LORDS GAVE UP MOST OF HIS GODLY POWER IN ORDER TO SEAL AWAY MORO'S MAGIC.
YOU GALACTIC POLICE BOYS CAN HANDLE IT FROM HERE.
YES, SIR.
UNABLE TO FIGHT BACK, MORO WAS LOCKED AWAY IN THE GALACTIC PRISON.
KLAK
WELL, MORO WAS STILL A CAPABLE FIGHTER, EVEN WITHOUT MAGIC, SO...
...HE WAS SENTENCED TO DEATH. UNFORTUNATELY, NOBODY COULD ACTUALLY KILL HIM, SO HE WAS INSTEAD GIVEN LIFE IMPRISON-MENT.
AND THIS MORO IS STILL ALIVE AFTER TEN MILLION YEARS?
YES.
WHOA... THIS GUY IS OLD.
SO HE MANAGED TO ESCAPE, HUH?
CORRECT. IT'S LIKELY THAT MORO HAS REGAINED HIS MAGIC, SO WE REQUIRE THE GREAT LORD OF LORDS' POWER TO CAPTURE THIS CRIMINAL ONCE AGAIN.

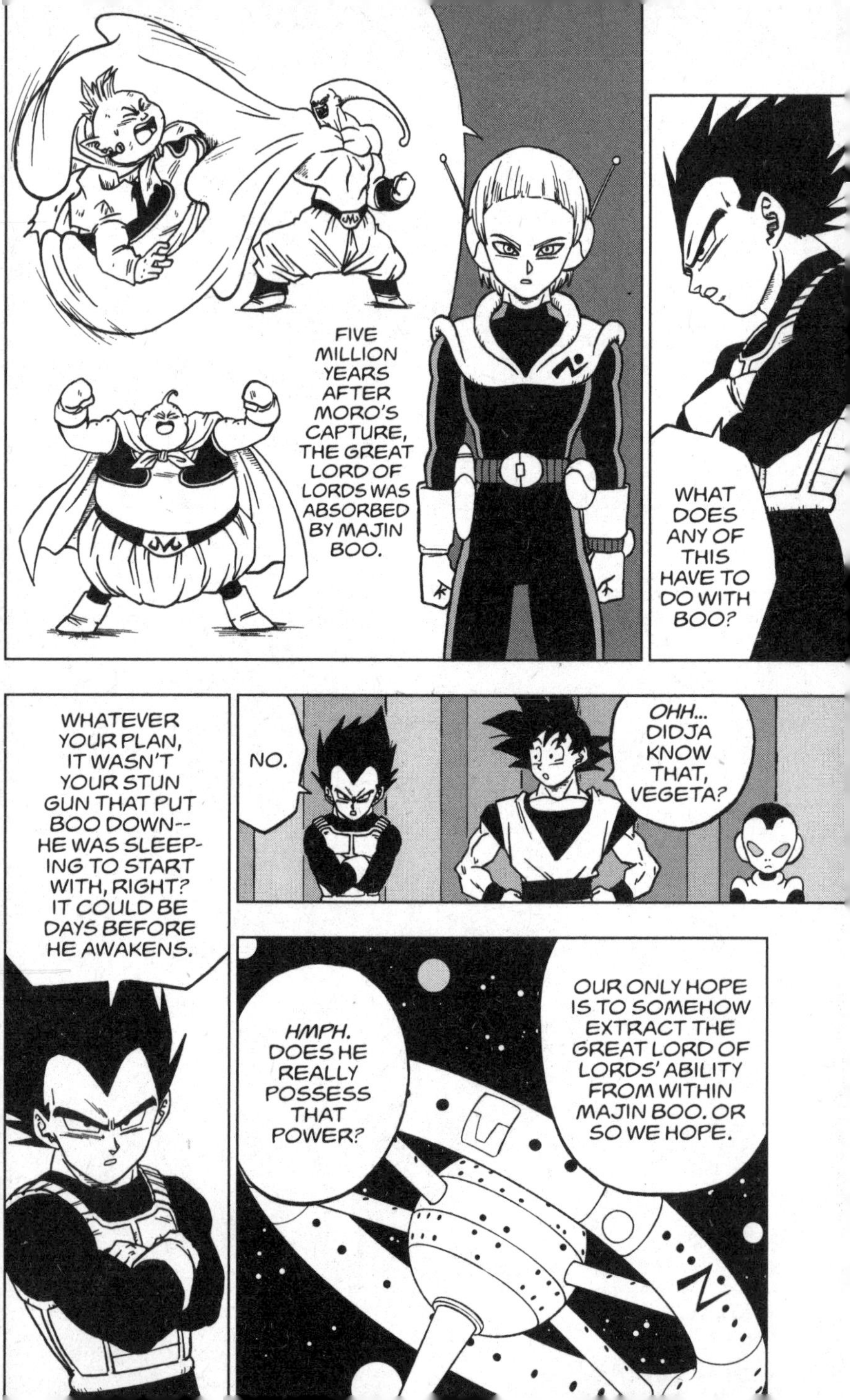
WHAT DOES ANY OF THIS HAVE TO DO WITH BOO?
FIVE MILLION YEARS AFTER MORO'S CAPTURE, THE GREAT LORD OF LORDS WAS ABSORBED BY MAJIN BOO.
OHH... DIDJA KNOW THAT, VEGETA?
NO.
OUR ONLY HOPE IS TO SOMEHOW EXTRACT THE GREAT LORD OF LORDS' ABILITY FROM WITHIN MAJIN BOO. OR SO WE HOPE.
HMPH. DOES HE REALLY POSSESS THAT POWER?
WHATEVER YOUR PLAN, IT WASN'T YOUR STUN GUN THAT PUT BOO DOWN--HE WAS SLEEPING TO START WITH, RIGHT? IT COULD BE DAYS BEFORE HE AWAKENS.

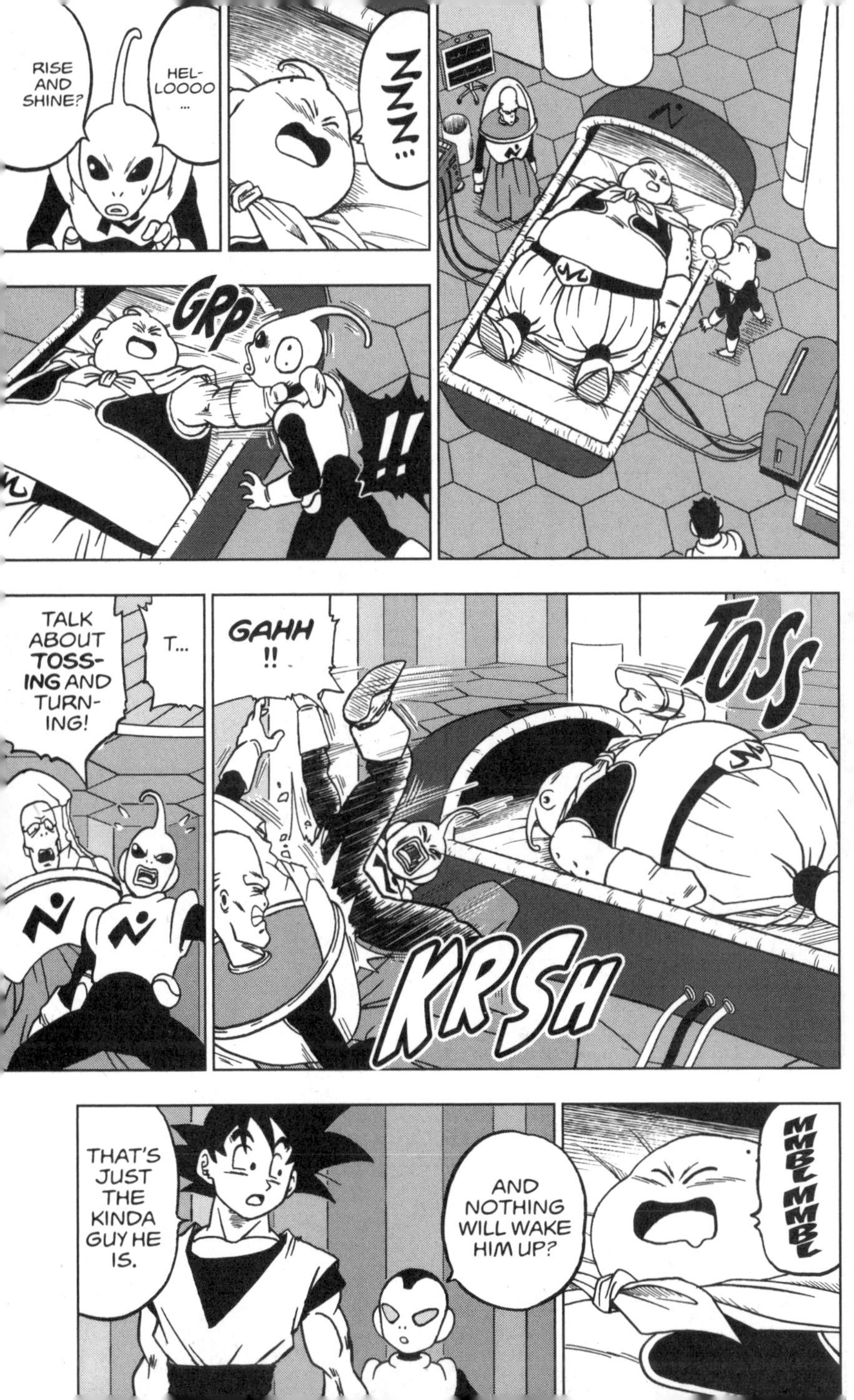
ZZZ...
HEL-LOOOO...
RISE AND SHINE?
GRP
!!
TOSS
GAHH!!
KRSH
T...
TALK ABOUT **TOSSING** AND TURNING!
MMBLMMBL
AND NOTHING WILL WAKE HIM UP?
THAT'S JUST THE KINDA GUY HE IS.

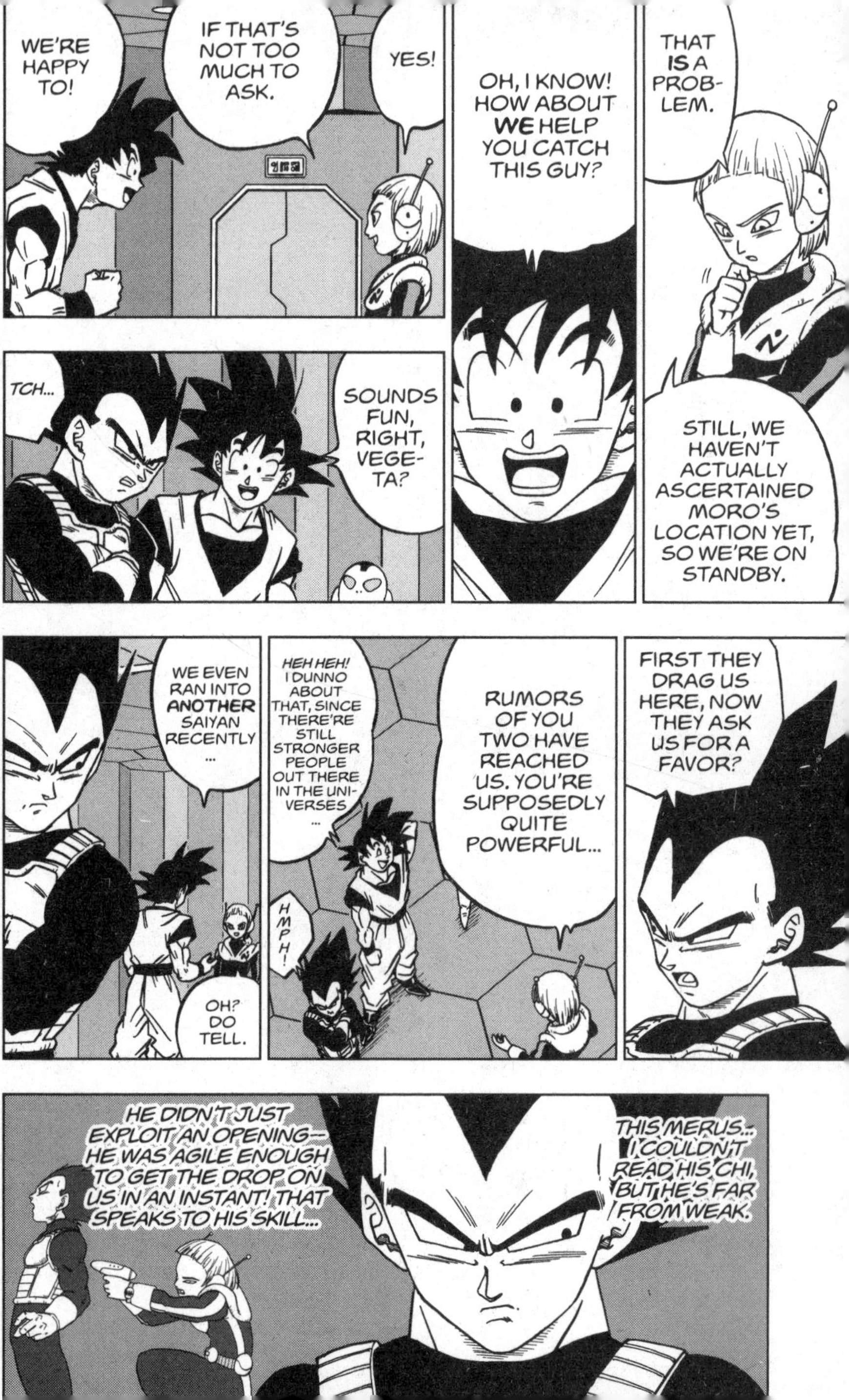
THAT **IS** A PROB-LEM.
STILL, WE HAVEN'T ACTUALLY ASCERTAINED MORO'S LOCATION YET, SO WE'RE ON STANDBY.
OH, I KNOW! HOW ABOUT **WE** HELP YOU CATCH THIS GUY?
YES!
IF THAT'S NOT TOO MUCH TO ASK.
WE'RE HAPPY TO!
SOUNDS FUN, RIGHT, VEGE-TA?
TCH...
FIRST THEY DRAG US HERE, NOW THEY ASK US FOR A FAVOR?
RUMORS OF YOU TWO HAVE REACHED US. YOU'RE SUPPOSEDLY QUITE POWERFUL...
HEH HEH! I DUNNO ABOUT THAT, SINCE THERE'RE STILL STRONGER PEOPLE OUT THERE IN THE UNI-VERSES...
HMPH!
WE EVEN RAN INTO **ANOTHER** SAIYAN RECENTLY...
OH? DO TELL.
THIS MERUS... I COULDN'T READ HIS CHI, BUT HE'S FAR FROM WEAK.
HE DIDN'T JUST EXPLOIT AN OPENING-- HE WAS AGILE ENOUGH TO GET THE DROP ON US IN AN INSTANT! THAT SPEAKS TO HIS SKILL...

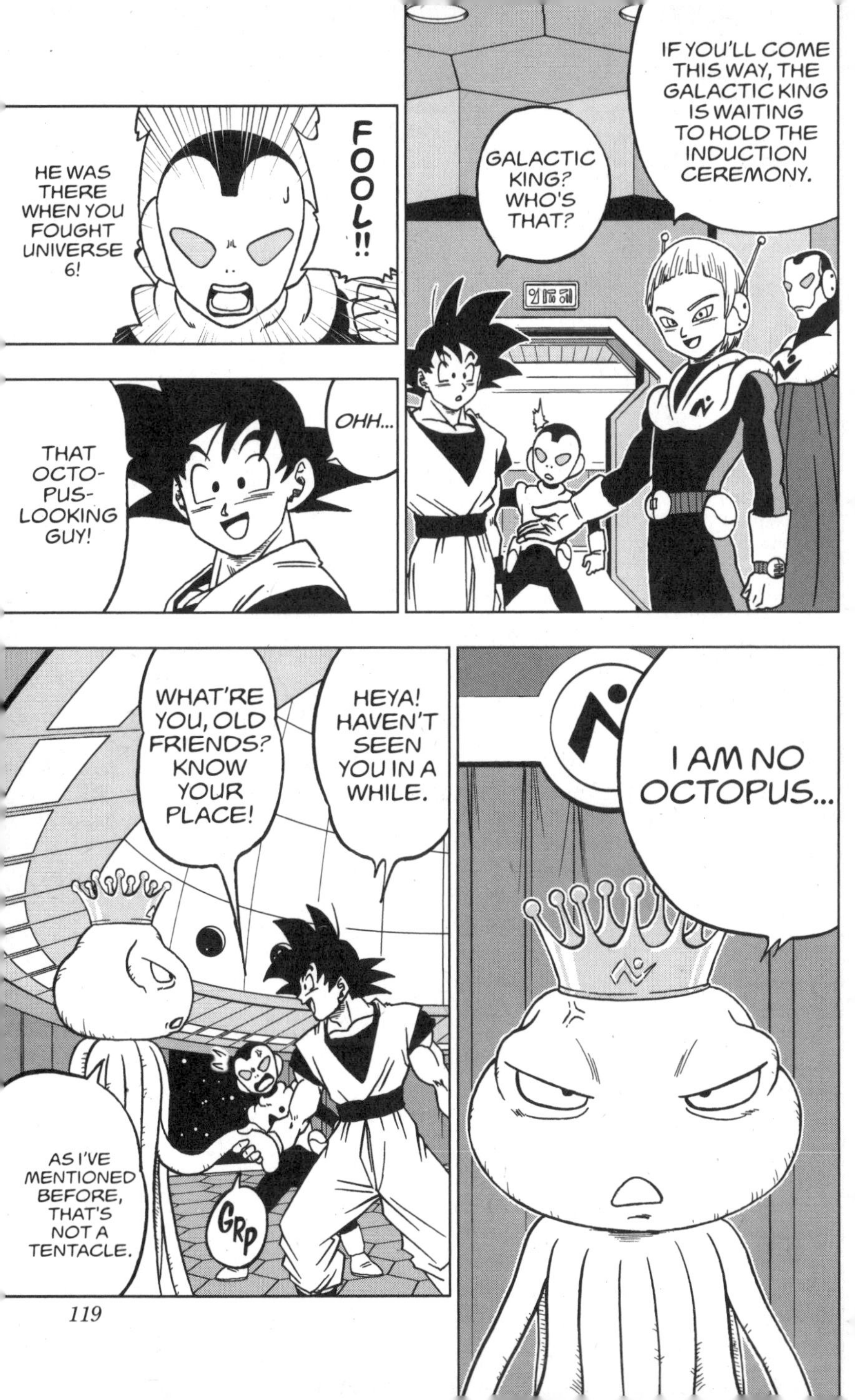

IF YOU'LL COME THIS WAY, THE GALACTIC KING IS WAITING TO HOLD THE INDUCTION CEREMONY.
GALACTIC KING? WHO'S THAT?
FOOL!!
HE WAS THERE WHEN YOU FOUGHT UNIVERSE 6!
OHH...
THAT OCTO-PUS-LOOKING GUY!
I AM NO OCTOPUS...
HEYA! HAVEN'T SEEN YOU IN A WHILE.
WHAT'RE YOU, OLD FRIENDS? KNOW YOUR PLACE!
GRP
AS I'VE MENTIONED BEFORE, THAT'S NOT A TENTACLE.

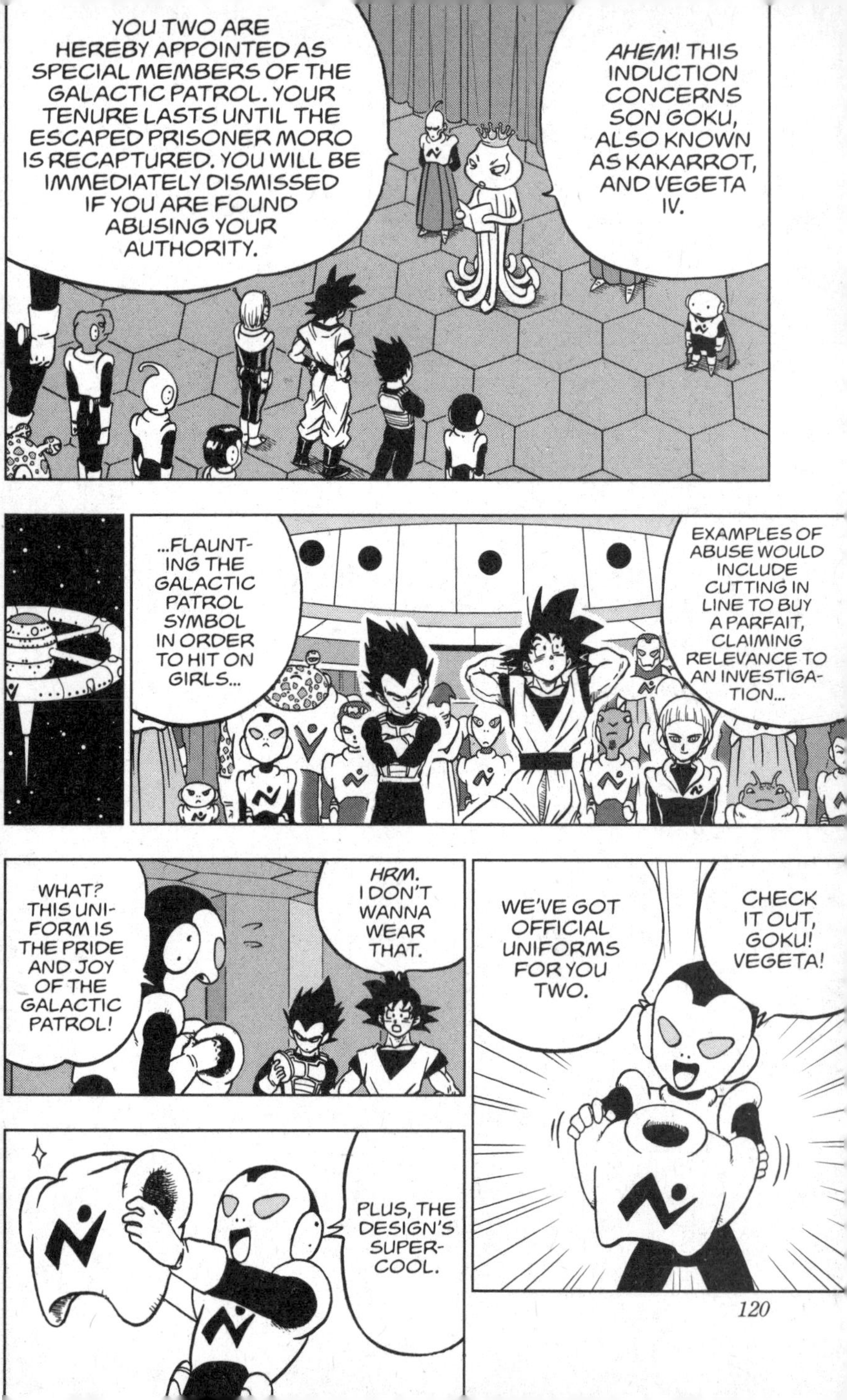
AHEM! THIS INDUCTION CONCERNS SON GOKU, ALSO KNOWN AS KAKARROT, AND VEGETA IV.
YOU TWO ARE HEREBY APPOINTED AS SPECIAL MEMBERS OF THE GALACTIC PATROL. YOUR TENURE LASTS UNTIL THE ESCAPED PRISONER MORO IS RECAPTURED. YOU WILL BE IMMEDIATELY DISMISSED IF YOU ARE FOUND ABUSING YOUR AUTHORITY.
EXAMPLES OF ABUSE WOULD INCLUDE CUTTING IN LINE TO BUY A PARFAIT, CLAIMING RELEVANCE TO AN INVESTIGATION...
...FLAUNTING THE GALACTIC PATROL SYMBOL IN ORDER TO HIT ON GIRLS...
CHECK IT OUT, GOKU! VEGETA!
WE'VE GOT OFFICIAL UNIFORMS FOR YOU TWO.
HRM. I DON'T WANNA WEAR THAT.
WHAT? THIS UNIFORM IS THE PRIDE AND JOY OF THE GALACTIC PATROL!
PLUS, THE DESIGN'S SUPER-COOL.

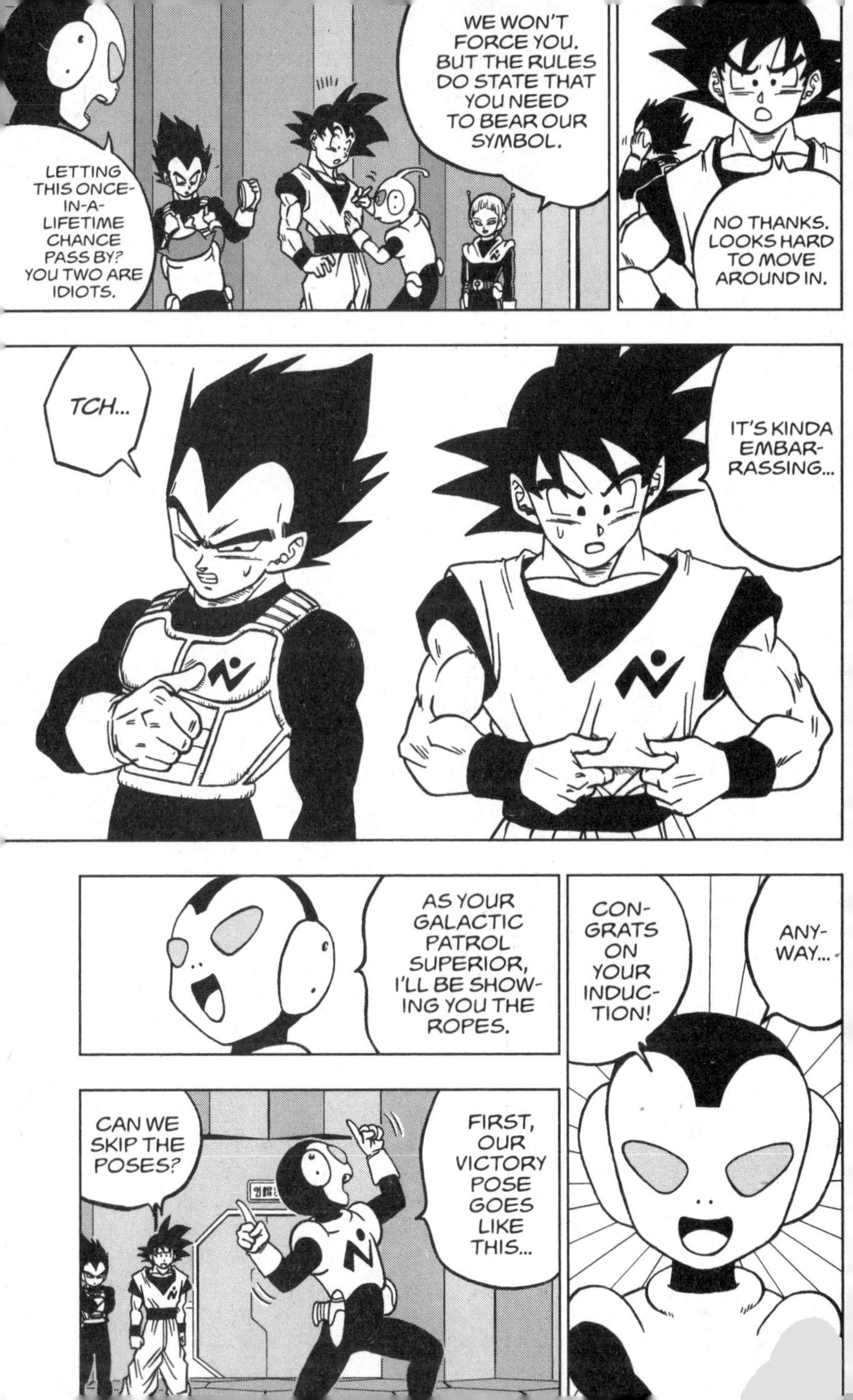
NO THANKS. LOOKS HARD TO MOVE AROUND IN.
WE WON'T FORCE YOU. BUT THE RULES DO STATE THAT YOU NEED TO BEAR OUR SYMBOL.
LETTING THIS ONCE-IN-A-LIFETIME CHANCE PASS BY? YOU TWO ARE IDIOTS.
IT'S KINDA EMBAR-RASSING...
TCH...
ANY-WAY...
CON-GRATS ON YOUR INDUC-TION!
AS YOUR GALACTIC PATROL SUPERIOR, I'LL BE SHOW-ING YOU THE ROPES.
FIRST, OUR VICTORY POSE GOES LIKE THIS...
CAN WE SKIP THE POSES?

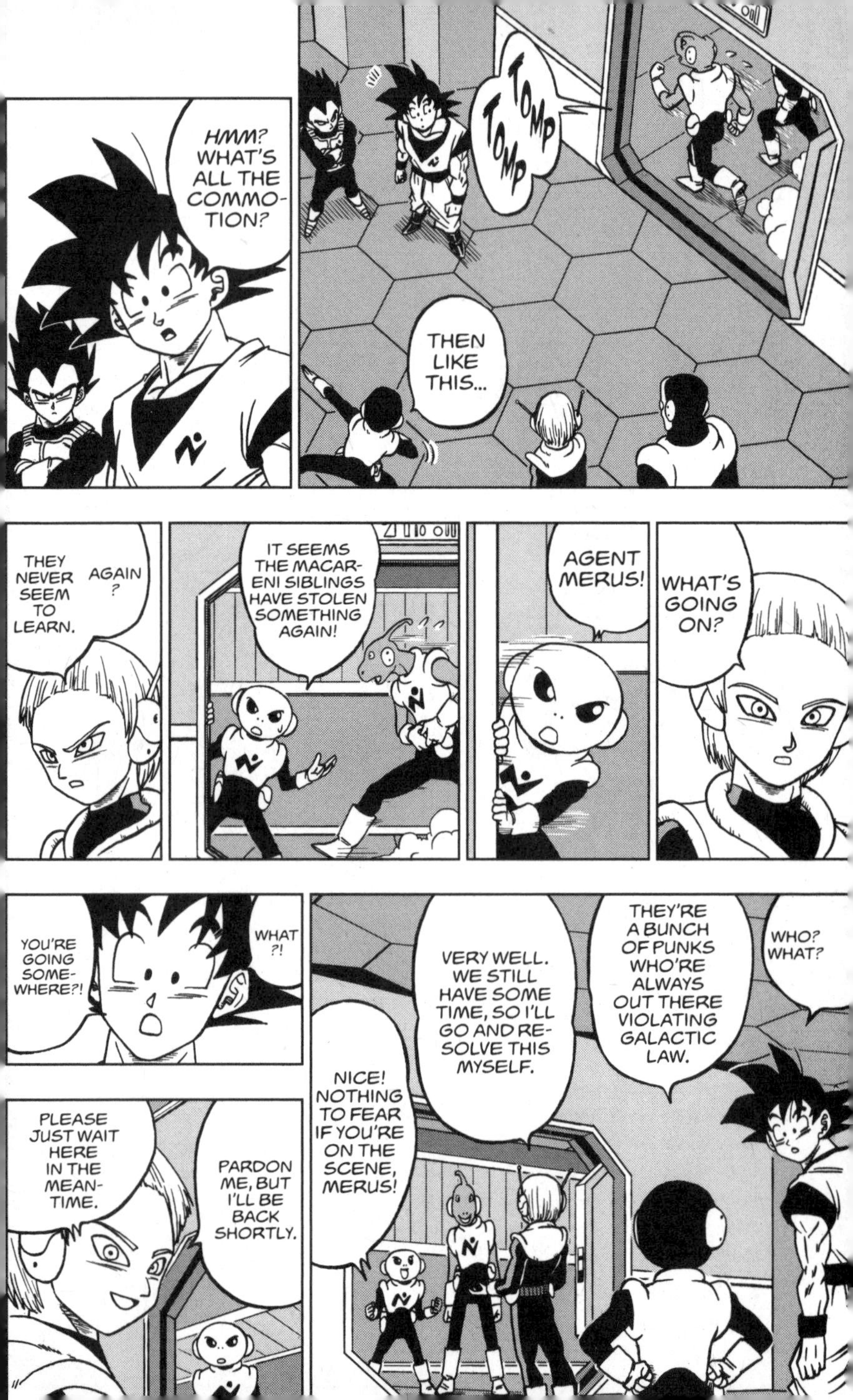
TOMP TOMP
THEN LIKE THIS...
HMM? WHAT'S ALL THE COMMOTION?
WHAT'S GOING ON?
AGENT MERUS!
IT SEEMS THE MACARENI SIBLINGS HAVE STOLEN SOMETHING AGAIN!
AGAIN?
THEY NEVER SEEM TO LEARN.
WHO? WHAT?
THEY'RE A BUNCH OF PUNKS WHO'RE ALWAYS OUT THERE VIOLATING GALACTIC LAW.
VERY WELL. WE STILL HAVE SOME TIME, SO I'LL GO AND RESOLVE THIS MYSELF.
NICE! NOTHING TO FEAR IF YOU'RE ON THE SCENE, MERUS!
WHAT?!
YOU'RE GOING SOMEWHERE?!
PARDON ME, BUT I'LL BE BACK SHORTLY.
PLEASE JUST WAIT HERE IN THE MEANTIME.

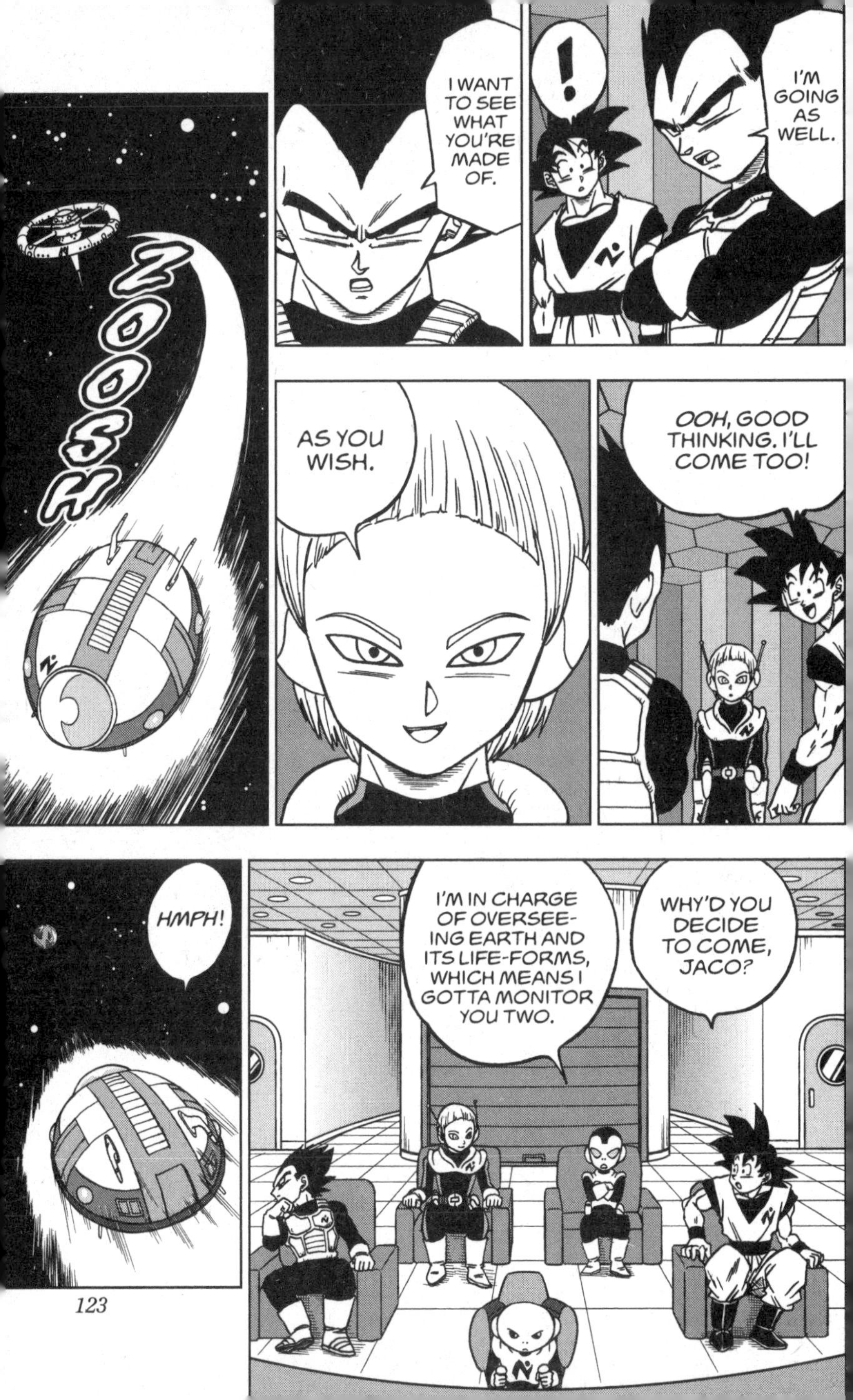
I'M GOING AS WELL.
!
I WANT TO SEE WHAT YOU'RE MADE OF.
OOH, GOOD THINKING. I'LL COME TOO!
AS YOU WISH.
ZOOSH
WHY'D YOU DECIDE TO COME, JACO?
I'M IN CHARGE OF OVERSEE-ING EARTH AND ITS LIFE-FORMS, WHICH MEANS I GOTTA MONITOR YOU TWO.
HMPH!

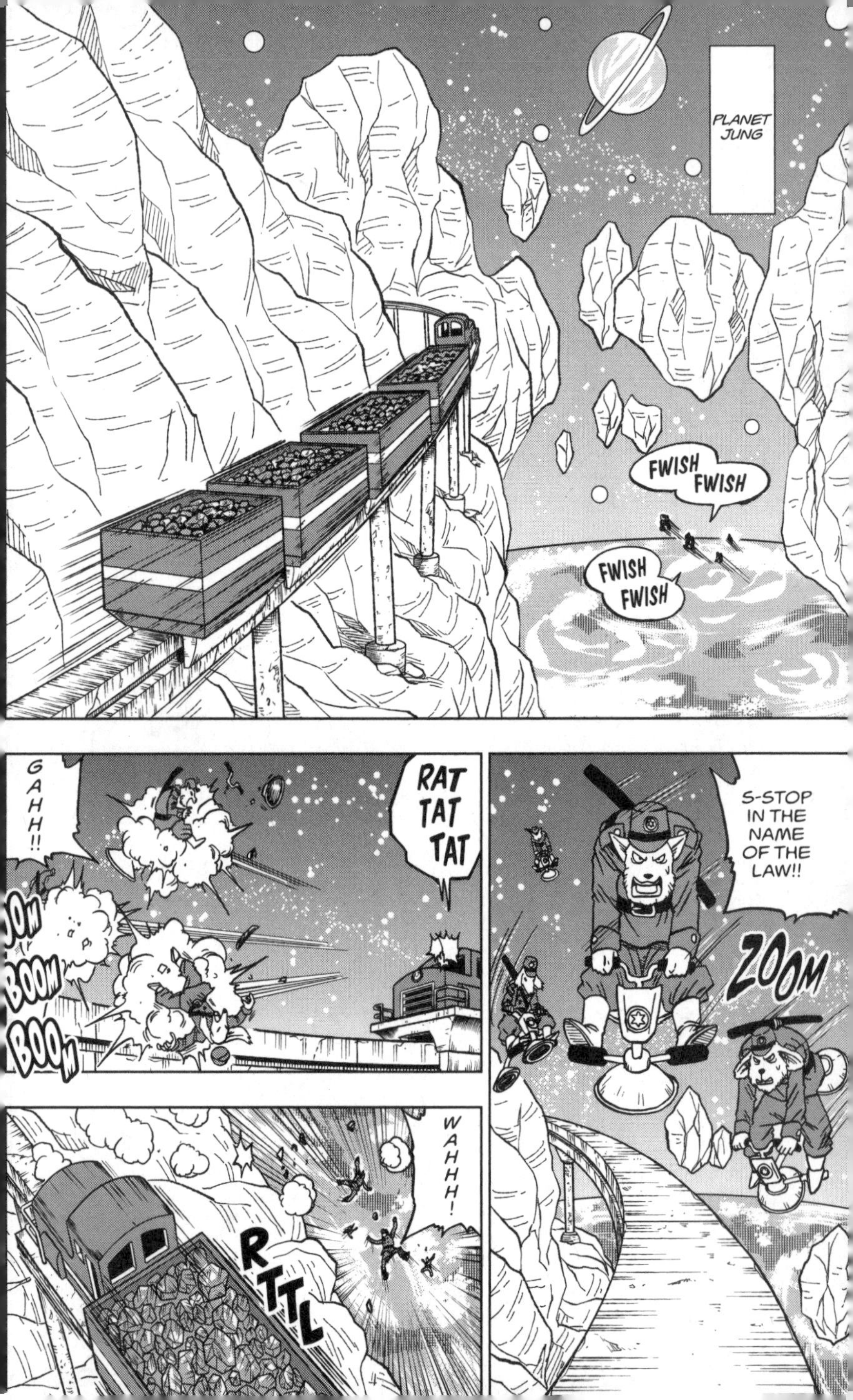
PLANET JUNG
FWISH FWISH
FWISH FWISH
S-STOP IN THE NAME OF THE LAW!!
ZOOM
RAT TAT TAT
GAHH!!
BOOM
BOOM
WAHHH!
RTTL

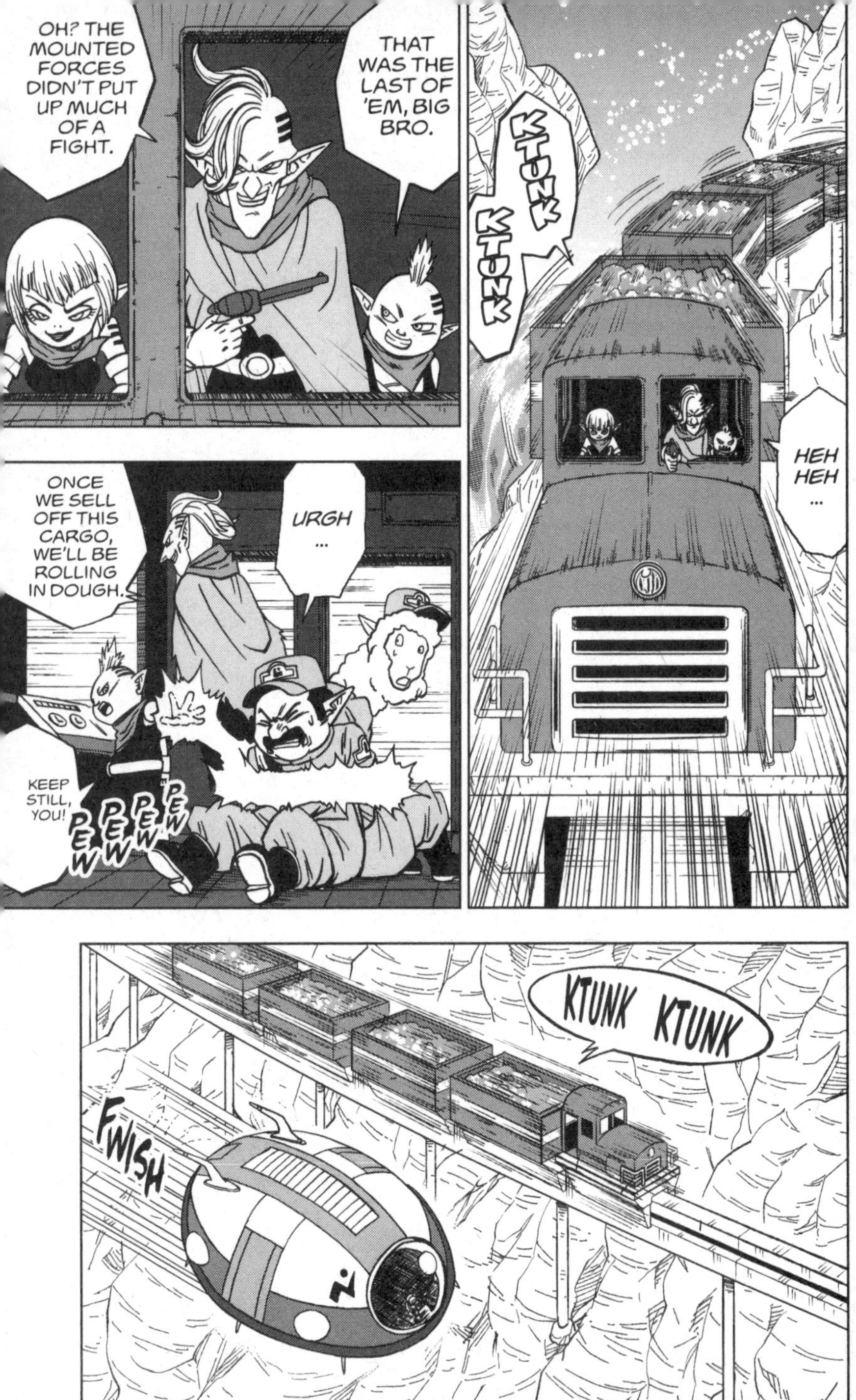
KTUNK KTUNK
HEH HEH ...
THAT WAS THE LAST OF 'EM, BIG BRO.
OH? THE MOUNTED FORCES DIDN'T PUT UP MUCH OF A FIGHT.
URGH ...
ONCE WE SELL OFF THIS CARGO, WE'LL BE ROLLING IN DOUGH.
KEEP STILL, YOU!
PEW PEW PEW PEW
KTUNK KTUNK
FWISH

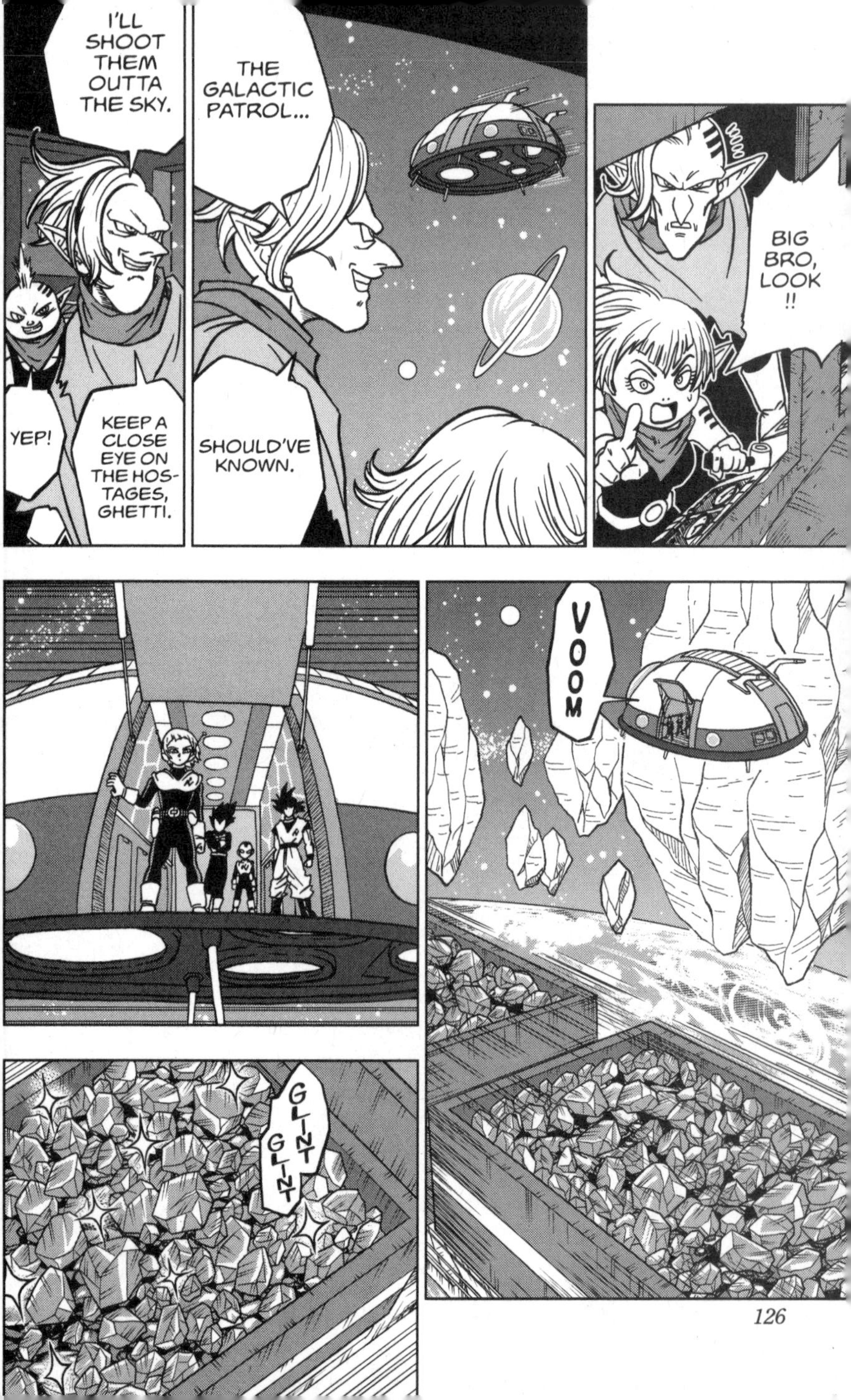
BIG BRO, LOOK!!
THE GALACTIC PATROL...
SHOULD'VE KNOWN.
I'LL SHOOT THEM OUTTA THE SKY.
KEEP A CLOSE EYE ON THE HOSTAGES, GHETTI.
YEP!
VOOM
GLINT GLINT

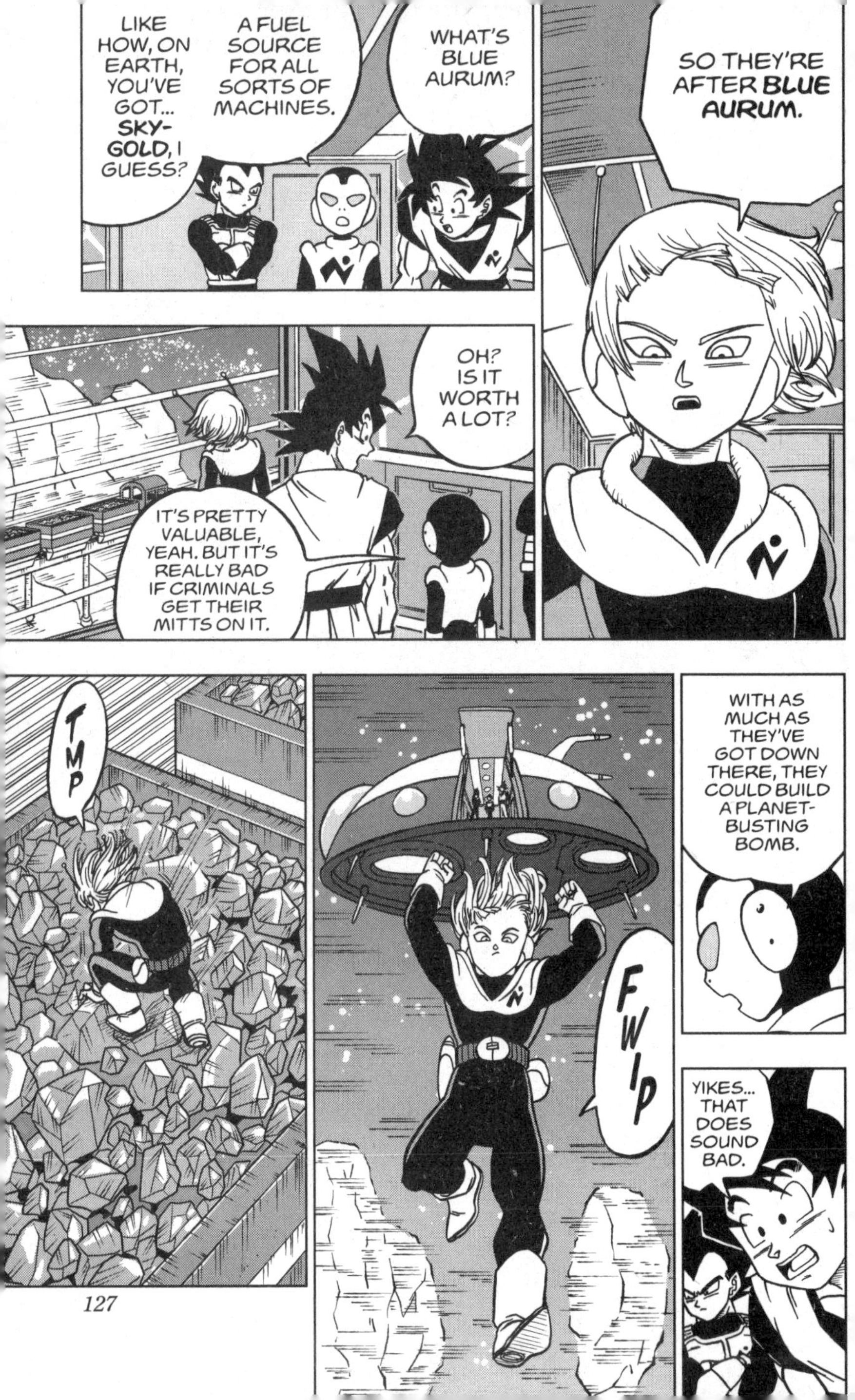
SO THEY'RE AFTER **BLUE AURUM.**
WHAT'S BLUE AURUM?
A FUEL SOURCE FOR ALL SORTS OF MACHINES.
LIKE HOW, ON EARTH, YOU'VE GOT... **SKY-GOLD,** I GUESS?
OH? IS IT WORTH A LOT?
IT'S PRETTY VALUABLE, YEAH. BUT IT'S REALLY BAD IF CRIMINALS GET THEIR MITTS ON IT.
WITH AS MUCH AS THEY'VE GOT DOWN THERE, THEY COULD BUILD A PLANET-BUSTING BOMB.
YIKES... THAT DOES SOUND BAD.
FWIP
TMP

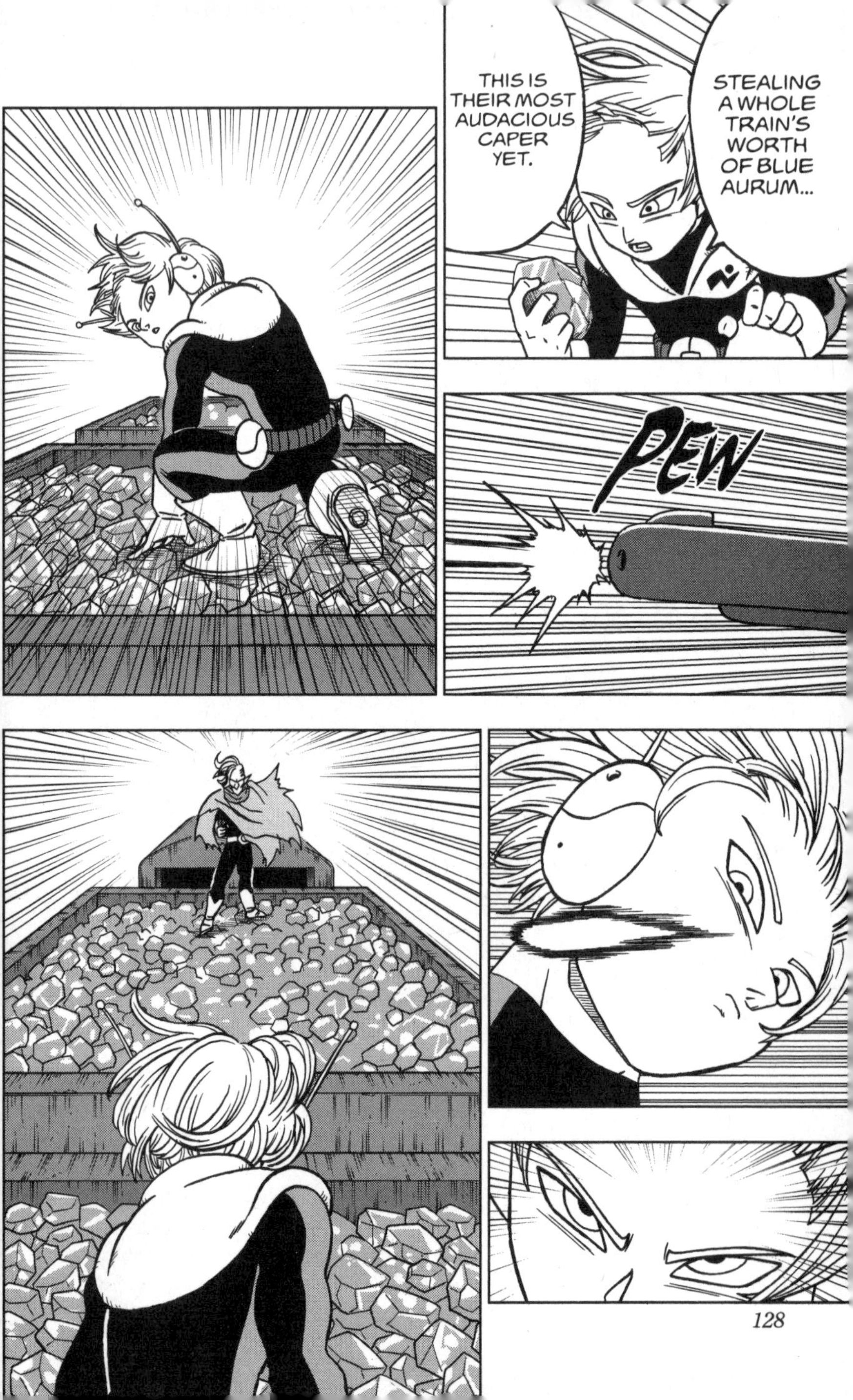
STEALING A WHOLE TRAIN'S WORTH OF BLUE AURUM...
THIS IS THEIR MOST AUDACIOUS CAPER YET.
PEW

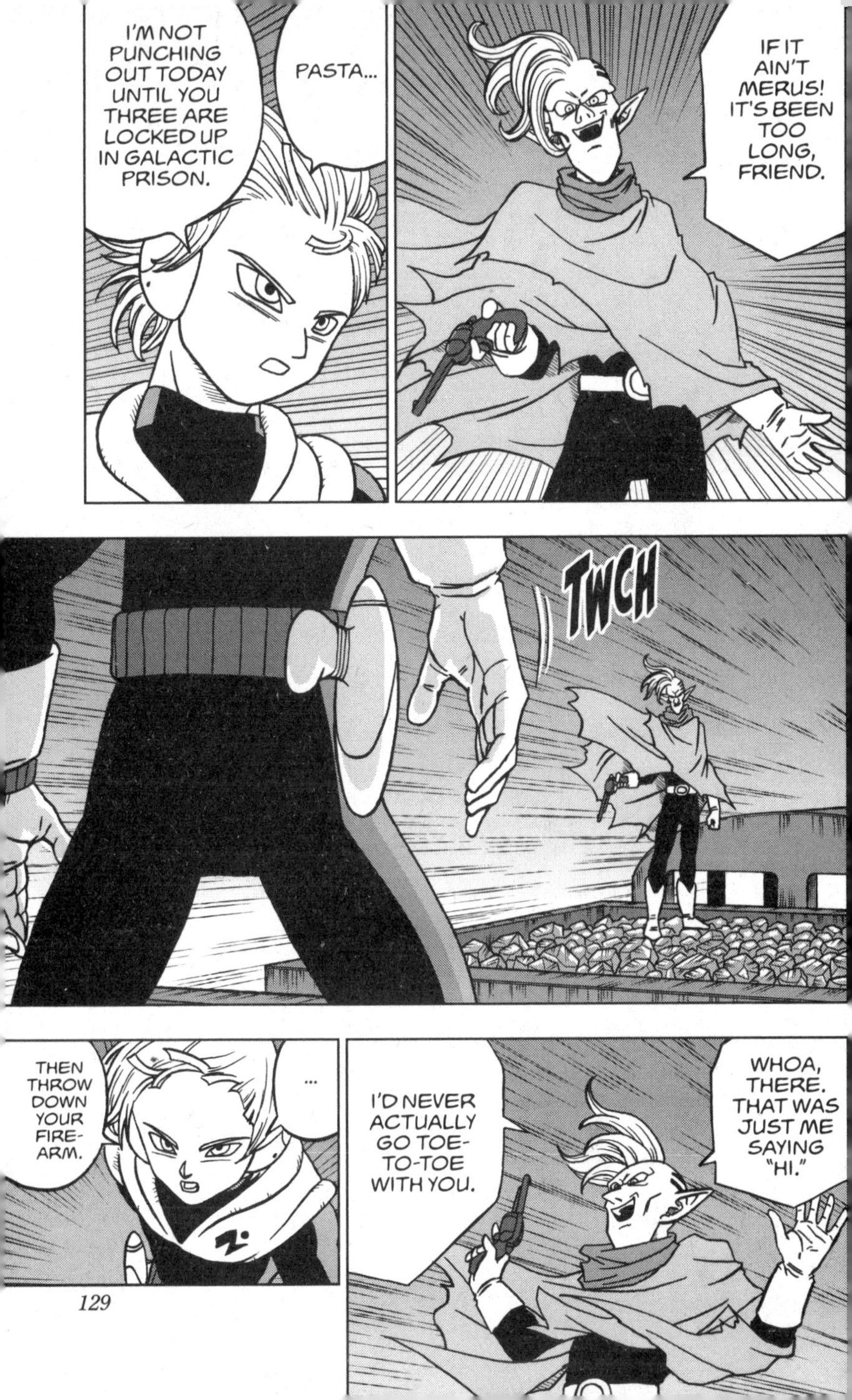
IF IT AIN'T MERUS! IT'S BEEN TOO LONG, FRIEND.
PASTA...
I'M NOT PUNCHING OUT TODAY UNTIL YOU THREE ARE LOCKED UP IN GALACTIC PRISON.
TWCH
WHOA, THERE. THAT WAS JUST ME SAYING "HI."
I'D NEVER ACTUALLY GO TOE-TO-TOE WITH YOU.
...
THEN THROW DOWN YOUR FIRE-ARM.

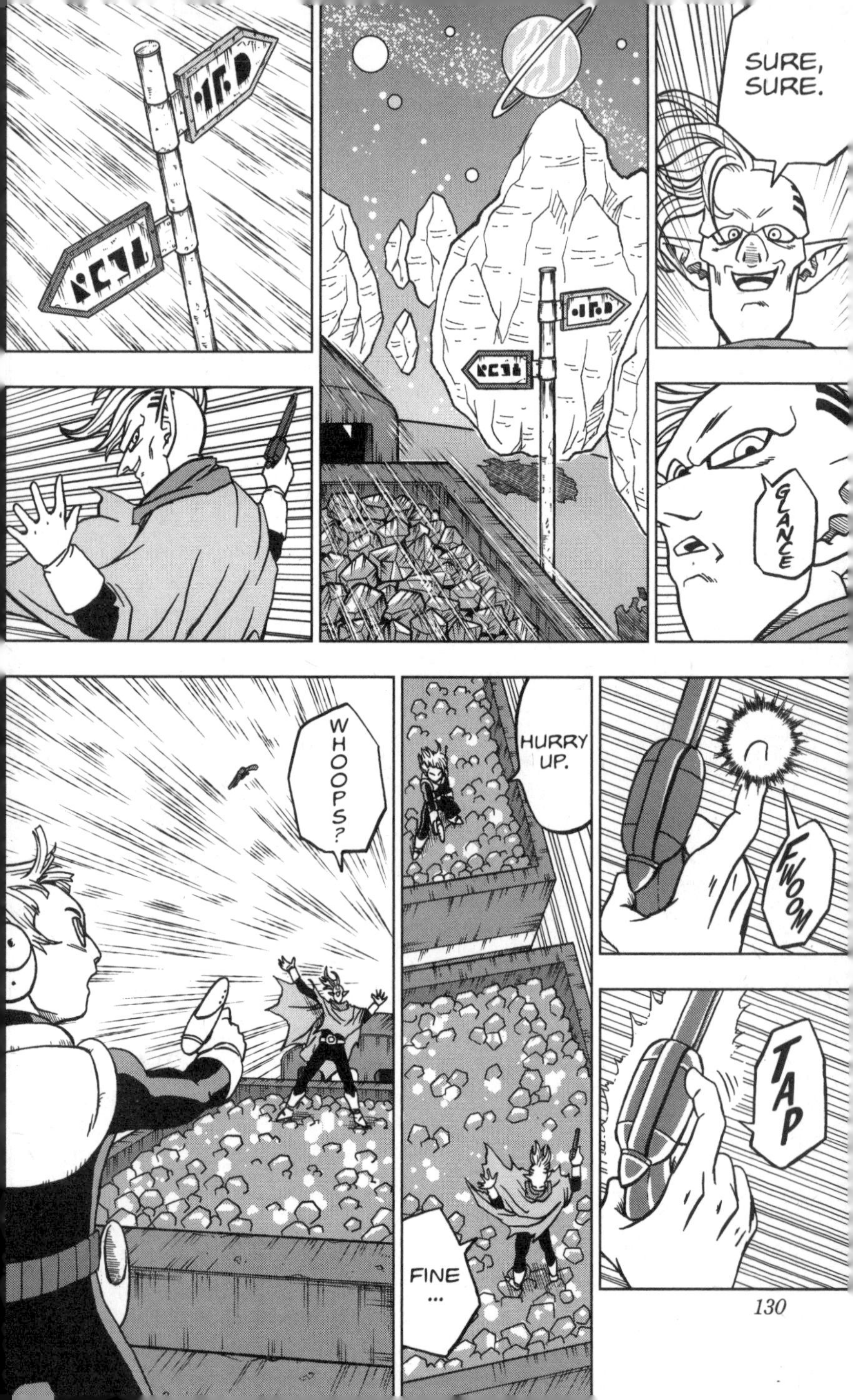
SURE, SURE.
GLANCE
FWOOM
TAP
HURRY UP.
FINE ...
WHOOPS?

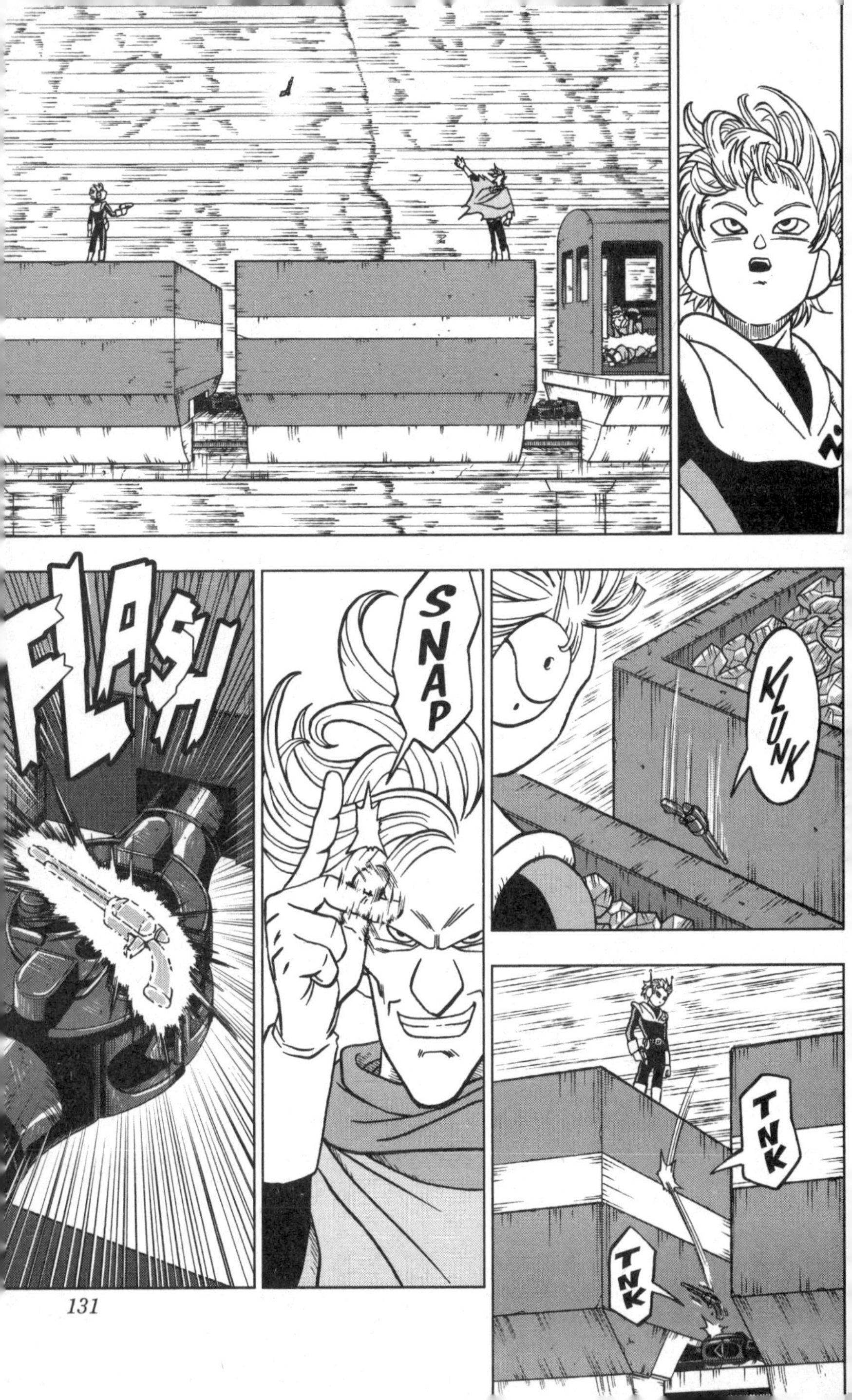
KLUNK
TNK
TNK
SNAP
FLASH

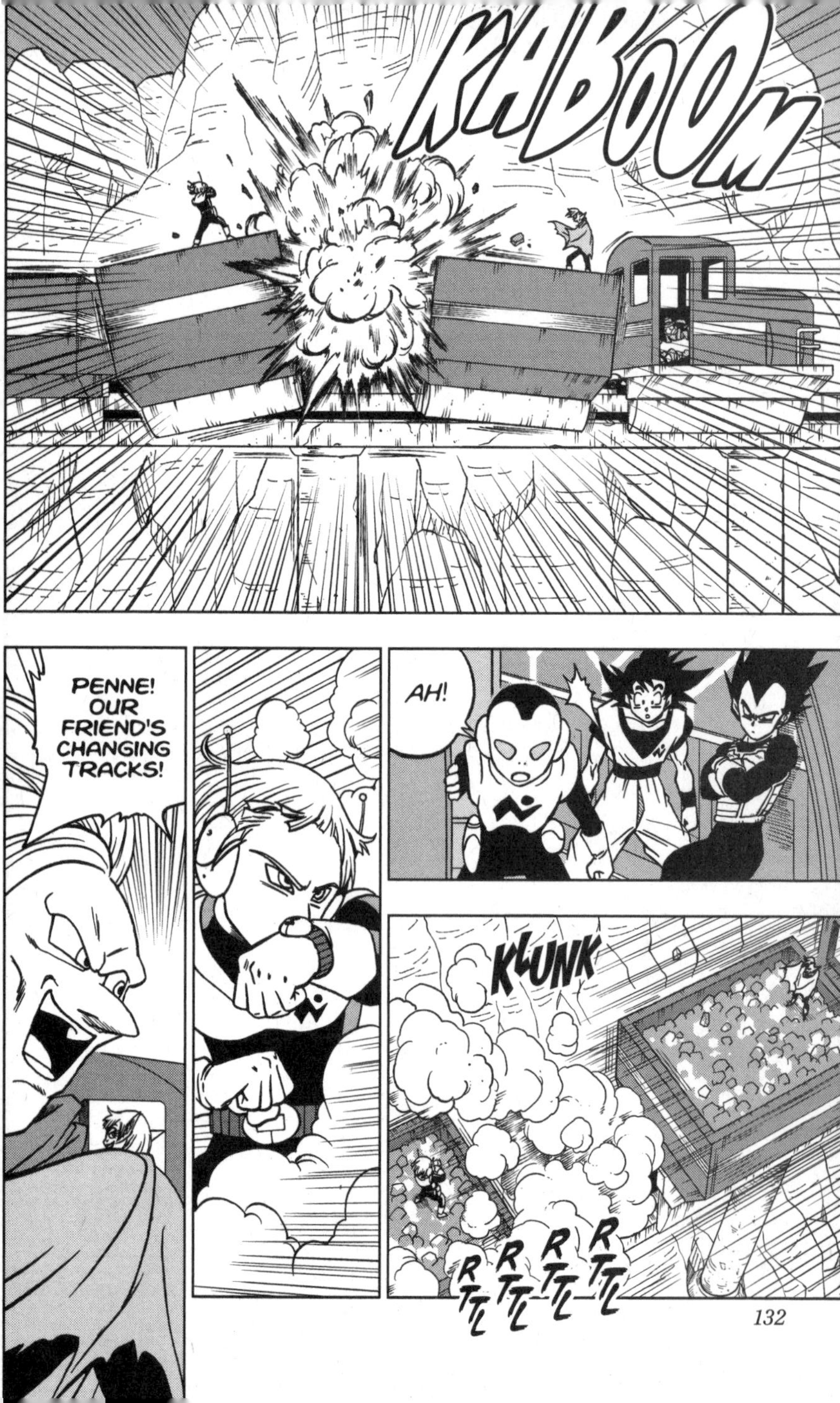
KABOOM
AH!
KLUNK
RTTL
RTTL
RTTL
RTTL
PENNE! OUR FRIEND'S CHANGING TRACKS!

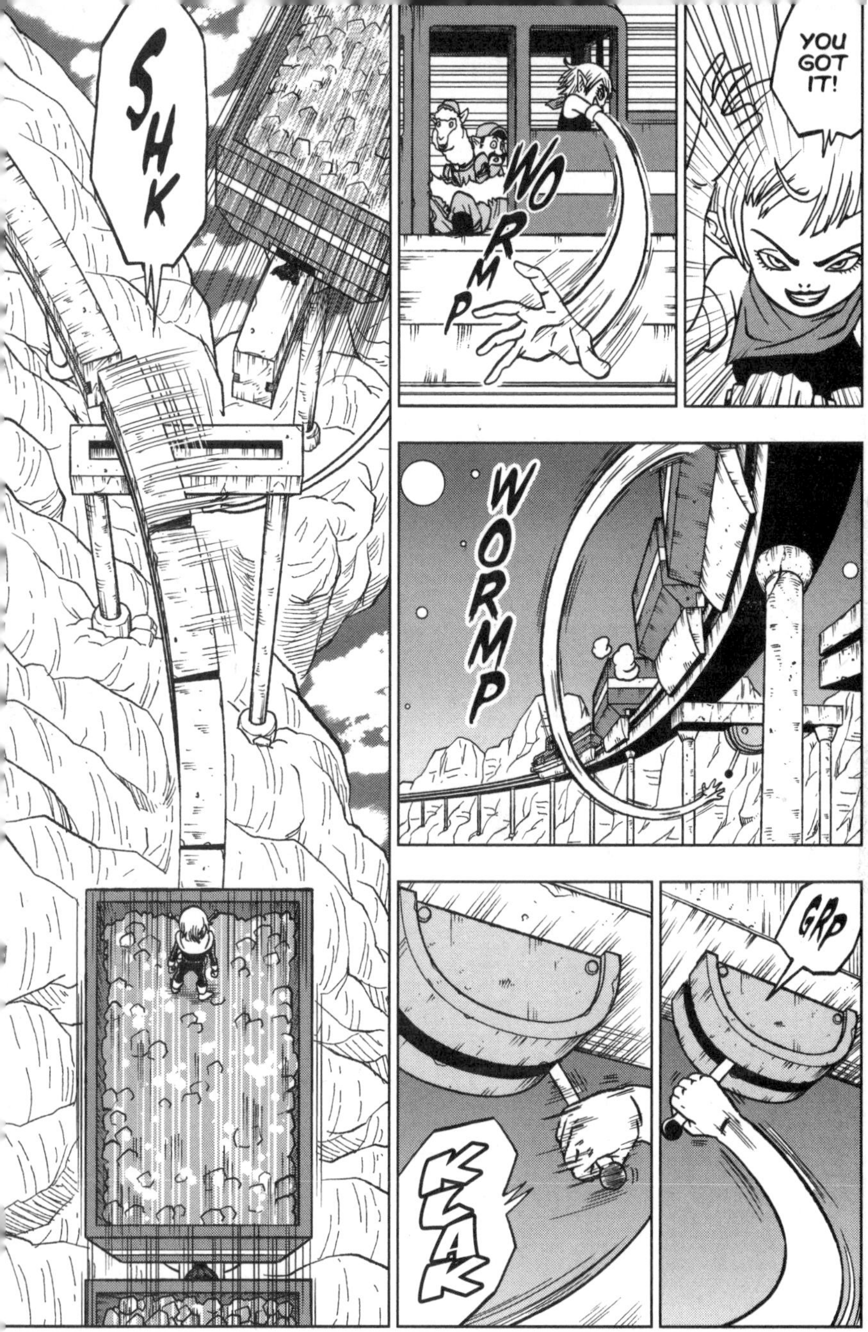
YOU GOT IT!
WORMP
WORMP
GRP
KLAK
SHK

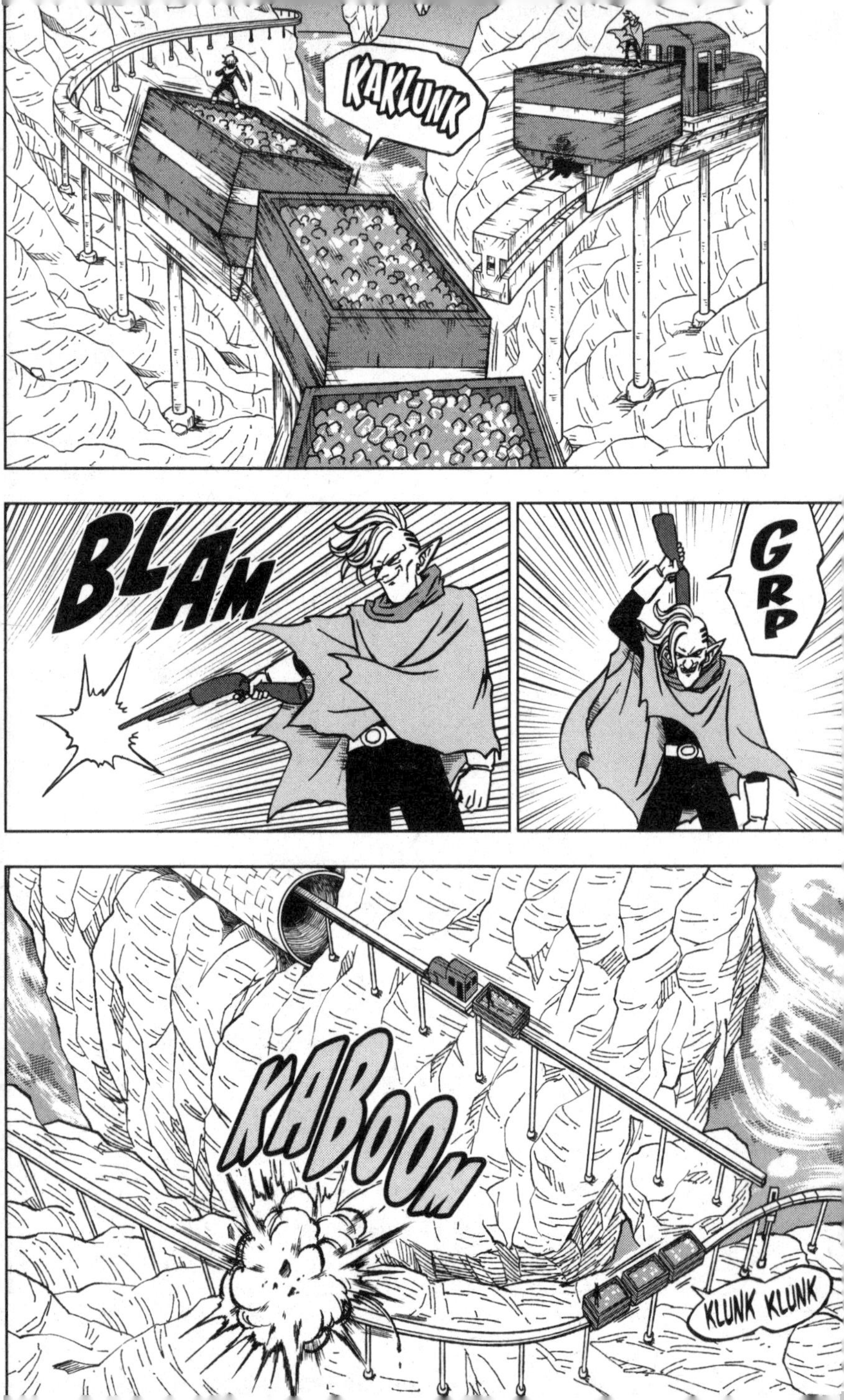
KAKLUNK
GRP
BLAM
KABOOM
KLUNK KLUNK

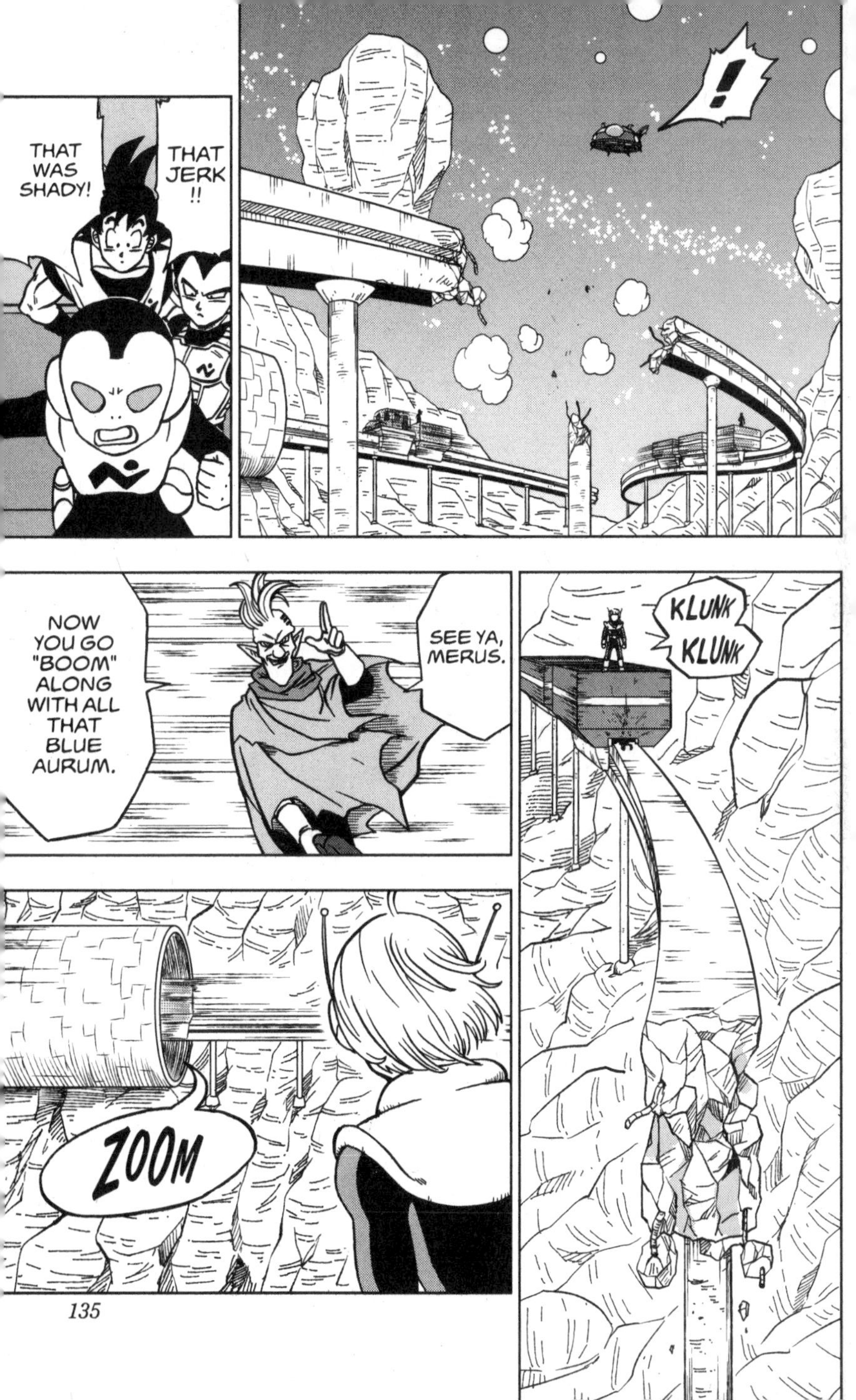
!
THAT JERK !!
THAT WAS SHADY!
KLUNK KLUNK
SEE YA, MERUS.
NOW YOU GO "BOOM" ALONG WITH ALL THAT BLUE AURUM.
ZOOM

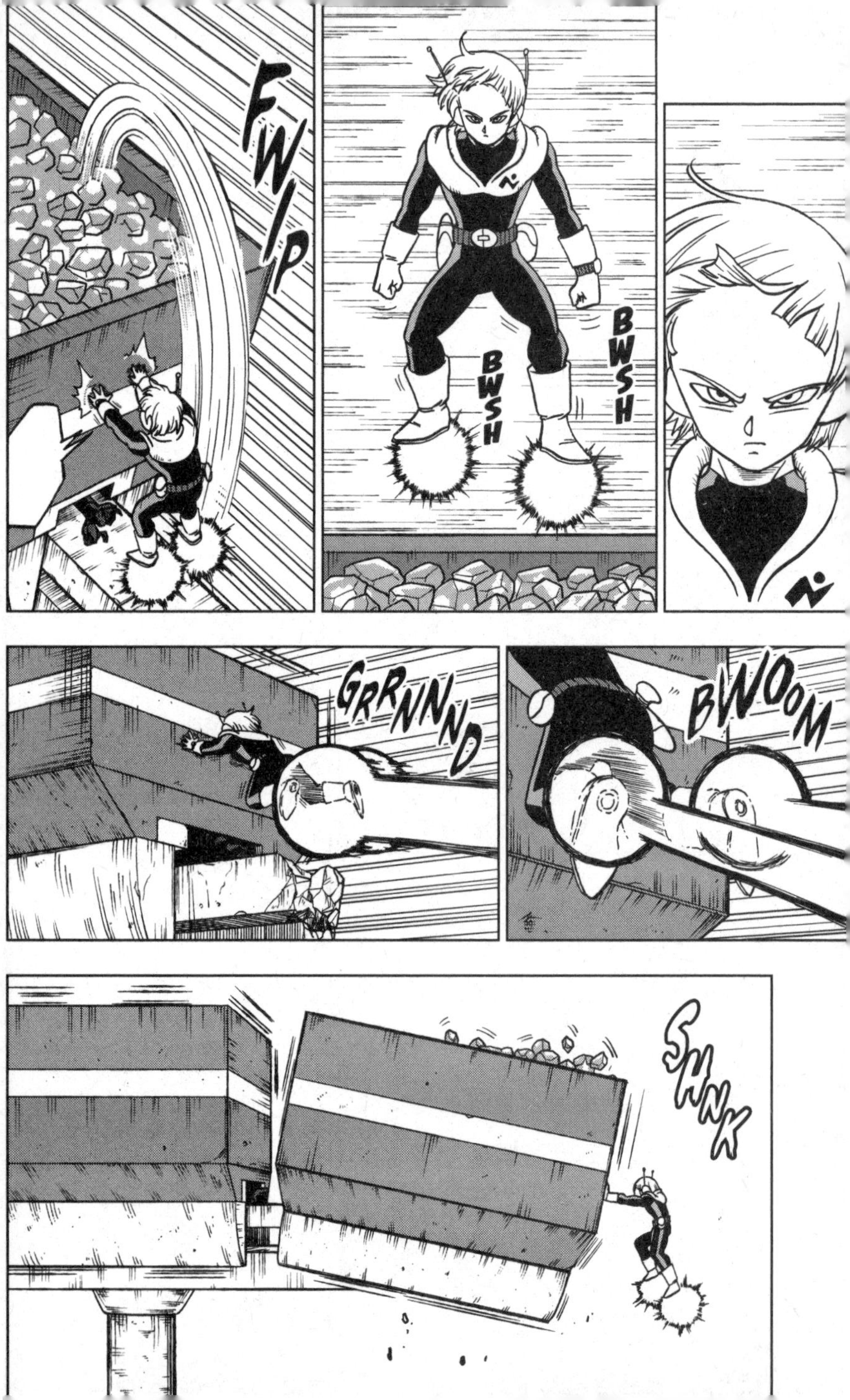
BWSH
BWSH
FWIP
BWOOM
GRRNNND
SHNK

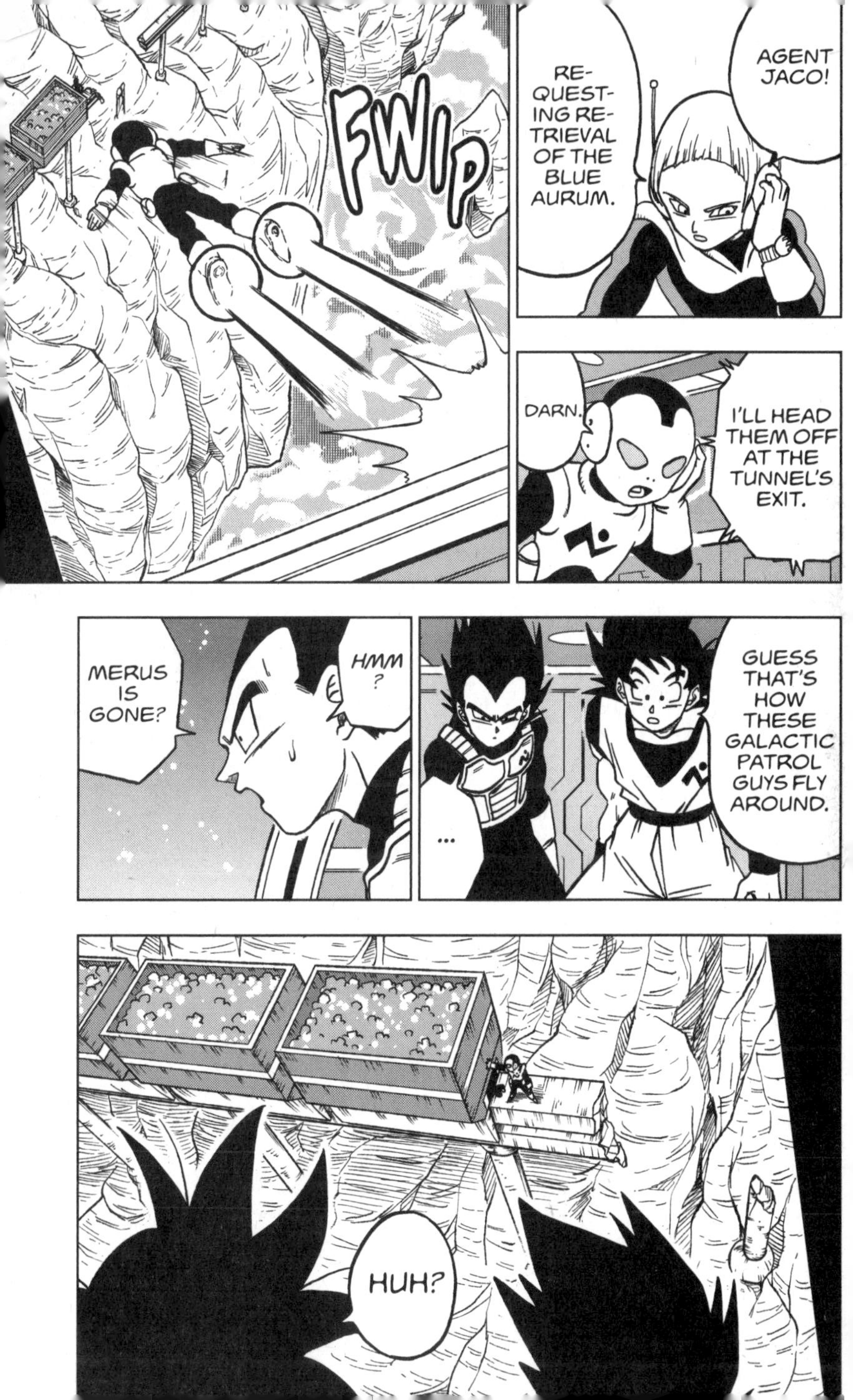
AGENT JACO!
REQUESTING RETRIEVAL OF THE BLUE AURUM.
I'LL HEAD THEM OFF AT THE TUNNEL'S EXIT.
DARN.
FWIP
GUESS THAT'S HOW THESE GALACTIC PATROL GUYS FLY AROUND.
...
HMM?
MERUS IS GONE?
HUH?

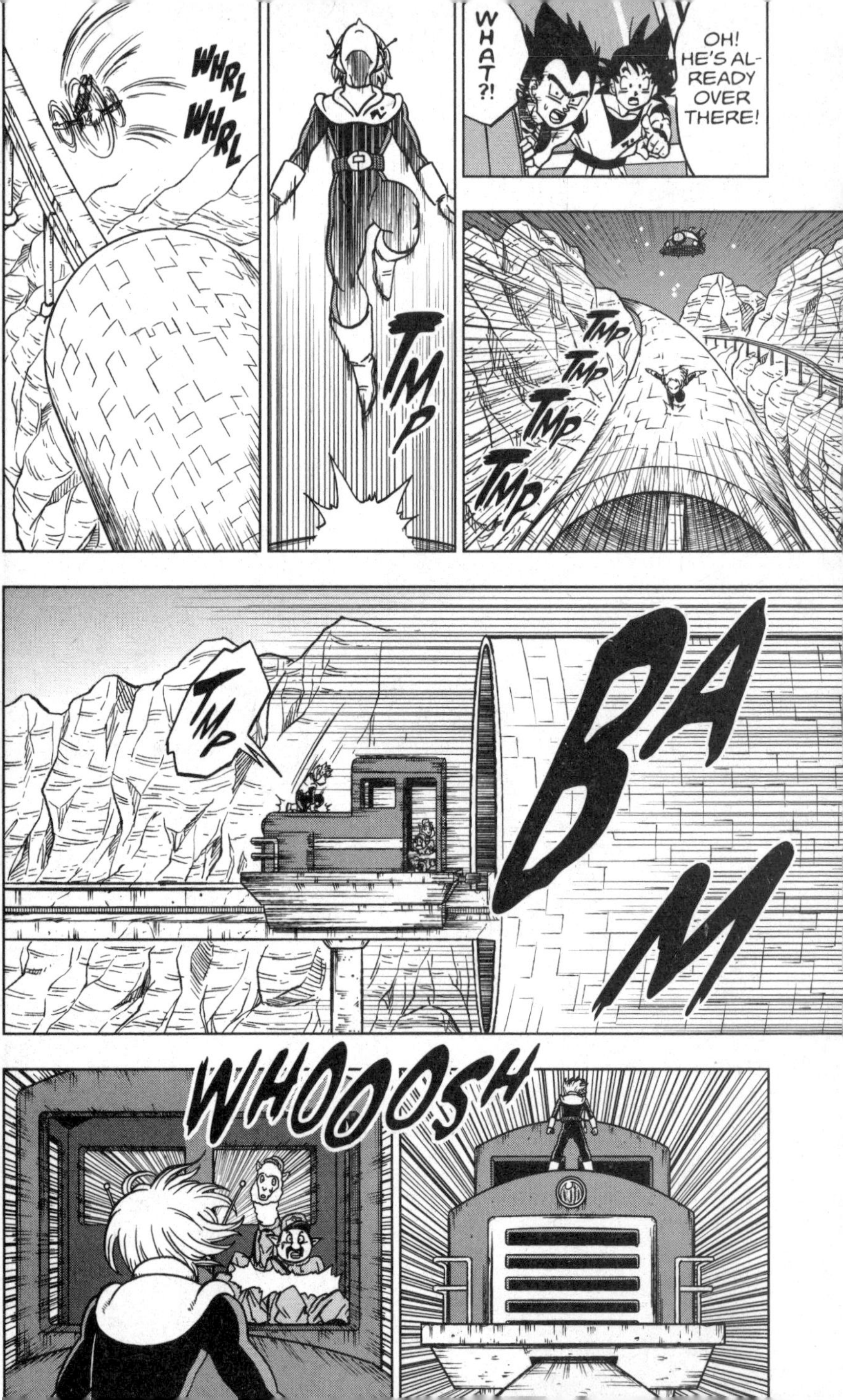
OH! HE'S AL-READY OVER THERE!
WHAT?!
TMP TMP TMP TMP
TMP
WHRL WHRL
BAM
TMP
WHOOOSH

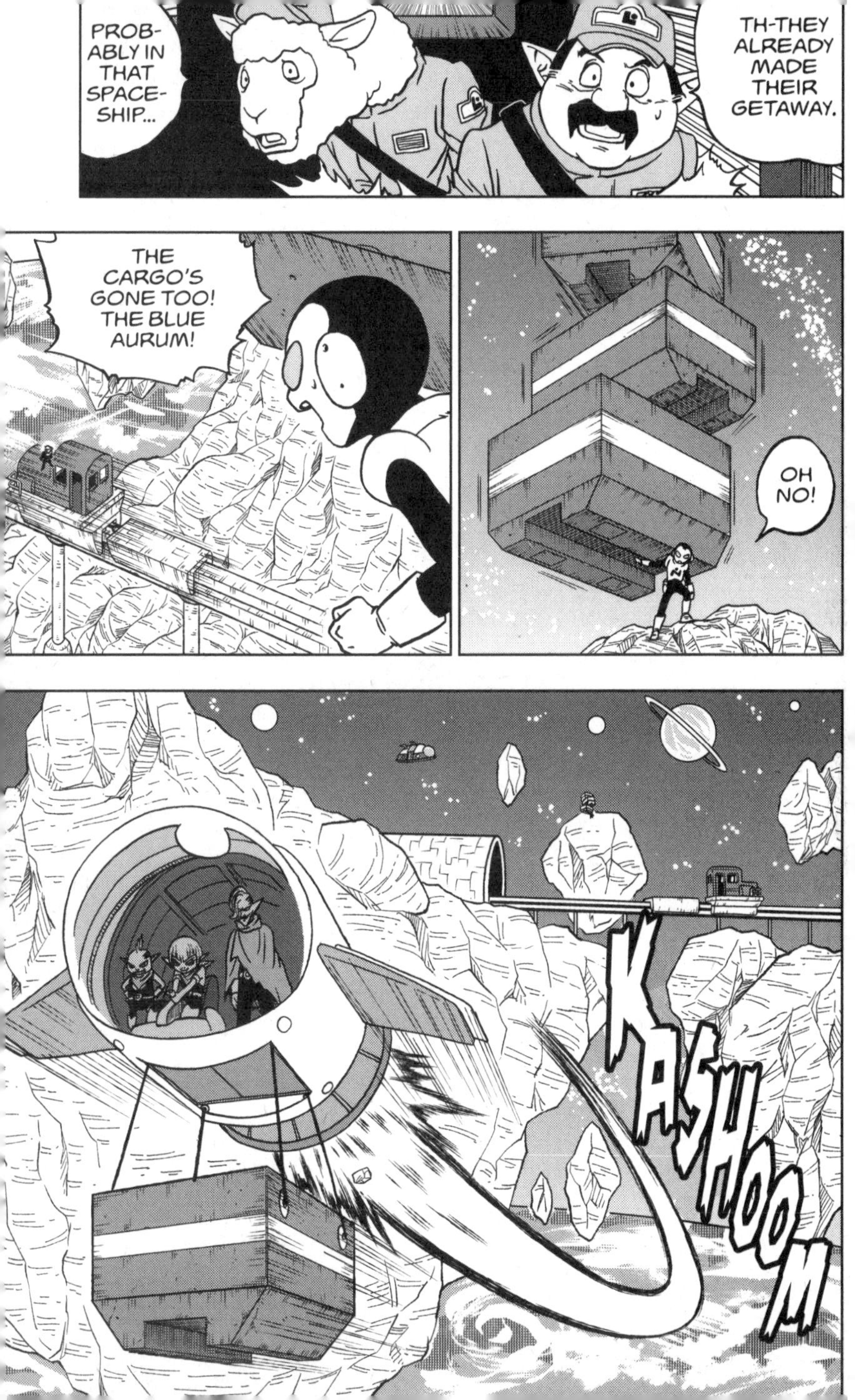
TH-THEY ALREADY MADE THEIR GETAWAY.
PROB-ABLY IN THAT SPACE-SHIP...
OH NO!
THE CARGO'S GONE TOO! THE BLUE AURUM!
KASHOOM

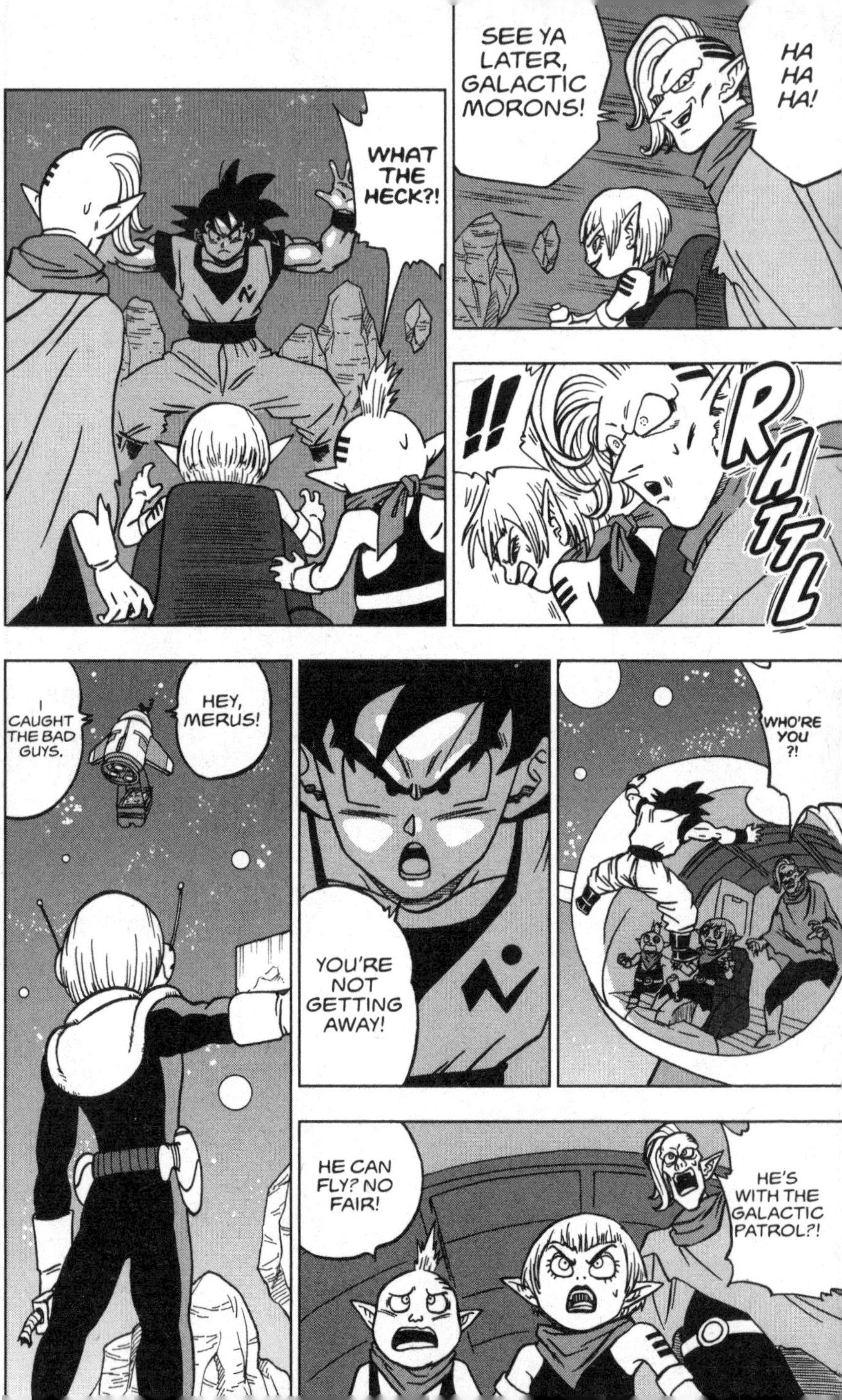
HA HA HA!
SEE YA LATER, GALACTIC MORONS!
RATTL
!!
WHAT THE HECK?!
WHO'RE YOU ?!
YOU'RE NOT GETTING AWAY!
HE'S WITH THE GALACTIC PATROL?!
HE CAN FLY? NO FAIR!
HEY, MERUS!
I CAUGHT THE BAD GUYS.

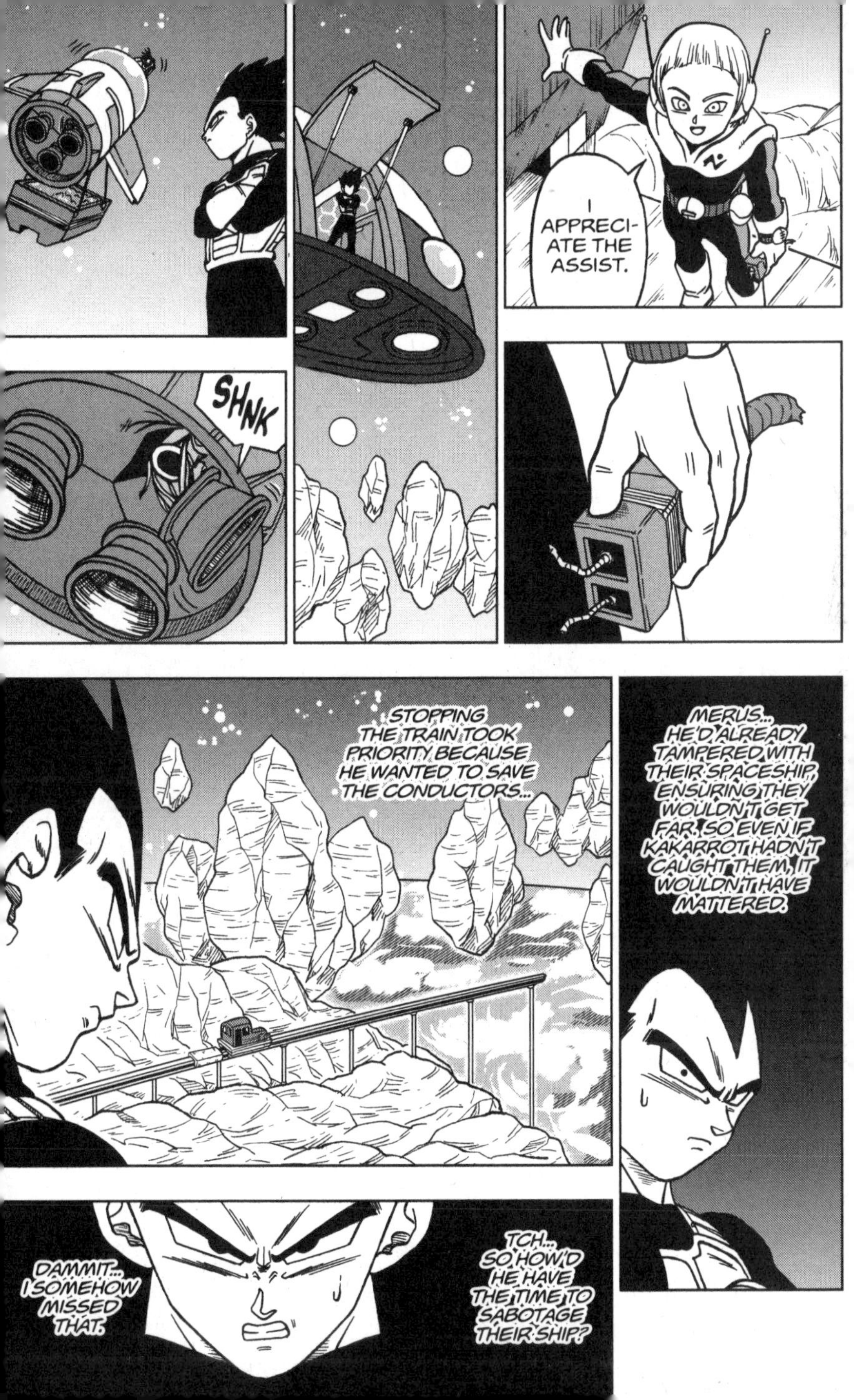
I APPRECIATE THE ASSIST.
SHNK
MERUS... HE'D ALREADY TAMPERED WITH THEIR SPACESHIP, ENSURING THEY WOULDN'T GET FAR, SO EVEN IF KAKARROT HADN'T CAUGHT THEM, IT WOULDN'T HAVE MATTERED.
STOPPING THE TRAIN TOOK PRIORITY BECAUSE HE WANTED TO SAVE THE CONDUCTORS...
TCH... SO HOW'D HE HAVE THE TIME TO SABOTAGE THEIR SHIP?
DAMMIT... I SOMEHOW MISSED THAT.

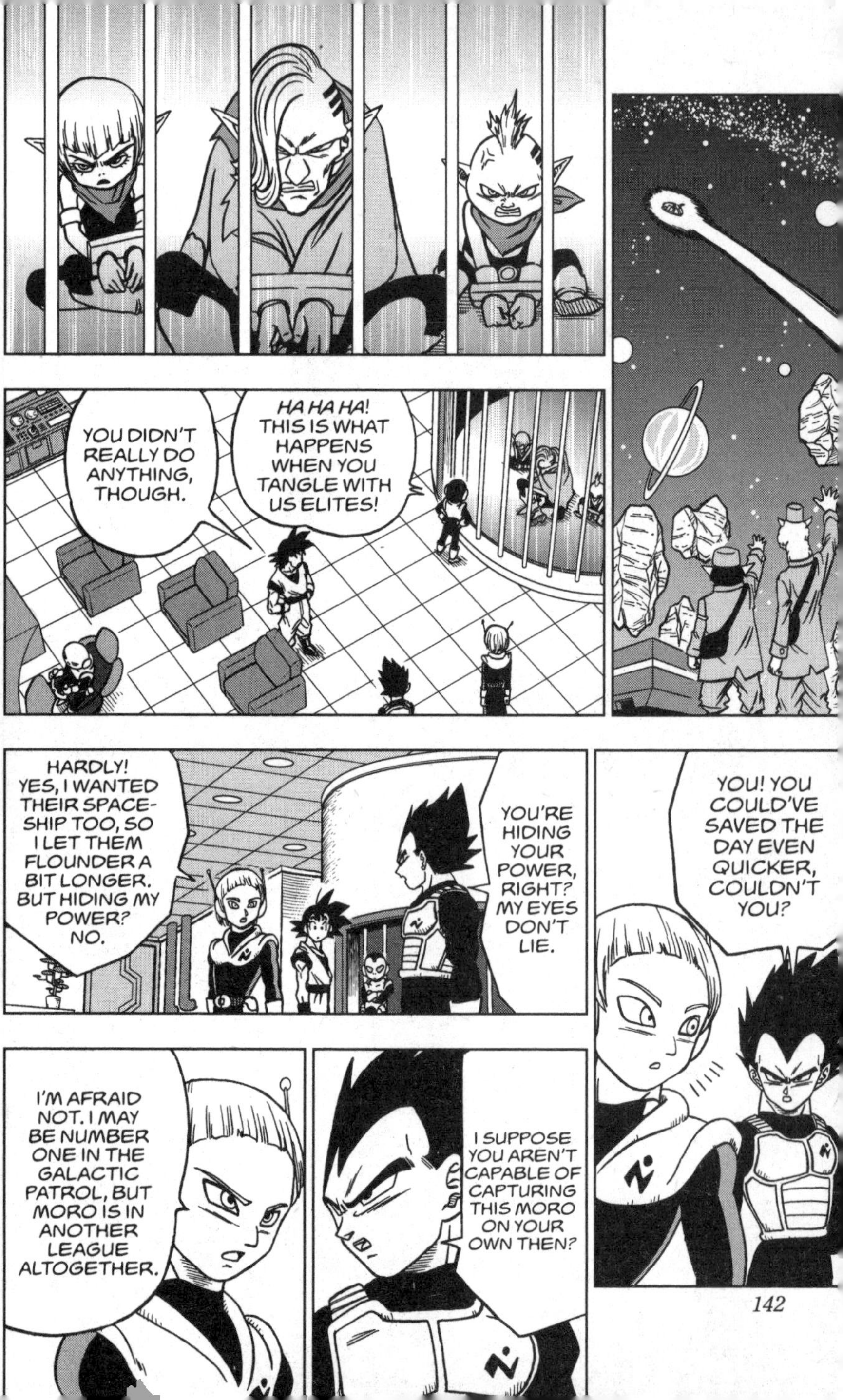
HA HA HA! THIS IS WHAT HAPPENS WHEN YOU TANGLE WITH US ELITES!
YOU DIDN'T REALLY DO ANYTHING, THOUGH.
YOU! YOU COULD'VE SAVED THE DAY EVEN QUICKER, COULDN'T YOU?
YOU'RE HIDING YOUR POWER, RIGHT? MY EYES DON'T LIE.
HARDLY! YES, I WANTED THEIR SPACE-SHIP TOO, SO I LET THEM FLOUNDER A BIT LONGER. BUT HIDING MY POWER? NO.
I SUPPOSE YOU AREN'T CAPABLE OF CAPTURING THIS MORO ON YOUR OWN THEN?
I'M AFRAID NOT. I MAY BE NUMBER ONE IN THE GALACTIC PATROL, BUT MORO IS IN ANOTHER LEAGUE ALTOGETHER.

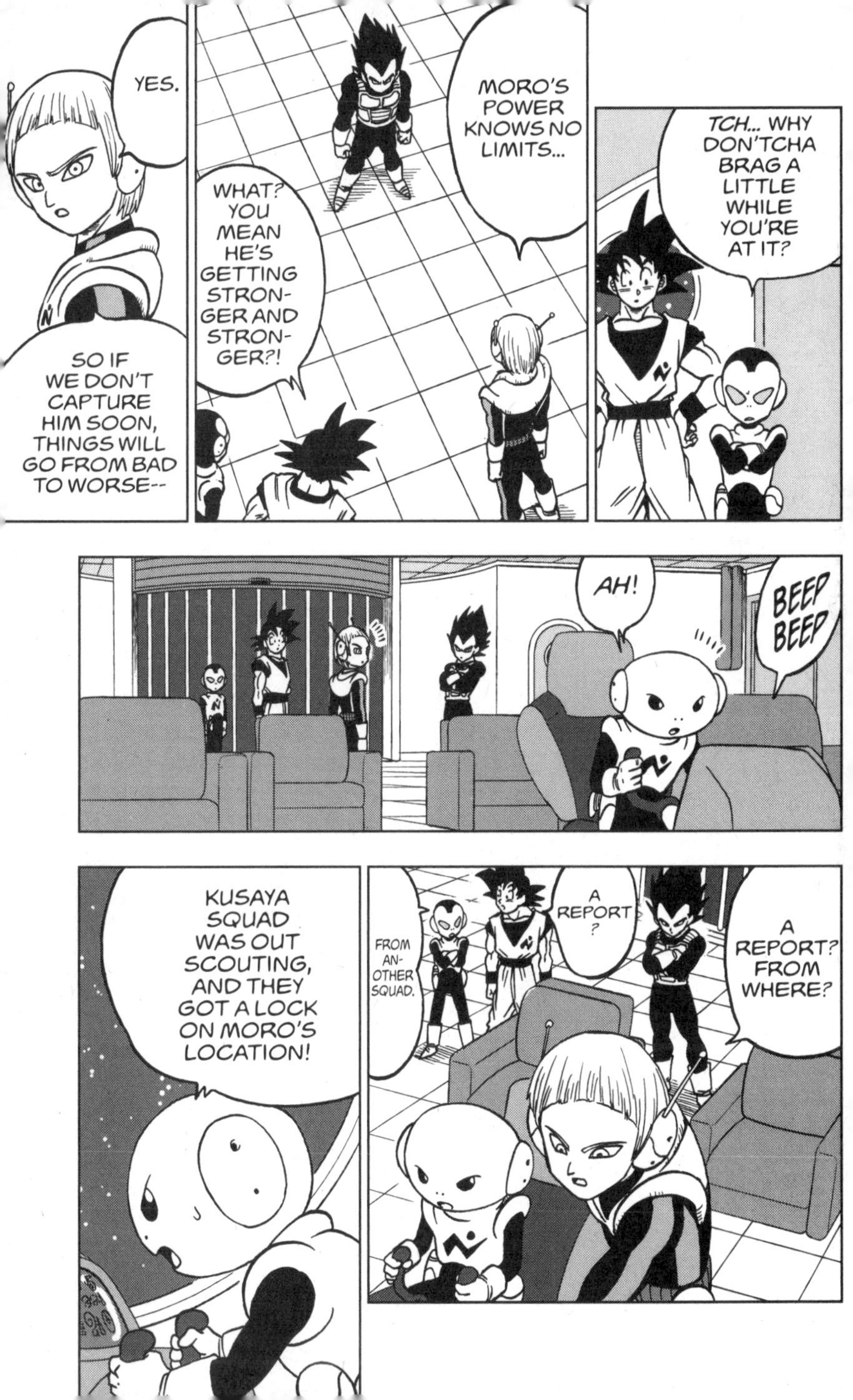
TCH... WHY DON'TCHA BRAG A LITTLE WHILE YOU'RE AT IT?
MORO'S POWER KNOWS NO LIMITS...
WHAT? YOU MEAN HE'S GETTING STRONGER AND STRONGER?!
YES.
SO IF WE DON'T CAPTURE HIM SOON, THINGS WILL GO FROM BAD TO WORSE--
BEEP BEEP
AH!
A REPORT? FROM WHERE?
A REPORT?
FROM ANOTHER SQUAD.
KUSAYA SQUAD WAS OUT SCOUTING, AND THEY GOT A LOCK ON MORO'S LOCATION!

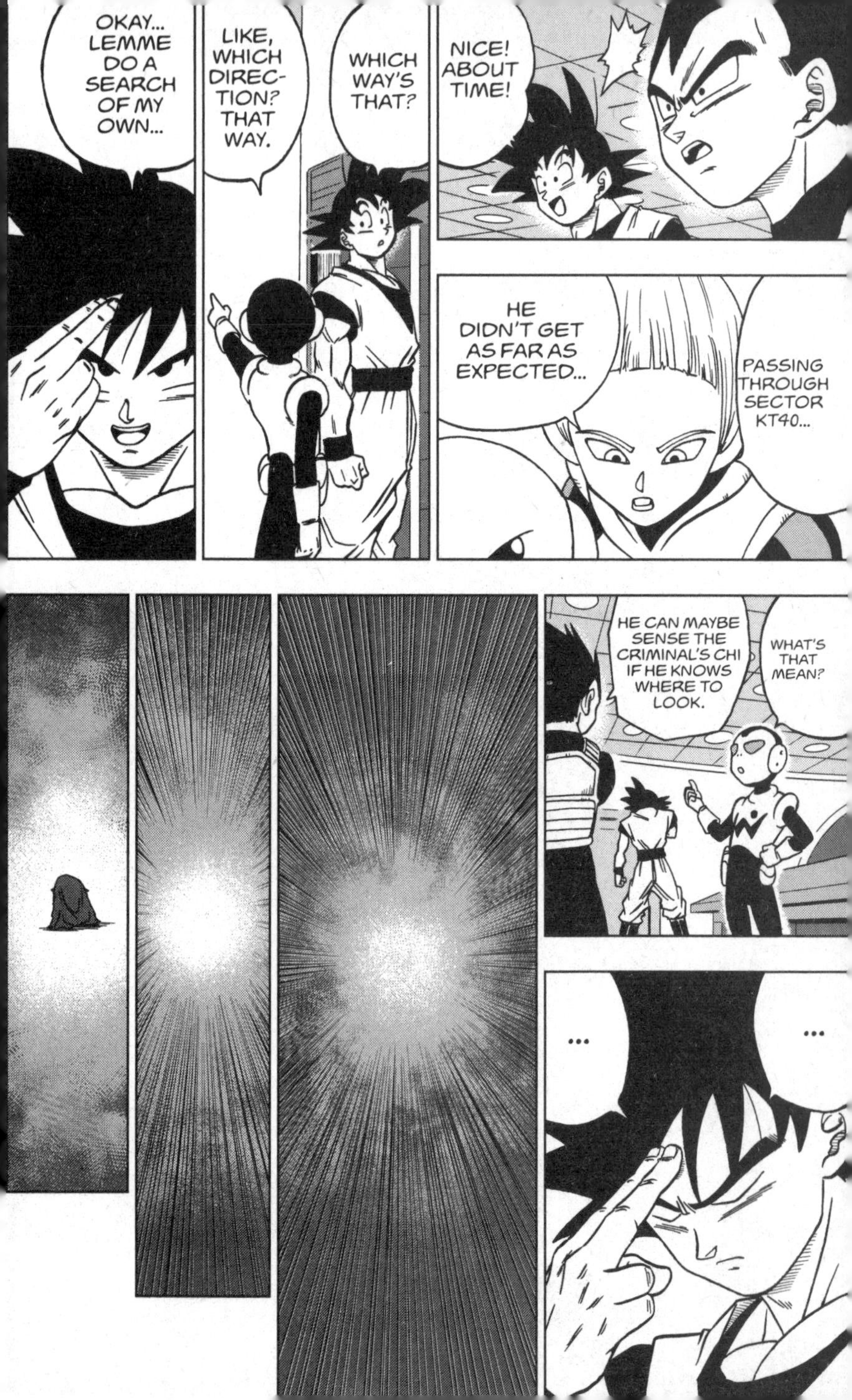
NICE! ABOUT TIME!
PASSING THROUGH SECTOR KT40...
HE DIDN'T GET AS FAR AS EXPECTED...
WHICH WAY'S THAT?
LIKE, WHICH DIRECTION? THAT WAY.
OKAY... LEMME DO A SEARCH OF MY OWN...
WHAT'S THAT MEAN?
HE CAN MAYBE SENSE THE CRIMINAL'S CHI IF HE KNOWS WHERE TO LOOK.
...
...

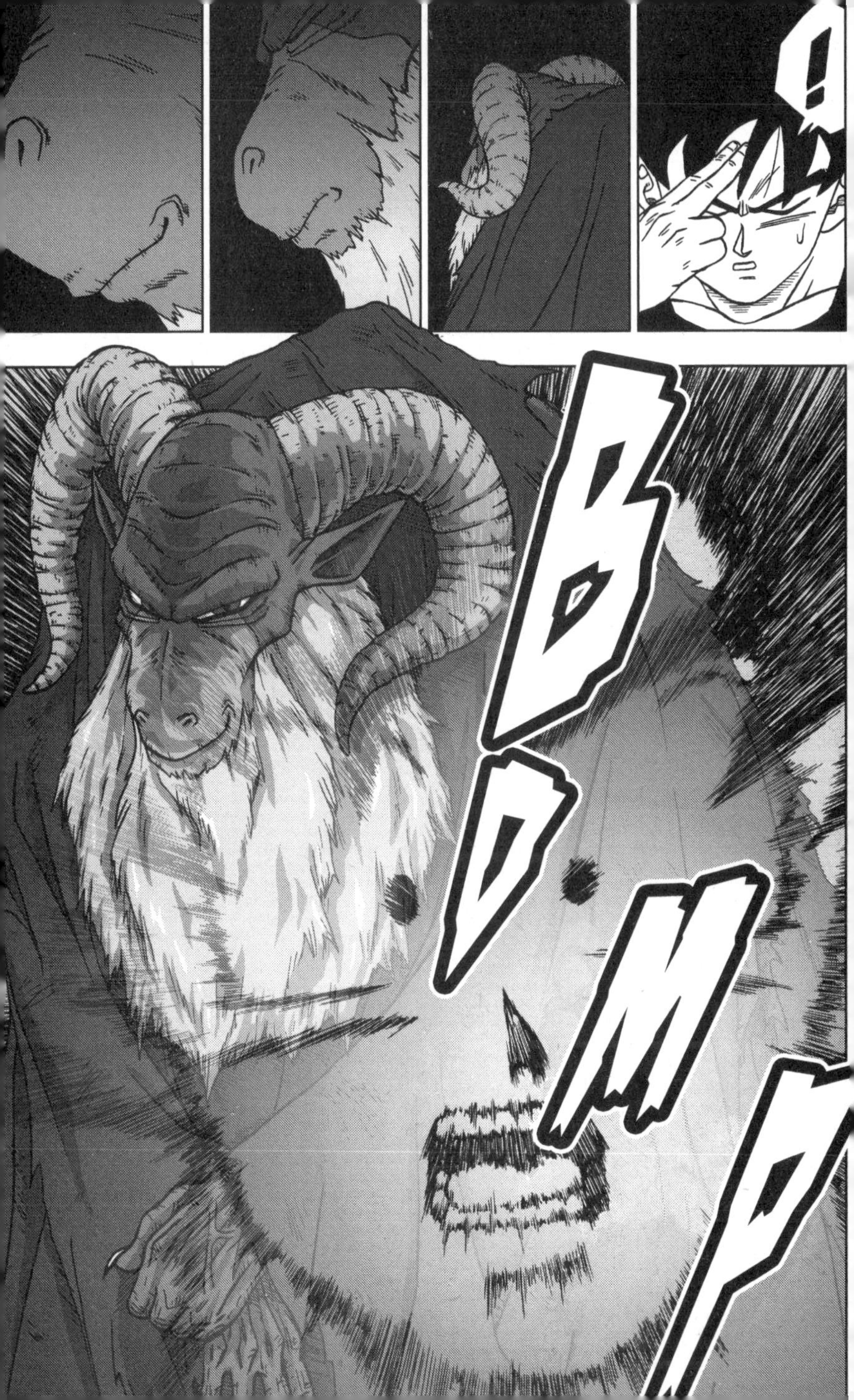
!?
BDMP

DRAGON BALL SUPER

CHAPTER 44: ESCAPED PRISONER MORO

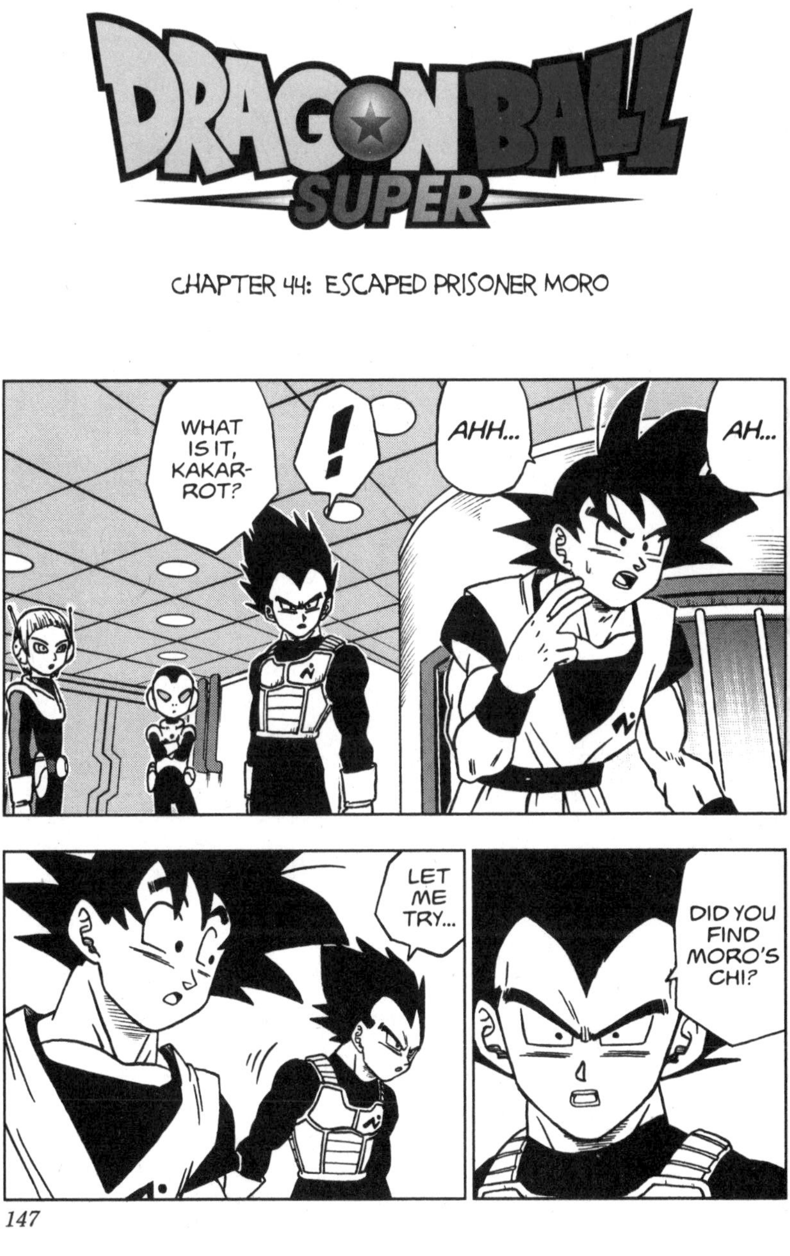
AH...
AHH...
!
WHAT IS IT, KAKARROT?
DID YOU FIND MORO'S CHI?
LET ME TRY...

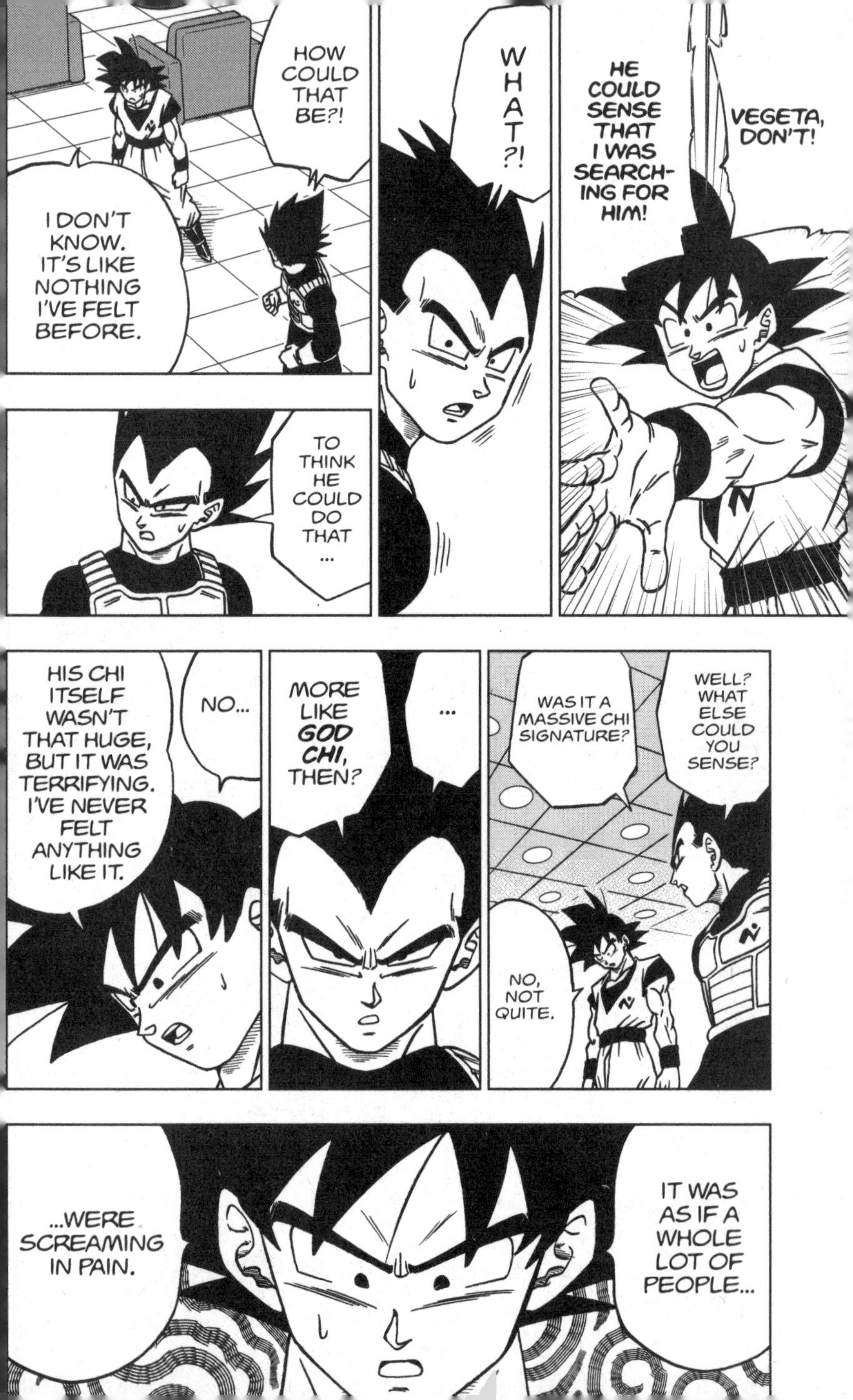
VEGETA, DON'T!
HE COULD SENSE THAT I WAS SEARCHING FOR HIM!
WHAT?!
HOW COULD THAT BE?!
I DON'T KNOW. IT'S LIKE NOTHING I'VE FELT BEFORE.
TO THINK HE COULD DO THAT...
WELL? WHAT ELSE COULD YOU SENSE?
WAS IT A MASSIVE CHI SIGNATURE?
NO, NOT QUITE.
...
MORE LIKE ***GOD CHI***, THEN?
NO...
HIS CHI ITSELF WASN'T THAT HUGE, BUT IT WAS TERRIFYING. I'VE NEVER FELT ANYTHING LIKE IT.
IT WAS AS IF A WHOLE LOT OF PEOPLE...
...WERE SCREAMING IN PAIN.

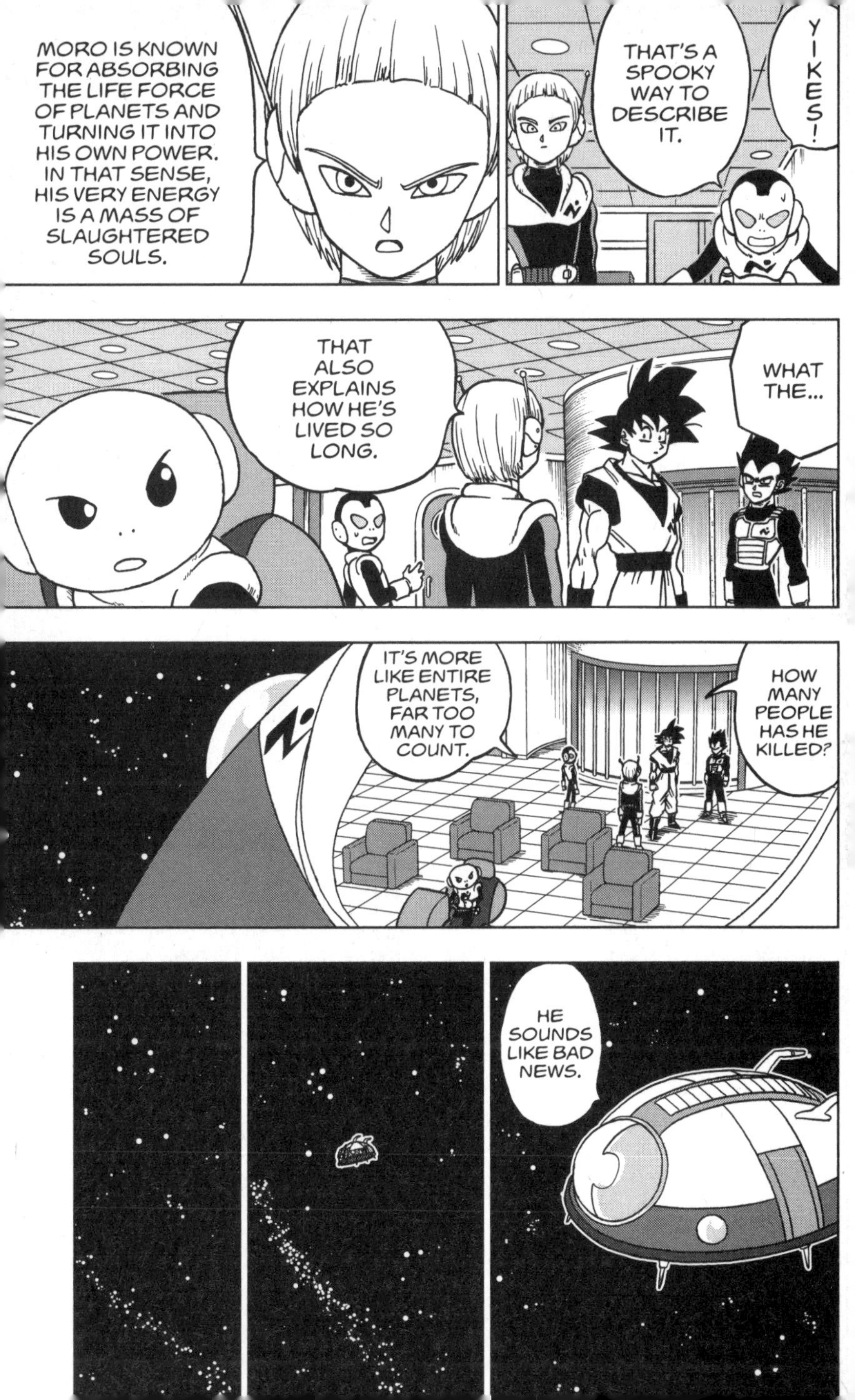
YIKES!
THAT'S A SPOOKY WAY TO DESCRIBE IT.
MORO IS KNOWN FOR ABSORBING THE LIFE FORCE OF PLANETS AND TURNING IT INTO HIS OWN POWER. IN THAT SENSE, HIS VERY ENERGY IS A MASS OF SLAUGHTERED SOULS.
WHAT THE...
THAT ALSO EXPLAINS HOW HE'S LIVED SO LONG.
HOW MANY PEOPLE HAS HE KILLED?
IT'S MORE LIKE ENTIRE PLANETS, FAR TOO MANY TO COUNT.
HE SOUNDS LIKE BAD NEWS.

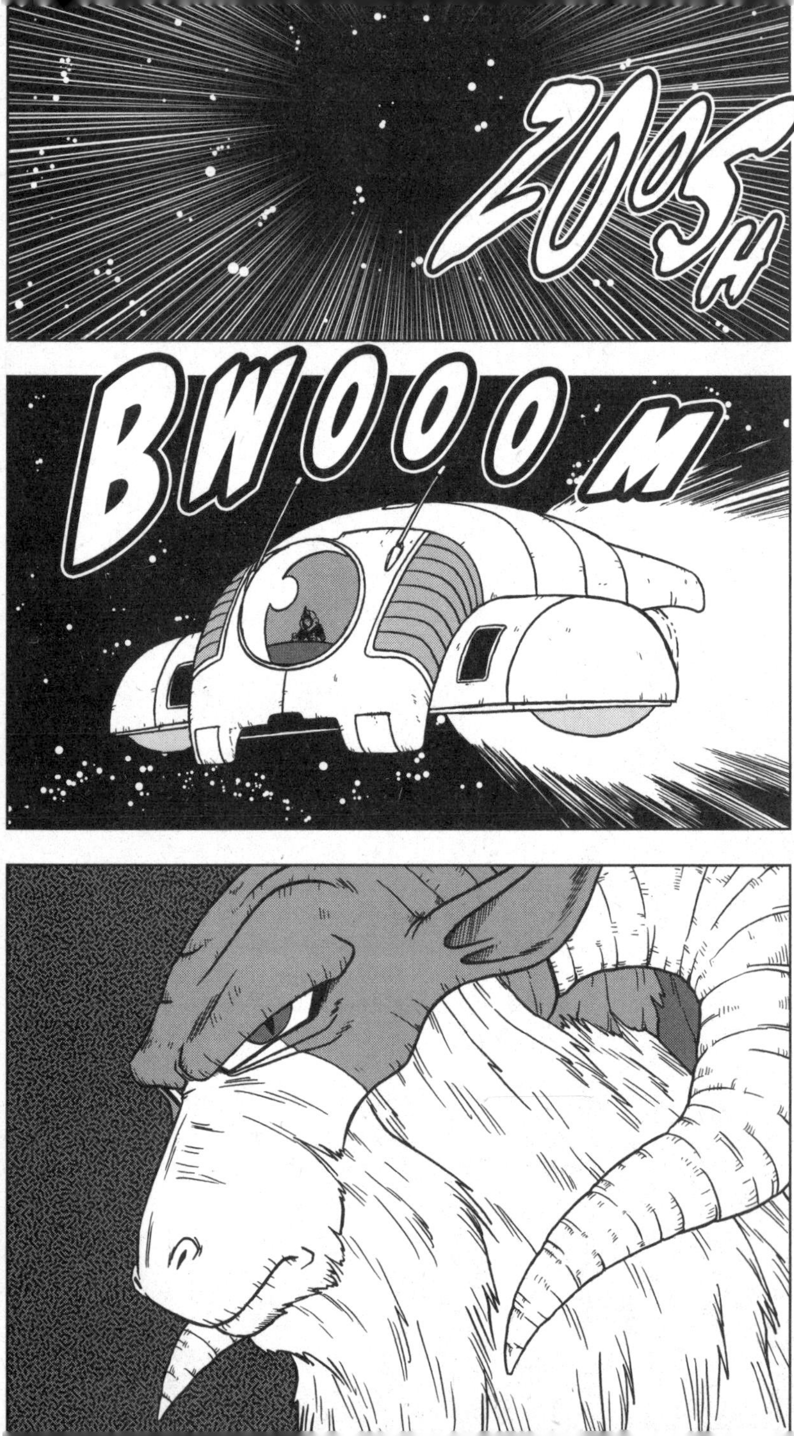
ZOOSH
BWOOOM

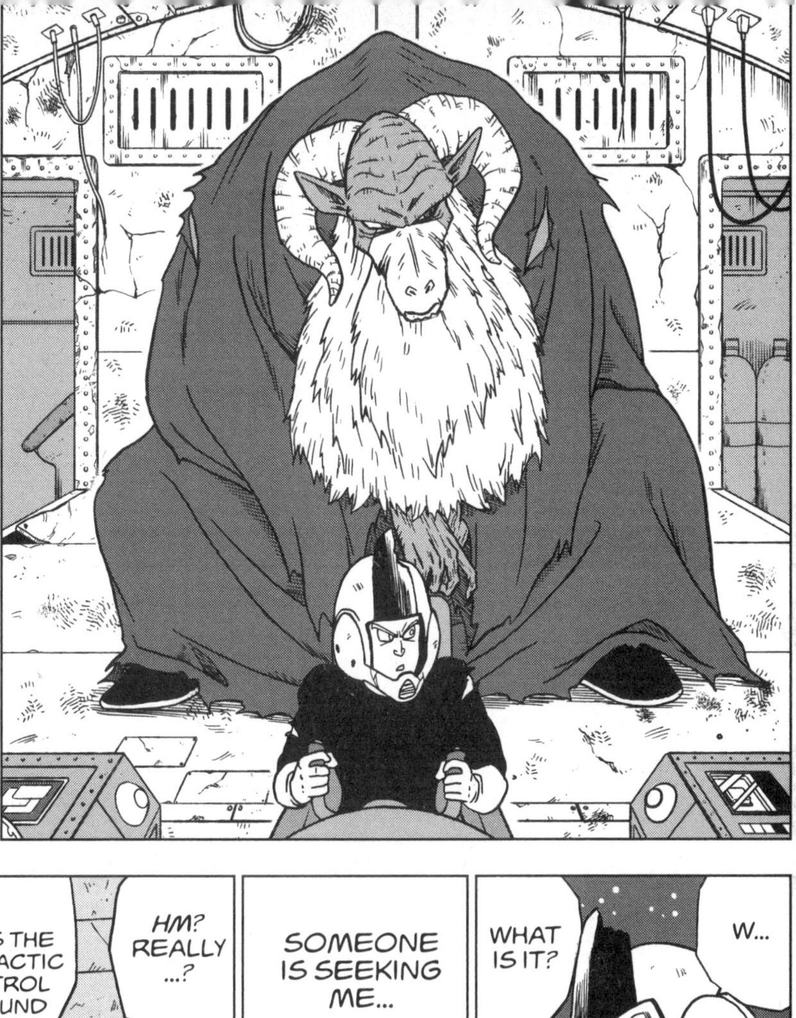

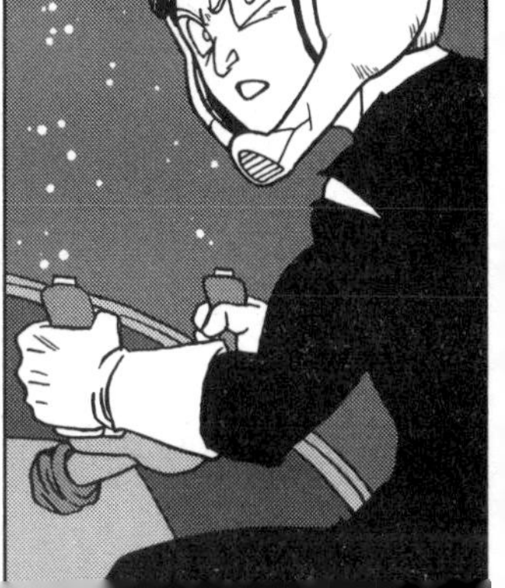
W...
WHAT IS IT?

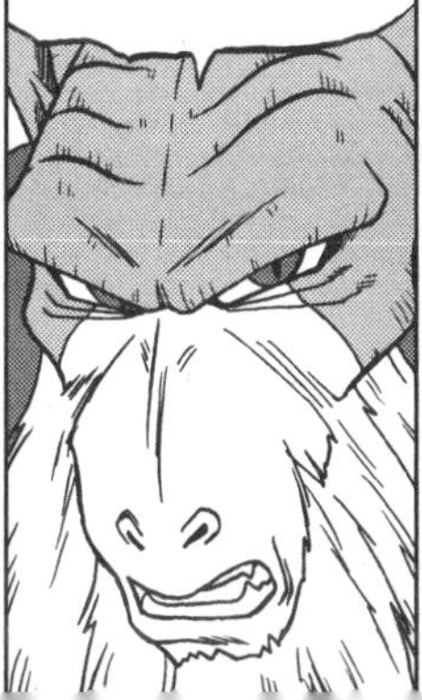
SOMEONE IS SEEKING ME...

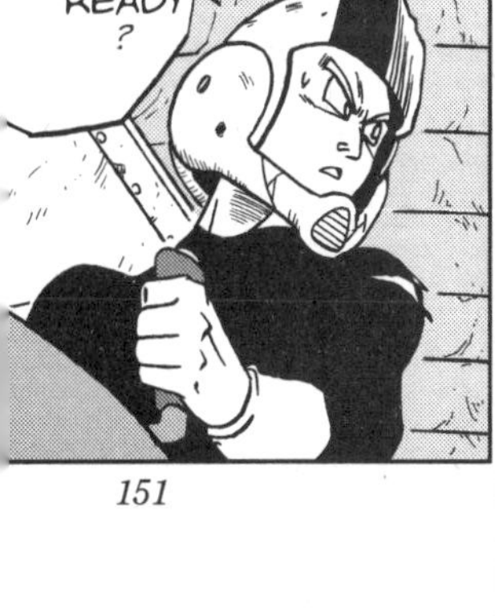
HM? REALLY ...?
HAS THE GALACTIC PATROL FOUND US AL-READY?

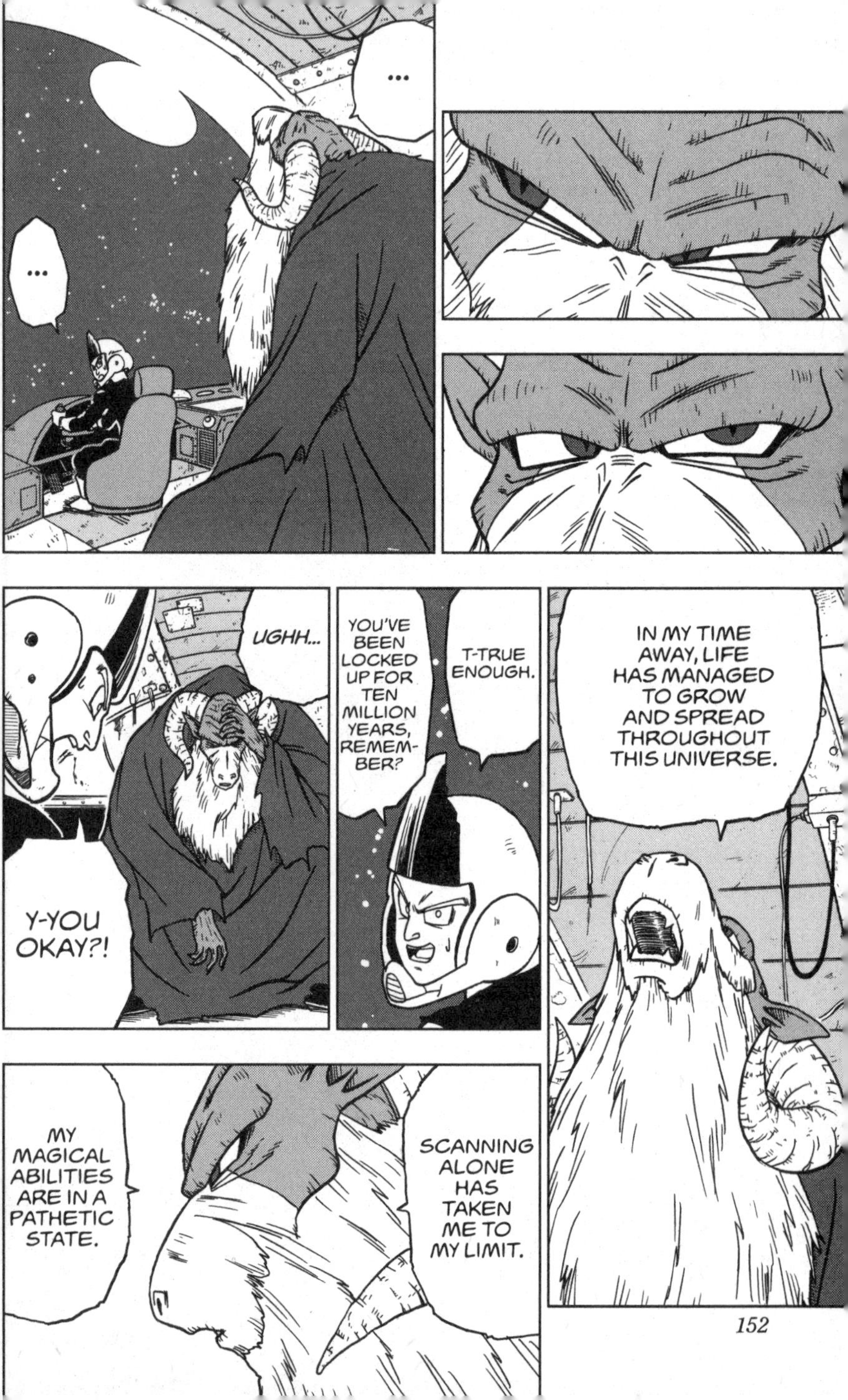
...
...
IN MY TIME AWAY, LIFE HAS MANAGED TO GROW AND SPREAD THROUGHOUT THIS UNIVERSE.
T-TRUE ENOUGH.
YOU'VE BEEN LOCKED UP FOR TEN MILLION YEARS, REMEMBER?
UGHH...
Y-YOU OKAY?!
SCANNING ALONE HAS TAKEN ME TO MY LIMIT.
MY MAGICAL ABILITIES ARE IN A PATHETIC STATE.

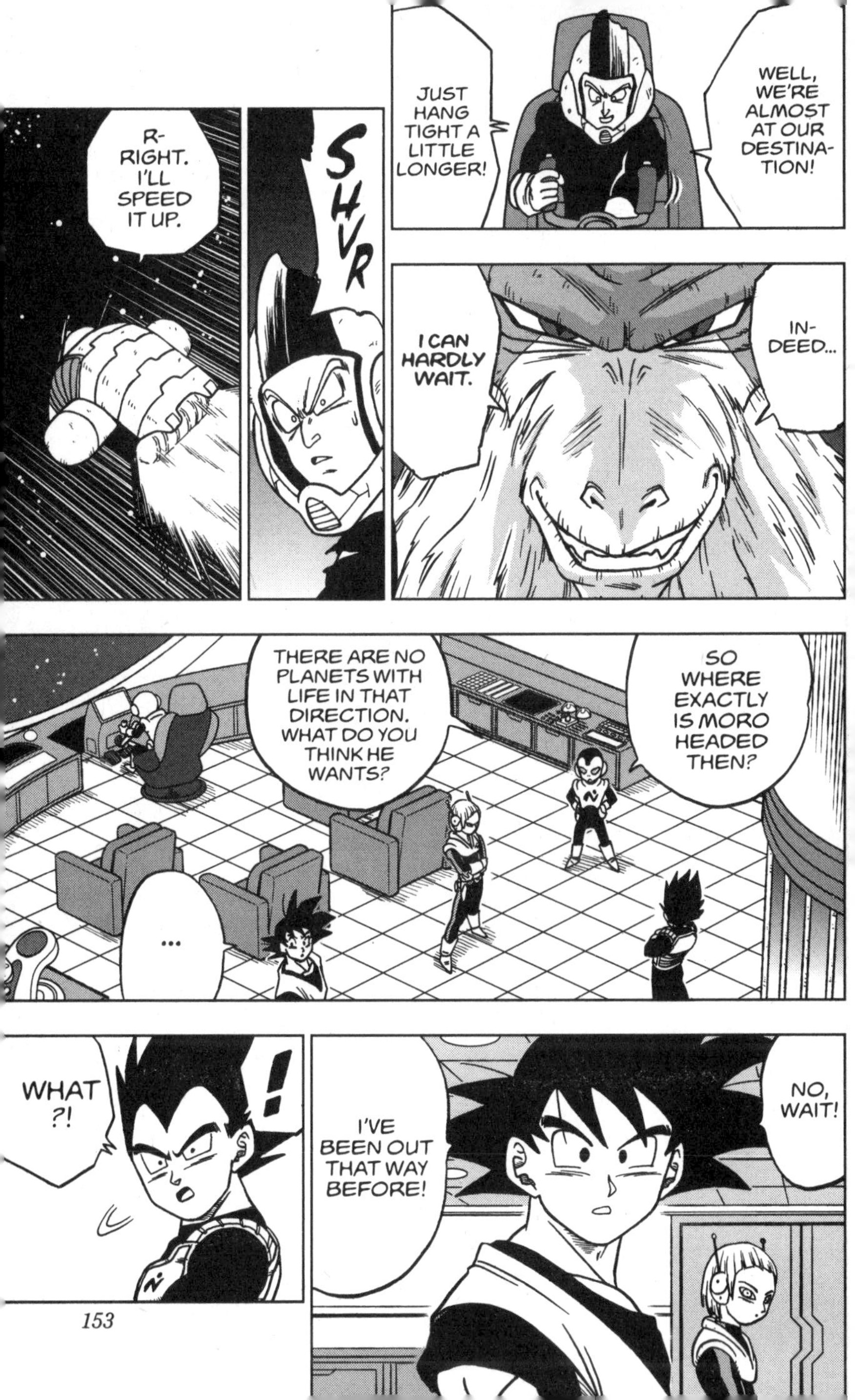
WELL, WE'RE ALMOST AT OUR DESTINATION!
JUST HANG TIGHT A LITTLE LONGER!
IN-DEED...
I CAN HARDLY WAIT.
SHVR
R-RIGHT. I'LL SPEED IT UP.
SO WHERE EXACTLY IS MORO HEADED THEN?
THERE ARE NO PLANETS WITH LIFE IN THAT DIRECTION. WHAT DO YOU THINK HE WANTS?
...
NO, WAIT!
I'VE BEEN OUT THAT WAY BEFORE!
!
WHAT?!

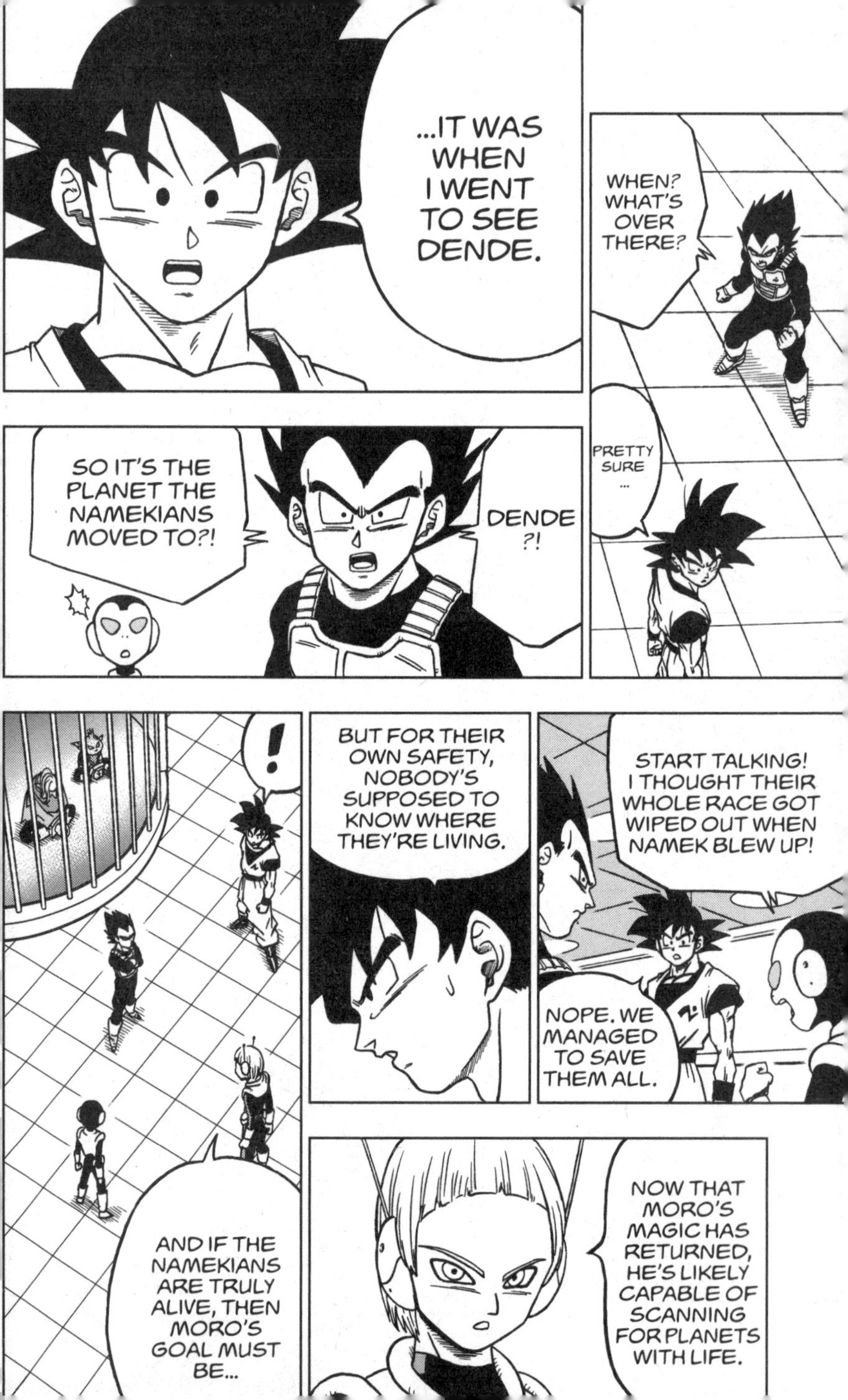
WHEN? WHAT'S OVER THERE?
PRETTY SURE ...
...IT WAS WHEN I WENT TO SEE DENDE.
DENDE ?!
SO IT'S THE PLANET THE NAMEKIANS MOVED TO?!
START TALKING! I THOUGHT THEIR WHOLE RACE GOT WIPED OUT WHEN NAMEK BLEW UP!
NOPE. WE MANAGED TO SAVE THEM ALL.
BUT FOR THEIR OWN SAFETY, NOBODY'S SUPPOSED TO KNOW WHERE THEY'RE LIVING.
NOW THAT MORO'S MAGIC HAS RETURNED, HE'S LIKELY CAPABLE OF SCANNING FOR PLANETS WITH LIFE.
!
AND IF THE NAMEKIANS ARE TRULY ALIVE, THEN MORO'S GOAL MUST BE...

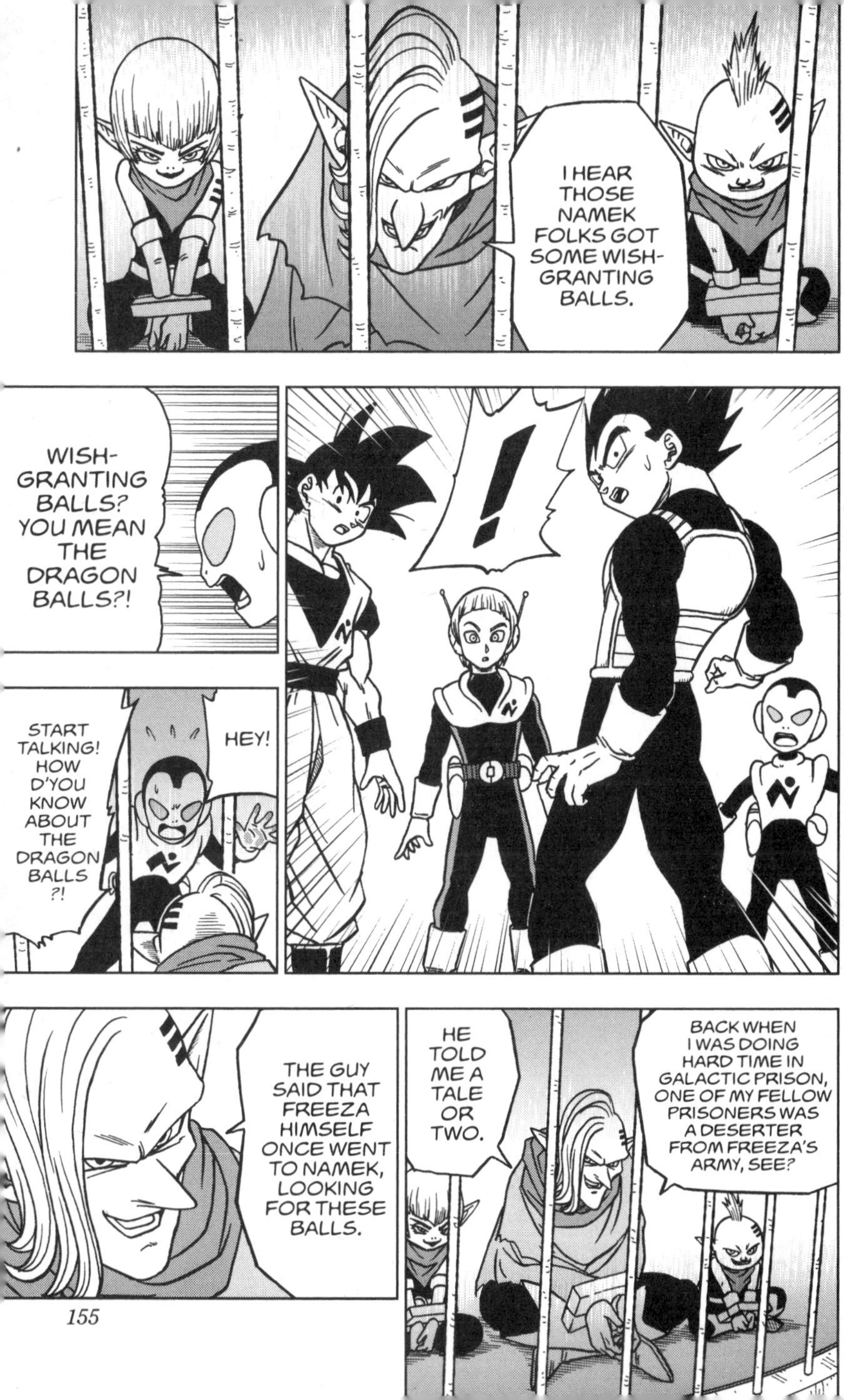
I HEAR THOSE NAMEK FOLKS GOT SOME WISH-GRANTING BALLS.
!
WISH-GRANTING BALLS? YOU MEAN THE DRAGON BALLS?!
HEY!
START TALKING! HOW D'YOU KNOW ABOUT THE DRAGON BALLS?!
BACK WHEN I WAS DOING HARD TIME IN GALACTIC PRISON, ONE OF MY FELLOW PRISONERS WAS A DESERTER FROM FREEZA'S ARMY, SEE?
HE TOLD ME A TALE OR TWO.
THE GUY SAID THAT FREEZA HIMSELF ONCE WENT TO NAMEK, LOOKING FOR THESE BALLS.

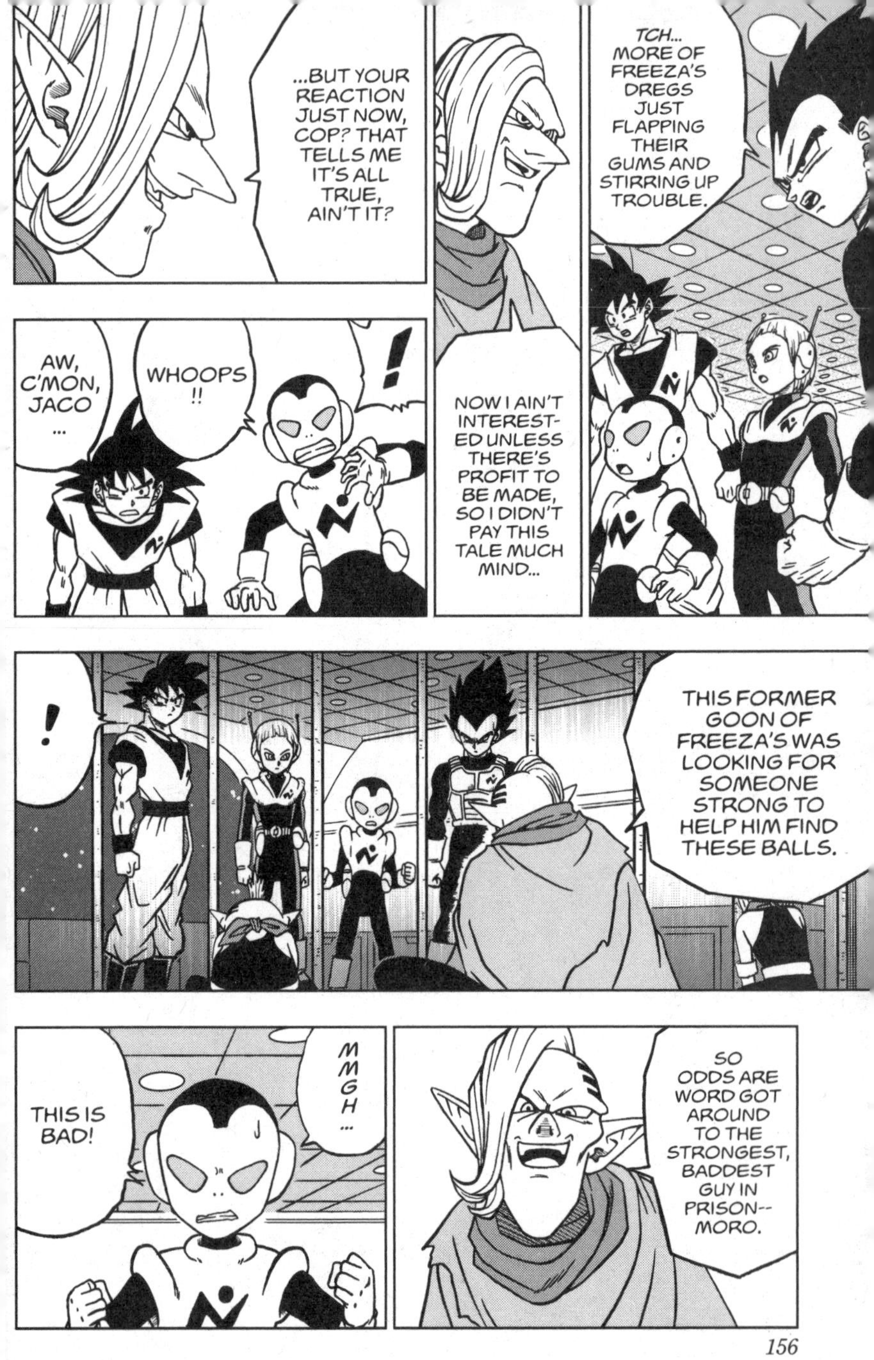
TCH... MORE OF FREEZA'S DREGS JUST FLAPPING THEIR GUMS AND STIRRING UP TROUBLE.
NOW I AIN'T INTEREST-ED UNLESS THERE'S PROFIT TO BE MADE, SO I DIDN'T PAY THIS TALE MUCH MIND...
...BUT YOUR REACTION JUST NOW, COP? THAT TELLS ME IT'S ALL TRUE, AIN'T IT?
!
WHOOPS !!
AW, C'MON, JACO ...
THIS FORMER GOON OF FREEZA'S WAS LOOKING FOR SOMEONE STRONG TO HELP HIM FIND THESE BALLS.
!
SO ODDS ARE WORD GOT AROUND TO THE STRONGEST, BADDEST GUY IN PRISON-- MORO.
MMGH ...
THIS IS BAD!

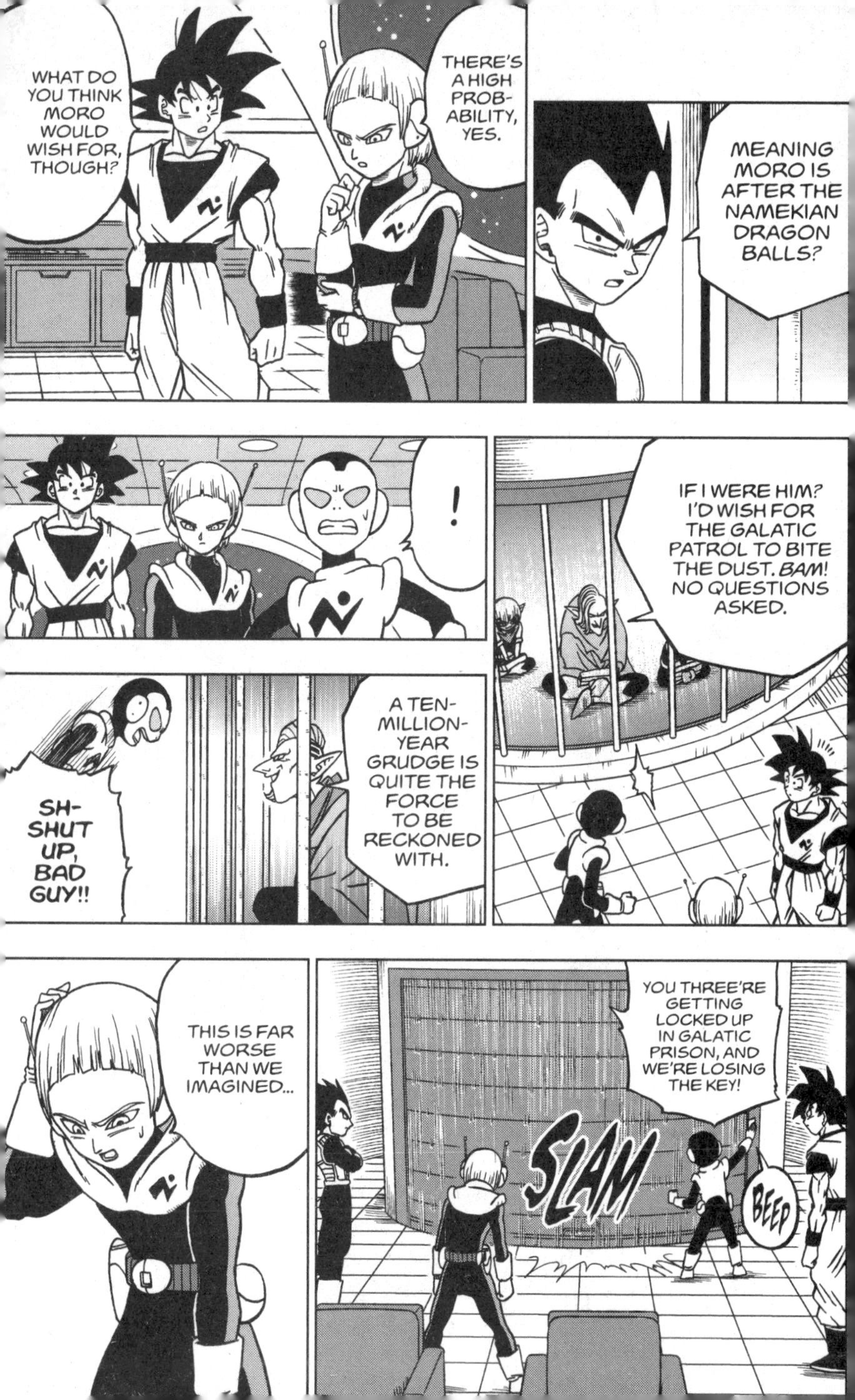

MEANING MORO IS AFTER THE NAMEKIAN DRAGON BALLS?
THERE'S A HIGH PROBABILITY, YES.
WHAT DO YOU THINK MORO WOULD WISH FOR, THOUGH?
IF I WERE HIM? I'D WISH FOR THE GALATIC PATROL TO BITE THE DUST. *BAM*! NO QUESTIONS ASKED.
!
A TEN-MILLION-YEAR GRUDGE IS QUITE THE FORCE TO BE RECKONED WITH.
SH-SHUT UP, BAD GUY!!
YOU THREE'RE GETTING LOCKED UP IN GALATIC PRISON, AND WE'RE LOSING THE KEY!
SLAM
BEEP
THIS IS FAR WORSE THAN WE IMAGINED...

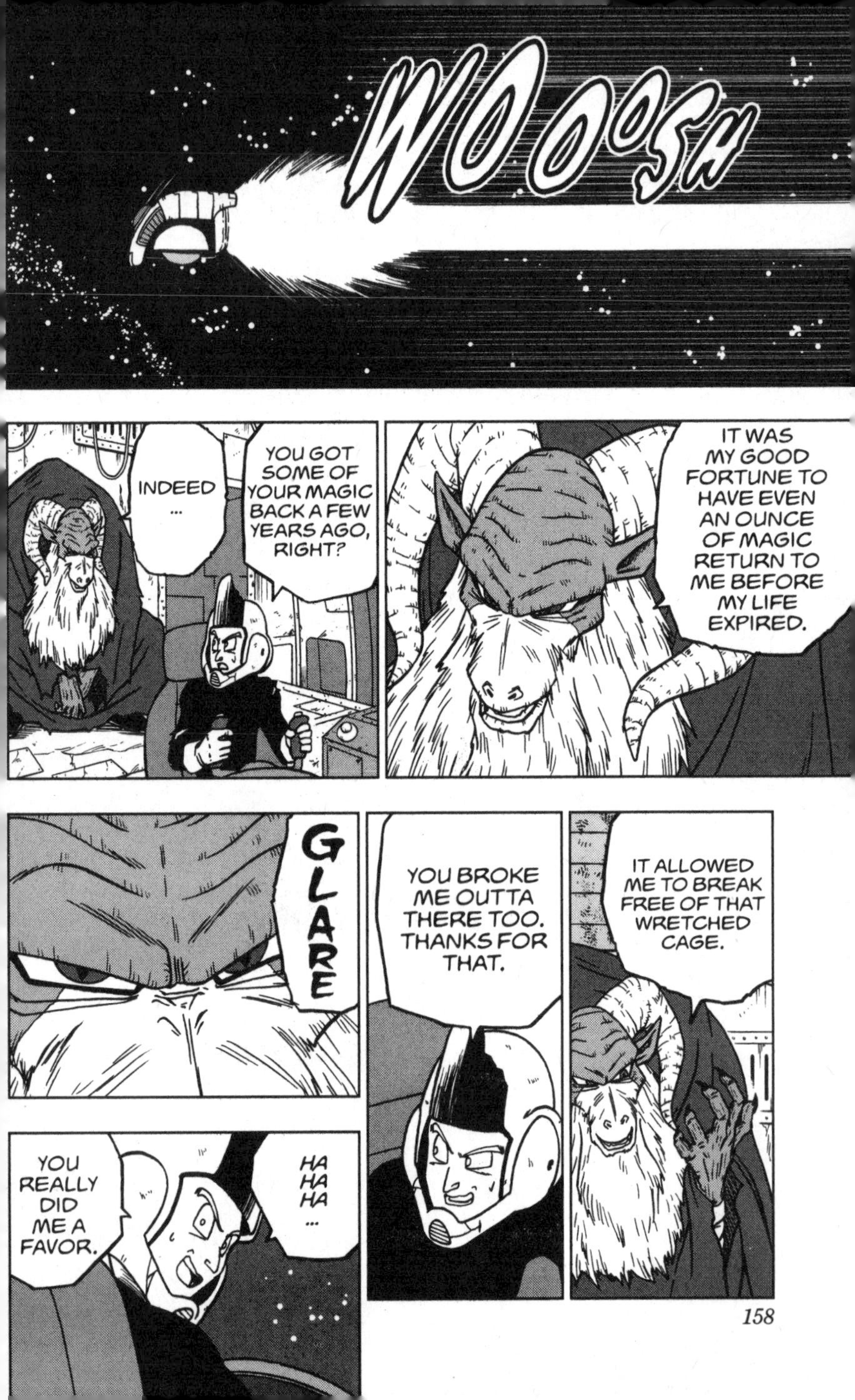
WOOOSH
YOU GOT SOME OF YOUR MAGIC BACK A FEW YEARS AGO, RIGHT?
INDEED ...
IT WAS MY GOOD FORTUNE TO HAVE EVEN AN OUNCE OF MAGIC RETURN TO ME BEFORE MY LIFE EXPIRED.
IT ALLOWED ME TO BREAK FREE OF THAT WRETCHED CAGE.
YOU BROKE ME OUTTA THERE TOO. THANKS FOR THAT.
GLARE
HA HA HA ...
YOU REALLY DID ME A FAVOR.

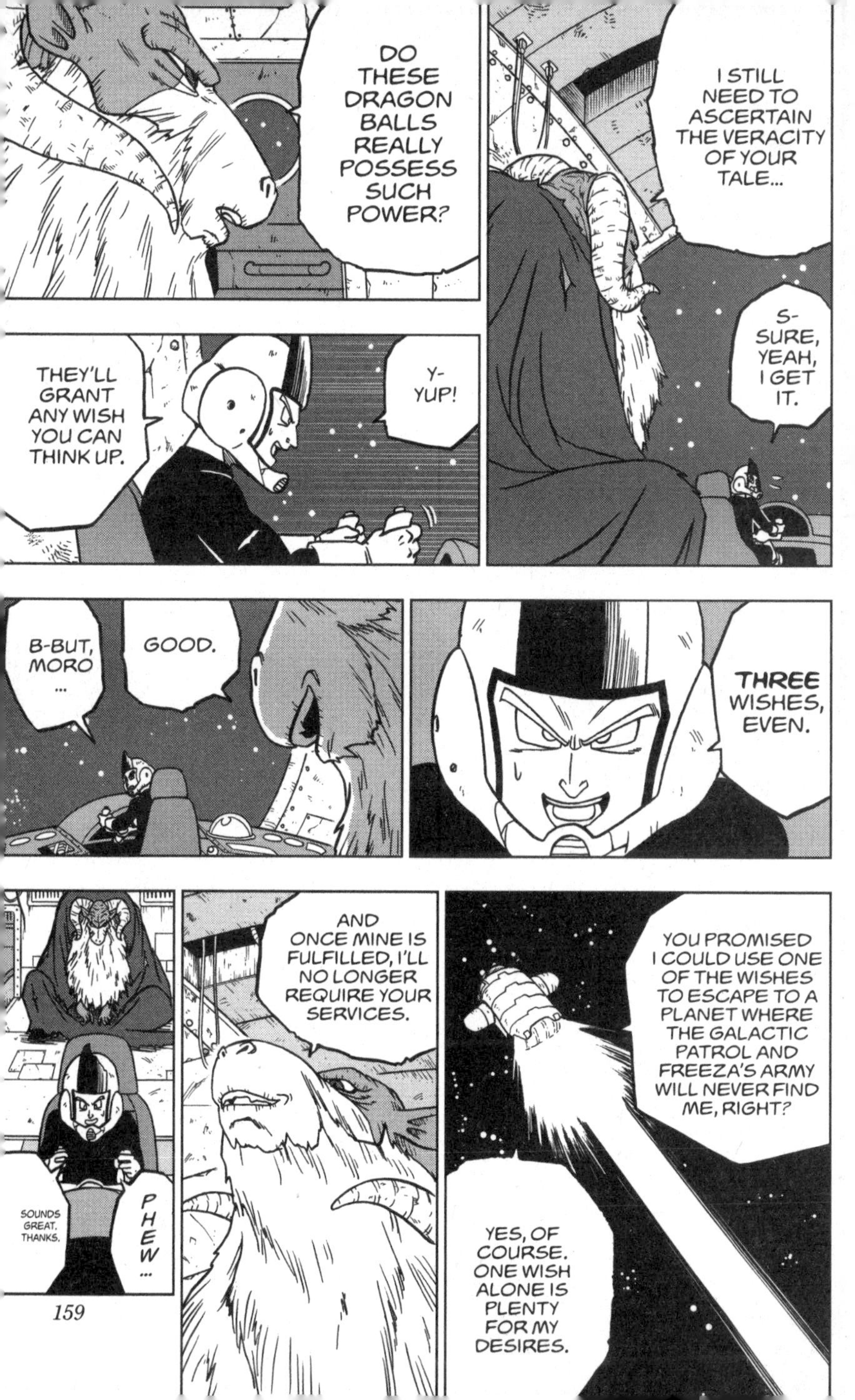

I STILL NEED TO ASCERTAIN THE VERACITY OF YOUR TALE...
S-SURE, YEAH, I GET IT.
DO THESE DRAGON BALLS REALLY POSSESS SUCH POWER?
Y-YUP!
THEY'LL GRANT ANY WISH YOU CAN THINK UP.
THREE WISHES, EVEN.
GOOD.
B-BUT, MORO...
YOU PROMISED I COULD USE ONE OF THE WISHES TO ESCAPE TO A PLANET WHERE THE GALACTIC PATROL AND FREEZA'S ARMY WILL NEVER FIND ME, RIGHT?
YES, OF COURSE. ONE WISH ALONE IS PLENTY FOR MY DESIRES.
AND ONCE MINE IS FULFILLED, I'LL NO LONGER REQUIRE YOUR SERVICES.
PHEW...
SOUNDS GREAT. THANKS.

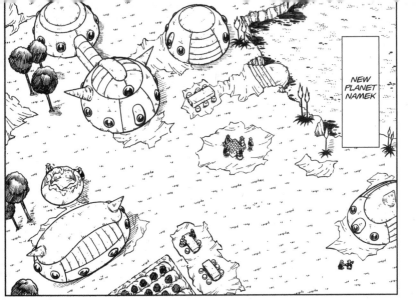

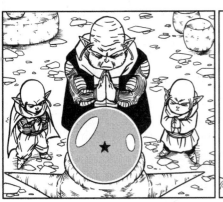

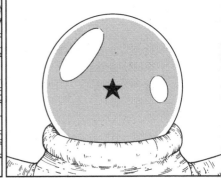

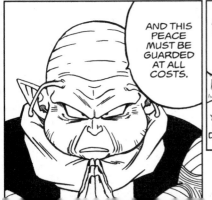

NEW PLANET NAMEK
IT IS THANKS TO THE PROTECTION OF THE GODS THAT WE MAY LIVE IN PEACE.
WE MUSTN'T FORGET TO BE GRATE-FUL.
YES, EL-DER.
AND THIS PEACE MUST BE GUARDED AT ALL COSTS.

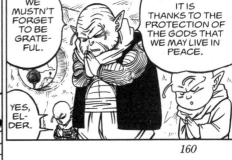

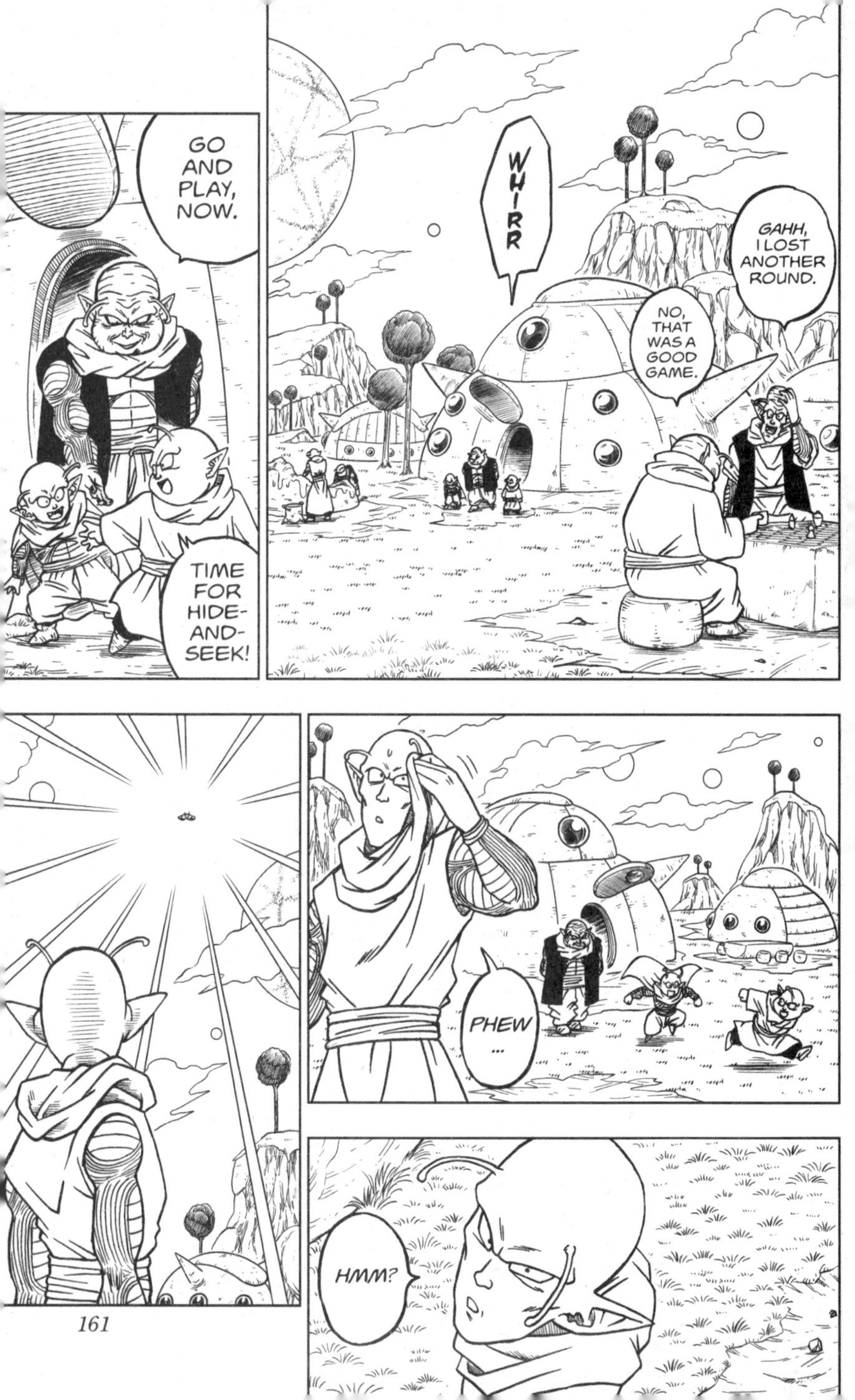
WHIRR
GAHH, I LOST ANOTHER ROUND.
NO, THAT WAS A GOOD GAME.
GO AND PLAY, NOW.
TIME FOR HIDE-AND-SEEK!
PHEW...
HMM?

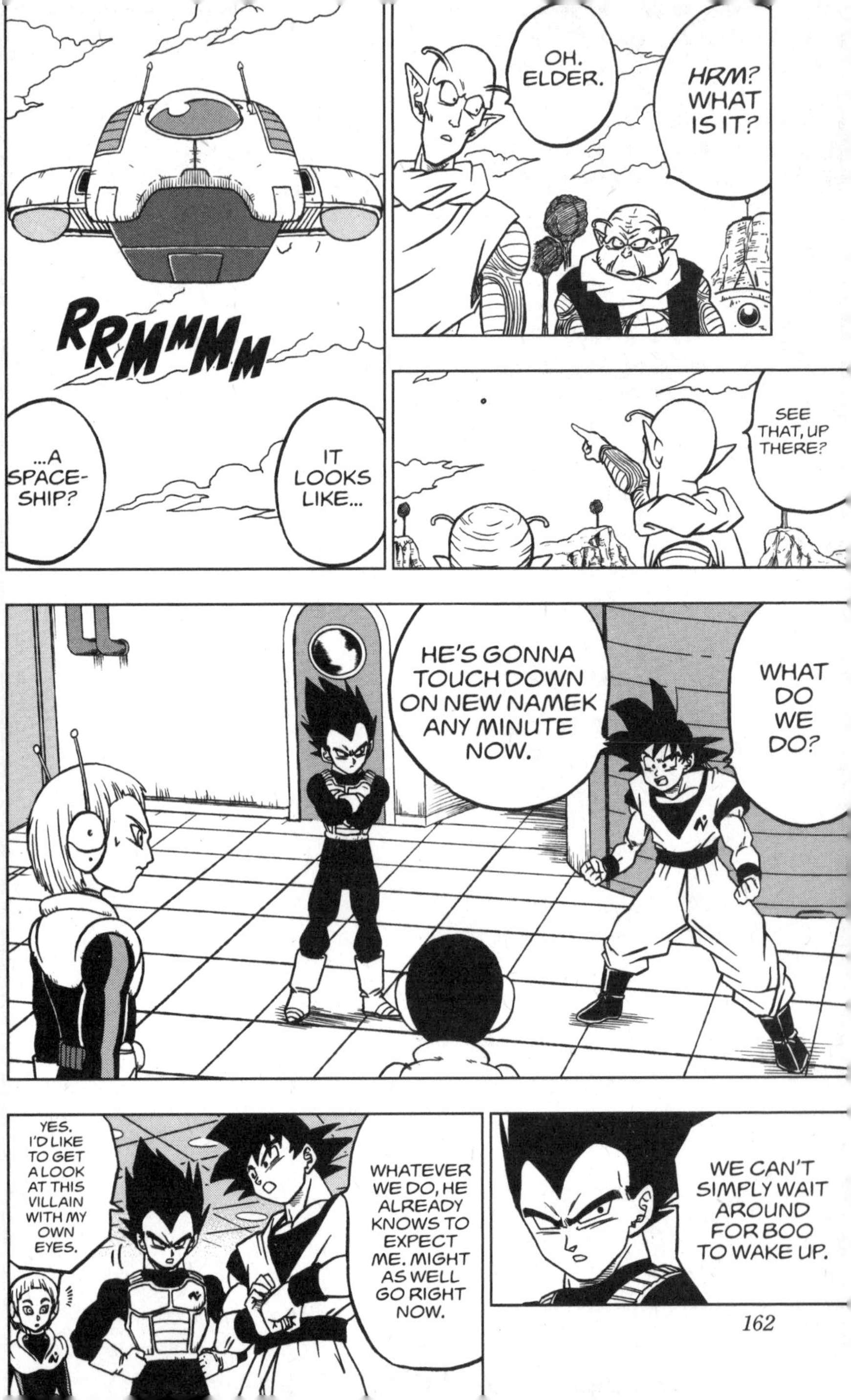
HRM? WHAT IS IT?
OH. ELDER.
SEE THAT, UP THERE?
RRMMMMM
IT LOOKS LIKE...
...A SPACE-SHIP?
WHAT DO WE DO?
HE'S GONNA TOUCH DOWN ON NEW NAMEK ANY MINUTE NOW.
WE CAN'T SIMPLY WAIT AROUND FOR BOO TO WAKE UP.
WHATEVER WE DO, HE ALREADY KNOWS TO EXPECT ME. MIGHT AS WELL GO RIGHT NOW.
YES. I'D LIKE TO GET A LOOK AT THIS VILLAIN WITH MY OWN EYES.

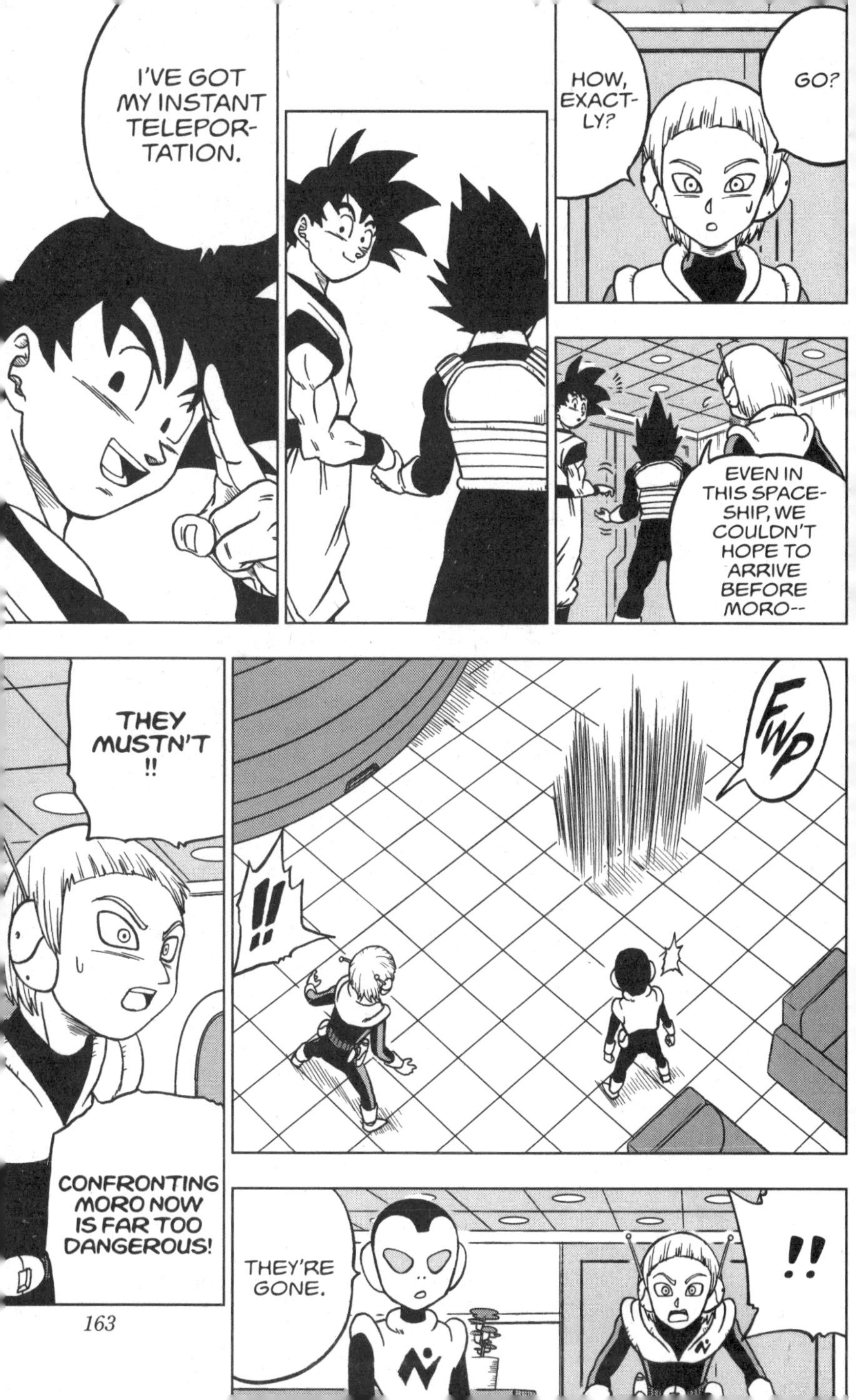
GO?
HOW, EXACT-LY?
EVEN IN THIS SPACE-SHIP, WE COULDN'T HOPE TO ARRIVE BEFORE MORO--
I'VE GOT MY INSTANT TELEPOR-TATION.
FWP
!!
!!
THEY'RE GONE.
THEY MUSTN'T!!
CONFRONTING MORO NOW IS FAR TOO DANGEROUS!

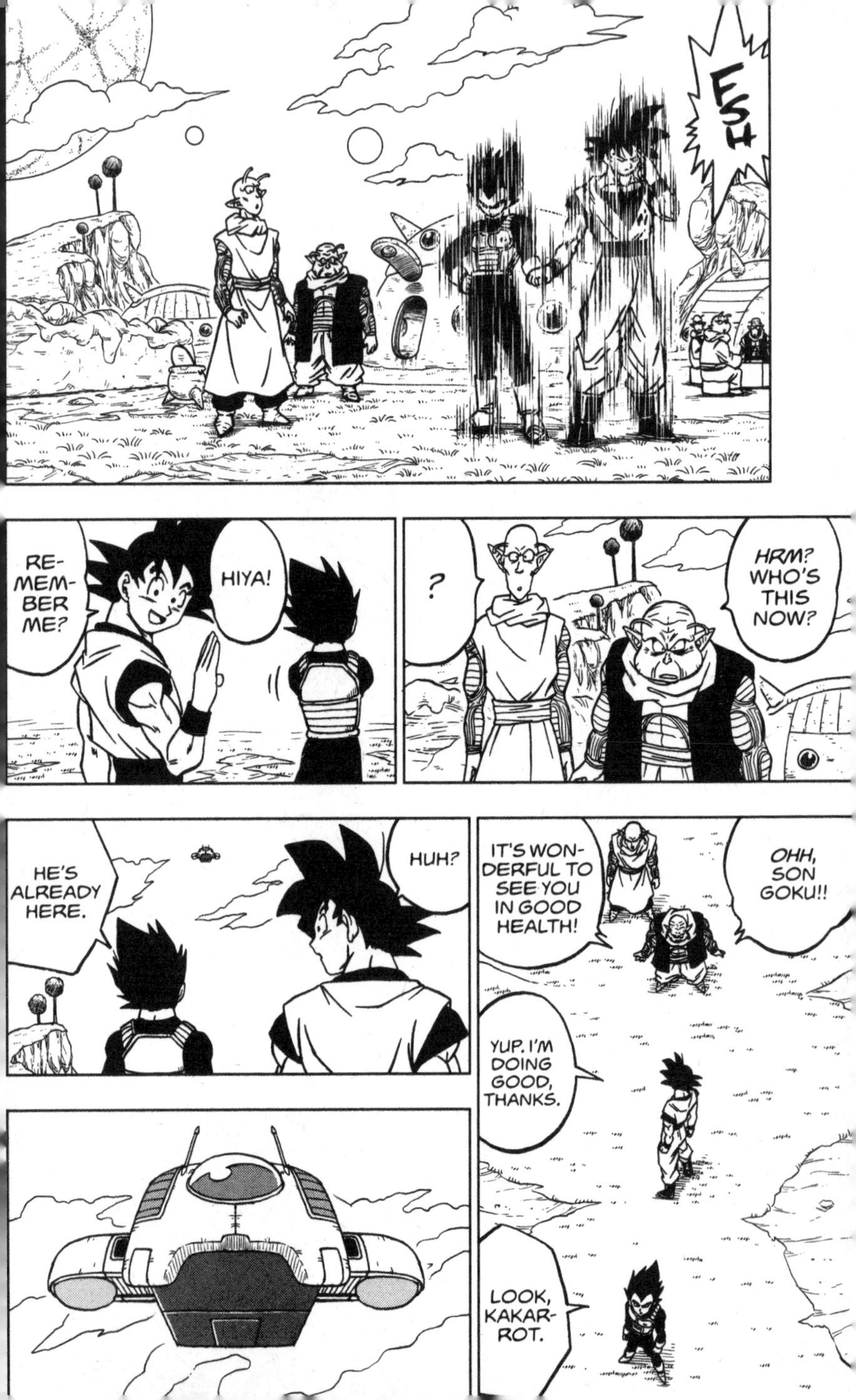
ESH
HRM? WHO'S THIS NOW?
?
HIYA!
REMEMBER ME?
OHH, SON GOKU!!
IT'S WONDERFUL TO SEE YOU IN GOOD HEALTH!
YUP. I'M DOING GOOD, THANKS.
LOOK, KAKARROT.
HUH?
HE'S ALREADY HERE.

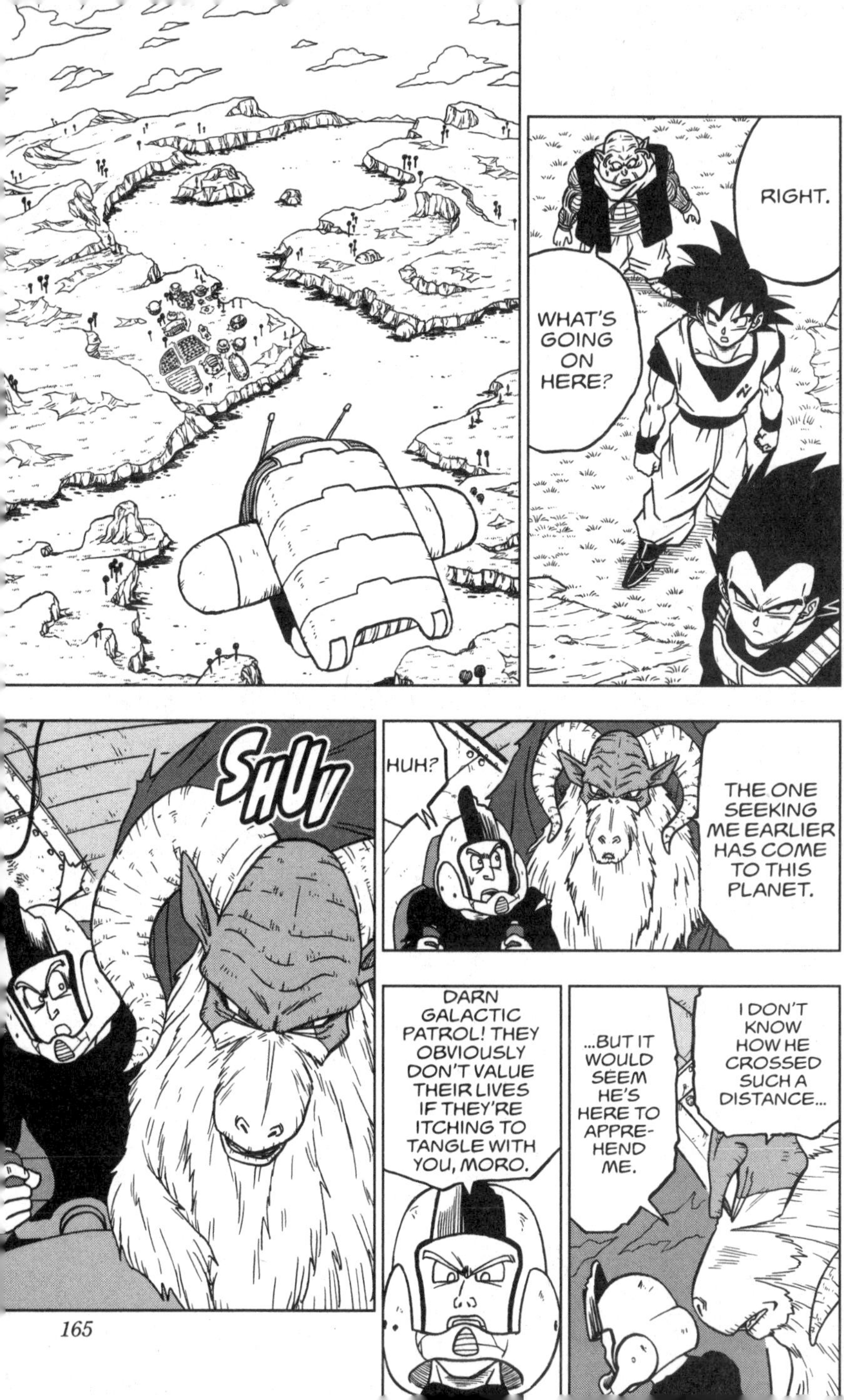

RIGHT.
WHAT'S GOING ON HERE?
THE ONE SEEKING ME EARLIER HAS COME TO THIS PLANET.
HUH?
I DON'T KNOW HOW HE CROSSED SUCH A DISTANCE...
...BUT IT WOULD SEEM HE'S HERE TO APPRE-HEND ME.
DARN GALACTIC PATROL! THEY OBVIOUSLY DON'T VALUE THEIR LIVES IF THEY'RE ITCHING TO TANGLE WITH YOU, MORO.
SHUV

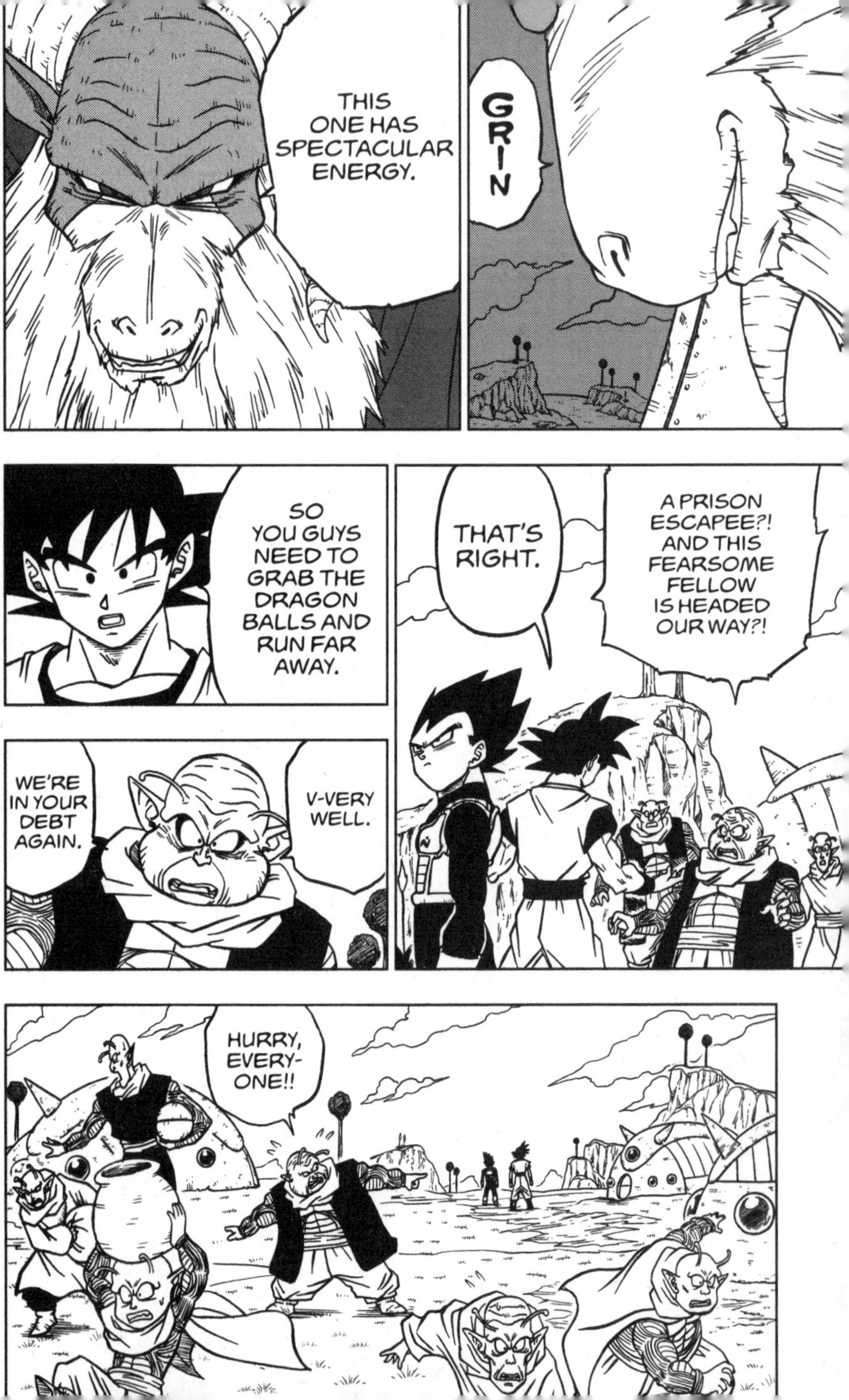
GRIN
THIS ONE HAS SPECTACULAR ENERGY.
A PRISON ESCAPEE?! AND THIS FEARSOME FELLOW IS HEADED OUR WAY?!
THAT'S RIGHT.
SO YOU GUYS NEED TO GRAB THE DRAGON BALLS AND RUN FAR AWAY.
V-VERY WELL.
WE'RE IN YOUR DEBT AGAIN.
HURRY, EVERY-ONE!!

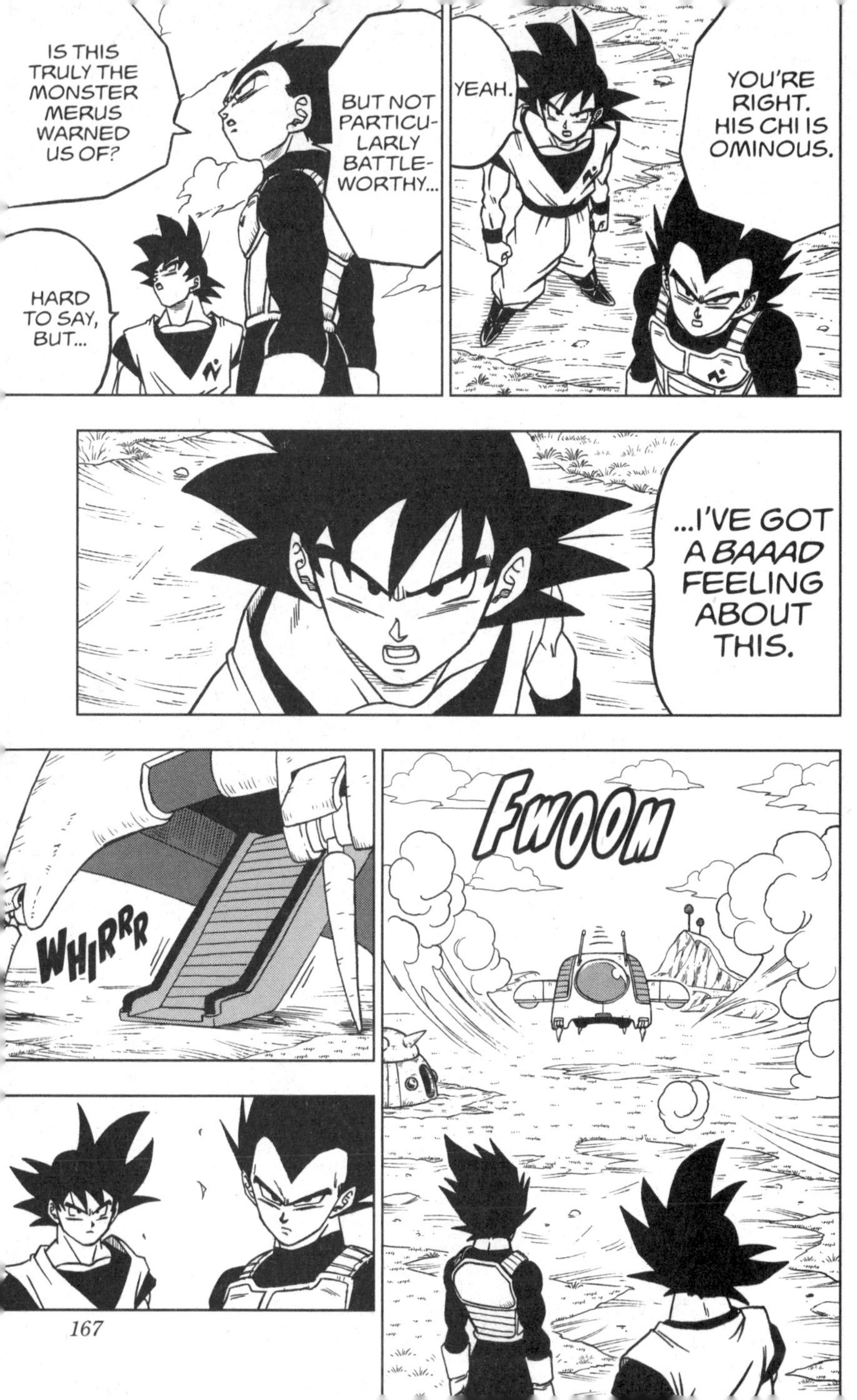
YOU'RE RIGHT. HIS CHI IS OMINOUS.
YEAH.
IS THIS TRULY THE MONSTER MERUS WARNED US OF?
BUT NOT PARTICULARLY BATTLE-WORTHY...
HARD TO SAY, BUT...
...I'VE GOT A *BAAAD* FEELING ABOUT THIS.
FWOOM
WHIRRR

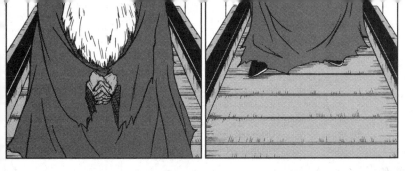

168

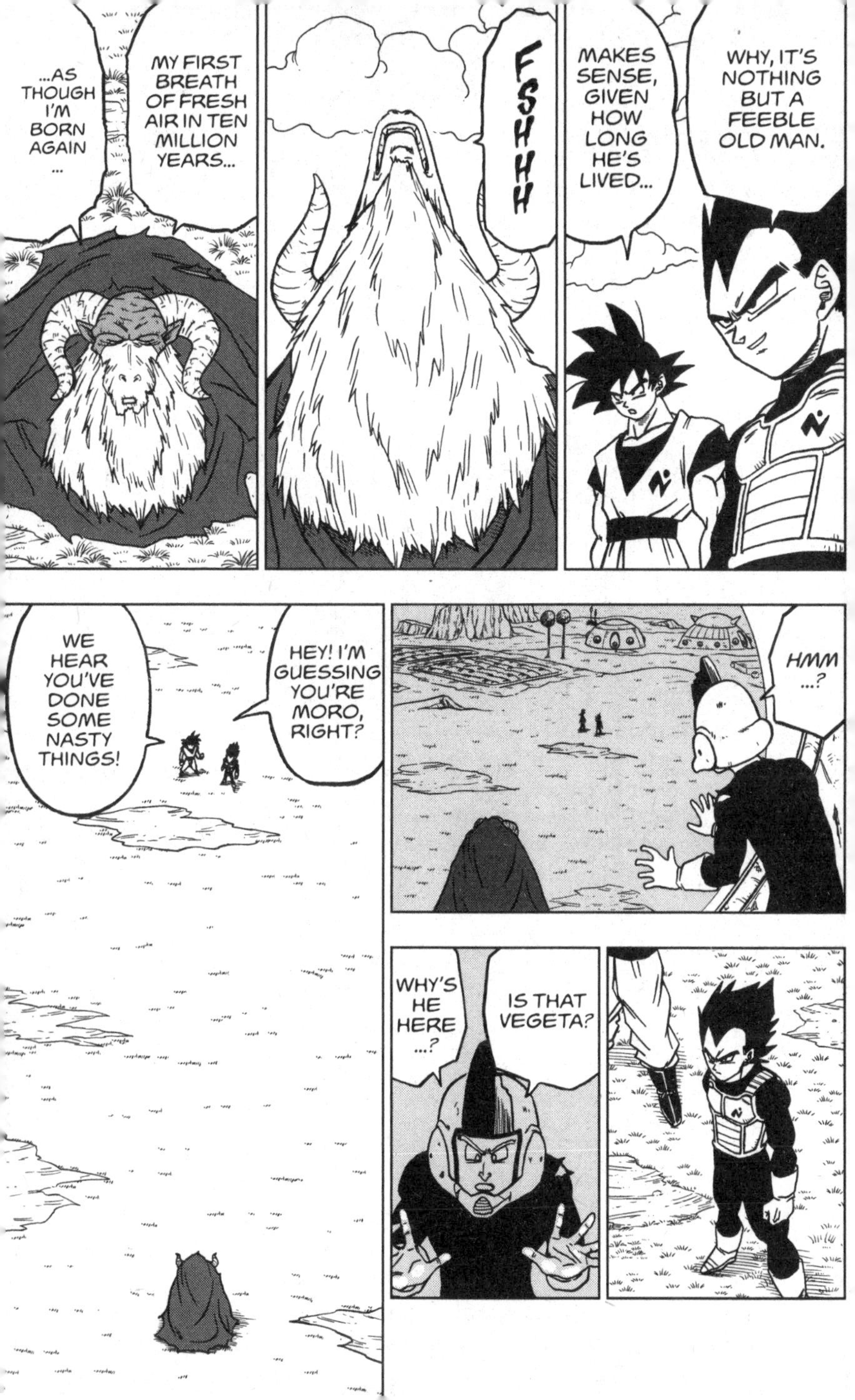
WHY, IT'S NOTHING BUT A FEEBLE OLD MAN.
MAKES SENSE, GIVEN HOW LONG HE'S LIVED...
FSHHH
MY FIRST BREATH OF FRESH AIR IN TEN MILLION YEARS...
...AS THOUGH I'M BORN AGAIN...
HMM...?
IS THAT VEGETA?
WHY'S HE HERE...?
HEY! I'M GUESSING YOU'RE MORO, RIGHT?
WE HEAR YOU'VE DONE SOME NASTY THINGS!

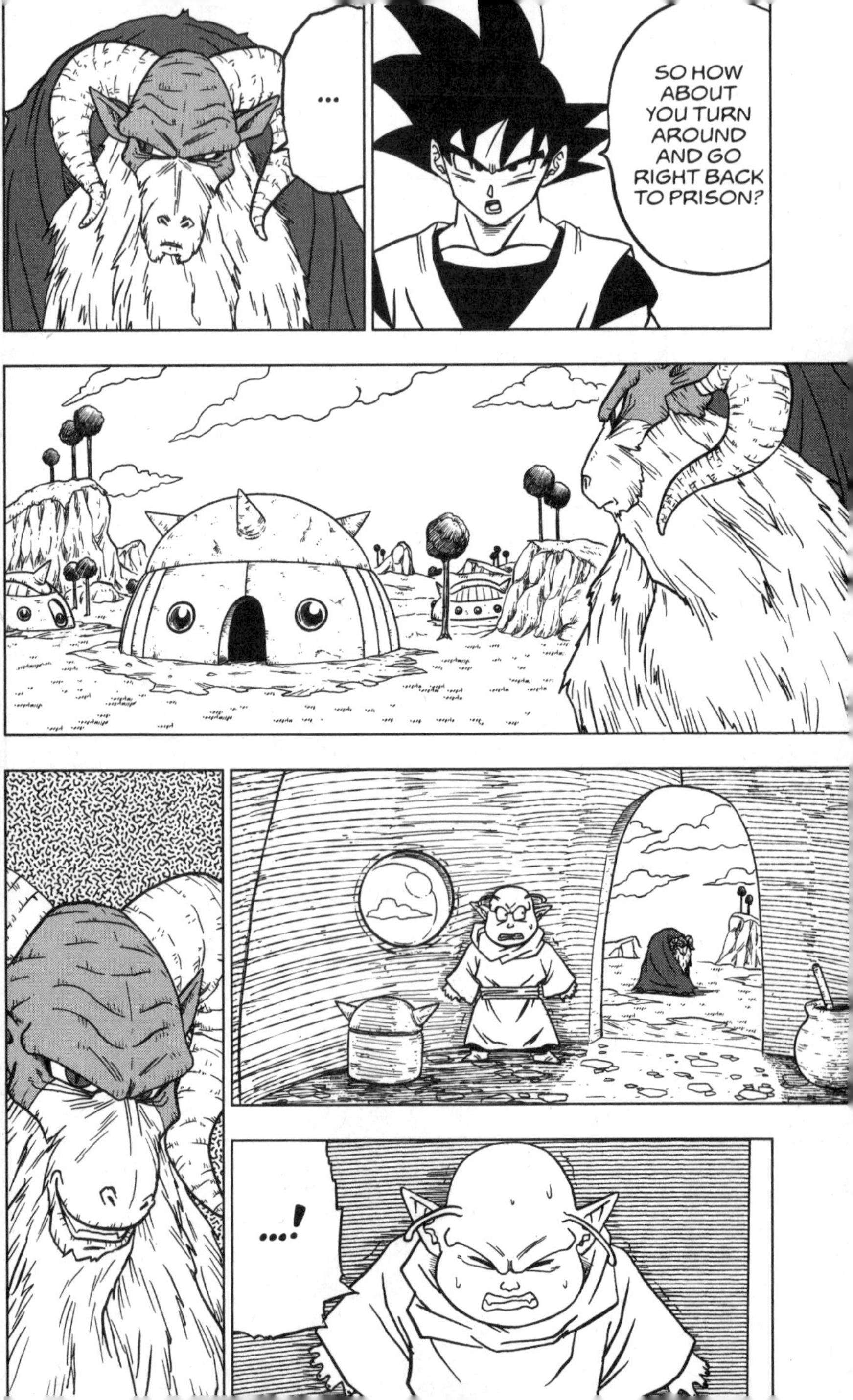
SO HOW ABOUT YOU TURN AROUND AND GO RIGHT BACK TO PRISON?
...
...!

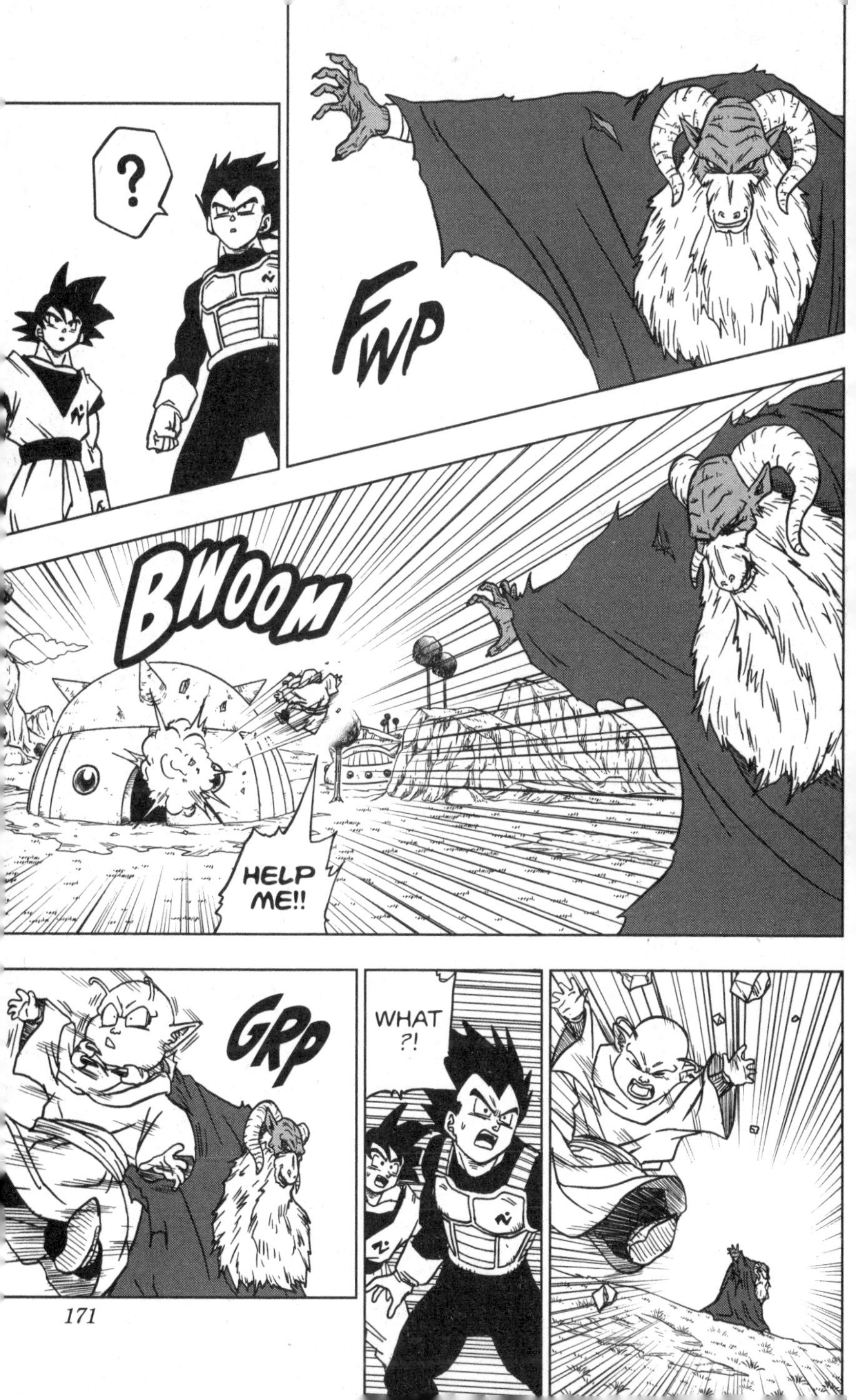
FWP
?
BWOOM
HELP ME!!
WHAT ?!
GRP

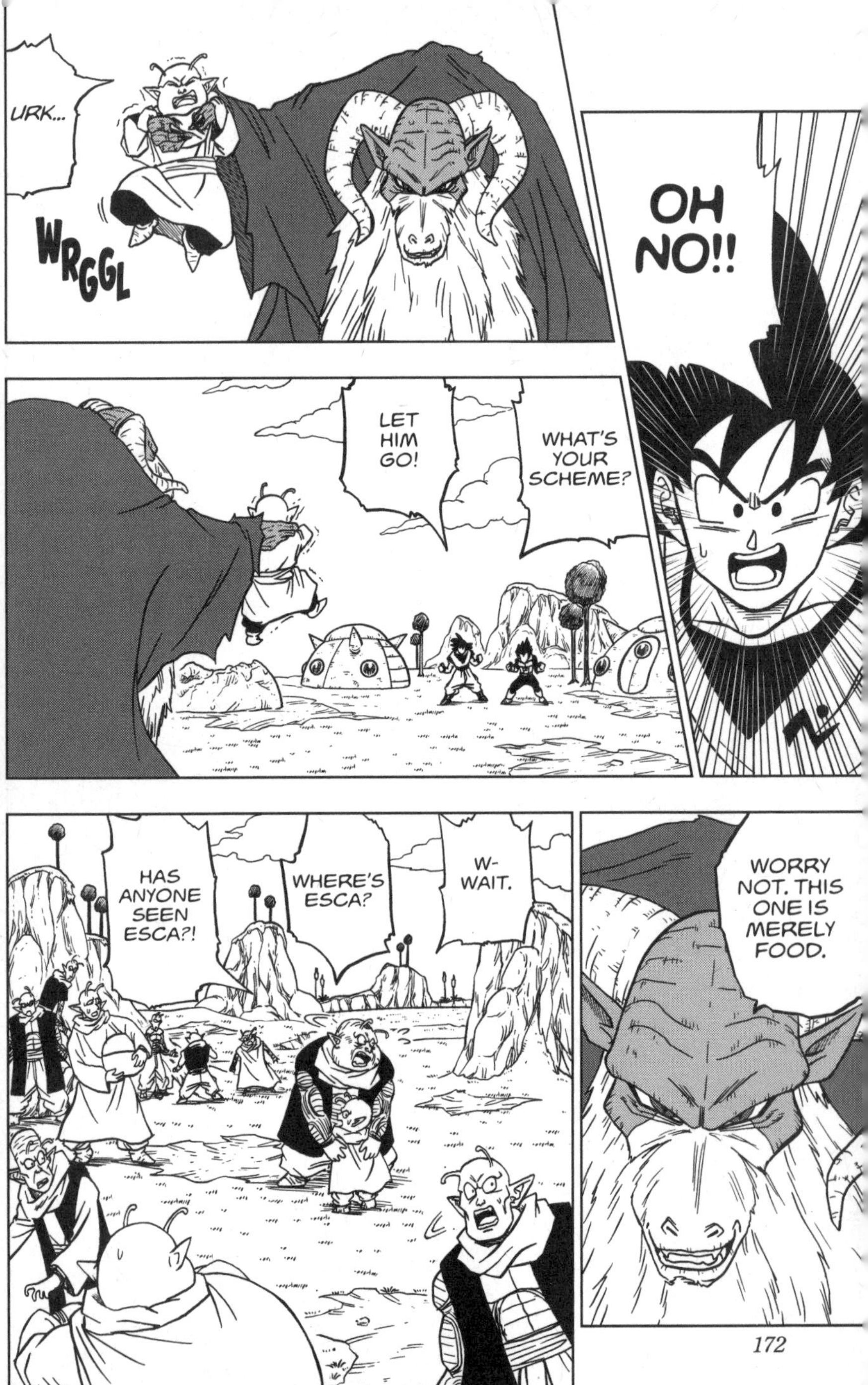
OH NO!!
URK...
WRGGL
WHAT'S YOUR SCHEME?
LET HIM GO!
WORRY NOT. THIS ONE IS MERELY FOOD.
W-WAIT.
WHERE'S ESCA?
HAS ANYONE SEEN ESCA?!

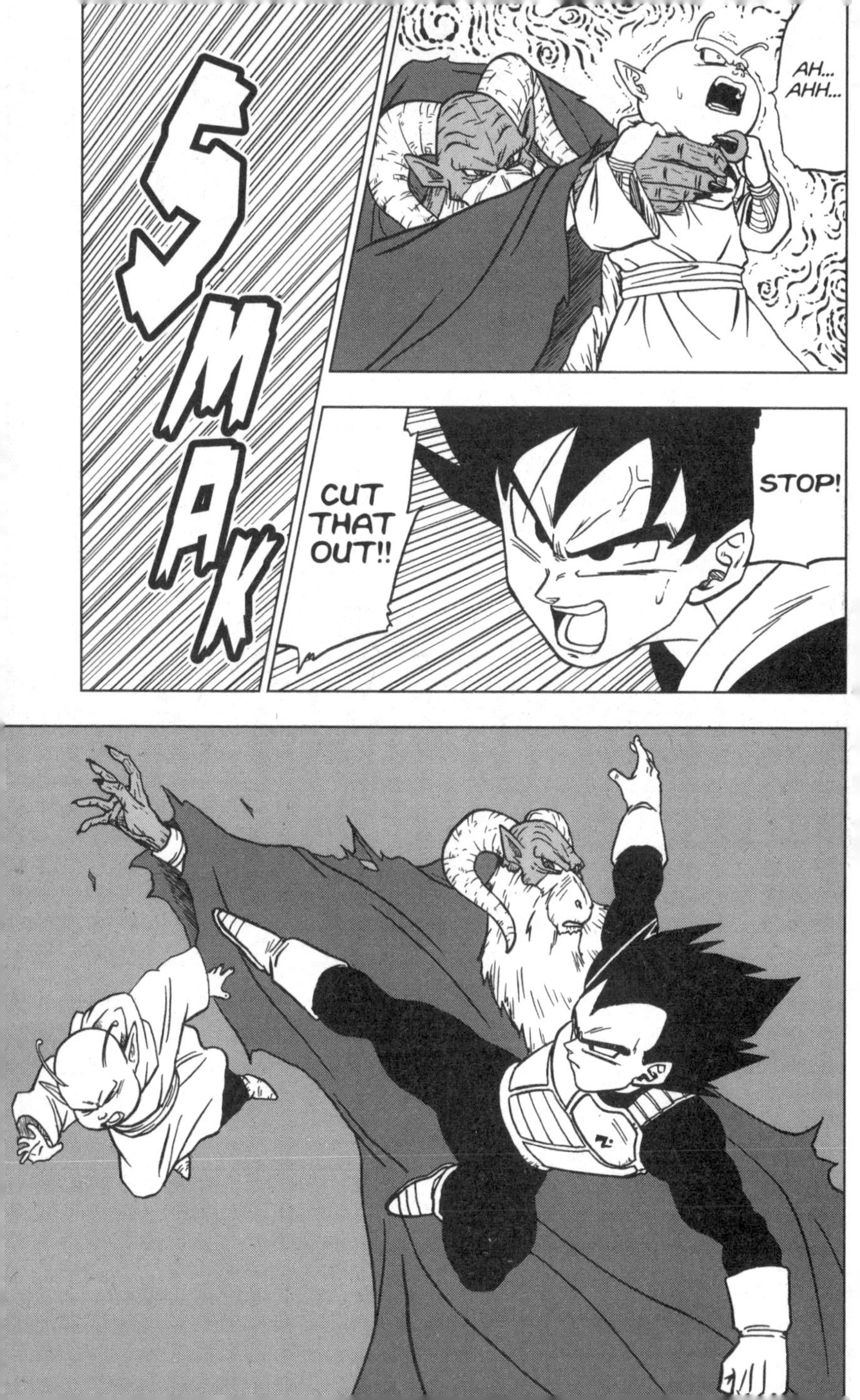
AH... AHH...
STOP!
CUT THAT OUT!!
SMAK

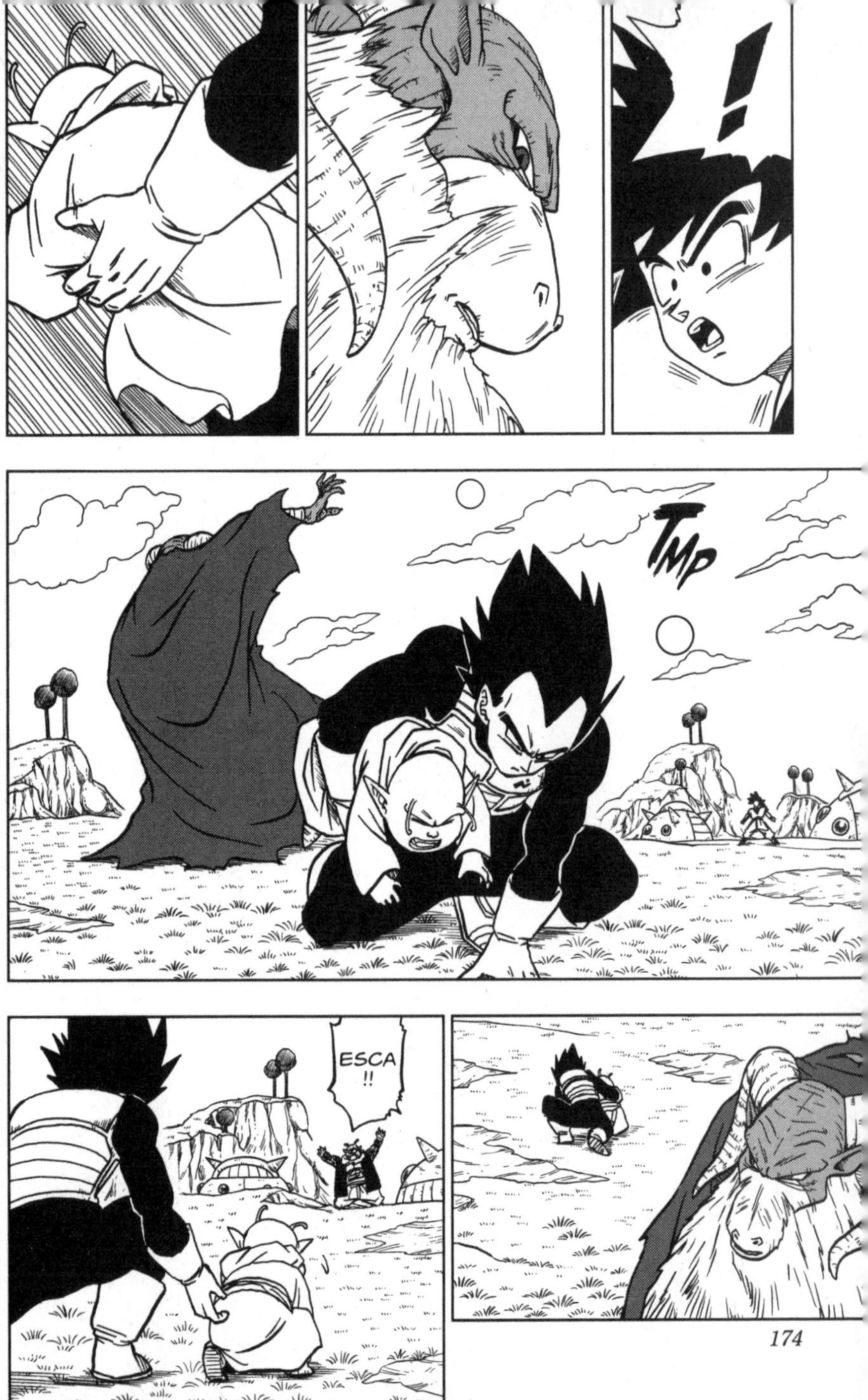
!
TMP
ESCA
!!

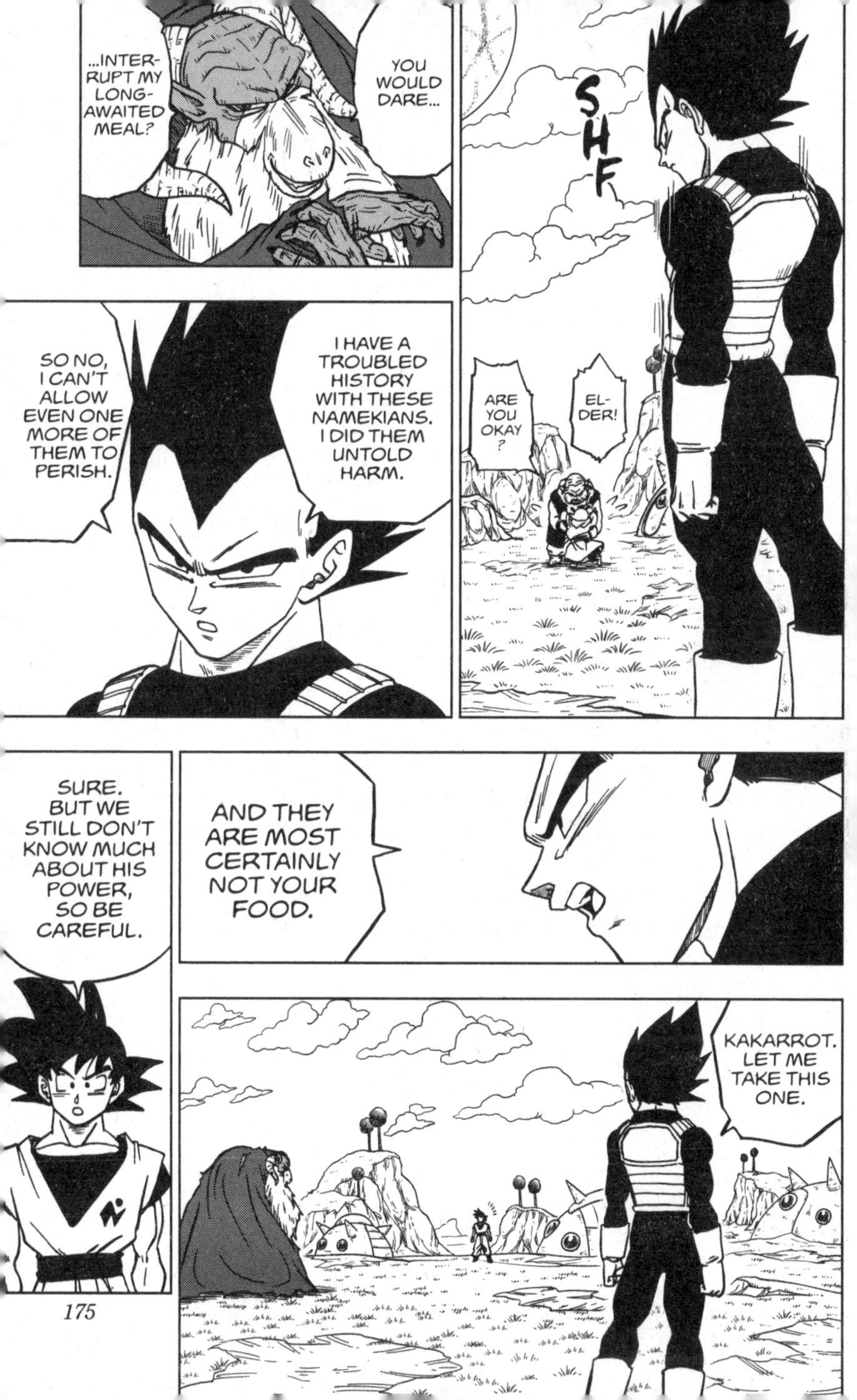

SHF
EL-DER!
ARE YOU OKAY?
YOU WOULD DARE...
...INTERRUPT MY LONG-AWAITED MEAL?
I HAVE A TROUBLED HISTORY WITH THESE NAMEKIANS. I DID THEM UNTOLD HARM.
SO NO, I CAN'T ALLOW EVEN ONE MORE OF THEM TO PERISH.
AND THEY ARE MOST CERTAINLY NOT YOUR FOOD.
KAKARROT. LET ME TAKE THIS ONE.
SURE. BUT WE STILL DON'T KNOW MUCH ABOUT HIS POWER, SO BE CAREFUL.

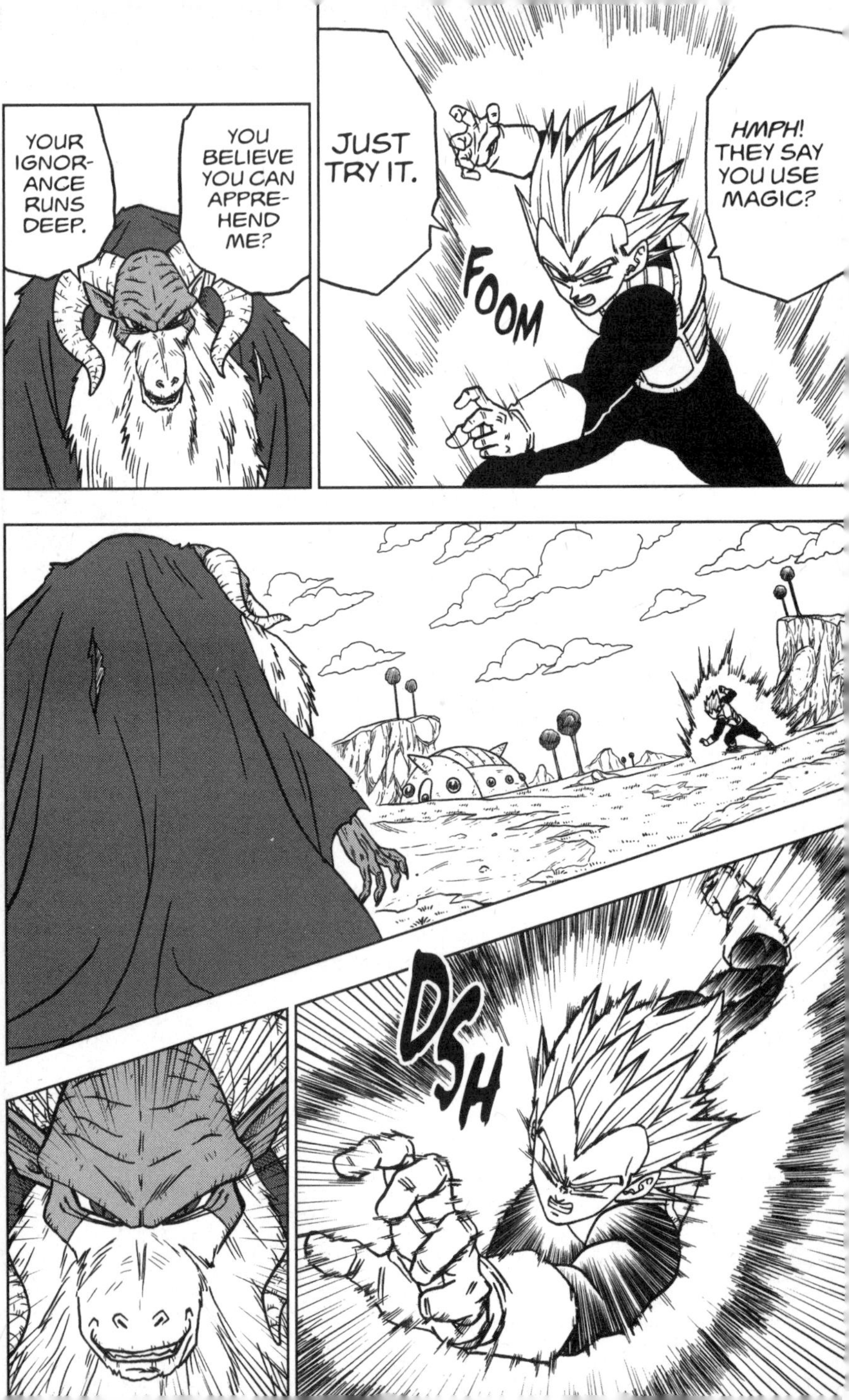
HMPH! THEY SAY YOU USE MAGIC?
JUST TRY IT.
FOOM
YOU BELIEVE YOU CAN APPREHEND ME?
YOUR IGNORANCE RUNS DEEP.
DSH

WHF

ZOOSH

FWOOSH

WHF

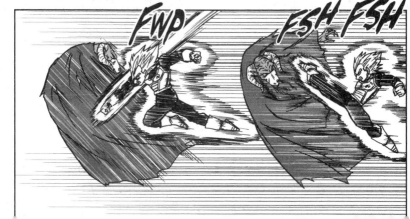

FWP

FSH FSH

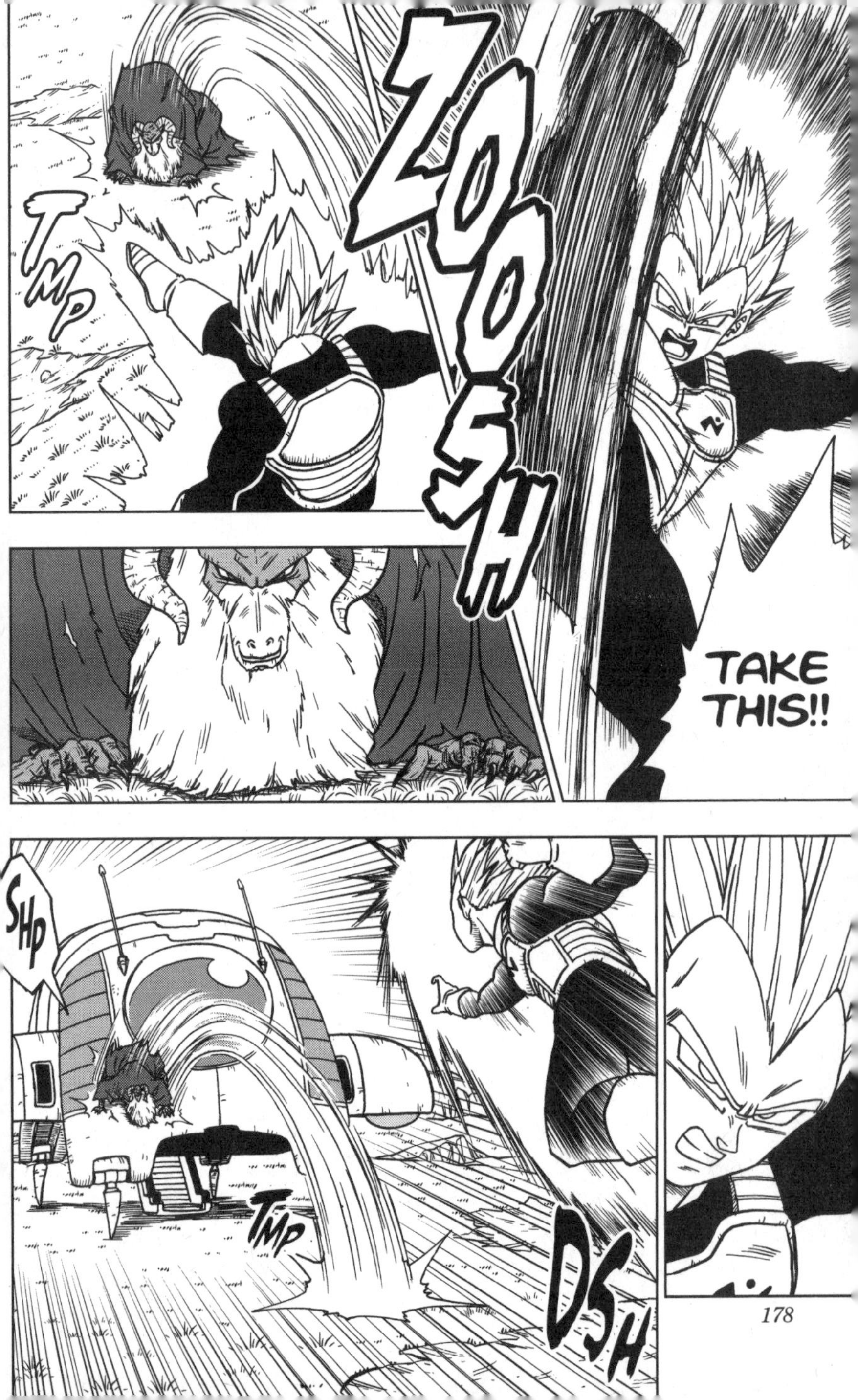
TAKE THIS!!
ZOOOSH
TMP
SHP
TMP
DSH

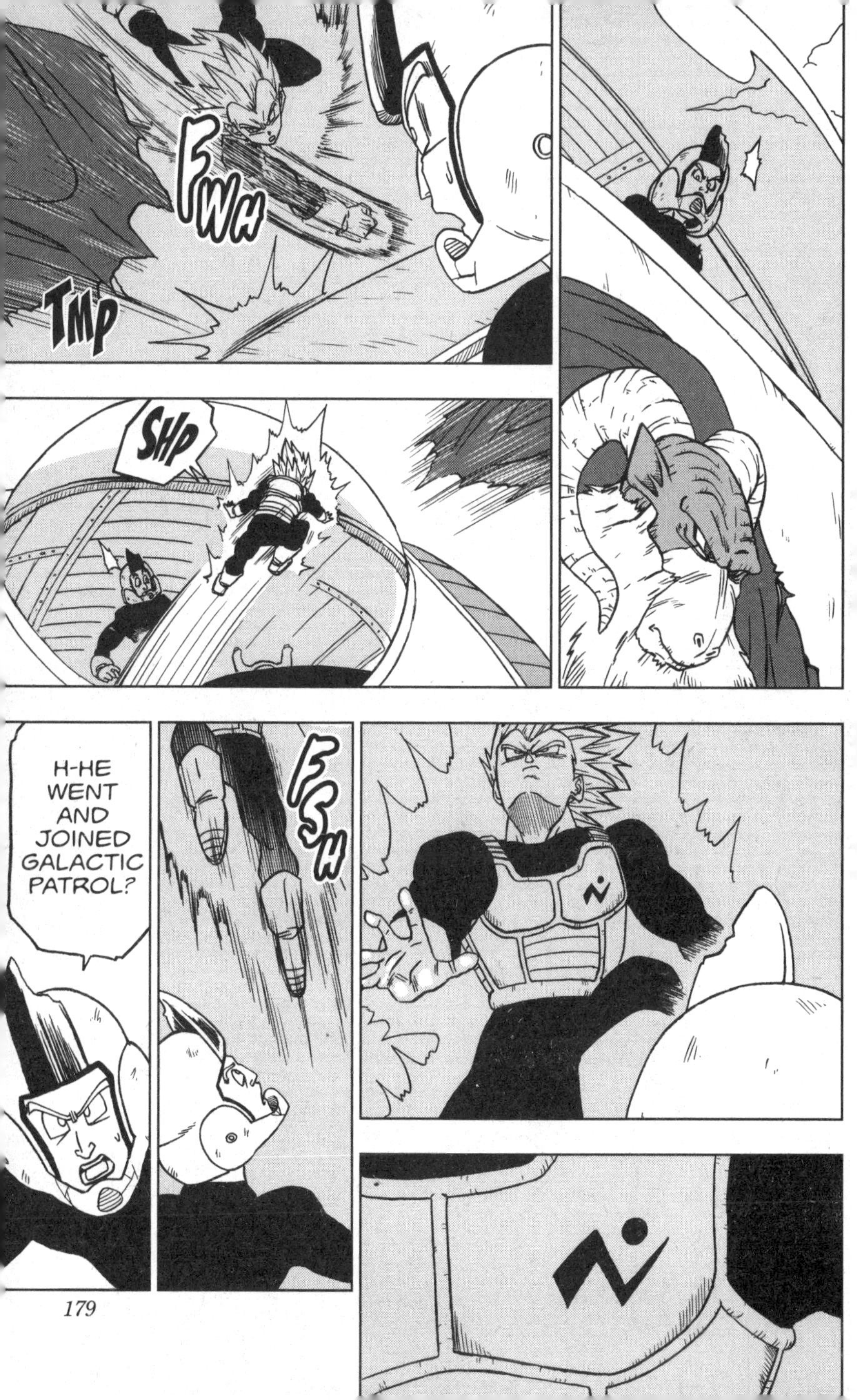
FWH
TMP
SHP
FSH
H-HE WENT AND JOINED GALACTIC PATROL?

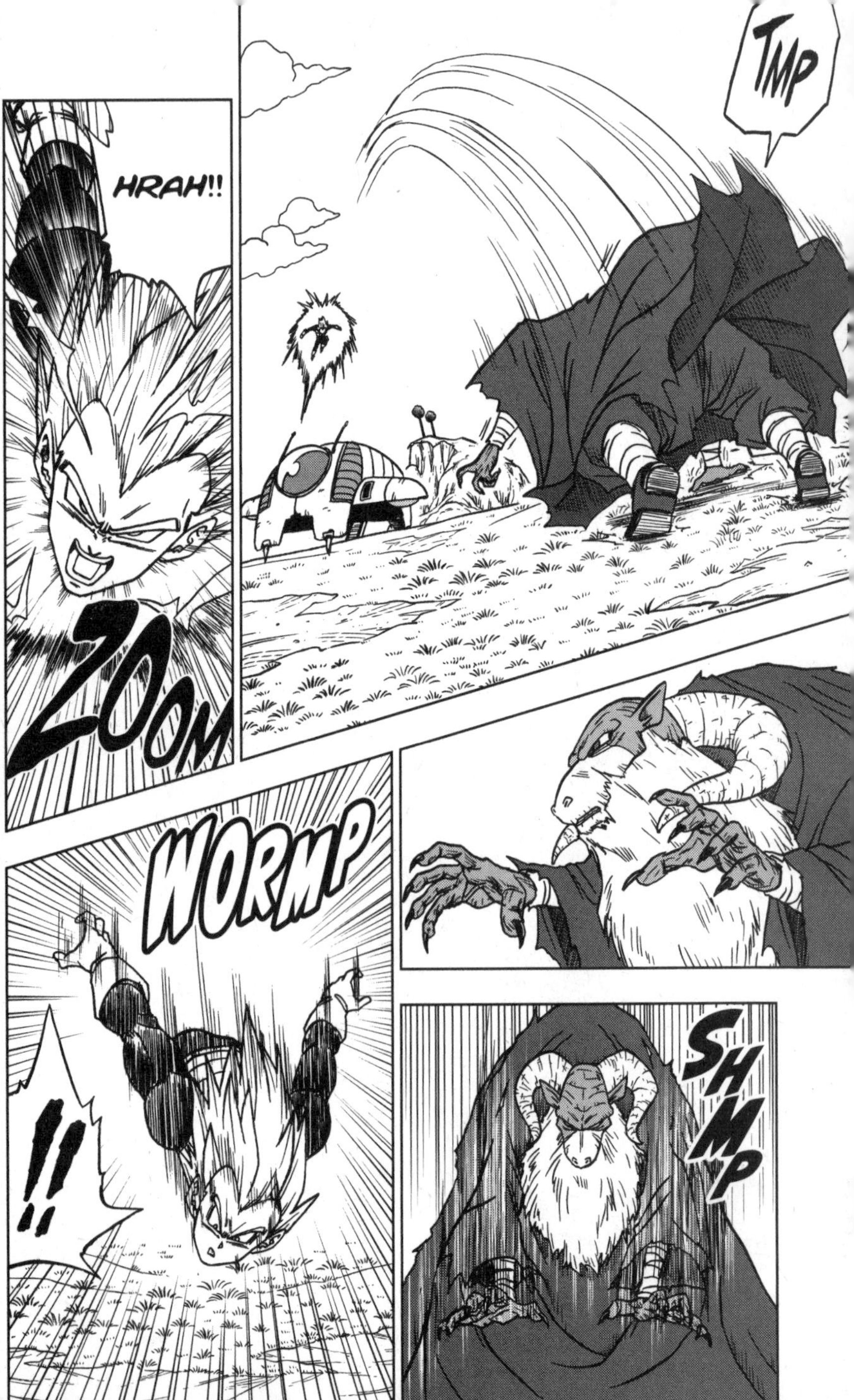
TMP
HRAH!!
ZOOM
SHMP
WORMP
!!

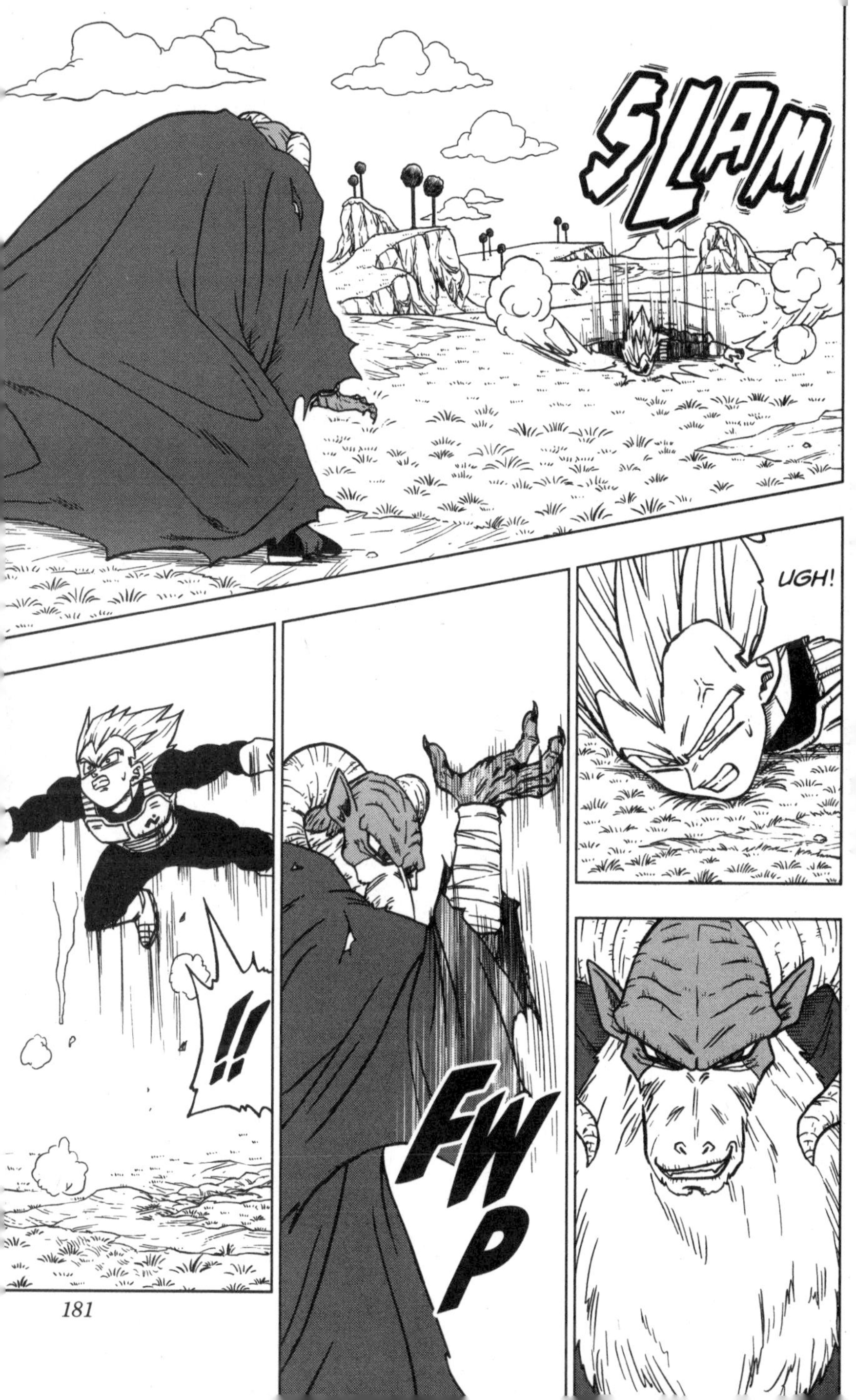
SLAM
UGH!
FWP
!!

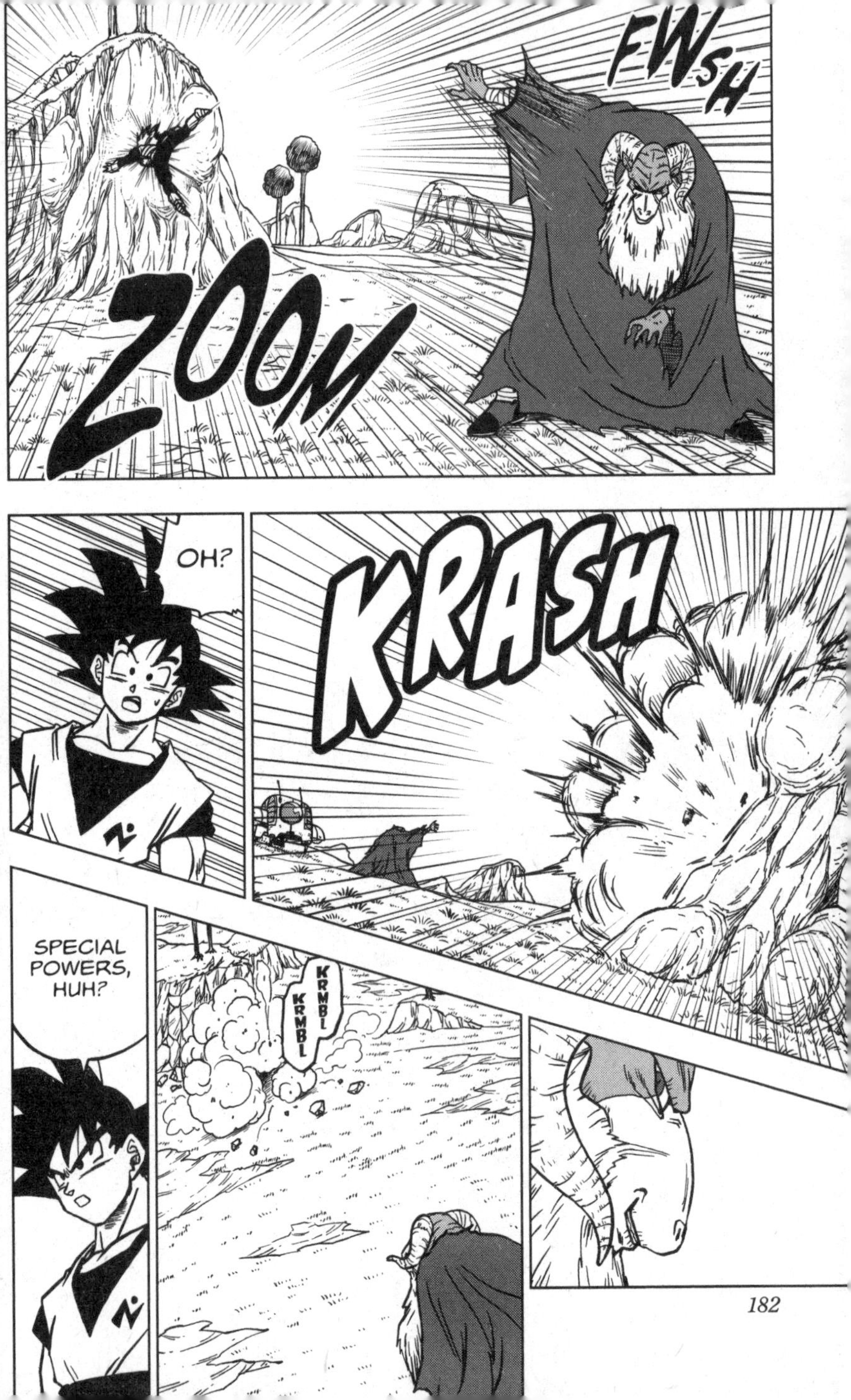
FWSH
ZOOM
KRASH
OH?
KRMBL KRMBL
SPECIAL POWERS, HUH?

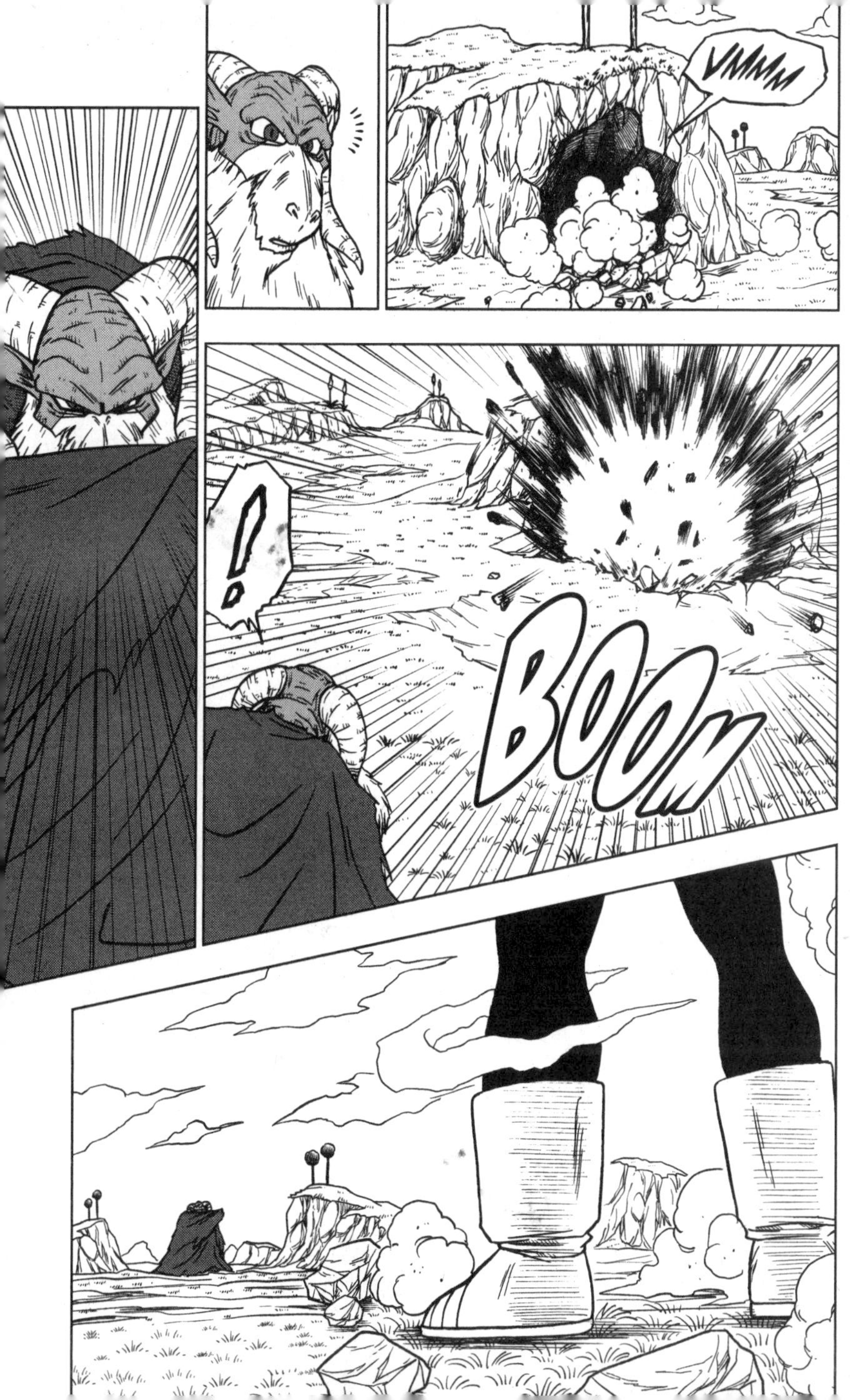
VMMM
!
BOOM

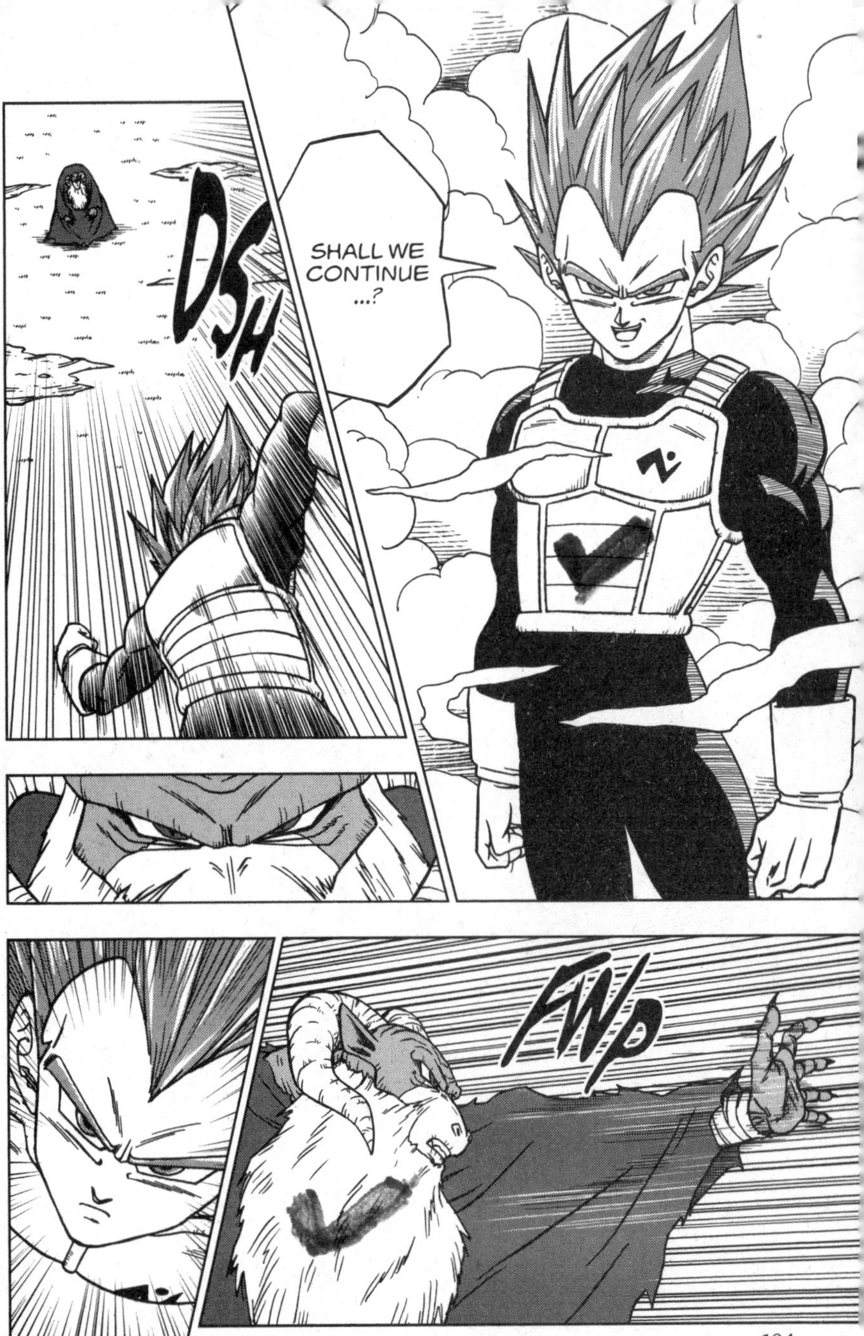
SHALL WE CONTINUE ...?
DSH
FWP

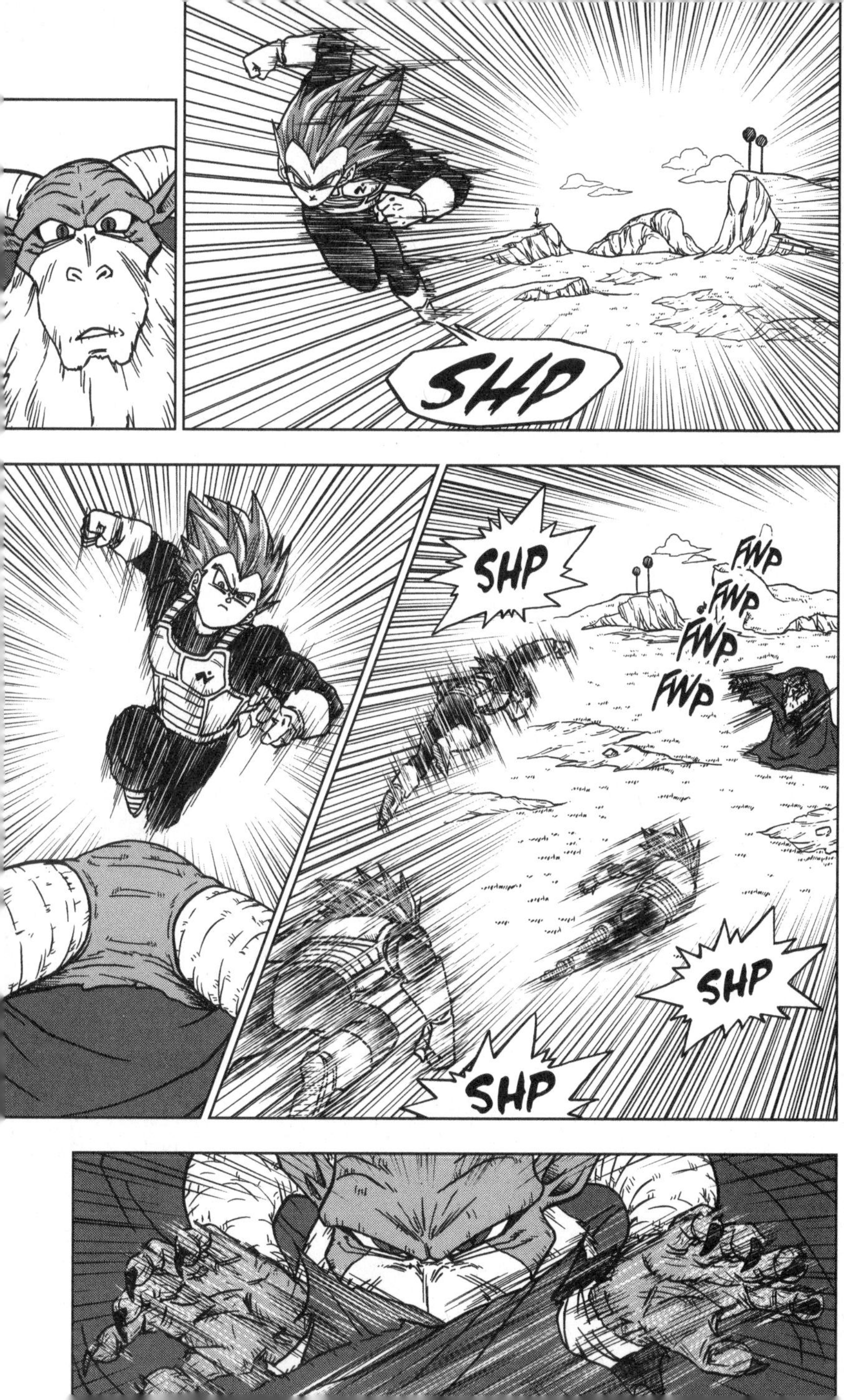
SHP
FWP
FWP
FWP
FWP
SHP
SHP
SHP

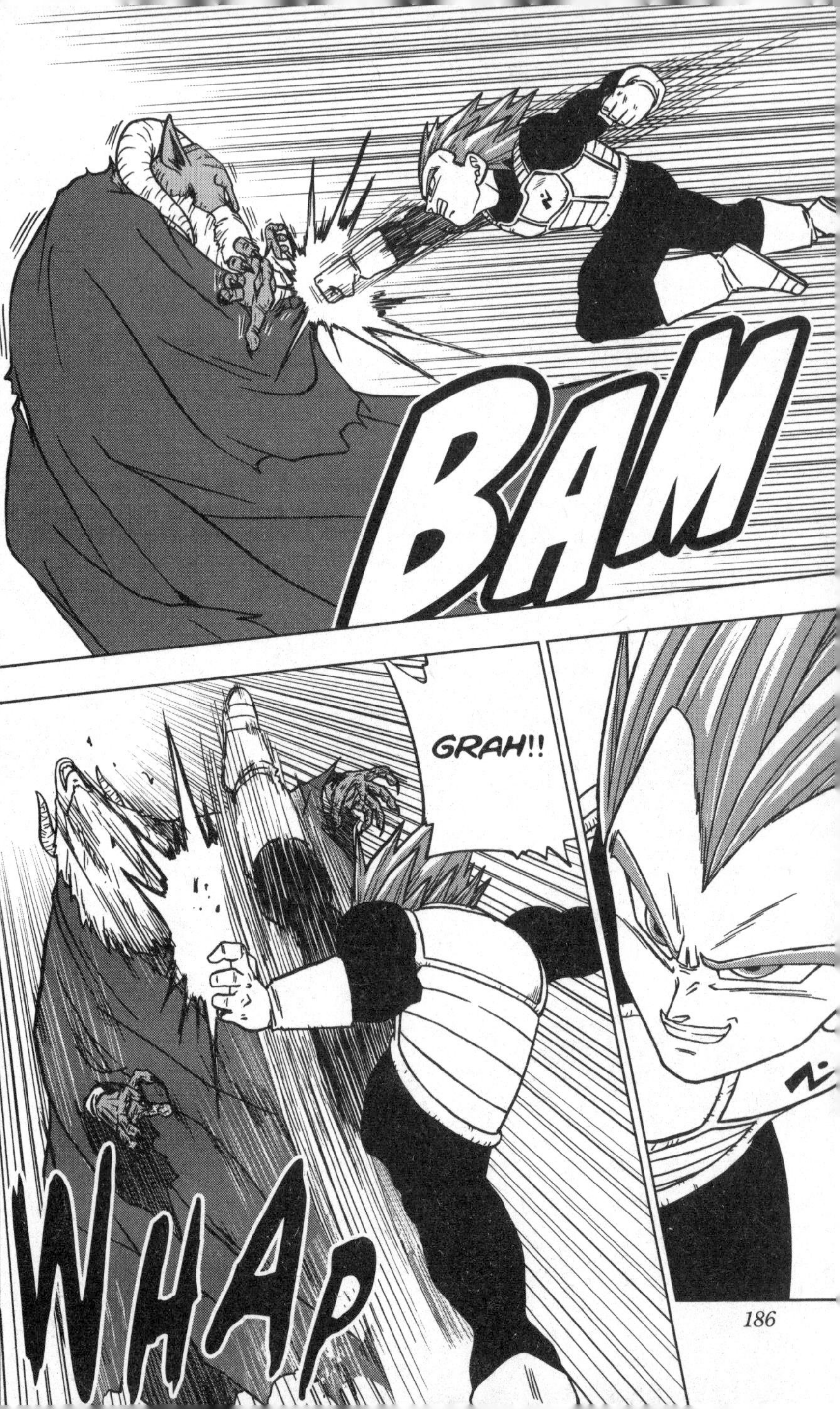
BAM
GRAH!!
WHAP

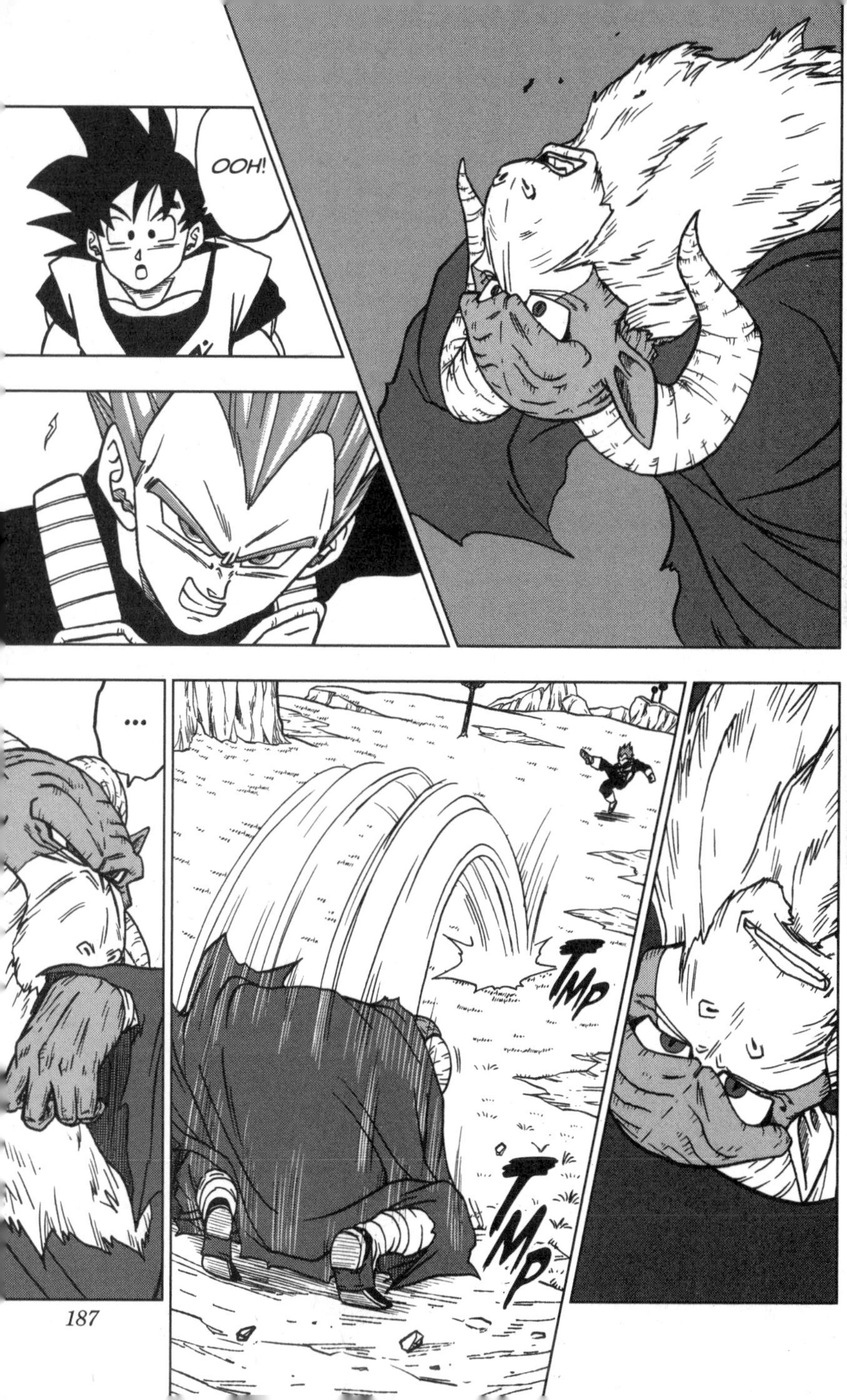
OOH!
TMP
TMP
...

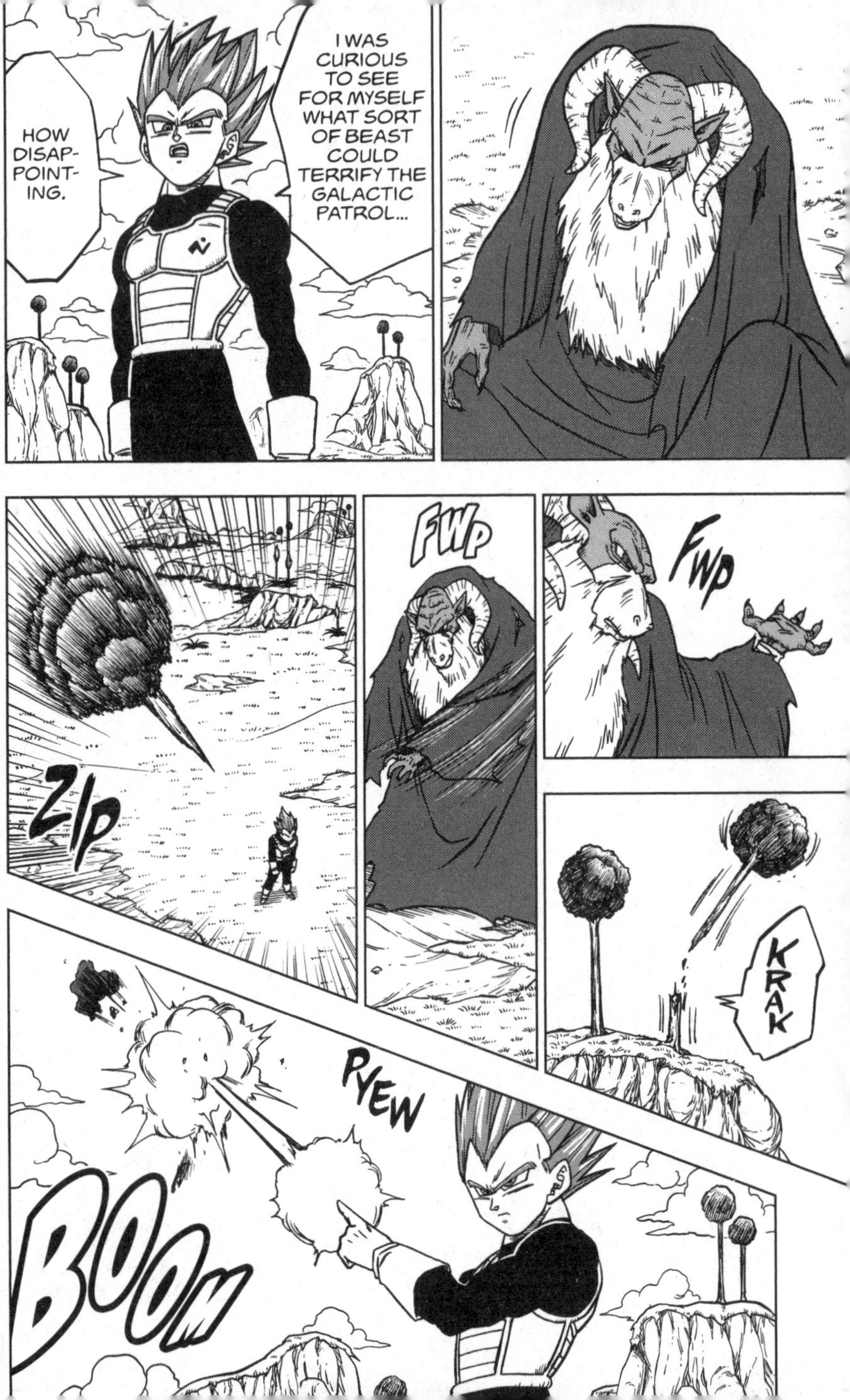

I WAS CURIOUS TO SEE FOR MYSELF WHAT SORT OF BEAST COULD TERRIFY THE GALACTIC PATROL...
HOW DISAP-POINT-ING.
FWP
KRAK
FWP
ZIP
PYEW
BOOM

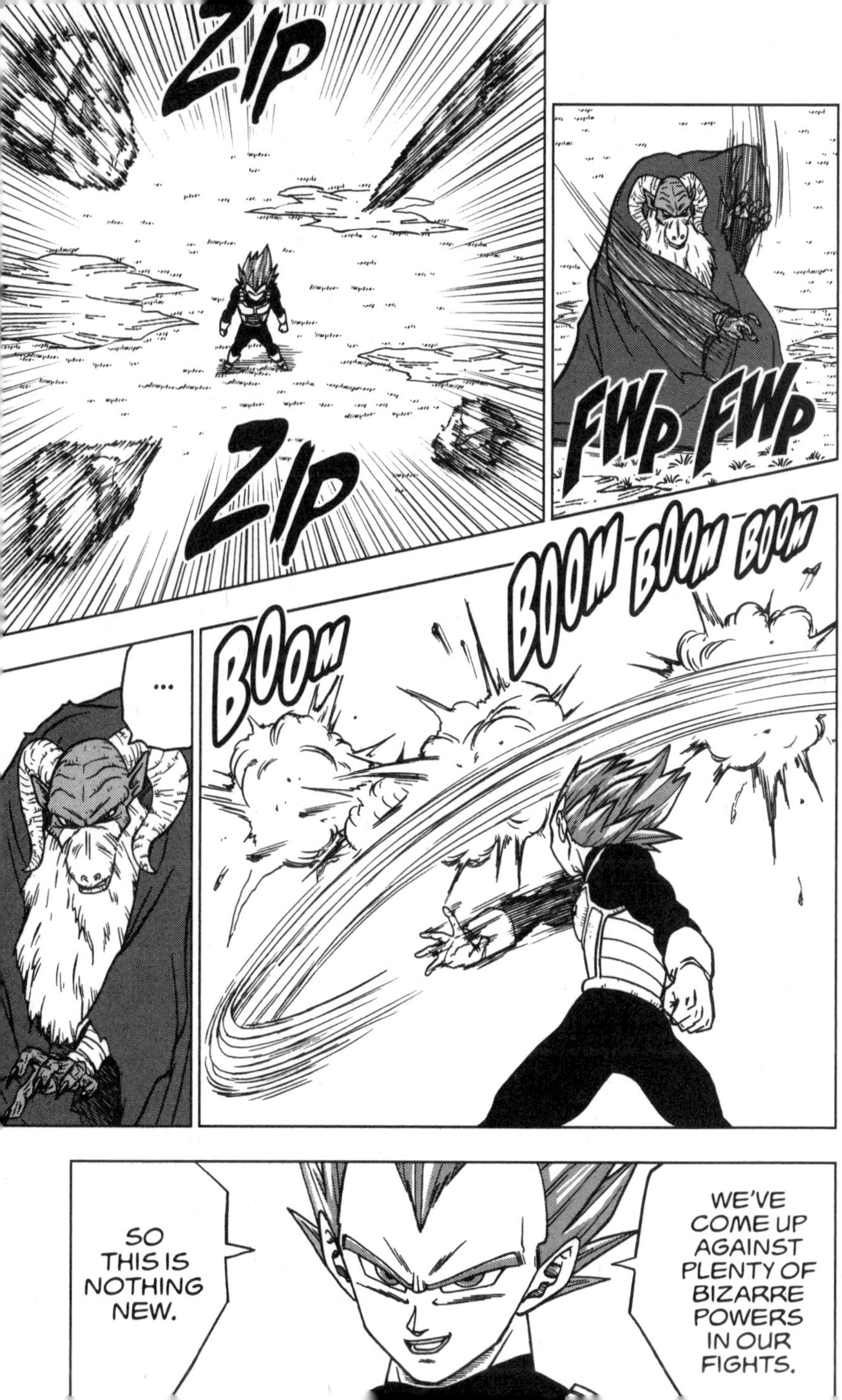
FWP FWP
ZIP
ZIP
BOOM BOOM BOOM
BOOM
...
WE'VE COME UP AGAINST PLENTY OF BIZARRE POWERS IN OUR FIGHTS.
SO THIS IS NOTHING NEW.

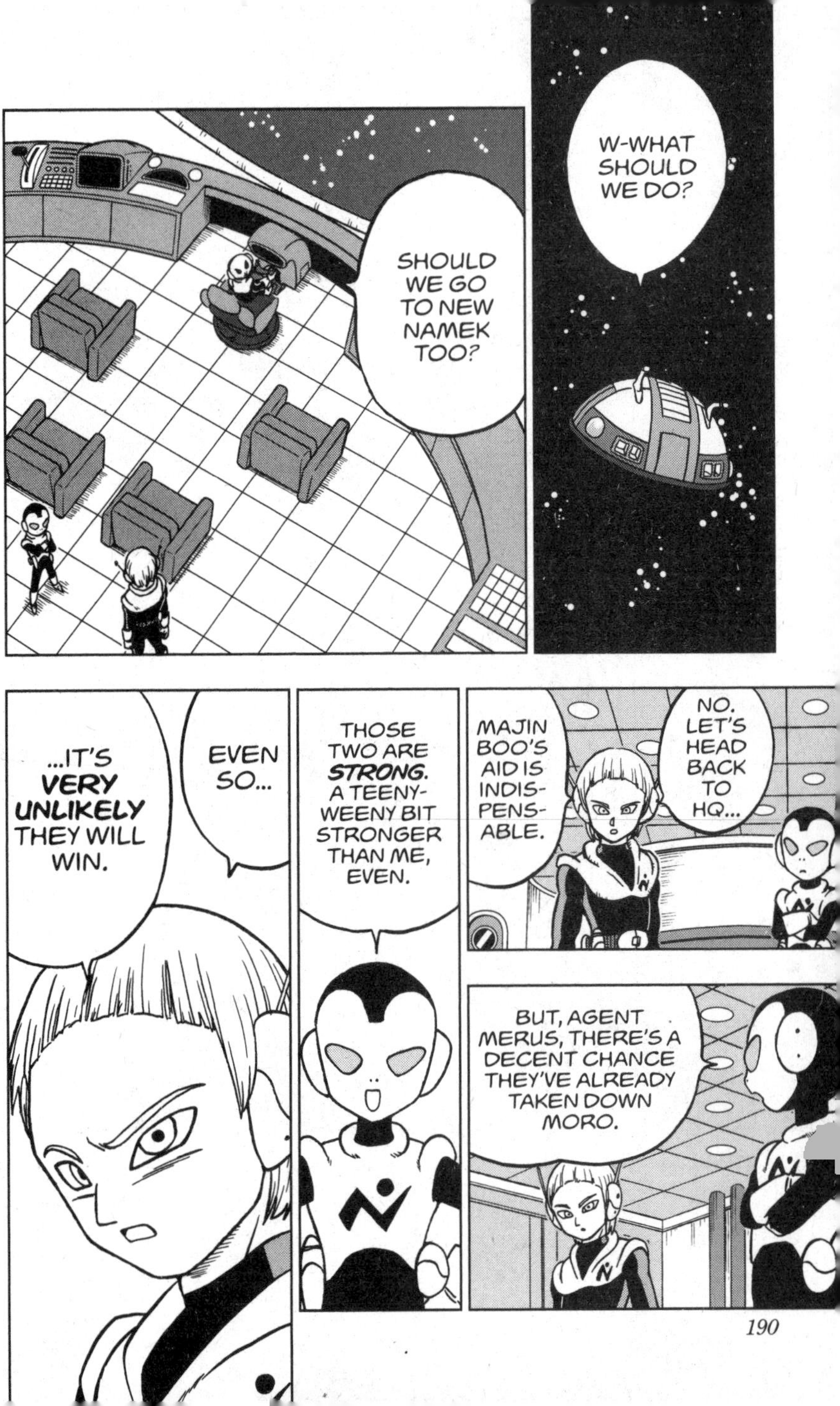
W-WHAT SHOULD WE DO?
SHOULD WE GO TO NEW NAMEK TOO?
NO. LET'S HEAD BACK TO HQ...
MAJIN BOO'S AID IS INDIS-PENS-ABLE.
BUT, AGENT MERUS, THERE'S A DECENT CHANCE THEY'VE ALREADY TAKEN DOWN MORO.
THOSE TWO ARE **STRONG**. A TEENY-WEENY BIT STRONGER THAN ME, EVEN.
EVEN SO...
...IT'S **VERY UNLIKELY** THEY WILL WIN.

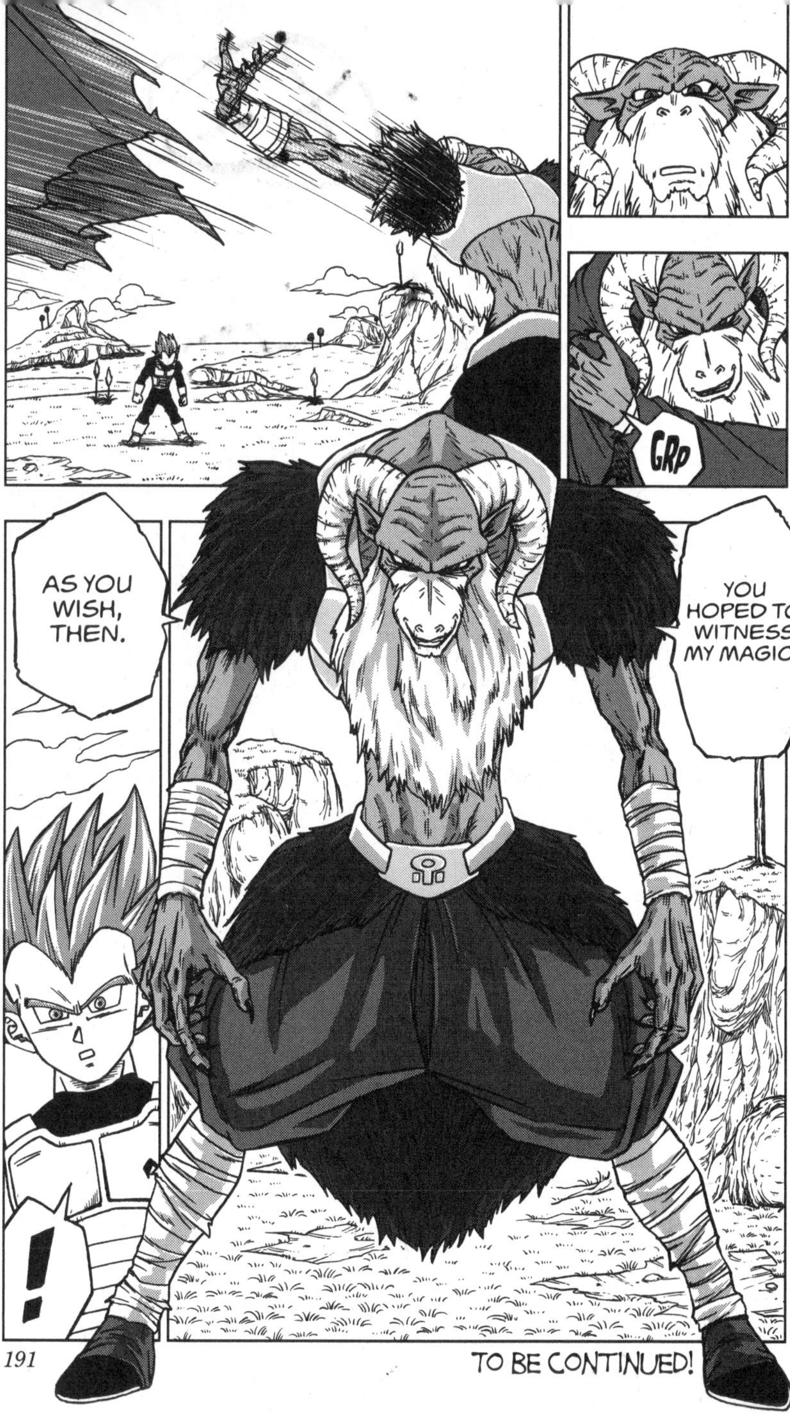
GRP
YOU HOPED TO WITNESS MY MAGIC?
AS YOU WISH, THEN.
!

TO BE CONTINUED!

YOU'RE READING
THE WRONG WAY!

Dragon Ball Super reads from right to left, starting in the upper-right corner. Japanese is read from right to left, meaning that action, sound effects, and word-balloon order are completely reversed from English order.